Unconditional Surrender

THE ROMANCE OF JULIA AND ULYSSES S. GRANT

written by:

Patricia Cameron

First Edition

ISBN: 1-4392-3619-4 (paperback)
ISBN: 9781439236192

10 9 8 7 6 5 4 3 2 1

Library of Congress Cataloging-in-Publication Data available upon
request.

QUANTITY PURCHASES
Companies, professional groups, clubs, and organizations may
qualify for special terms when ordering quantities of this title. For
information, e-mail: info@grantgeek.com

Manufactured in the United States of America.

For my mother.
I will love you forever, Mommy.

My main sources for this book were:
The Papers of Ulysses S. Grant
edited by John Y. Simon

The Personal Memoirs of Julia Dent Grant
edited by John Y. Simon

and

The Personal Memoirs of Ulysses S. Grant

and

Special thanks to
the Huntington Library
San Marino, CA.
for use of the West Point
account book of Cadet U.S. Grant

In the page index of
General Grant's Personal Memoirs,
amid the names of generals and battlefields,
I found this sweet little listing of page references:

It gave me a warm, cozy feeling.

Unconditional Surrender
THE ROMANCE OF
JULIA AND ULYSSES S. GRANT

Contents

PROLOGUE

I have felt a great deal of empathy for General Ulysses S. Grant since I was a little girl. I recall seeing a line-up of all the presidents when I was about six, and immediately President Grant caught my attention. From that moment, he became my favorite president.

As an adult, I began researching his life. I had heard negative things about him, like his drinking and his brutality in war, but I was amazed to find out what a good man he was, and what a beautiful romance he shared with his Southern belle wife, Julia. She was one of a big family that owned a huge plantation, and many slaves. He was a Yankee.

I was drawn to their romance to such a degree, that I joined the Grant Association. At the first convention I attended, in Washington D. C., I was incredibly lucky to get to see some of his original letters at the Library of Congress—not microfilm or copies, but the actual letters! His love letters were poetic and wonderfully romantic, written when lonely and far from home in military service.

From reading his Memoirs, I could tell he was a brilliant writer, but his Memoirs contained almost no mention of Julia and their love. Not until I read his love letters did I discover his passion.

I decided to research their romance in depth and went to some of the places around the country from which he wrote his love letters. One trip seemed to lead to another and, before I knew it, I had traveled to twenty-two places important to Julia and Ulysses, and to their love. My journey also led me to little known facts, and important discoveries. I hope that after you read this book, you will want to make that journey with me, as ensuing books will invite you along to where they courted, to where they loved, and to where he died and left her with a broken heart.

This book is devoted to Ulysses' love letters to Julia. Through these deep and heartfelt missives, one can better know the man. One can also better understand his Southern wife, who loved him beyond his death and until her own, even though she had to watch him destroy her entire way of life. To do so, Julia had to give herself to him completely. I hope you will enjoy her "Unconditional Surrender."

Patricia Cameron

CHAPTER ONE
Lap of Luxury

The story of U.S. Grant is the story of loneliness—a terrible loneliness healed only by love. The source of this healing love was a woman. Her name was Julia.

She was born Julia Boggs Dent in Gravois County, Missouri, just south of St. Louis, near the banks of the sleepy Mississippi River. "Miss Julia" was cuddled in the lap of luxury on a Southern plantation, drenched in the very culture her Yankee husband would someday destroy.

Miss Julia and her family lived at White Haven, a thousand acres of flowers and fruit trees—and slaves.

By Julia's own account, "Our home was really the showplace of the county." In her sentimental memory, "Life seemed one long summer of sunshine, flowers, and smiles to me and to all at that happy home."

Miss Julia was the "pet" of the family, the first daughter coming after four boys, John, George, Fred and Louis. She was followed by two younger sisters, Nellie and Emmy, but Julia was clearly her father's favorite. Her family, and father in particular, lavished her with affection. With her adoring parents, Julia's life was one big love fest, a vivid contrast to the cold childhood of her future husband, Ulysses S. Grant.

Julia grew up in a warm, gracious world full of hugs and kisses—while poor little Ulysses' mother starved him of affection. Hannah and Jesse Grant, while possessing many other noble qualities such as being hard workers with good common sense, did not squander affection on their children. In fact, by most accounts, Ulysses' mother never even kissed him at all.

Ulysses S. Grant was born in a crude, one room cabin in Point Pleasant, Ohio, on the 27th of April, 1822. He was the eldest son of Jesse Grant, a hard working but braggadocios tanner, and Hannah Grant, a stoic, silent woman. Sensitive Ulysses hated the tannery and was squeamish at the sight of blood. But he loved horses and from a tender age, did all the family work relating to horses, such as furrowing, ploughing, and hauling wood.

When little Ulysses was sick, his mother never fussed over him. She'd give him a spoon of castor oil and say, "Oh, he'll be all right." When neighbors saw him hanging upside down from a horse, they were worried about him, but not Hannah. "He can take care of himself. He'll be all right," she said unemotionally, and went back to her housework.

Grant's coolness in battle can be traced back to his mother's quiet confidence in him. But her cold, unemotional approach left him starving for female attention.

There was no laughing, kissing, and playfulness in Ulysses' house, like there was in Julia's home. And it left him with a great emptiness inside. He was painfully shy, especially with girls. He had a dreamy, romantic streak that for now, went unshared and unexpressed. His happiest times were spent alone and on horseback, enjoying the beauty of nature.

At the age of seventeen, Ulysses' father got him an appointment to West Point Military Academy. One day his father simply said, "Ulysses, I believe you will get the appointment."

"What appointment?" asked Ulysses.

"To West Point. I have applied for it."

Ulysses protested, "But I won't go."

Years later, General Grant recalled of his father, "He said he thought I would, *and I thought so, too, if he did.*"

When Ulysses left home for West Point, Hannah was silent and undemonstrative. "He'll be all right," was all she said.

Ulysses went to say good bye to a neighbor woman, Mrs. Bailey, who had always liked him. Mrs. Bailey wept. Ulysses was astonished.

"Why, Mrs. Bailey," he said, "They didn't cry at our house."

And so, Ulysses went off to West Point to learn how to be a soldier. But his mind was never far from romance. He wrote a long account of the rigors of West Point to his cousin. In training, he had slept for two weeks on only one blanket, but even worse, "I haven't even spoken to a lady in over four months," Ulysses wistfully complained, "I wish some of the pretty girls of Bethel were here, just so I could look at them."

Ulysses spent more time in his room reading novels and

painting than studying. One of his paintings features a Mexican woman nursing her baby. Ulysses' desire for womanly warmth presents itself at every turn.

Ulysses' best friend at West Point was James Longstreet, a dashing, tall tree of a man from South Carolina who was as outgoing as Ulysses was shy. Longstreet and his Southern pals took the bashful Yankee lad under their wing. They gave him a slew of affectionate nicknames such as "Country Sam" "Uncle Sam" and just plain "Sam." And they introduced him to the mysteries of "Brag," an early form of poker. Ulysses was a terrible card player, but he enjoyed the manly camaraderie.

"Country Sam" Ulysses faired poorly with the girls in comparison with his gallant Southern comrades. He never had a sense of rhythm, and once remarked of dancing, "I'd be all right, if it wasn't for the music."

Surprisingly, one of Ulysses' first purchases as a cadet at West Point was a pair of dancing shoes! Carefully recorded in his account book amid items like cakes of soap and quill pens, it appears he made at least one poignant attempt to dance. But since many of his classmates never remember even seeing him at a dance or cotillion party, it appears Ulysses soon gave up dancing as a means to meet the ladies.

On a leave from West Point, women were still on Ulysses' mind. He befriended two local girls, Mary King and Kate Lowe, with whom he visited.

In later years he recalls, "I enjoyed this period of my life above all others." His wife probably didn't like this comment, for during this "happiest time of my life" he hadn't met her yet. But it was a carefree time. He had not yet met the woman who would be his salvation—but also his Achilles heel. Falling in love with her he later described as "having something serious the matter with me." Once he fell for Julia, if he couldn't be with her, he was utterly miserable. Once he fell for Julia, he went from being a carefree youth to, being, frankly, a lovesick moose!

Young Ulysses enjoyed his visits with Mary King and Kate Lowe, but he evidently cast no spell over them, for when he returned to West Point, both girls married other men. This must have been a disappointment to the shy young man who yearned for a romance like the ones described in the novels he was always reading in his room. Little did he know, his own real life romance would surpass them all.

While the wistful Ulysses returned to the rigid training of drills and deprivation at West Point, teenage Julia was at Miss Mauro's fashionable finishing school in St. Louis. Its purpose was to turn Southern girls into proper Southern ladies.

Teenage Julia was "well formed for her age" with a "beautiful figure," long black hair and creamy white skin. She had "the slenderest prettiest foot, and the smallest hands ever seen on a woman." Most attractive about her seemed to be her sweet, vivacious personality, good manners and fun-loving playfulness. She was "delightfully feminine." Before meeting Ulysses, she had many suitors and it was rumored she had "already had several affairs of the heart."

There were lots of parties, dancing and girlish giggling at the finishing school, and the pretty young students gossiped about who among the eligible Southern young men they would marry. It seemed that bubbly Julia certainly could have her pick, but when she returned home after graduation, she had not yet met anyone especially special.

Following his graduation from West Point, bashful Ulysses was still hoping to meet somebody special, who would think he was special. Before returning home to Ohio, Ulysses anticipated the reward for his four years of grueling work: a fancy new uniform.

Anxiously waiting to receive his new clothes, Ulysses recalled: "I was impatient to get on my uniform and see how it looked, and probably wanted my old schoolmates, particularly the girls, to see me in it."

But when Ulysses rode through town in his new uniform, imagining the girls were admiring him, a couple of local boys mocked his pride. One, a ragged little street urchin, called, "Soldier, will you work? No sir—ee! I'll sell my shirt first!" And a scrawny stable boy paraded the streets, barefoot, in a pair of sky-blue pantaloons—just the color of Ulysses' uniform trousers—with a strip of white cotton sheeting sewn down the outside seams in imitation of the young cadet. The neighbors all got a huge laugh at Ulysses' expense. The sensitive Ulysses was mortified. His wistful attempt to impress the girls resulted in a distaste for military uniform from which he never recovered.

His senior year at West Point, Ulysses' roommate was Frederick Dent, Julia's older brother. After graduation, Frederick went West, while Ulysses was posted with the Fourth Infantry at Jefferson Barracks, not far from White Haven, the Dents' estate. Frederick extended an open invitation to Ulysses to visit Frederick's family.

Despite his shy ways, Ulysses was always hungry for warmth and companionship. It was early October, 1843, when Ulysses first found his way out to White Haven on horseback.

White Haven was in the throes of a brilliant autumn. As Ulysses approached the sprawling estate, trees swayed and sighed all around him, shimmering with their sensual shades of fall, groaning beneath the weight of juicy, golden apples that tempted him to linger and take a bite. Jewel colored leaves rained down upon him like confetti hailing a hero, and decorated his path to the Dents' door.

At White Haven, the old year, 1843, was passing away with the falling leaves. Their world was slowly passing away, as well. With the arrival of Ulysses S. Grant, it would never be the same again.

Julia's little sister, Emmy, never forgot seeing Ulysses invade White Haven for the first time.

As Ulysses approached White Haven for his maiden visit, Emmy was collecting birds' nests with the slave girls. She heard someone approaching on horseback. Lieutenant Ulysses came into view, dressed in his uniform. He gazed down at Emmy with his translucent blue eyes.

"How do you do, little girl. Does Mr. Dent live here?" he asked Emmy. Emmy could only stare up at him in awe.

"Why, he's as pretty as a doll!" she gasped to herself.

At home in Ohio, Ulysses had tried and failed to make an impression on the girls in his uniform. Now, he was succeeding without even trying.

His cheeks, Emmy noted, were round and plump and rosy. His hair was "fine and brown, very thick and wavy; his eyes were "a clear blue and full of light." He was "slender and well-formed" and whenever he moved, Emmy thought he was graceful.

Yes, Ulysses was handsome in a frail, haunting sort of way. He still suffered from a desperate cough he acquired at West Point called

"Tyler's Grip," which left him painfully thin. Yet, combined with his sensitive, vulnerable aura, there was also the manly bearing of a soldier.

"He looked like a little prince," Emmy recalled.

But something else lit the shy lieutenant's presence which was irresistible to the women of White Haven—a quality which made him the most compelling male to ever cross their threshold.

He needed loving, bad.

Julia was still staying with friends in St. Louis, but all the other women at White Haven fell instantly in love. Mrs. Dent offered elixirs to cure his cough, and Julia's sisters, seven year old Emmy and fifteen year old Nelly, giggled and flirted and bickered over which one of the two would have him. Ulysses visited twice a week, and thoroughly enjoyed the female attention. Of course, the girls were way too young for him, but it was fun and harmless to play with them.

And then, Miss Julia came home.

And after their first meeting, Ulysses came over everyday.

At seventeen, she was closer to his age. More mature than her sisters, she didn't try to flirt with him. She didn't need to. Right from the start, she answered every longing he had in his heart, his body and his soul.

Where his mother was unsmiling, Julia was merry and "full of fun." Where his mother was austere, Julia wore lacy petticoats and pretty satin bows. Where his mother was thin as a rail, Julia was voluptuous. Where his mother was cold, Julia was warm. She took his hands in her tiny hands and welcomed him into her world—a world of sunshine, laughter and affection.

Yes, Julia made him feel welcome. Later he would write her from the Mexican War, *"If I could only spend an hour per day in your parlor, what a recreation it would be!"*

After the harshness of his home life, West Point and the army barracks, what a tonic she was!

As Julia and Ulysses' feelings awakened for each other, White Haven was awakening from winter.

Acres of flowers were just starting to open, peach trees with their filmy white blossoms beginning to bloom. As the dreamy, romantic Ulysses beheld White Haven each day, it must have seemed like Eden. Compared to the austerity of camp life, and the coldness of his own home, he surely felt like the man in the song, "Stranger in Paradise."

At age twenty-one, with no serious romantic experience, Ulysses was primed to fall in love. And what better place for it to happen than in this fragrant fantasyland?

More beautiful to him than the scenery of White Haven, was sweet Miss Julia. With her, his shyness unfolded, like petals on a flower, exposing the yearning young heart beneath.

Soon after meeting her, he wrote in his journal, "My new friends are becoming very interesting!"

After a lifetime of no nonsense meals of cucumbers and gruel, to Ulysses, Julia was like a lacy little box of Southern bon bons, her laughter, her softness, her playfulness like delightful little treats just waiting for him to pluck and enjoy.

They shared a silly sense of humor, a side most never noticed in Ulysses. When Julia's pet canary died, Ulysses arranged a "solemn" funeral for the bird, complete with tiny yellow coffin, with him and his fellow officers as pall bearers, all in formal dress uniforms. It is hard to imagine them all keeping straight faces through such a funny affair!

Miss Julia had a lovely flower garden. He liked to hear her tell him about all the kinds of flowers and their hidden meanings. She gave him little nosegays to brighten up his barracks. They shared joyous horseback rides before breakfast, and long walks and talks along the nearby Gravois Creek at sunset. He escorted her to all the local parties. He didn't like to dance, but he liked to watch her dance. He didn't talk much, but he liked to listen to her gaily prattle away.

Both were having so much fun, neither realized they were falling in love. Not the way her sisters had fallen for him, but something deeper, more powerful, more spiritual.

What did they talk about on their walks along the Gravois Creek? Certainly horses and nature. And much more. It was early spring, and as the delicate flowers opened up, so they opened up to each other their own delicate dreams. Whatever thoughts and feelings they shared bonded him more closely to her than to any other living human being.

Julia had planned to come home and resume the pampered life of a plantation princess. Instead, she was being swept away by something far more powerful. In Miss Julia, Ulysses aroused unexpected feelings of romantic and sexual love.

But was this not improper, she must have wondered? She was supposed to marry a Southern gentleman and be the mistress of a grand Southern home, just like her mama. Her feelings for this bashful young Yankee were very confusing. Why, he couldn't even dance!

But Ulysses was not confused. He knew what he wanted. He wanted Miss Julia.

Ulysses planned a short visit to his parents in Ohio. Before leaving, he sat alone with Miss Julia on the piazza at White Haven. As usual, he said little, while she prattled on about fanciful things like flowers and parties. He listened, and as usual, felt happy just being near her warm presence.

He had once confided to Julia that when he gave his class ring to a lady, it would be as an engagement ring. He was recalling this, as she finally stopped chatting. They sat quietly a few moments. She smiled at him, and he smiled back. Perhaps this was the right moment? His cheeks flushing pink, his heart pounding with a mixture of love and fear, he shyly offered Miss Julia his class ring. Perhaps she would accept it, and spare him an actual declaration of his love.

Julia was surprised. She was enjoying their days together, but as yet had not had to confront the reality that he was a Yankee, and unacceptable for her as a husband. Flustered, trying to fight off her ever blossoming feelings for him, Julia gave the acceptable response of a proper Southern belle.

"Oh, no!" she gasped, "Mama would never approve of my accepting a gift from a gentleman!" Her mama and papa's approval still had a stronger pull on Miss Julia than her feelings for her handsome young suitor.

For Julia and Ulysses, the Civil War had begun.

But her surrender was still not at hand.

Ulysses was hurt. "He was rather put out," as Julia described it many years later. "And soon after, he took his leave. But he lingered near me long enough to ask if I would miss him." Afraid of her feelings, feelings which "mama" and "papa" did not approve, Julia merely murmured, "I am happy when you are near, but that is all."

It was the Southern belle equivalent of "I just like you as a friend!"

Disappointed, but taking it like a man, Ulysses tore himself away from White Haven to visit his parents in Bethel, Ohio. When he returned, he told himself, there was no reason he could not continue his visits to Miss Julia.

While he was gone, Julia missed him terribly.

She was totally surprised by how lonely she was without him.

About that time, Miss Julia was given a new, four poster bed. The genteelly bred young lady named one of her bedposts "Lieutenant Grant." And that night, she dreamed that he paid her a visit.

Miss Julia's romantic dream was about to come true. While Ulysses was with his parents in Ohio, he received word that he was to be transferred away from Jefferson Barracks. Away from Julia! Ulysses awoke as if from a dream, with the realization that he might never see her again. And if he did see her some day in the distant future, she might be married to someone else.

Ulysses remembered, "I now discovered that I was exceedingly anxious to get back to Jefferson Barracks, and I understood the reason without explanation from anyone."

Meanwhile, Miss Julia herself heard the news about her friend's transfer. "Lieutenant Hazlitt assured us that if Mr. Grant were not out to see us within a week from the following Saturday week, we must understand that he had gone on down the Mississippi and would not be back at the Barracks again. Saturday came and no Lieutenant. I felt very restless and, ordering my horse, rode alone towards the Barracks, not feeling afraid. I halted my horse and waited and listened, but he did not come. The beating of my own heart was all the sound I heard. So I rode slowly and sadly home, where I found two young ladies and two gentlemen had arrived to remain over Sunday."

The comfortable life went on at White Haven, but for Miss Julia, it just wasn't the same without her shy, sweet Lieutenant.

Meanwhile, a desperate Ulysses was driven to declare his love immediately.

"I immediately procured a horse and started for the country, taking no baggage with me, of course." He recalled. Ulysses alluded to his ardor many years later, the ardor of a young man so in love, he doesn't even take time to pack a bag for his trip.

Ulysses galloped toward White Haven as fast as he could ride. When he began his journey, the sky was clear, because he had not prepared for rain. But on his way, the heavens opened up and it began to pour. The Gravois Creek, which he had to cross to get to his beloved, was normally placid and dry. As Ulysses describes it, "There was usually not enough water in it to even run a coffee mill." But tonight, like everything else about this night, it was different.

When Ulysses arrived at the Gravois Creek, the pounding rain storm had turned the creek into a raging torrent! It was too dangerous to cross, but it was the only way he could get to his love.

One of the young officer's superstitions had always been, to never turn back until the thing intended was accomplished. So he struck into Gravois Creek on his horse, and in an instant, he was swept away by the wild current! The love struck lieutenant nearly drowned.

Thunder rolled and crashed around White Haven. The Dents were all safe and snug in their beds while out in the rain, Lieutenant Grant was fighting for his life.

Flailing in the raging torrent, and gasping for breath, Ulysses managed to grab hold of his horse's reins. Clutching them like his lifeline, he somehow made it to the other side of the bank, alive, but soaked to the skin.

When the normally dignified soldier showed up at White Haven that night, dripping wet, "his clothes flapping about like rags," the Dents all laughed at him. But they noticed he wasn't laughing. He was on a life or death mission.

Her heart surely pounding, Julia got dressed and came out to greet Ulysses, who was right outside of her door and "seemed to be expecting me." Julia's sister Nelly told Ulysses that he had shown up for a visit, just as Julia dreamed he would.

Ulysses turned and looked at Julia with his bedroom eyes. "Have you been dreaming of me?" he murmured. Julia surely must have melted. She admitted she had indeed been dreaming of him. And she innocently admitted she had named her bedpost after him, too.

That night, Ulysses slept at the Dents' house. Surely, he kept re-living Julia's words. She was dreaming of him, and she had named her bedpost after him. She *must* have feelings for him, he reasoned. In the darkness, he dared himself to hope. As so often occurred in the future, when Ulysses was a general, he was the only one who knew the true object of his mission.

Lying awake in her own bedroom, Julia's willpower was weakening.

For the next day or two, Julia and Ulysses said nothing about love, but it was in the air. He was struggling to get his courage up for a marriage proposal. His shyness tied his tongue so badly that it was torture to even think of coming out with the truth. But it had to be done.

Just like in his famous battles of the Civil War, the time had come for Ulysses to risk all, to do what all the other Union generals failed to do, "confront the terrible moment of truth."

Julia and Ulysses had been invited to a wedding. Just as he would someday maneuver Robert E. Lee to surrender, Ulysses maneuvered to get Miss Julia alone. He offered to lend Julia's brother his own saddle horse, if he could have the honor of driving Miss Julia in the carriage. Julia's brother shrugged and complied, and Ulysses finally got her all to himself.

Julia's heart was fluttering at Ulysses' close proximity. As usual, he looked so handsome. But he was so quiet and serious today. Not his usual fun-loving self.

As they rode along in silence, they reached an old plank bridge over a creek, which, like Gravois Creek, was swollen from the rain. Julia was frightened. She kept asking Ulysses if he thought the water was too dangerous to breast. Perhaps they should turn back? Ulysses quietly insisted that there would be no turning back.

Just as they were about to cross the bridge, she warned him, "Now, if anything happens, I shall cling to you, no matter what you say to the contrary."

He said simply, "All right," in his brief way.

As he drove them over the bridge, she noticed as never before, his quiet strength, how she trusted him to take care of her, how perhaps her "threat" to cling to him really was no threat at all, but her deepest desire.

As soon as the buggy was safely over the bridge, Ulysses pulled over to the side of the road. This was it. The terrible moment of truth! Just as when approaching what he supposed would be his first field of battle during the Civil War, Ulysses' heart was in his throat.

General Grant has often been chided in his Memoirs for his "emotionally repressed" rendition of his marriage proposal to Julia. But it is charming in its own way, revealing the awkwardness he still felt, even at the age of sixty-two, even as he was dying and writing his memoirs, to admit the depth of his feelings for her: "Before I returned, I mustered up courage to make known, in the most awkward manner imaginable, the discovery I had made on learning that the 4th infantry had been ordered away from Jefferson Barracks. The young lady afterwards admitted that she too, although until then she had never looked upon me other than as a visitor whose company was agreeable to her, had experienced a depression of spirits she could not account for when the regiment left. Before separating, it was definitely understood that at a convenient time we would join our fortunes, and not let the removal of a regiment trouble us."

Julia's own memory of the moment is, true to her own personality, more open and outwardly emotional. "He declared his love and told me that without me, life would be insupportable."

Miss Julia could fight her feelings no more. Her Southern belle pretenses fluttered away like the peach blossoms, uncovering at last her naked adoration for him. To his great joy, she confessed that she loved him, too.

One thing is certain, since neither one had ever revealed their feelings for each other before, this was the first time they kissed. And it must have been one beautiful, incredible, powerful kiss!

Because of Ulysses' shyness with girls, and the fact he had no other serious romances, combined with the Victorian formality of the times, it is quite possible that this was the first time he had ever held a woman in his arms and kissed her.

So began a lifelong passion for Julia and for kissing, as Ulysses' love letters from Mexico, California and the Civil War contain countless instances of his sending kisses through the mail to the woman he loved. His usual signature was, "A thousand kisses to you, dear, dear Julia." They kissed leaves and sent them to each other. They wrote the word "KISS" on the bottom of their love letters so they could kiss the same spot that their beloved had kissed.

Other men might take kissing for granted, but never General Grant! Because his mother never kissed him, he was a man who craved, appreciated and enjoyed kissing to its fullest all of his life.

A Civil War staff officer recalls of then Lieutenant-General Grant, Supreme Commander of the Union Army: "Smooching his wife in full view of staff officers, holding her hand at every free moment, and battling the hell out of everyone."

Something so simple as a kiss, and his missing her kisses, led him to drink during the Civil War and put the fate of the Union at risk. Is it any wonder General Grant is the true romantic icon of American History?

And it all began with their first kiss on the old plank bridge.

Ulysses wanted to marry Miss Julia immediately, though he only had a few more days left of his leave. It would have been quite shocking at that time, in 1844, to have but a three day engagement! But once Ulysses S. Grant made a decision, a fire burned in him to move ahead. At the outset of the war, when he was just one of many brigadier generals, and both sides were taking their sweet time in confronting each other, a frustrated Ulysses wrote to his wife, "What I want to do is advance." And now, with his true love in his arms at last, he wanted to advance to the intimacy of marriage as fast as possible.

Julia was in love with Ulysses, but she seemed frightened by the prospect of actually marrying him. She had just turned eighteen, was fresh home from finishing school, and had no notion of leaving home. It was all so sudden. She needed more time.

Julia recalls, "When he spoke of marriage, I simply told him I thought it would be charming to be engaged, but to be married—no! I would rather be engaged. I do not think he liked this arrangement, but as he was going away and could not have taken me with him—he let the matter rest."

Ulysses was probably crushed that he would have to wait to consummate his passion. By waiting now, it would be four long years before they were finally united. But these were four long years to stoke the fires of their devotion to a white heat and to produce the most heart-rending love letters in American history.

Following their mutual declaration of love, the young couple proceeded in a daze to the wedding of Julia's friend. Julia was a bridesmaid and Ulysses a guest. They kept their engagement a secret, but inside, their minds and hearts were surely swirling.

In her memoirs, the ever popular Julia recalls, "At this wedding party several young gentleman citizens were very devoted to me. They seemed determined to monopolize all of my time to the exclusion of the Lieutenant. I do not think I half liked their attentions, as I thought I would greatly prefer a little of Mr. Grant's company, but he was near me all evening, and I was, in a measure, happy."

In later years, Julia was fond of reminiscing, "We were always happy in each other's company." Yet, she let him ride out of her life and off to war in Mexico, without marrying him.

Why?

Julia must have sensed that marrying this man was not to be taken lightly. Perhaps she even felt a sense of foreboding. She would be leaving a life of luxury to live with the Army, married to a Yankee, no less, in a free state, with no slaves to wait upon her. And the disapproval-of her beloved Papa breathing down her neck. She was so conflicted, she even made Ulysses promise not to tell anybody about their engagement, especially her slave-owning, Yankee-hating Papa.

No, Miss Julia was not ready for unconditional surrender just yet.

So began four years of passionate love letters from Ulysses S. Grant to his "dear, dear Julia," during the Mexican War. He was by far the more punctual writer, her letters were inconsistent. This caused the lovelorn soldier much pain. Ironically, her love letters cannot be found, but she saved every single one of her lieutenant's letters, even the ones scolding her for not writing more often.

It is humorous that at the very beginning of their correspondence, he avoids actually speaking of love, and she chides him for it. She *wants* him to tell her of his love! This is a woman who wasn't afraid to ask for what she wanted, and she got it, for this romantic request opened the floodgates for the lovesick lieutenant to pour out his heart with increasing intensity.

No description could be as eloquent as the real thing, so following are love letters from Ulysses S. Grant, age twenty-two, to Miss Julia Dent, age eighteen, before the start of the Mexican War:

A PERSONAL NOTE FROM THE AUTHOR

I must admit to you, I love reading these love letters. It makes me feel happy to read them, because it is so rare for a man to be so open about his feelings, especially such tender feelings. Julia was indeed a lucky woman! In typing Ulysses' love letters for this book, I noticed little gems I had missed in reading them for the first time, so I will point them out to you as we go along. Also, I decided to choose my favorite line from each love letter to use as a sort of a title. If I couldn't decide between a couple of my favorite lines, my seven year old son, Teddy, helped me in my selection. He was very serious about helping me. He would listen to a romantic line, then say, impressed, "That's pretty good!"

I think Teddy loves General Grant, too.

I left in all of Ulysses' original misspellings. There is, to me, something so poignant about them.

Patricia Cameron

THE LOVE LETTERS OF
ULYSSES S. GRANT TO MISS JULIA DENT

Notice the way Ulysses, in his very first love letter, hints around about love in a shy, humorous way, while managing to avoid actually saying the word "love." You can practically see the words "hint hint!" in parentheses after many of his bashful statements, especially this one:

"I <u>know</u> the climate, &c. (&c. meaning much more than what precedes it) about St. Louis suits me well."

Camp Salubrity
Near Nachitoches Louisiana
June 4th, 1844

My Dear Julia
I have at length arrived here with the most pleasing recollections of the short leave of absence which prevented my accompanying my Regiment; and as well, with the consequences of the leave. I arrived here on Monday at the 3rd Ins; I believe just the day that I told you I thought I should arrive. My journey to N. Orleans was a pleasant one, on a pleasant boat, with pleasant passengers and officers, but was marked with no incident worth relating, except that as we approached the South the Musquetoes become troublesome, and by the time I left N. Orleans my hands and face bore the strongest testamony of their numbers and magnitude.—I spent something over a day in N. Orleans, and its being a tolerably large place, and my Bump of Acquisitiveness prompting me on to see as much of the place as possible, the result was that I went over the town just fast enough to see nothing as I went, stoped long enough at a time to find out nothing atall and at the end found myself perfectly tired out. But I saw enough to convince me that a very pleasant season might be passed there; and if I <u>can't</u> get back to <u>Jeff. Bks</u> again will make no objections to the contemplated change which sends me here. But I am not disposed to

*give up a known good for an untried one, and as I <u>know</u> the climate
&c. (&c. meaning much more than what precedes it) about St. Louis
suits me well, I will by no means fail to take up with any offer which
will take me back.—My journey up the Red River was not so pleasant
as the other. The boat was quite small and considerably crouded
with passengers, and they not of the most pleasant sort; a number of
them being what are usually called <u>Black</u> <u>Legs</u> or Gamblers; some
of them with very cut throat appearances. There was some of them
that I should very much dislike to meet unarmed, and in a retired
place, their knowing I had a hundred dollars about me. Likely I judge
harshly. The monotony of the Journey though was somewhat broken
by the great difference in the appearance of the Red River country
and anything else I had ever seen. The first hundred miles looks like
a little deep and winding canal finding its way through a forest so
thickly set, and of such heavy foliage that the eye cannot penetrate.
The country is low and flat and overflown to the first limbs of the
trees. Aligators and other revolting looking things occupy the swamps
in thousands; and no doubt the very few people who live there shake
with the ague all Summer. As far up the river as where we are the
land is high and healthy, but too poor to bear anything but one vast
pine forest. Since Mr. Hazlitt wrote to you our Encampment has been
moved to a much more pleasant and higher situation. We are on
top of a high ridge, with about the best spring of water in Louisiana
runing near. There is nothing but pine woods surrounding us and
they infested to an inormaus degree with Ticks, Red bugs, and a
little creeping thing looking like a Lizard, that I dont know the name
of. This last vermin is singularly partial to society, and become so
very intimate and sociable on a short acquaintance as to visit our
tents, crawl into our beds &c. &c. Tis said they are very innocent
but I dont like the looks of th(em).—Nearly the first person I met here
was Hazlitt, (or) Sly Bob, with one of those Stage driver's round top
wool hats and a round jacket, trying to take the heat as comfortably
as possible. He drew me into his tent; which by the way is a little
linen affair just like your Fishing tent, with the ground covered with
Pine leaves for a floore. It took me one day to answer his questions,
and you may rest assured that a number of them were about Ellen
and yourself together with the rest of the family. When you write*

to him tell him how Clarra is comeing on.—Since I first set down to write we have had a hard shower and I can tell you my tent is a poor protection. The rain run through in streams. But I will have a shed built in a few days then I will do better. You have been to Camp Meeting, and know just how the people cook, and sleep, and live there? Our life here is just about the same. Hazlitt probably told you all about how we live here. While I think of it he sends his love to you and Ellen and the rest of the family, and to Wrenshall Dent's family. Mine must go to the same.—

I was detained a day longer in St. Louis than I expected and to make time pleasantly pass away I called on Joe Shurlds and had a long talk of three or four hours, about—about!—let me see: What was the subject? I believe it was the usual topic. Nothing in particular, but matters generally. She pretends to have made a great discovery. Can you concieve what it was?

Julia! I cannot express the regrets that I feel at having to leave Jeff. Bks. at the time that I did. I was just learning how to enjoy the place and the <u>Society</u>, at least a part of it. Blank _____ _____

_____ _____ _____ _____ _____ _____ _____ _____

_____ _____ _____ _____ _____ _____ _____

_____ _____ _____ _____ Read these blank lines just as I intend them and they will express more than words.—You must not forget to write soon and what to seal with. Until I hear from you I shall be,— I don't know what I was going to say—but I recon it was your most humble (lover) and Obt. friend.

Ulysses S. Grant

Miss Julia Dent
Gravois Mo.

P.S. Did you get the Magazines I sent you, one from Memphis the other from N. Orleans? Usg

Ulysses keeps his engagement a secret but can't resist hinting at it in this poignant letter to Mrs. Bailey, the neighbor who cried when he left for West Point, though there were no tears at his own house:

"Tell me of all the weddings &c. &c..."

Camp Salubrity
Near Nachitoches Louisiana
June 6th 1844

Mrs. Bailey
 My journey fortunately is at an end, and agreeably to your request, and my own pleasure, I hasten to notify you of my safe arrival here. It always affords me pleasure to write to old acquaintances, and much more to hear from them, so I would be pleased if the correspondence would not stop here. As long as my letters are answered, if agreeable to you I will continue to write.—
 My trip to this place "forty days journey in the wilderness" was marked with no incident, Save one, worth relating and that one is laughable curious, important, surprising &c. &c. but I cant tell it now. It is for the present a secret, but I will tell it to you some time. You must not guess what it is for you will go wrong.

Ulysses goes on to describe his trip to Camp Salubrity, as he did to Julia. Then, the eager young soldier, secretly engaged, can't help but turn the subject back to romance.

 I should be happy to get an answer to this as early as possible; if nothing more, a Post Script from the Young ladies. Ladies are always so much better at giving the news than others, and then there is nothing doing or said about Georgetown that I would not like to hear. They could tell me of all the weddings &c. &c. that are talked of. Give my love to evry body in Georgetown.

Lt. U S Grant
4th Infantry

To Mrs. G. B. Bailey
Georgetown Ohio

P.S. I give my title in signing this not because I wish people to know what it is, but because I want to get an answer to this and put it there that a letter may be directed so as to get to me.

Ulysses' second love letter to Julia reveals many things. One is a telling sentence about someone selling whiskey which he hastily crossed out, revealing he thought better of bringing up the subject of alcohol. He may have already sensed he had a problem, and doesn't want to call attention to it to his betrothed. He clearly prefers the thought of fighting to being "doomed to stay safe." The following passage shows his courage at declaring his love for Julia that day on the bridge, when he was still unsure of her feelings.

That bridge, for them, was indeed a bridge to a new world—the world of passion and romance.

"Never before was I satisfied that my love for you was returned, but you then assured me that it was."

Camp Salubrity
Near Nachitoches
July 28th 1844

My Dear Julia.

Mr. Higgins has just arrived from Jefferson Barracks and brings word that he saw you well on the 4th Inst. He delivered your message and says that he promised to bring some letters from you but supposes that you expected him out at your house to recieve them. You can hardly immagine how acceptable your message was but when I found that I might have expected a letter from you by his calling for it, I took the Blues (You told me that you had experienced the same complaint) so badly that I could resort to no other means of expelling the dire feeling than by writing to My <u>Dear</u> <u>Julia</u>. It has been but few days since I wrote to you but I must write again. Be as punctual in writing to me Julia and then I will be compensated in a slight degree,—nothing could fully compensate—for your absence.—In my mind I am constantly turning over plans to get back to Missouri, and until today there has been strong grounds for hoping that the whole of the 4th Regiment would be ordered back there; but that hope is blasted now. Orders have arrive from Washington City that no troops on the frontier will be removed. Fred's Regiment as well as mine will *have to remain. Mexico has appropriated four millions of dollars for the purpose of raising an Army of thirty thousand men for the reconquering of Texas, and we are to remain here to preserve neutrality between the United States and the belligerent parties. Who knows but Fred. and me may have something to do yet? Though it may be something short of the conquest of Mexico, or the overpowering of some other big country. Would you not be glad to hear of something of the kind after the difficulty was all over and we were safely out (of the difficulty)? I think there is no danger, however, from any present causes, of anything of the kind taking place. Fred. and me are doomed to stay safe and quietly in the woods for some time yet. I may be able to get to the same post with Fred. by transfering with Lt. Elting. I have written to Towson on the subject. If I should get there Fred. and me will be great friends as we always have been, and no doubt will spend many pleasant hours together talking over the pleasant times both of us have spent on the Gravois. No doubt your brother will have many pleasant things to relate of the place, and to me they will be doubly interesting because Julia Dent is there. Many a pleasant hour have I spent at Camp Salubrity thinking over my last visit to Mo. and its results. Never before was I satisfied that my love for you was returned, but you then assured me that it was. Does Mrs. Dent know of the engagement between us? I believe from Freds letter that he half suspects it, though he mentions nothing of the kind. I would be perfectly willing that he should be acquainted with the fact though of course, would not tell him myself.—Mr. Higgins gives us an account of the Barbeque on the Gravois the 4th of July. Billy Long kept whiskey to sell in one corner, and Miss Lucy entertained the gentle(men) is his account. No doubt Miss Fanny Morrison was in all her glory with her returned intended! Does Fanny call out to see you often? What does she say about me? What is the reason I cant be there myself to hear? evry body els is going. Col. Garland, Captain Morris and Capt. Barber are just starting, and in a few days Capt. Morrison will be off.—Julia write to me soon and give a long account of how you pass your time. No doubt it is much more pleasantly spent than mine in the hot pine woods of Louisiana. Hazlitt and me visit each other, at our linen Mansions about three times per day, and our calls are so unfashionable that the three calls lasts from morning until bed time.*

The subjects of our conversations are usually Missour(i) Turn over and commence reading the cross lines on the first page.
To Miss Julia Dent. Yours most constantly U S Grant and the people of Missouri—Miss J. & E Dent in particular and our future prospects and plans. We have big plans laid for visiting Mixico and Texas this winter and Missouri too soon. Sometimes we get to talking about your house I almost immagine myself there. While speaking of Mr. Hazlitt let me tell you that he has just left my tent and the last words he said was for me to be sure and give you and Ellen, and the rest of the family his very best love. He says that he expects a partnership letter from you two.—I wish Julia that you and Ellen could be here for one hour to see our mode of living. When any body calls to see me we have very cozily to take our seats side by side on the bed for I have no chair. If I could only be in your parlor an hour per day what a recreation it would be. Since I arrived here it has been so very hot that I but seldom go out of Camp. Once I was over at Fort Jesup and saw Mr. Jarvis. Tell Ellen that he fell a good deal more than half in love with her. He seemed very anxious to know what word she had sent him by me. Has Miss Fanny ever tried to convince you since, that she is in possession of all my secrets and knows just who I love best? Dont you think it strange that a young lady will talk so. I am afraid that you will find difficulty in reading the crossed lines. I will therefore conclude on the page left for directing the letter, u.s.g. Julia I would not presume so much as to send this letter without having recieved an answer to either of my others if Mr. Higgins had not mentioned that you told him you had rec'd letters from Mr. Hazlitt and me, which led me to suppose that Mr. & Mrs. Dent knew of your recieving them and make no objection. I have too an opportunity of sending it to Jeff. Bks. to be mailed.—Be shure and answer it and all my others soon—I am sorry Julia that I wrote the letter sent in one of Mrs. Porters. Burn it up wont you? I would feel much freer if the consent desired in that letter was obtained, but as it is not, I will have to wait until I get back there to get it; unless you can satisfy me that there is no parental objection.—What is the reason that John Dent has not written to me? He must have been much engaged electioneering this Summer! Give my love to Ellen and the rest of the family. Again, be shure and write soon and relieve from suspense your most Devoted and Constant l____

U S G

P.S. I have carefully preserved the lock of hair you gave me. Recollect when you write to seal with the ring I used to wear: I am anxious to see an impression of it once more.

U s g

Poor Ulysses! He is so worried about every little thing that might alter Julia's feelings for him. Yet he still can't bring himself to say the word "love" in a romantic way. Signing his name, he simply places an "l" and a blank space where he obviously wanted to write the word "lover."

At last, he receives letters from Julia, his very first ones. In her very first letter, she reveals she has been dreaming of him. This begins a lifelong theme between the lovers of dreaming of each other, and sharing their dreams in letters, when they are apart.

"You say Julia that you often dream of me!"

Camp Necessity La.
Grand Ecore & Texas Road
Aug. 31st 1844

My Dear Julia
Your two letters of July and August have just been received and read you can scarsely immagine with how much pleasure. I have waited so long for an answer to my three letters (I have written you three times Julia one of them you probably had not time to get when you wrote yours) that I began to dispare of ever recieving a line from you; but it come at last and how agreeable the surprise! Take example in punctuality by me Julia, I have rec'd your letters only to day and now I am answering them. But I can forgive you since the tone of your last letter, the one in pencil, is so conclusive of constancy. I am sorry to hear that Mrs. Dent thinks there is nothing serious in our engagement with me nothing is more serious or half as pleasant to think of—Since the arrival of your letters I have read them over and over again and will continue to do so until another comes. I have not been into Camp Salubrity yet to deliver to Mr. Hazlitt verbally the messages you sent him, but I wrote him a note this morning containing them. Mr. Hazlitt has been quite unwell for a few days past—You probably have heard from Mr Porters letters that for the last three weeks my company have been road making—The day we came out it rained very hard all day— the men had heavy Knap sacks to carry through the mud and rain for a distance of about five miles and no shelter to go under at the end of their journey—My fare was just the same only I had nothing but myself to carry—The first night we had to lay our wet beds on the still damper ground and make out the best we could—Musketoes and Wood ticks

by the hundreds pestered us—On the whole I spent a few miserable nights and not much better days at the begining of my first experience at campaigning, but now I find it much better—We will probably be through and return to Camp Salubrity in ten days more—I have just rec'd a letter from Fred, he is about my most punctual correspondent, he speaks of Louise Stribling. I think (s)he certainly is not married nor wont be unless she gets Fred—Fred is very well but hartily tired of Fort Towson—He proposes that (him) and (me) should each get a leave of absence next Spring and go to Missouri I would accept his proposal but I intend going sooner—I shall try very hard to go in the Fall—The happiness of seeing you again can hardly be realized, and then like you I have so much that I would like to say and dont want to write.—Julia do tell me the secrets that Georgia M disclosed to you—I think I can guess them from what follows in your letter—Georgia M is a very nice modest and inexperienced girl and can very easily be made to believe anything her oldest sister tells her—I know very well that Fanny told her that I was in love with her and she foundes her reasons for thinking so upon what followed took place at you house— You remember the occurrence of the apple seeds? Fany has tried to find out from Mr. Hazlitt which I loved best Georgia or Julia—Mr. Hazlitt would not tell her which he thought because to please her he would have to tell what he believed to be a story, and to have said you (as he believed though of course he new nothing about certain) he thought would give unnecessary offense. Hazlitt told me of the conversation he had and it displeased me so much with Miss F. that I said things of her which I would not commit to paper—Believe me my dear Julia what ever Miss Georgia may have told you she no doubt believed herself, but in believing she has allowed herself to be the dupe of one older than she is, but whose experience in <u>love</u> <u>affairs</u>, ought to be worth a great deel more than it is.—Tell me what she said in your next letter— Dont let Mrs. Dent see this part of my letter for of all things I don't like to have to speak ill of a third person, and if I do have to speak so I would like as few as possible to know it.—I am very far from having forgotten our promise to think of each other at sun seting—At that time I am most always on parade and no doubt I sometimes appear very absent minded—You say you were at a loss to ascribe a meaning to t(h)e blank lines in my first letter! Nothing is easyer, they were onl(y) *intended to express an attachment which words would fail to express Julia do not keep anything a secret from me with persons standing in the relation that we do to each other there should be no backwardness about making any request—You commenced to make a request of me and checked yourself—Do not be afraid that any thing you may request will not be granted, and just think too the good you might .do by giving good advice—No one is so capable of giving good advice as a lady, for they always practice just what they would preach—No doubt you have laid down to Fred. just the course he ought to take, and if he follows the advice he must do well—How fortunate he must feel himself to have a sister to correspond with I know I should have been proud to have had such a one to write to me all the years of my absence. My oldest sister is old enoug(h) to write now and I intend to direct all my home letters to her—She loves you and Ellen already without ever having seen you just from what she has heard me say—You say Julia that you often dream of me! Do tell me some of your good ones; dont tell me any more of the bad ones; but it is an old saying that dreams go by contraries so I shall hope you will never find me in the condition you drempt I was in—And to think too that while I am writing this the ring I used to wear is on your hand—Parting with that ring Julia was the strongest evidence I could have given you (that is—in the way of a present) of the depth and sincerity of my love for you—Write to me soon, much more than the last time and if Mrs. Porter is not there, or not writing at the time take a little ride and put your letter in the Post Office—On the road think of some of the conversations we used to have when we rode out together*

Most Truly and Devotedly Your Lover
Ulysses

To Julia

P S I think in the course of a few days Julia I will write to Col. Dent to obtain his consent to our correspondence; I will ask nothing more at present but when I get back to St. Louis I will lay the whole subject before him Julia do not let any disclosed secrets such as Miss Georgia told you, make you doubt for a moment the sincerity depth *and constancy of my feeling, for you and you alone out of the whole acquaintance. Find some name beginning with "S" for me Julia You know I have an `S in my name and dont know what it stand for.*

U.S.G.

P.P.S. Tell Ellen that I have not been into Camp yet to see the playthings she sent Mr. Hazlitt but I will go tomorrow morning if I have to walk. I think there is no danger of us quarreling since we have agreed so long together; but if we do get into a scrape I will let her know it. Remember me to Miss Ellen, Mrs. Porter Mrs. Mary Dent and your Fathers family all.

USG

When selecting this line as our favorite, I asked my "editor," my seven year old son Teddy, "I wonder what she wanted to tell him, but couldn't write down?" He quickly replied, "I love you."

"Another of our little walks up or down the creek would be so pleasant, and then too you could tell me what you say you want to tell and cant write."

Camp Salubrity La
Near Nachitoches
Sept. 7th 1844

My Dear Julia
I have just written the letter you desired I should, and which I have long thought it a duty to write. You can scarsely conceive the embarrassment I felt in writing such a letter, even in commencing the first line. You must not laugh at it Julia for you have the chance I send it unsealed that you may read it before delivering it. I wrote it at our little camp in the woods on the road to Texas while alone by my self, at night. I immagined all the time that I saw your Pa & Ma reading it and when they were done, raising all kinds of objections. Youth and length of acquaintance I feared might be brought against us but assure them my dear Julia that the longest acquaintance, or a few years more experience in the world could not create a feeling deeper or more durable. While I have been writing this there has been three or four officers in the tent bothering and talking to me all the time but they have just gone out thank fortune. They do not suspect that I am writing to you. It has only been a few days since I received your letters. I answered them immediately, wont you be as punctual in answering mine in the future? You dont know Julia with how much anxiety and suspense I await there arrival. But here I am asking you to write soon and in the same letter asking permission to have you write, and without knowing that the favor will be granted. If the proper consent is obtained I know you will follow the example of punctuality I have set.
I wrote to Fred a day or two ago: I told him I would accept his

invitation to go to Mo. next Spring if I did not go sooner, but at present the prospect is so fair for the 4th Regiment going to Jefferson Barracks to spend next winter that I am in hopes that shorter leaves will be long enough for me to visit Gravois. You dont know how much I want to get back there once more. Another of our little walks up or down the creek would be so pleasant, and then too you could tell me what you say you want to tell and cant write. In your next wont you tell me all about the secrets Miss Georgia made known to you. I do assure you Julia that you need not let anything she can tell you, about me, give the least trouble.

Mrs. Capt. Page and Mrs. Alden have each written to their husbands that they saw General Scott lately and he says that he intends sending our Regiment up the Mississippi as soon as possible; and if he does we will get to Jeff. Bks. about November where we will have to stay until the river breaks up above which will be about next May. It is now about Eleven o'clock P.M. and Mr. Porter and me are each sitting writing letters to go to Gravois. All the time I am writing mine I am thinking that probably Julia has on, the ring that I left her, and who knows but just at this time she may be dreaming of me! How much I flatter myself dont I? To think that your thoughts might be upon me during your sleep.

Mr. Porter is through writing his letter and waiting to get this to seal them up. You know he is Post Master? He says that when you write to me again you must put a little cross on the outside that he may know the letter is for me. The last one he opened before he found it out—Mr. Hazlitt I believe I told you has been sick. His health is improving gradually, but he is very tired of this country. He says he does not consider it (living)g atall; but merely spining out an existance. He d(esir)es to be remembered to you and Ellen and the rest of the family. He has never seen any of the play things yet that Ellen sent him. Possibly they will be here to-morrow for I understand that Mr. Wallen's baggage is just arriving. Mr. Hazlitt says he wishes you would write him just one letter—Remember me to all the people at Gravois little Davy and all.

Ulysses

P.S. Julia don't let any one but your Pa. & Ma read the letter I have directed to them will you?

U

This letter to a friend reveals Ulysses' attraction to gambling, and his already cemented status at it of "loser." But it also reveals Ulysses' sense of humor with the boys.

"I was there every day and bet low, generally lost."

To Robert Hazlitt

December 1, 1844

There were five days' races at Natchitoches. I was there every day and bet low, generally lost. Jarvis and a number from Jessup were there. Jarvis was pretty high and tried to be smart all the time. He fell over the back of a bench at the racecourse and tumbled over backward in his chair in front of Thompson's Hotel during his most brilliant day. He undertook to play brag at our camp and soon succeeded in ridding himself of twenty dollars in quarters. The game of brag is kept up as lively as ever. I continued to play some time after you left and won considerable, but for some time back I have not played and probably will never play again—no resolution, though.

This was one of my favorite discoveries. While reading this love letter, I kept wondering, "Why is Ulysses going on and on in such detail about Mr. Hazlitt falling off of his donkey?" Ah. Then I realized, it was all so he could nobly point out that he was being faithful to Julia, because Hazlitt fell off his donkey on the way to a ball, and—

"I was not at the ball myself..."

> *Camp Salubrity*
> *Near Nachitoches La.*
> *January 12th 1845*

My Dear Julia
> *It has now been nearly two months since I heard from you and about four months since I wrote the letter to your parents to which I hoped so speedy an answer. Of course I cannot argue any thing very strong in favor of my request being granted from their not answering it, but at the same time they do not say that I shall not write to you, at least as a friend, and therefore I write you this Julia, and direct it to Sappington P.O. expecting your Pa and Ma to know that you get it. The fact is I thought I must hear from you again—The more than ordinary attachment that I formed for yourself and family during my stay at Jeff. Bks. cannot be changed to forgetfulness by a few months absence. But why should I use to you here the language of flattery Julia, when we have spoken so much more plainly of our feeling for each other? Indeed I have not changed since and shall hope that you have not, or will not, at least until I have seen all of you once more. I intend to apply for a leave in the spring again and will go to St. Louis. For three months now I have been the only officer with my company and of course cannot leave even for one week. Julia can we hope that you Pa will be induced to change his opinion of an army life? I think he is mistaken about the army life being such an unpleasant one. It is true the movements of the troops from Jeff. Bks. so suddenly and to so outlandish a place would rather create that opinion, but then such a thing hardly occurs once a lifetime.*

Mr. Hazlitt returned about one month ago looking as lazy and healthy as ever. I was away from camp when he returned and did not get home until about midnight. I woke him up and him and me had a long talk from that until morning. He told me all about what a pleasant visit he had at Jeff. Bks. or rather on the Gravois. Was he plagued much about Miss Clara while there? You don't know how much I wished to be along with him! He regrets very much that he didnot return by St. Louis.—I must tell you something about Mr. Hazlitt since he returned. He has got him a little pony about the size of the one I had at Jeff. Bks. it is a little "Jim a long Josy" of a thing and if you were to see it you would think it was going to drawl out "y-e-s im hisn" just as you know Mr. Hazlitt does himself; he rode his pony to a Ball four or five mile from camp a few days ago and as he was jogging along the road, neither pony nor man thinking of anything I suppose, the little thing stumbled and away went Hazlitt over its head rolling in the dust and dirt. When he got up he must have turned a complete summer-set. I was not at the Ball myself, and therefore didnot see Hazlitts exhibition and it was several days before he told me of it. He could'nt keep it a secret. You ought to be here a short time to see how we all live in our winter houses. They are built by puting posts in the ground as if for a fence and nailing up the outside with shingles. I have plank for my house but there is but one or two other officers that have. The chimneys are of mud and sticks and generally are completed by puting a barrel or two on top to make them high enough. Mr. Porter, Wallen & Ridgley have built themselves fine houses expecting their families here. Mr. Por(ter) went three or four weeks ago to visit his wife (.....) the mouth of Red river. If they were here they might live very pleasantly for the weather is so warm that we need but little or no fires. Mr. Hazlitt and me keep bachilors hall on a small scale and get along very pleasantly. We have an old woman about fifty years old to cook for us and a boy to take care of our horses so that we live as well as though we were out of the woods—Mr. Hazlitt wishes to be remembered to all of you. He says that you must write to him right off.—I hear from Fred. very often. He was well the last time he wrote. Julia you must answer this quick wont you? I know you can. Give my love to all the family.

Fare well, Ulysses

To Bvt. Brig. Gen. Roger Jones

> *Camp Salubrity La.*
> *March 11th 1845*

Sir,

    I have rec'd my commission as a Bvt. 2d Lieut. in the army of the U. States and hasten to acknowledge my acceptance of the rank it confers.

> *I am Sir*
> *Your Obt. Svt.*
> *US Grant*
> *Bvt. 2d Lt. 4th Inf*

To Gen. R. Jones Adj. Gen

TIME FOR ACTION

Ulysses wrote to Miss Julia's father, the cantankerous Colonel Dent, asking permission to write to her, but never received a reply. He begged Miss Julia for more letters, but got no response. It was time for Lieutenant Grant to take action!

CHAPTER TWO
The Lieutenant Takes on a Colonel

One year after his departure with the Army, Ulysses returned to White Haven to ask Julia's father for her hand. When Lieutenant Ulysses S. Grant stood before "Colonel" Dent to ask for his daughter's hand in marriage, it was surely the first battle of the Civil War.

Both the Colonel and the Lieutenant had military titles. Ulysses had earned his title the hard way, through boot camp and deprivation, long marches and monotonous drilling.

"Colonel" Dent earned his title simply by being rich. It was a tradition in the Old South for wealthy landowners to spontaneously become known as "Colonel."

Both the Colonel and the Lieutenant were romantics, but again, in very different ways.

Lieutenant Grant was in love with a woman, Colonel Dent was in love with a dream: the dream of being a Southern plantation owner.

Born and raised in Maryland, Colonel Dent had worked all his life in pursuit of his dream. (Well, actually, his slaves had worked all his life in pursuit of his dream.)

Like many wealthy landowners of the era, Colonel Dent felt he was a member of Southern aristocracy, a sort of rural royalty, with a front porch instead of a throne. While his slaves did all the work, the Colonel lounged on his front porch, nursing his mint julep and his dream. He would pass along this dream to future generations of his family, a dream he believed would last forever.

Julia was his first and favorite daughter, and as little sister Emmy Dent recalled, "Papa would give Julia anything she wanted, anything at all." But this did not include the poor, frail Yankee Lieutenant standing determinedly before him.

Colonel Dent had always envisioned his favorite daughter, through an advantageous marriage, upgrading the Colonel to even higher status in his exclusive, imaginary club. Her upbringing and seven years at Miss Mauro's Finishing School had certainly prepared her for this destiny—to be a great Southern lady and continue the traditions so dearly cherished by her doting Papa.

And now, here was this pathetic little fellow with the sensitive eyes and obstinate mouth, trying to ruin it all.

Penniless, a stranger, a Yankee, worst of all, Lieutenant Grant had nothing to give Colonel Dent's daughter but love.

And Julia was attracted like a hummingbird to nectar.

To Julia, her Lieutenant's love was worth more than all the wealth, glamour, and creature comforts in the world.

For this reason, Julia Dent must surely go on record as the greatest female romantic icon in American history.

In one of his earliest military strategies on record, Ulysses carefully planned to accost Colonel Dent as he was preparing to leave on a trip, taking him by surprise and giving him as little time to think about it as possible. A flustered Colonel Dent suddenly found himself face to face with the man who would not only take his little girl away, but someday destroy the Colonel's entire way of life.

Colonel Dent was the first Southerner to face Ulysses S. Grant—he wouldn't be the last.

One can imagine the scowling "Colonel" receiving the stubborn little Lieutenant. Colonel Dent, clothed in his elegant black frock coat, the uniform of the South, and the sturdy soldier, Ulysses, in the military uniform of the United States Army.

As usual, Ulysses got straight to the point.

"Mr. Dent, I want to marry your daughter, Miss Julia."

"The roving life of the military would not suit my Julia at all," the Colonel drawled, confidently making his first move.

Already knowing, from Julia's letter, her father's negative position, Ulysses had been thinking this one out, as well.

"Then, I will resign the military and become a math teacher," Ulysses calmly countered.

Colonel Dent looked the stubborn little soldier over.

"You belong in the military," Colonel Dent was forced to admit, either because he felt it, intuitively, or because it was a good way for this damned Yankee to get himself killed.

Opening his heart a little, Ulysses promised that if life in the Army did not suit his bride, "I will make her happy."

No doubt flustered by the Yankee's noble intentions, Colonel Dent countered that they were too young for marriage. But the Lieutenant wasn't budging. Finally, Colonel Dent came up with a good one. He said that if, in a *couple of years,* they did not change their minds, he would give his consent.

Colonel Dent, like Robert E. Lee in the future, figured time would wear out Ulysses' determination. They were both wrong.

After winning the Colonel's reluctant permission for them to correspond, Ulysses drank up the remaining days of his leave with his love.

As Julia recalls, "Mr. Grant passed the next ten or twelve days at White Haven, and such a two weeks! It was May, and the country was beautiful. The days were passed in reading, walking, and riding, and full of such pleasant, pleasant memories to me. The locust trees were more heavily laden than usual with their white plumes. The forests were more tenderly green, and our seat on the piazza was one bower of eglantine and white jessamine. I remember how pleasantly the hum of the bees in that bower of ours and how near the swallows would come as they whirled past us making music with the fluttering of their wings."

How romantic and appropriate that Julia and Ulysses were serenaded by the birds and the bees.

After spending two weeks with her lover, Julia's feelings for Ulysses began to heat up.

But so did tensions between the United States and Mexico.

Ulysses returned to Camp Salubrity, with dreamy memories of his sojourn with Julia.

I had only planned to select one favorite line from each love letter, but now I see it may be too hard for me to resist putting in a couple of my favorite lines:

"I shall always look back on my short trip to Missouri as the most pleasant part of my life."

"I am going to follow your advice, Julia, and have me a good and comfortable house."

Camp Salubrity
Near Nachitoches La.
Tuesday, May 6th 1845

My Dear Julia
　　I have just arrived at Camp Salubrity after a tolerably pleasant trip of only one week from St. Louis, with one days detention at the mouth of Red river. I am here just in time; one day later I would probably an excuse to write. Whilst at the mouth of Red river I met with Lt. Baker who is strait from Fort Towson. He left there only about one week ago. Fred. is very well, and would have been in Missouri with me but his commanding officer refused him a leave. It was right mean in him was'nt it?—Evry thing at Camp Salubrity looks as usual only much greener from the contrast between the advancement of the season here and in the North. Though we are so far South and vegetation so far advanced a fire this evening is very comfortable. The officers are all collected in little parties discussing affairs of the nation. Annexation of Texas, war with Mexico, occupation of Orregon and difficulties with England are the general topics. Some of them expect and seem to contemplate with a great deal of pleasure some difficulty where they may be able to gain laurels and <u>advance</u> <u>a</u> <u>little</u> <u>in</u> <u>rank.</u> Any moove would be pleasant to me since I am so near promotion that a change of post would not affect me long. I have advanced three in rank very lately, leaving only

five between me and promotion.—Mr. Hazlitt has gone to Fort Jesup and wont be back for a week; he left this morning before I got here.— It seems very strange for me to be siting here at Camp Salubrity writing to you when only a little more than one short week ago I was spending my time so pleasantly on the Gravois.—Mrs. Porter started a few days ago for Washita and of course took little Dave. along so that I could not give him the kiss you sent him. Mr. Porter was very particular in his enquiries about all of you, and if he knew that I was writing he would send his love. When I got to Nachitoches I found Mr. Higgins and Beaman there just ready to start on a leave of absence. I am sorry that Miss Fanny dont know that he is on the way. I wanted him to tell me if he intended to bring her to Salubrity with him but he would not say yes or no. Tell me what the probablities are.—Have you heard yet from Col. Dent? I suppose Brand must have written you a very amusing account of his adventures in the East.—I suppose Capt. Cotton has taken Lizzy to Green Bay before this. Does John pretend to be as much as ever in love?—The first thing I did after geting here was to get my letters from the Post Office. I found one from Miss J.B.D. that afforded me a great deel of pleasure, and one from home that had come by the way of St. Louis. Is Miss Jemima Sappington married yet?—Tell John not to take it so hard as he appeared inclined to when he first heard of it.—I wrote to Fred. on my way down the Mississippi and told him of the pleasant visit I had, and how disappointed you all were that he was not along. I shall always look back to my short visit to Mo. as the most pleasant part of my life. In fact it seems more like a pleasant dream than reality. I can scarsely co(nvince) myself of the fact that I was there so short a ti(me) ago. My mind must be on this subject something like Hercules Hardy's was whilst he was a prisoner among the Piannakataws in Guiana. I send you the story that you may read it.—Remember me very kindly to Mrs. Dent and Ellen and Emmy and your brothers and to your Aunt Fielding and your Cousins. Don't neglect to write as soon as you get this.

I am most devotedly your
Ulysses S. Grant

Julia

P.S. I promised to write to Lewis Dent as soon as I got here but I am so busily engaged building myself a new house that I will not have much time for awhile. Mrs. Wallen is here safe and looks very delicate.—I am going to follow your advice Julia and have me a good and comfortable house.

U.

The letter you wrote me before I went to Mo. was very different from what I expected to find it. It was not near so cold and formal as you led me to believe. I should not have written this last Post script should I?

u

Poor Ulysses! After spending such a blissful two weeks with Julia, he doesn't hear a word from her for months. She seems to be scatterbrained. But perhaps her beloved papa, after finding out Ulysses' romantic intentions to his daughter, is pressuring her to break it off. This is speculation, but it makes sense. Julia's inner conflict was always love of Ulysses versus love of her Southern belle lifestyle, which included "Mama" and "Papa's" approval.

If Ulysses can't get Julia to write via his own charms, he hopes perhaps the neighbor's inquiries about her will spur her pen to action. Notice how he signs his name, not with the usual "yours most devotedly," but with the downbeat, "Yours as ever."

"You dont know how tired I am geting of this place! I believe it is because I never hear from you."

"Mrs. Wallen is very well; she enquires when I heard from you last when ever she sees me but unfortunately I have to tell her that I never hear."

Camp Salubrity La.
Near Nachitoches
June 1845

My Dear Julia
It is now seven weeks since I wrote to you and about three weeks since I began anxiously to expect an answer, but as none has come yet I conclude that either you have never received my letter or els you have rec'd and answered it and the answer has been miscarried. Is it not so Julia, for I know you intended to be punctual when writing to me. If you knew how much I prized a letter from you you certainly would be. I do not expect to receive many more letters from you while at this place, judging from present appearances. All due preparations are now going on for our removal. The Texan Congress has already met and it is thought will soon accede to our

terms of Annexation and then in we go without delay, that is, some of the troops from these parts will. The 4th is hardly considered as one bound for Texas unless in case of difficulty with Mexico, but if we do not go there will be some place else, and I know that I shall be glad enough to get any place away from here. If any difficulty with the Mexicans takes us across the Western frontier the 6th will be as likely to go as the 4th and then I may have the pleasure of meeting Fred. on the <u>Rio</u> <u>Grande</u>. We will be excellent friends you may depend upon it when we get so far away. That will be the time for Fred. to prove himself a second Napoleon as you always said he would. I got a letter from Fred. a few days ago. He is in good health, he says he scarsely ever gets a letter from home. The last one he says was from Ellen, and that now you, John, Lewis, Wrenshall and your pa are all indebted to him a letter. So Julia I am not the only one you are negligent in writing to! But I don't believe you deserve so severe a charge as negligence. Are you all well on the Gravois? At Camp Salubrity it is very healthy although it is warm enough to throu a Regiment into a fever. You dont know how tired I am geting of this place! I believe it is because I never hear from you. Your Pa has returned before this time I suppose. Did he have a pleasant trip? Brand no doubt has a great many amusing adventures to relate. Write to me Julia as soon as you recieve this whether you have written to me before or not. Col. Dent told me that he would write to me as soon as he returned from the East; if he has not done it yet, wont you remind him of his promise. Remember me to your Aunt Fieldings family. I will wind up this time Julia with a short letter with the very good intention of writing you a very long one in answer to the first one I get from you. Mr. Porter has not heard from Mrs. Porter since she arrived at her mothers infact has not heard that she did arrive. She has been gone now nearly two months. Mrs. Wallen is very well; she enquires when I heard from you last when ever she sees me but unfortunately I have to tell her that I never hear. Miss Fanny Morrison is married I presume. The Captain is building a very comfortable house for her and Higgins. He says he expects Miss Clara along. Mr. Hazlitt wishes to be reminded to all at White Haven.

Yours as ever, Ulysses

Not only is Ulysses pleading for Julia to write him, now he is pleading for Colonel Dent to write to him, too. Like father, like daughter. Colonel Dent is counting on it.

"If you knew how happy I am to get a letter from you you would write often."

"Remind your pa about writing to me and you plead for us wont you Julia?"

N. Orleans Barracks La.
July 6th 1845

My Dear Julia
I received your letter a day or two before leaving Camp Salubrity but after we knew that we were to go. You dont know how glad I was to get it at that time. A weeks longer delay in writing to me and I probably would not have heard from you for months, for there is no telling where we are going or how letters will have to be directed so as to reach us. Our orders are for the Western borders of Texas but how far up the Rio Grand is hard to tell. My prediction that I would recieve but few letters more at Camp Salubrity has proven very true. I hope you have sent me a letter by Mr. Higgins. How unfortunate Miss Fanny has been. The Brevets that are going to Texas are probably better off than those of higher rank. I am perfectly rejoiced at the idea of going there myself for the reason that in the course of five or six months I expect to be promoted and there are seven chances out of eight that I will not be promoted in the 4th so that at the end of that time I shall hope to be back in the U. States, unless of course there should be active service there to detain me and to take many others there.—I was very much in hopes Julia that I would receive a letter from your pa before leaving Camp Salubrity giving his full consent to our engagement. Now—that I am going so far away and dont know how long it may be before I can hear from you I shall be in

a greatdeal of suspense on the subject. Soldiering is a very pleasant occupation generally and is so even on this occation except so far as it may be an obsticle in the way of our gaining the unconditional consent of your parents to what <u>we</u>, or at least I, believe is for our happiness.—Mrs. Wallen will soon go to Jefferson Barracks to remain until her husband has quarters comfortably arranged for her where the troops may be posted. She will be writing to Mr. Wallen, wont you ask her how she directs her letters and write to me? If you knew how happy I am to get a letter from you you would write often. Mrs. Wallen asked me if I would not have a letter for her to carry when she went to St. Louis and I told her that I would so if you will call on her when she arrives which will probably be about the 1st of August you may find another letter from me.—From what I have seen N. Orleans Barracks is the most pleasant place I have ever been stationed at. It is about four miles below the city, but it is so thickly settled all the way along that we appear to be in town from the start. The place is much more handsomely fixed than Jefferson Barracks.—In a few days the 3d Infantry will join us here, and not long after two companies are expected from Fort Scott. I dont know what the probabilities are for Fred. going to Texas, I know he is anxious to go and I should be happy to meet him there.—You ask if Fred. has done any thing out of the way that his commanding officer (w)ould not give him a leave! Certa(inly) he (has) (n)ot; the comd.g off. probably thin(ks) that he has not been long enough in s(e)rv(ice) to have a leave, or els there is too many officer(s) absent already, or something of the kind. There are but few Commanding officers as indulgent about giving young officers leaves of absence as the one I am serving under. (Col. Vose). I received a letter from Fred. but a few weeks ago and he said nothing to me about being ordered farther into the wilderness. Probably some of the Indians in those parts have been pestering the frontier setlers. Dont be frightened about his geting home again and I shall hope too to be with him. Next time I ask for a leave of absence it will be for six months, <u>to take a trip North</u>.

Give my love to all your family, and your Aunt Fieldings also. Mr. Hazlitt wishes to be remembered. He says that he was not two months in answering your letter.

48

Write without failing and I will trust to providence for geting the letter, for ever yours most devotedly

u s Grant

Julia

P.S. Remind your pa. about writing to me and you plead for us wont you Julia? I will keep an account of all the Mexicans and Comanches that we take in battle and give you a full account. I have a black boy along to take along as my servant that has been in Mexico. He speaks English Spanish and French I think he may be very useful where we are going. Fare well my Dear Julia for a scout among the Mexicans.

U.

Wait a minute! I just had a revelation. I never noticed until reading the above letter for the umpteenth time. Ulysses begs Julia to "plead for us" to her pa. This proves that when Ulysses visited St. Louis to ask Colonel Dent for her hand, just two months ago, Colonel Dent did not give his consent, or anything close to it. Julia was just putting her usual positive spin on Papa. She says in her memoirs, "We considered the matter settled," but it was far from it. Or else why would Ulysses have to ask Julia to "plead for us?" Through out the rest of his letters, let's see how many times Ulysses tries to get Papa's consent to their marriage.

Ulysses is about to leave New Orleans with his regiment, bound for Texas. This letter is full of poignant little gems. It shows how much Ulysses needs to have someone who cares for him, even if she rarely writes. He needs to feel he matters to somebody. And that somebody is his dear, dear Julia.

"In going away now I feel as if I had some one else than myself to live and strive to do well for."

N. Orleans Barracks La.
July 11th 1845

My Dear Julia

I wrote you a letter a few days ago in which I promised to write again by Mrs. Wallen. It was my intention then to write you a very long one but she starts much sooner than I expected so that I will only trouble you with a short note, and it too will probably reach you before the letter sent by Mail. There is now no doubt Julia but we will all be in Texas in a very short time. The 3d Infantry have arrived on their way and in a week or so we will all be afloat on the Gulf of Mexico. When I get so far away you will still think of and write to me I know and for my part I will avail my self of evry opportunity to send you a letter. It cannot well be many months that i will be detained in that country unless I be promoted to one of the Regiments stationed there and the chances are much against that. I have never mentioned any thing about <u>love</u> in any of the letters I have ever written you, Julia, and indeed it is not necessary that I should, for you know as well as I can tell you that you alone have a place in my <u>my</u>—What an out I make at expressing any thing like love or sentiment: You know what I mean at all events, and you know too how acquerdly I made known to you for the first time my love. It is a scene that I often think of, and with how much pleasure did I hear that my offer was not entirely unacceptable? In going away now I feel as if I had some one els than myself to live and strive to do well for. You can have but little idea of the influance you have over me Julia, even while so far away.

If I feel tempted to do any thing that I think is not right I am shure to think, "Well now if Julia saw me would I do so" and thus it is absent or present I am more or less governed by what I think is your will.

Julia you know I have never written anything like this befor and wont you keep any one from seeing it. It may not be exactly right to keep it from your parents, but then you will get a letter from me by Mail about the same time which they will probably see. Am I giving you bad advice? If you think so act just as you think you ought.—Mrs. Wallen will give you all the news afloat here. Dont forget to ask her how she intends to direct her letters to Mr. Wallen and send mine to the same address, and now I must close with sending the most devotional love of

U S G

To Julia

After reading the above letter, one wonders what things Ulysses was tempted to do, but stopped, when he imagined Julia watching him. He was too honest to steal, too monogamous to be unfaithful. It seems obvious he was tempted to drink, and just thinking of her helped keep him from it.

He was emotionally dependent on her from the start. He instinctively knew she was his salvation. Without her, he had nothing to live for. She alone had seen into his soul and still loved him. Nobody else had ever done that before. No one had ever kissed him, touched him, really seen deep inside of him. It was devastating.

One of the ongoing side soap operas in Julia and Ulysses' romance, is someone who seems determined to ruin their happiness almost as much as Colonel Dent. Her name is Fanny Morrison. If you'll recall, Ulysses was worried about Fanny spreading rumours that he loved her sister, "Miss Georgia," and not Julia. Now, married and with a new name, "Mrs. Higgins," Fanny is trying to hurt them again by telling Ulysses some terrible news:

"She says I have a dangerous rival in Missouri, and that you do not intend to write to me anymore"

(July 17, 1845)
N. Orleans Barracks La.

My Dear Julia
I wrote to you several days ago expecting that Mrs. Wallen would start the next day for St. Louis and would be the bearer of my letter, but at the time that she expected to get off she was taken sick and has not been able to start until now, so my Dear Julia I write you a second sheet hoping that any addition to one of my letters will be as agreeable to you as a Post Script to one of your letters is to me. Since I wrote you the first sheet several things of importance, or at least new, have taken place. One company of Artillery is now this and the mouth of the Mississippi river to join us for Texian service. Mr. and Mrs. Higgins have arrived and appear to be as happy as you please. Mrs. Higgins for some time persisted in accompanying her husband into the field but she has at length given it up.—Something melancholy has taken place too. On the evening of the 15th Inst. Col Vose, for the first time since I have been in the Army, undertook to drill his Regiment. He was probably some what embarassed and gave his commands in a loud tone of voise; before the drill was over I discovered that he put his hand to his breast when ever he commenced to give any command, and before he was through with the parade he was compelled to leave the field and start for his qarters, which were hardly fifty paces off, and just upon arriving there he

fell dead upon the poarch. He was buried to-day (July the 15th) with military honors.

That evening late I was sent to town to have the Obituary notice published; the next evening I was sent again to have the order and time of the funeral put in the papers and was returning between 1 and 2 o'clock at night when I discovered a man and woman that I thought I knew, footing it to the city carrying a large bundle of clothes. I galloped down to the Barracks to asc(er)tain if the persons I suspected were absent or not and found that they were. I was ordered immediately back to apprehend them, which by the assistance of some of the City Watchmen I was able to do. I had the man put in the watch house and brought the <u>lady</u> back behind me on my horse to her husband, who she had left asleep and ignorent of her absence. Quite an adventure was'nt it?

Mrs. Higgins and husband have arrived just in time to find us <u>en</u> <u>route</u> for Texas. I believe she will return to Jeff. Bks. in a day or two. She brings news Julia which if I did not believe she was mistaken in would give me some trouble of thoughts. She says that I have a dangerous rival in Missouri, and that you do not intend to write to me any more &c. &c. Of course Julia I did not believe this, yet the fact of any one saying it was so gave me some uneasiness. I knew, or at least I thought I knew, that even if any thing of the kind was so that you would let me know it and not tell it to a disinterested person. I am right in this am I not? You must not think Julia that I have been questioning and pumping to get the above information; it was voluntarily given and not to me but to another who come and told me. You will write to me soon wont you and contridict the above statement. Mrs. Higgins told me to-day that she would carry any letters or packages that I might have to send you. I will send these by Mrs. Wallen and when the other asks me for my letters I will tell her that I understand that you do not intend writing to me any more and of course cant expect me to be writing to you. If you direct your letters to me at N. Orleans La. or Corpus Christi Texas they will be forwarded to where I am. This makes five letters I have written to you since I was in Mo. Wont you in turn write me one immediately and another in two or three weeks after? Give my love to all your fathers and Aunt Fieldings families.

53

Yours affectionately
U S Grant

Julia

P.S. We will start for Texas in the course of three or four days. While you are reading this I will be thinking of you at Corpus Christi, that is if so fortunate as to get there safely. In a few months I shall hope to be back promoted. I now have but three now between me and promotion; a few months ago I had nine or ten, dream of me Julia and rest assured that what I have heard has not weight enough to chang my love for you in the slightest.

U S G to Julia

(in an envelope marked "Politeness of Mrs. Wallen")

I love the way he tells her to "dream of me."

In this next letter, Julia reproaches Ulysses for not writing to her more often! This is amazing, since she is the one that almost never wrote to him. She shows herself to be a woman who speaks up when she wants more attention. It also shows, despite her inner conflict about Ulysses, he does have a hold on her heart that she can't shake, try as she, and her precious Papa, might.

For Ulysses' part, he is ecstatic with any attention she gives him. As he honestly puts it:

"Your letters always afford me a greatdeal of happiness because they assure me again that you love me still."

Corpus Christi Texas
Sept. 14th 1845

My Dear Julia
I have just received your letter of the 21st ultimo in which you reproach me so heavily for not writing to you oftener. You know my Dear Julia that I never let two days pass over after recieving a letter from you without answering it; But we are so far separated now that we should not be contented with writing a letter and waiting an answer before we write again. Hereafter I will write evry two or three weeks at farthest, and wont you do the same Julia? I received your letter before the last only about three weeks ago and answered it immediately. Your letters always afford me a greatdeal of happiness because they assure me again that you love me still; I never doubted your love Julia for one instant but it is so pleasant to hear it repeated, for my own part I would sacrifice everything Earthly (...) to make my Dear Julia my own forever. All that I would ask would be that my Regiment should be at a healthy post and you be with me, then I would be content though I might be out of the world. There are two things that you are mistaken in Julia, you say you know that I am in an unhealthy climate and in hourly expectation of War: The climate is delightful and very healthy, as much so as any climate in the world and as for war we dont believe a word of it. We are so numerous here

*now that we are in no fear of an attack upon our present ground.
There are some such heavy storms here on the coast the later part
of Sept. and October however that we will probably be moved up the
Nuices river to San Patricio, an old deserted town, that the Indians
have compelled the inhabitants to leave.—Since the troops have been
at Corpus Christi there has not been a single death from sickness, but
there has been two or three terrible visitations of providence. There
has been one man drownd in the breakers; a few weeks ago a storm
passed over camp and a flash of lightning struck a tent occupied
by two black boys killing one and stuning the other, and day before
yesterday the most terrible accidents of all occured. For the last
few weeks there has been an old worn out Steam Boat, chartered by
government, runing across the bay here, and day before yesterday
there happened to be several officers and a number of soldiers
aboard crossing the bay; the boat had scarsely got out of sight when
the boilers bursted tearing the boat into atoms and througing almost
evry one aboard from twenty to fifty yards from the wreck into the
Briny Deep. Some were struck with iron bars and splinters and killed
immediately others swam and got hold of pieces of the wreck and
were saved. Among the killed was Lt. Higgins and Lt. Berry both of
the 4th Infantry. It will drive Fanny almost mad I fear. Capt. Morrison
takes Mr. Higgins' death very hard. When he was killed he was
standing talking with several officers; the others were uninjured. The
number killed and wounded I have not heard accurately state(d), but I
believe there was 9 killed and about 17 wounded one or two mortally.*

*Do you hear much about War with Mexico? From the accounts
we get here one would supposed that you all thought the Mexicans
were devouring us. The vacancies that have lately occured brings
me about first for promotion and if by chance I should go back to the
States I may have the pleasure of seeing my Dear Julia again before
the end of the year; what happiness it would be to see you again
so soon! I feel as though my good fortune would take me back. If I
should be promoted to a Regt. in Texas I will have to remain untill
an(...) affairs look a little more setled and we become permanent in
this country, which is a delightful one so far a(s) climate and soil is
concerned, but where no one lives scarsely except the troops, and
then I will go back and either remain there, or—May I flatter myself*

that one who I love so much would return with me to this country, when all the families that are now absent join their husbands?—If so Julia you know what I would say.

The mail is just going to close so I must stop writing. I intended to have written another sheet but I will have to put off my long letter until next time. Give my very best love to all your family and also Mrs. Fieldings. Don't neglect writing to me very soon Julia for you dont know how anxious I always am to get a letter from my Dear Dear Julia and how disappointed I always feel when I am a long time without one from her. I very often look at the name in the ring I wear and think how much I would like to see again the one who gave it to me. I must close, so good by my Dear Julia

U S Grant

It is heartbreaking to read of Ulysses' desperate longing for a letter. He tries to keep their love alive by reminding her of happy memories they shared. I love this description of Texas, because it shows how much he enjoys being out in nature, riding free. But he needs someone he loves to ride with him, even if it is only in his imagination. Surely, he was imagining the two of them together when he wrote of Texas:

"It is just the kind of country Julia that we have often spoken of in our most romantic conversations. It is the place where we could gallop over the prairies and start up Deer and prairie birds and occasionally see droves of wild horses or an Indian wigwam."

Corpus Christi Texas
Oct. 10th 1845

My Dear Julia
Yesterday evening we had a mail which was the first for several weeks and as it was a very large one I was in hopes that I would hear from you, but how disappointed I was! Not a single letter out of several hundred to the officers at this place was directed to me. I wrote you my third letter since I have been in Texas a few days ago but finding an opportunity of sending a letter all the way by politeness I write to you again Mr. Reeves will deliver this in person and no doubt will have a great deal to tell you about us all here. What we are to do is hard to surmise, but as I have told you in several previous letters it is supposed that we will remain until spring and then a large proportion return to the States. Those that remain will probably commence puting up quarters for a permanent post, and really I dont know but it would be desirable to remain in Texas. It is just the kind of country Julia that we have often spoken of in our most romantic conversations. It is the place where we could gallop over the prairies and start up Deer and prairie birds and occasionally see droves of wild horses or an Indian wigwam. The climate is delightful and healthy and the soil fertile, and when protected by troops no

doubt will be settled very rapidly.—The more we see of the Mexicans the more improbable it seems that we can ever get into war with her. Yucatan, one of Mexico's most powerful states has told Mexico to do their own fighting for they wont assist, besides this they are on the eve of revolution with their own subjects, and so far as we have seen, the poorer and less ambitious and much the most numerous class of Mexicans are much better pleased with our form of government than their own; infact they would be willing to see us push our claims beyond the Rio Grande if we would promise not to molest them in their homes and possessions.—The weather is geting quite cold here and no doubt we will suffer conciderably this winter, but it is all for glory you know so we should never complain.—When I wrote to you last I mentioned that I had been promoted, and I believe I said, to the 4th Inf.y, but I was mistaken in my calculation. I am promoted but the news has not yet had time to come from Washington, but I believe I go to the 8th Inf.y so I will of course remain in Texas this winter. Next Summer though I shall go back to the States either with my Regiment or on leave.

Have you seen Mrs. Higgins since the death of her husband? She must have taken it very hard. Capt. Morrison could not have taken it harder if Mr. Higgins had been a son instead of a son-in-law.

Have you heard from Fred. lately? I have not heard from him since I have been in Texas. Tell John that if he wants to come into the army, this Winter will probably be his chance. It is strongly rumored at Washington that there will be two Regiments of Infantry and one of Dragoons raised this comeing session of Congress and if so there will be a great many citizens appointed. Tell him to apply to Mr. Benton to use his influence right off. Are you all well on the Gravois? Remember me to evry one I know there. Write to me soon Julia and be assured that I am ever yours devotedly

U S Grant

Julia

You can see for yourself, Ulysses' greatest desire, in the following quote:

"Don't you think it time for us to begin to settle upon some plan for consumating what we believe is for our mutual happiness? After an engagement of sixteen or seventeen months, ought we not to think of bringing that engagement to an end, in the way that all true and constant lovers should?"

(Oct. 1845)
Corpus Christi Texas

My Dear Julia

    In my last letter I promised to write to you evry two or three weeks and it is now about that time since I wrote and you see how punctual I am. I fear Julia that there was a long time between the receipt of my letters from N. Orleans and my first from Texas but you must reflect that I had writen you three without having received an answer and before writing again I wanted to hear from my <u>Dear</u> <u>Dear</u> Julia. I always do and always will answer your letters immediately and if you knew how delighted I always am to hear from yourself you would write often too.

    The late casualty in the 4th Infantry promotes me so that I am now permanently at home in the Regiment. I should have prefered being promoted to a Regiment that is now in the States, because then I would get to see again, <u>soon</u>, one who is much dearer to me than any commission, and because too, there is hardly a probability of active service in this remote quarter of our country, and there is nothing els, excepting a fine climate and soil, to make one wish to stay here.—There is now over half of the Army of the U. States at Corpus Christi, and there must of course be a breaking up and scatterment of this large force as soon as it is found that their services will not be required in this part of the country. It is the general opinion that on account of the length of time the 4th has already been encamped, here and at Camp Salubrity, the general unsettled position that it has been *in since the begining of the florida war, that we will be the first out of Texas. Once in quarters again no doubt we will remain for a good long time.*

The most of the talk of war now comes from the papers of the old portion of the U. States. There are constantly bands of Mexican Smugglers coming to this place to trade, and they seem to feel themselves as secure from harm here as though they were citizens of Texas, and we on the other hand, although we are occupying disputed Territory, even acknowledging our right to Texas, feel as secure from attacks as you do off in Missouri. There was a time since we have been here when we were in about half expectation of a fight and with a fare prospect of being whipped too; that was when there was but few of us here and we learned that General Arista and other officers of rank were on the Rio Grande ready to march down upon us. We began to make preparations to make as stout a defence as possible. Evry working man was turned out and an intrenchment began and continued for about a week and then abandoned.

Now my Dear Julia that a prospect is ahead for some perminancy in my situation dont you think it time for us to begin to settle upon some plan for consumating what we believe is for our mutual happiness? After an engagement of sixteen or seventeen months ought we not to think of bringing that engagement to an end, in the way that all true and constant lovers should? I have always expressed myself willing you know my dear Julia to resign my appointment in the army for the sake of overcomeing the objections of your parents, and I would still do so; at the same time I think they mistake an army life very much. No set of ladies that I ever saw are better contented or more unwilling to change their condition than those of the Army; and you Julia would be contented knowing how much and how dearly devoted I am to you—I cannot help writing thus affectionat(ely) since you told me that no one but yourself reads my letters.

Your Pa asks what I could do out of the Army? I can tell you; I have at this time the offer of a professorship of mathematics in a tolerably well endowed College in Hillsboro, Ohio, a large and flourishing town, where my salary would probably equal or exceed my present pay. The Principle of the Institution got my father to write to me on the subject; he says I can have until next spring to think of this matter. The last letter I wrote was to make all the enquiries I could about the situation and if the answer proves favorable I shall give this matter serious concideration.

I am now reading the Wandering Jew, the copy that belonged to Mr. Higgins and the very same numbers read by yourself. How often I think of you whilst reading it. I think well Julia has read the same words that I am now reading and not long before me. Yesterday in reading the 9th No I saw a sentence marked around with a pencil and the word <u>good</u> written after it. I thought it had been marked by you and before I knew it I had read it over three or four times. The sentence was a sentiment expressed by the Indian Prince Djalmo on the subject of the marriage of two loving hearts, making a compareison you may recollect. Was it you that marked the place. I have written so long a letter that I must close. Remember me to evry body on the Gravois. Mr. Hazlitt also wishes to be remembered.

Give my love to Ellen. How is Ellen's soft eyed lover comeing on that she wanted me to quiz somebody down here about? She did not say so but I know she wanted some of her friends here to hear of him just to see how jealous she could make them.

Good bye my Dear Julia and dont forget to write soon.

Yours most affectionately
Ulysses

The speech of Prince Djalmo which Ulysses hoped that Julia had marked, reads:

"—for two drops of dew blending in the cup of a flower are as hearts that mingle in a pure and virgin love; and two rays of light united in one inextinguishable flame, are as the burning and eternal joys of lovers joined in wedlock."

It says right here in this next letter that Colonel Dent continues to "disapprove of the match." For Ulysses to know this, Julia must have told him in her letter. It was her first letter in two months, and clearly states that Papa still disapproves of the match. Her Papa had a huge influence over her. If he disapproved, he would be actively doing everything he could to keep her from writing. And very shortly after, he shipped Julia and her sister off to St. Louis to participate in the winter social season, no doubt hoping she would meet a suitable Southern suitor. Ulysses still pleads his case, assuring her that:

"Any one so much loved as you are Julia must be contented."

Corpus Christi Texas
Nov. 11th 1845

My Dear Julia
I was gratified this morning with recieving a letter from you which was the first in two months. You dont know how disappointed I have always felt for the last month when I go to the Post Office and find no letter from my Dear *Dear* Julia*. I do not recollect what the report was that you say I spoke of in one of my last letters, but it was nothing concerning either of us and certainly nothing like what you suspected.— Next Spring at farthest I think the 4th Infantry will be going back to the United States and no doubt will be permanent for many years unless some other difficulty should spring up to make it necessary to make us miserable again for another year or two. I always feel as though any place would be pleasant if I could only often see my Dearest Julia, and without that I will always be more or less discontented. How can your Pa continue to disapprove of a Match which so much affects the happiness of both? I say both because I judge you by myself. Dont you think he will finally yeald? How can I say finally though when we have been waiting already so long? I think my* Dear Julia *that the question of our marriage should be fully and irrevocably settled soon in justice to you. You know my Dear Julia that evry one who knows either of us believes that we*

are engaged and if it should turn out after all (I can scarsely bear to think such a thing possible though) that the engagement should be broken off by the objections of your parents, wont people say that I have done very rong and acted very unjustly to you not to have had a decission of the question much sooner. You know my views my Dear Julia on the subject of the interferance of parents in matters of such vast importance. You know that I think that evry thing possible should be done to reconcile parents to a marriage, at the same time, before an engagement is allowed to run on for years the party should make up their mind as to how they should act in case of a final refusal. I have always thought that you were of the same opinion as myself on this subject; am I not right Julia? I am fully satisfied that we could be happy and at the same time independent of the world. Any one so much loved as you are Julia must be contented. Wont you write to me soon and tell me if you think as I do. I would not propose any thing that I did not think would be for your own happiness for believe me I am not altogether selfish, I think of Julia as much as I do myself.—I believe I told you some time ago that I am promoted such is the case anyhow but I was not fortunate enough to get in a Regiment in the U.S. I go to the 7th Infantry which is encamped here but I have made application to transfer with Lt. Gardner of the 4th Inf.y and no doubt will be able to get back. No doubt Mr. Rieves has answered the questions you ask me about the particulars of the death of Mr. Higgins. I intend writing to Fred. to day. He owes me a letter but I shant be particular about that. He is very much like his sister Julia about writing he likes to have about two letters for one. No reproach upon you though Julia, if I thought you would write me one letter for evry two I would write about twice a week—The portion of the Army at Corpus Christi (amounting to between four and five thousand) would no doubt spend a very unpleasant winter if we didnot have such a fine climate. We have no quarters but our linen tents and or course cannot have fires, but we are so far South the cold is but little felt. I dont see that there is much difference between the winters and the summers in fact, except that there is more rain in the winter. Give my love to Ellen and the rest of the family at White Haven and if you can do write to me soon. The letter you speak of Julia as having read over so often could have been nothing but the most affectionate for I have not felt any other way. I do not recollect a word of what I wrote. I have written this in a great hurry and in consequence have told you but little news but I will write soon again and write much longer. I shall look for a letter from you very soon now in answer to the one Mr. Rieves delivered to you

Ulysses

To Julia

P.S. You have no doubt heard that Mexico has consented to appoint commissioners to settle the question of the boundary between this country and their own without any fighting. No doubt the whole affair will be settled by spring and the troops here will be distributed. Some two or three Regiments no doubt will have to remain to build and Garrison posts on the frontier of this country.

Julia at home they are very anxious to have me resign evry letter I get is on the subject of resignation. I have the offer of a professorship in a college in Ohio which they would prefer my taking to remaining in the Army but I have not concluded to accept the offer. I will come to some conclution on the subject between this and Spring. What do you think about it Julia? No one now can have more influance than just yourself. Tell me plainly what you think about my resigning for a place of the kind. If you can muster courage mention the matter to your Pa.

Adieu
U S G

Julia

He also refers to *both* of her parents disapproving of their engagement. Interesting, since Julia's mother is always represented as having liked Ulysses. But liking him and choosing him to be her daughter's husband are two different matters.

While Ulysses was plaintively wailing to be united with his dear dear Julia, Julia was off partying in St. Louis and passing "such a happy winter." She seemed to have no idea how badly she was hurting him by her neglect. In her memoirs, she clearly savored those days, recounting trivial details of parties, rather than her feelings for Ulysses. It shows that even in her old age, she didn't realize how miserable Ulysses was without her. To her, at this time, their romance just seemed like a lark. She was not brooding about it, as he was. She was trying to hold on to the carefree old days as long as she could.

Her unconditional surrender was still not at hand.

It called to her in the moonlight when she read one of her lonely soldier's letters. But she could merely tuck the letter away and go to sleep in the peace and security of her downy, Southern bed—for now.

You can feel Ulysses' pain in this line:

"I was so much in hopes that I would have a letter from you that I could scaresely bear to leave the office without one."

And in this line, you fully feel his love for her.

"The subject spoken of as being upermost, is my love for <u>my</u> <u>dear</u> <u>Julia</u> and the consequence (matrimony) of a love so pure."

(Nov.-Dec., 1845)

My Dear Julia
> *There is one subject that is ever upermost with me and I have alluded to it several times before but I could not resist this fine opportunity, when I know you will get my letter, to mention it again. I take an extra sheet for it not that I have said so much on the first but: I cant tell why—*
> *I was so much in hopes that I would have a letter from you that I could scaresely bear to leave the office without one, I wanted to write such a long one to you and wanted it to be an answer; but I know very well My Dear Julia that letters are a long time traveling as far as we are separated, and then too ladies think themselves punctual if they answer a letter in a month after it is recieved. This is no reproach upon you Julia for I have had two—and beautiful ones too—since the 4th has been in Texas; but you will write oftener even than this in the future wont you. You have often heard me say how delighted I always am to get a letter and now that you are so far away I believe I feel still more anxiety about hearing from you. It is not true that absence and distance conquer love.*
> *The subject spoken of as being ever upermost, is my love for <u>my</u> <u>Dear</u> <u>Julia</u> and the consequence (matrimony) of a love so pure. It is now about a year and a half Julia since I first confessed my love for you, and since that time we have been engaged, and yet but little*

*has been said as to when we should be united We have always lived
in hope that your Pa would remove the only obsticle in our way and
I took his answer to me as almost a complete removal. He told me
that before giving a positive answer he would have to speak to you. I
thought that he would decide as you wished, and I thought I well knew
how that was. I cant believe yet my <u>Dear</u> <u>Dear</u> <u>Julia</u> but that he will
give his consent. I would do anything to gain his permission to our
engagement but if he should still refuse: have you ever decided how
we then should or ought to act? I shall always recollect Miss C.O'F's
views upon this subject; it was you who told me them, and I perfectly
agree with her. I think we should try to gain the consent of interested
parties as long as there was hopes but only allow the best of reasons
to change our intention. Do you think with me on this subject? The
Army seems to be the only objection and really I think there can be no
happyer place to live. As I told you in my last letter I am at this time
thinking strongly of resigning but I do not think I will ever half so well
contented out of the Army as in it.*

*I shall not believe my Dear Julia that the difficulties alluded
to above will ever be met with. I will continue to think that when my
Regiment is permanent at some post where the officers have their
families that you will consent to go there too, and there will be no
serious objections made. We have loved each other now so long and
without any abatement, so far as I am able to answer, that it seems
to me they (I mean your Father and Mother) must agree that even
admitting that we might possibly be unhappy after marriage we would
still be more so were they to break off the engagement. I say we
because I measure your love by my own Julia. It may be vanity but I
do not think so.*

*It is now 8 o'clock A.M. and I have to march on Guard this
morning so that I can have but a few more minuets to write.*

*I have been reading the Wandering Jew but I have only got 15
Numbers of it. If you have the numbers after fifteen will you send them
to me. I have no way of geting them except by writing to my friends to
send them and what one more properly than Julia?*

*Give my love to Ellen. Ask her how Mr. Some one in the
country is coming on. Write soon and very often and I will do the
same—Adieu*

Your most affectionate
Ulysses

I love the way Ulysses misspells "minutes" as "minuets." It is cute because he couldn't dance, and it's funny to imagine him doing "a few minuets."

CHAPTER THREE
Southern Seduction

It is heartbreaking to read of Ulysses' desperate desire for letters, and her frequent lack of response. Knowing how badly he wanted to hear from her, why didn't she write more often?

For one thing, while the lonely Ulysses was longing for love letters in Corpus Christi, Julia was being serenaded under her window by gallant Southern dandies.

Julia recalls, "It was customary fifty years ago in St. Louis for the sterner sex to make sweet music at the midnight hour beneath the window of their dulcineas, and dear old Mr. C., Mr. K., Mr. M., and Judge S. used to tell us that it was impossible for them to get rest enough as our serenades were continuous. We would ask these gentlemen what we could do, we cannot help it, and besides it is so pleasant to have a half-dozen nice, handsome, manly young fellows beneath one's window pouring out their very souls in song, and hear:

"Thou art fair as any flower, Lady mine, Lady mine, Thou art silver to the sheen, Thou art moonlight to the beam" or "Good night, good night, dearest" accompanied by two or more lutes or guitars. What could we do?"

It would be entirely natural for pampered Southern belle Julia to be having second thoughts about marriage to a poor Yankee soldier, with this life of carefree ease being laid at her feet every night. The serenading Southern dandies were as seductive as a sultry night in St. Louis, the scent of honeysuckle wafting through the open shutters along with their sweet songs.

Teenage Julia could stay happily on at White Haven, then marry any man of property in the county and live like a Queen, waited on by slaves for the rest of her life.

And yet, her heart still pined for Lieutenant Grant. His slender arms trembling as he held her. His love-lit blue eyes that looked straight into her soul. She often went weeks without writing him, then suddenly wrote again, ardently assuring him of her love.

Something about this young man haunted her.

It seems that at the core of their bond was one simple truth: he needed love, and she loved to give it to him.

She had been given to all her life, waited on, pampered, her slightest whim obeyed. But she was a woman who needed to give, too. And who more compelling to give to than this lonesome, love starved Lieutenant?

He was off serving his country, sleeping on the hard ground, marching in the hot sun, bearing all kinds of deprivation and preparing to risk his life in battle, all the while longing to be in her arms.

But despite her feelings for him, Julia continued to stall about setting a wedding date, her conflict of love versus lifestyle clearly tearing at her.

Despite the lonely soldier's pleas, Julia is still not writing. That is because she is off living the life of a Southern belle, courtesy of Papa. If Ulysses was not so persistent, the whole engagement would have just been dropped, forgotten—just as Colonel Dent planned. Colonel Dent's scheme was a good one. Disapprove of the match, then get Julia off into Southern society to forget about the boy. His strategy would have worked against anyone—anyone except Ulysses S. Grant.

"Here it is now 1846 Julia, nearly two years since we were first engaged and still a time when or about when our marriage is to be consummated has never been talked of."

"My happiness would be complete if a return mail should bring me a letter setting the time—not far distant—when I might "clasp that little hand and call it mine."

Corpus Christi Texas
Jan. 2d 1846

My Dear Julia
I have just returned from a tour of one month through Texas, and on my return I find but one single letter from my Dear Julia and that one but a few lines in length. You dont know how disappointed I

felt, for in my two or three last letters, which remain unanswered yet, I said something that I was somewhat impatient to receive an answer too.

On the 2d of Dec. myself and some fifteen other officers started for San Antonio which is about one hundred and fifty miles from here and laying beyond a district of country which heretofore has been rendered uninhabitable by some bands of Indians—the Commanches and others—who have always been the enemies of the white man. Of course we had to camp out during the journey and we had very disagreeable weather to do it in too. Some of the old Texans say they have scaresely ever seen as disagreeable a winter as this one has been. From San Antonio I went across to Austin, the seat of Government. The whole of the country is the most beautiful that I ever have seen, and no doubt will be filled up very rapidly now that the people feel a confidance in being protected. San Antonio has the appearance of being a very old town. The houses are all built of stone and are beginning to crumble. The whole place has been built for defence, which by the way was a wise precaution, for untill within three or four years it has been the scene of more blood shed than almost any place of as little importance in the world. The town is compact, the houses all one story high only, the walls very thick, the roofs flat and covered with dirt to the depth of two or more feet they have but few doors and windows and them very small so the town cant be burned down, and a few persons in side of a house can resist quite a number. Austin in importance or at least in appearance is about equal to Carondolett. The inhabitants of San Antonio are mostly Mexicans. They seem to have no occupation whatever.

I have but little doubt Julia but that my Regt. the 4th Inf.y (I was promoted to the 7th but I have transfered to the 4th) will go up the Miss. River in the course of a few months now, but so far as I am concerned myself I dont know but I would prefer remaining in Texas. On you account Julia I would prefer going back but even here I think you would be contented.

Here it is now 1846 Julia, nearly two years since we were first engaged and still a time when or about when our marriage is to be consummated has never been talked of. Dont you think it is now time we should press your father further for his concent? If you would speak to him on the subject I think he would give his concent; you know he told me that you never spoke to him of our engagement and infact would hardly give him a chance to speak to you of it. If you think it best I will write again to him.

 You know Julia what I think we would be justifiable in doing if his concent is still withheld and I hope you think nearly with me. Wont you give the matter a serious concideration and tell me soon, very soon if we agree. You alone Julia have it in your power to decide whether we carry our engagement into effect. You have only to decide for me to act. If you will set a tim(e) when I must be in Missouri I will be there no matter if my Reg.t is still in Texas. The matter is one of importance enough to procure a leave of absence, and besides for the love I bear my dear Julia I would not value my commission to highly to resign it. I ought not to commit this to paper where there is danger that it may be seen before you get it, but I cannot help it, it is what I feel and have expressed before. My happiness would be complete if a return mail should bring me a letter seting the time—not far distant— when I might "clasp that little hand and call it mine."

Your Devoted Lover
Ulysses

Julia

 I found it interesting that Ulysses took the time to visit Austin, Texas, referring to it as the "seat of government." It shows he was a thoughtful young man, interested in the world—who, of course, had no idea he would be president of the United States someday.

Ulysses finally gets a rise out of Julia, by offering to resign from the Army so they can be together. She vehemently tells him not to resign. This is curious in itself. Why wouldn't any woman in love want to have her lover out of harm's way and safe at home with her? It is possible she was having so much fun being a carefree belle, that she did not want him to come home now. Another reason could have been a premonition about his destiny. In her memoirs, Julia professes to have had many psychic dreams and instincts about Ulysses' future. What seems most obvious to me, however, is that "Ulysses the brave soldier" was a large part of her attraction to him. When she was a child, Julia tells of reading a book called "The Dashing Lieutenant," and how she decided right then and there that she wanted to marry a soldier. She was always proud of the way Ulysses looked in his uniform, and she encouraged him to wear it. Though she still clung to her childhood idyll of the South, the dashing Lieutenant still rode his horse through her nocturnal fantasies. She did not want him to be replaced by a math professor!

"You beg of me not to resign: it shall be as you say..."

Corpus Christi Texas
Jan. 12th 1846

My Dear Julia
    I have just been deligted by recieving a long and interesting letter from the one I love so much and from the tone of her letter I am left with the hope that for the remainder of the time that we two are not one, she will be punctual in answering my letters. You do not know the pleasure it gives me to recieve letters from you my Dear Julia or you would write oftener. I write to you very often besides answering all your letters. You beg of me not to resign: it shall be as you say Julia for to confess the truth it was on your account that I thought of doing so, although all the letters I get from my father are filled with persuasion for me to resign. For my own part I am contented with an army life, all that I now want, to be happy is for

Julia to become mine, and how much I would sacrifize if her parents would give now their willing concent. By Spring at farthest I hope to see the 4th Inf.y (You know that I have transferred from the 7th to the 4th) settled and that too on the Mississippi river, unless something should take place to give us active employment. Has Mr. Reeves ever delivered you the letters sent by him. It is astonishing Julia what a place Corpus Christi has become. Already there are two Theaters and a printing office evry night there is a play at one or the other. It seems strange to hear you talking of sleigh riding, for here we have although it is January weather warm enough for light clothing. Such a thing as a sprinkle of snow is rarely seen at Corpus Christi.

From my last letter you will see that I have been on a long trip through Texas and I think the country beautiful and promising. If it should turn out after all that my Regiment should be retained here (it is not the opinion of any one that it will be kept) I could have but little to complain of. Your letter, and indeed all your letters, show your willingness to accompany me to any permanent Military post. It is very pleasant to hear such confessions from the one we love and in return I have to say that I would make any sacrifice for my Julias happiness. But what an uninteresting letter I am writing you it seems to me that the more I write the worse I get.—I have not heard from Fred. since I have been in Texas. I have written to him once and I think twice since he wrote me last. Tel him he must write soon. Fred is now about 3rd for promotion. There has been two resignations at Corpus Christi that he has not heard of.—Mr. Ridgley and Mr. Sykes have gone to St. Louis on a sick leave; if I had known sooner that they were going I would have sent a letter by them.

I have written you several letters that remain (u)nanswered so I shall look for an(other) letter (in) evry Mail. Give my love to all at White Haven. Soon I hope to see you again my dear dear Julia and let us hope that it will be to never separate again for so long a time or by so great a distance.

Your Devoted
Ulysses

Now that she knows her soldier of love will remain the "dashing lieutenant," and not resign the Army, Julia goes right back to her flighty, neglectful ways. Perhaps she didn't have confidence to strike out on her own yet. She was still a teenager. Ulysses wasn't even there—but Papa was. And so was her old way of life—the one that would slip through her fingers as soon as she slipped on Ulysses' wedding ring.

Ulysses' regiment is about to begin their march to the Rio Grande, moving closer to war with Mexico. It is chilling to read his promise to Julia:

"Of course Julia I never even dremed of such a thing as asking you to come to a Camp or temporary unsettled and distant post with me."

Shows what he knows! Someday, not only would he ask her to do just that, the fate of the United States would depend upon it. His desperate need for her expressed itself in these heartfelt lines:

"If you have but a little to write say that, it gives me so much pleasure even to see your name in your own hand writing."

"In the evenings just think that one who loves you above all on this Earth is then resting on the ground (thinking of Julia) after a hard days march."

Corpus Christi Texas
Feb 5th 1846

My Dear Julia
Two or three Mails have arrived at Corpus Christi in the last few days and by each I confidently expected a letter from you, but

each time I was disappointed. As a consolation then I come to my tent and got out all the letters yo(u have) ever written me—How many do you think they amounted to? Only 11 Julia and it is now twenty months that we have been engaged. I read all of them over but two and now write to you again Julia in hopes that hereafter I will get a letter from you evry two or three weeks. You dont know with what pleasure I read your letters or you would write much oftener.

At present the prospect of the 4th Infantry, or any other Regiment, geting back to civilization is by no means flattering. Our march is still onwards to the West. Orders have been recieved here for the removal of the troops to the Rio Grand (to Frances Isabel) and before you get this no doubt we will be on our way.—Continue to direct your letters as before, the care of Col. Hunt N. Orleans and they will reach me. In all probability this movement to the Rio Grande will hasten the settlement of the boundary question, either by treaty or the sword, and in either case we may hope for early peace and a more settled life in the army, and then may we—you and I Julia—hope for as speedy a consent on the part of your parents to our union? You say they certainly will not refuse it. I shall continue to hope and believe that it will be as you say.

I wrote to you a short time ago that I thought our engagement should be carried into effect as early as possible. I still think so and would be very happy to have you set the time at no very distant day, with the condition if the troops are not actively emploid. Of course Julia I never even dremed of such a thing as asking you to come to a Camp or temporary and distant post with me. I would not wish to take you from a home where you are surrounded by evry comfort and where you are among friends that you know and love. That is not what I proposed. If you should consent that I might "clasp that little hand and call it mine" while the troops are still in their present unsettled state I would either resign as my father is anxious to have me do, or return by myself leaving my Dear Julia at a comfortable home while I was fighting the battles of our Country.—Has John made application for an appointment in one of the new Regiments that are to be raised I hope he has not let the oportunity slip. With Mr. Bentons influance he could probably get a Captaincy.—I got a letter from Fred. a few days ago. He is well and is now looking out for promotion. He is anxious to get to the 4th I(nf.y) and says that if he is not promoted to it h(e) intends to make a transfer to it if he can.— Dont neglect to write to me often Julia. If you have but a little to write say that, it gives me so much pleasure even to see your name in your own hand writing. About the time you get this I will be on a march (on foot of course) between this and San Isabel or Frances Isabel. In the evenings just think that one who loves you above all on this Earth is resting on the ground (thinking of Julia) after a hard days march.— Give my love to Ellen Emmy and the rest at White Haven.

> *Your most affectionately*
> *U S Grant*

Is this guy romantic, or what? Any man who is reading this is probably ready to give up on himself, at this point! Ulysses knew how to make war, and he knew how to make love.

CHAPTER FOUR
Soldier of Love

Julia's interest has been sparked again. She has probably returned home to White Haven after the winter social season. It is about the time she returned home two years ago, when she first met Ulysses. She insists she's been punctual in writing, and he kindly lets her off the hook.

Here, Ulysses reveals the dark side of a soldier's life. He does not exempt himself from the coarse lifestyle described. Is he making a confession to Julia?

"Soldiers are a group of people who will drink and gamble let them be where they may, and they can always find houses to visit for these purposes."

Still he assures her, the most important thing to him is:

"I first loved Julia I have loved no one else."

She has said something to him which she fears was too bold. What could it have been? Intriguing! He says she was answering a question he often asked. Was it "when are we finally going to get married?" Probably. What could have been a "bold" answer to such a question? Perhaps something like, "Once we are married, we'll be together night and day." Or "When we are finally one, the wait will have been worth it! Oh! I hope you won't think me too bold in saying this!" He assures her she is not. Whatever it was, the idea it conjures was very pleasant to Ulysses.

"Your letter was one of the sweetest you have ever written me and your answer to the question I have so often asked was so much like yourself, it was just what I wanted to hear you say; boldness indeed: no my Dear Julia that is a charge that can never be laid to you."

Corpus Christi Texas
Feb. 7th 1846

Dearest Julia

I have just been delighted by a long and interesting letter from my Dear Julia and although I wrote to you but two or three days ago I answer this with my usual punctuality. You say you write me letter for letter well I am satisfied that my love is returned and you know how anxious one is to hear from the one they love and it may appear to me that you do not write as often as you really do. Your letter was one of the sweetest you have ever written me and your answer to the question I have so often asked was so much like yourself, it was just what I wanted to hear you say; boldness indeed: no my Dear Julia that is a charge that can never be laid to you.—There is a part of your letter that is entirely incomprehensible to me. I dont know whether you are jesting or if you are serious. I first loved Julia I have loved no one else.—The chance of any of the troops getting out of Texas this spring is worse than ever, before long we will be on our way farther West but no doubt it will be but a few months until the boundary question will be settled and then we may look for a general dispersion of troops and I for one at least will see Missouri again.—Does your pa ever speak of me or of our engagement? I am so glad to hear you say that you think his consent will be given when asked for. I shall never let an opportunity to do so pass.—As to resigning it would not be right in the present state of affairs and I shall not think of it again for the present.—So John is again a Bachilor without a string to his bow. No doubt he will remain single all his life. The extract from some newspaper you send me is a gross exageration of the morals and health of Corpus Christi. I do not believe that there is a more healthy spot in the world. So much exposure in the winter season is

*of course attended with a goodeal of sickness but not of a serious
nature. The letter was written I believe by a soldier of the 3d Inf.y. As
to the poisning and robberies I believe they are entirely false. There
has been several soldiers murdered since we have been here, but
two of the number were shot by soldiers and there is no knowing that
the others were not. Soldiers are a group of people who will drink
and gamble let them be where they may, and they can always find
houses to visit for these purposes. Upon the whole Corpus Christi is
just the same as any other plase would be where there were so many
troops. I think the man who wrote the letter you have been reading
deservs to be put in the Guard house and kept there until we leave the
country. There he would not see so much to write about.—Do you get
the paper I send you evry week?—I know Julia if you could see me
now you would not know me. I have allowed my beard to grow two
or three inches long. Ellen would not have to be told now that I am
trying to raise whiskers. Give my love to all at White Haven.*

*Your Devoted lover
Ulysses*

In this letter, Ulysses anticipates leaving Texas for Mexico, hoping in vain to have comfortable enough quarters for Julia to join him. If he can't get her to set a wedding date in Missouri, he hopes to convince her to marry him in Mexico. Because their troops are on the move, there is no chance of him getting a leave of absence to go back to Missouri anymore, anyway. Colonel Dent and the seductive South have succeeded at least in postponing his daughter's leaving White Haven. Still, Lieutenant Grant continues to dream.

"This morning before I got awake I dreamed that I was some place away from Corpus Christi walking with you leaning upon my arm, your hand was in mine and I felt very happy."

Corpus Christi Texas
March 3d 1846

My Dear Julia
I have not received a letter from you since my last, but as I may not have an opportunity of writing to you again (for) several weeks I must avail my self of this chance of writing to my dear Julia. This morning before I got awake I dreamed that I was some place away from Corpus Christi walking with you leaning upon my arm, your hand was in mine and I felt very happy. How disappointed when I awoke and found that it was but a dream. However I shall continue to hope that it will not be a great while befor such enjoyment will be real and no dream.—The troops have not yet left this place but the movement is to commence now in a few days. The 4th Inf.y is the last to leave. We are to go into camp on this side of the Rio Grande just opposite to Matamoras, a town of considerable importance in Mexico, and as we are informed, occupied by several thousand troops who it is believed by many will make us fight for our ground before we will be allowed to occupy it. But fight or no fight evry one rejoises at the idea of leaving Corpus Christi. It is to be hoped that our troops being so close on the borders of Mexico will bring about a speedy settlement of the boundary question; at all events it is some consolation to

know that we have now got as far as we can go in this direction by
any order from Government and therefore the next move will be
for the better. We may be taken prisoners it is true and taken to the
City of Mexico and then when we will be able to get away is entirely
uncertain. From the accounts recieved here I think the chances of
a fight on our first arrival on the Rio Grand are about equal to the
chances for peace, and if we are attacked in the present reduced state
of the troops here the consequences may be much against us.—Fred
is now about 2d or 3d for promotion and I have no doubt but this
moove will make him a 2d Lieut.—But I have said enough on this
subject for the present. A few weeks more and we will know exactly
what is to take place and then the first thing, I will write to one who in
all difficulties is not out of my mind. My Dear Julia as long as I must
be separated from your dear self evry moove that takes place I hail
with joy. I am always rejoised when an order comes for any change of
position hoping that soon a change will take place that will bring the
4th Inf.y to a post where there are comfortable quarters, and where
my Dear Julia will be willing to accompany me. In my previous letters
I have spoken a great deal of resigning but of course I could not think
of such a thing now just at a time when it is probable that the services
of evry officer will be called into requisition; but I do not think that
I will stand another year of idleness in camp.—You must write to me
often Julia and direct your letters as heretofore. I will write to you
very often and look forward with a great deal of anxiety—to the time
when I may see you again and claim a kiss for my long absence.—Do
you wear the ring with the letters U.S.G. in it Julia. I often take yours
off to look at the name engraved in it.—While writing this I am on
guard of course for the last time (at) this place.—Give my love to all
at White Haven.

Mr. Hazlitt is well and also Capt. Morrison. Tell John not to
let his chance of geting into one of the new Reg.t that will probably be
raised, slip by unimproved.

Your Most Devoted
Ulysses

Interesting, Ulysses mentions "*I do not think that I will stand another year of idleness in camp.*" He was going to find he much preferred fighting to idleness, a personal theme which would both haunt him and save the United States:

In this letter written from the border of Mexico, we see how Ulysses first learned not to be frightened by posturing from the enemy:

"Already they have boasted and threatened so much and executed so little that it is generally believed that all they are doing is mere bombast and show intended to intimidate our troops."

Also, notice how he is already analyzing what the Mexican Army did wrong, and exactly how they should have responded. He already had the gift of war strategy, and he had not yet fired a shot!

"When the troops were in water up to their necks a small force on shore might have given them a great deel of trouble."

Not realizing he is already a general-in-training, Ulysses obsession is, as it will be for the rest of his life, his love for his Dear Dear Julia.

"I am still in hopes notwithstand all warlike appearances that in a few months all difficulties will be settled and I will be permitted to see again My Dear Dear Julia. The time will appear long to me until this event but hope that has so long borne me out, the hope that one day we will meet to part no more for so long a time, will sustain me again."

Camp Near Matamoras
March 29th 1846

My Dear Julia

    *A long and laborious march, and one that was threatened
with opposition from the enemy too, has just been completed, and
the Army now in this country are laying in camp just opposite to
the town of Matamoras. The city from this side of the river bears a
very imposing appearance and no doubt contains from four to five
thousand inhabitants. Apparently there are a large force of Mexican
troops preparing to attack us. Last night during the night they threw
up a small Breast work of Sand Bags and this morning they have
a piece of Artillery mounted on it and directed toward our camp.
Whether they really intend anything or not is doubtful. Already they
have boasted and threatened so much and executed so little that it is
generally believed that all they are doing is mere bombast and show,
intended to intimidate our troops. When our troops arrived at the
Little Colorado, (a river of about 100 yards in width and near five feet
deep where we forded it) they were met by a Mexican force, which
was represented by there commander to be large and ready for an
attack. A parly took place between Gen. Taylor and their commanding
officer, whose name I have forgotten, the result of which was, that if
we attempted to cross they would fire upon us. The Mexican officer
said that however much he might be prepossessed in our favor himself
he would have to obey the orders of his own Government, which
were peremptory and left him with but one course, and that was to
defend the Colorado against our passing, and he pledged his honor
that the moment we put foot into the water to cross he would fire upon
us and war would commence. Gen. Taylor replied that he was going
over and that he would allow them fifteen minuets to withdraw their
troop and if one of them would show his heads after we started over,
that he would fire upon them; whereupon they left and were seen no
more until we were safely landed on this side. I think after making
such threats and speaking so positivl(y) of what they would do and
then let so fine an opportunity to execute what they had threatened
pass unimproved, shows anything but a decided disposition to drive*

us from the soil. When the troops were in the water up to their necks a small force on shore might have given them a greatdeel of trouble.—During our whole march we have been favored with fine weather, and altogether the march has been a pleasant one. There are about forty miles between the Nuices and the Colorado rivers that is one continuous sandy desert waste, almost without wood, or water with the exception of the Salt Lakes. Passing this the troops of course suffered considerably.—here the soil is rich and the country beautiful for cultivation. When peace is established the most pleasant Military posts in our country I believe will be on the Banks of the Rio Grande. No doubt you suppose the Rio Grande, from its name and appearance on the map to be a large and magnificent stream, but instead of that it is a small muddy stream of probably from 150 to 200 yards in width and navigabl(e) for only small sized steamers. I forgot to mention (that) we received before we arrived here, the proclomation of Col. Majia the Commander-in-Chief I believe, of the Mexican forces. It was a long wordy and threatning document. He said that the citizens of Mexico were ready to expose their bare breasts to the Rifles of the Hunters of the Mississippi, that the Invaders of the North would have to reap their Laurels at the points of their sharpened swords; if we continued our march the deep waters of the Rio Grande would be our Sepulcher the people of our Government should be driven East of the Sabine and Texas re-conquered &c. &c. all of which is thought to mean but very little.

The most beliggerent move that has taken place yet occured yesterday. When we had arrived near this place a party of Mexican soldiers siezed upon two of our Dragoons and the horse of a Bugler boy who had been sent in advance to keep an eye in the direction of the enemy and to communicate if they saw any movement towards our column. The prisoners are now confined in the city. It is quite possible that Gen. Taylor will demand the prisoners and if they are not given up march over and take the city or attempt it.

I am still in hopes notwithstand all warlike appearances that in a few months all difficulties will be settled and I will be permitted to see again My Dear Dear Julia. The time will appear long to me until this event but hope that has so long borne me out, the hope that one day we will meet to part no more for so long a time, will sustain me again. Give my love to all at White Haven and be sure to write soon and often. I have not heard from Fred. very lately. Vacancies have occured here which make him I think 2d from promotion and another will probably take place soon in the case of an officer who is to be tried for being drunk on duty.—I will write again in a few days, but dont put off answering this until you get my next.

Ulysses

Waiting to see if there will be war with Mexico, listening to Mexican threats which never materialize, Ulysses still dreams of Julia.

"At all events I shall try to get a leave of absence as soon as there ceases to be a probability of difficulties, and then my Dear Julia may I hope to claim you as my partner for life."

Camp Near Matamoras Tex.
April 20th 1846

My Dearest Julia
I have just rec'd your letter of the 19th of last month. You may judge with how much gratification when I tell you that it is the first letter I have got from you for about ten or twelve weeks with the exception of a few lines about seven weeks ago which come along with the copy of the Wandering Jew you sent me. Evry thing is very quiet here. We are only seperated by a narrow stream from one of the largest Cities of Mexico yet not a soul dare cross. Evry thing looks beliggerent to a spectator but I believe there will be no fight. The Mexicans are busily engaged in throwing up fortifications on their side and we are engaged in the same way on ours. Occationally they make a threa(t) but as yet their threats have all ended in bombast. I believe I told you of their threats when we cross the Colorado? We have been threatened of just as certain violance since that. About ten days ago Gen. Ampudia arrived at Matamoras with additional forces, reported at three thousand; he gave Gen. Taylor notice that he must

retire from this ground to go East of the Nuices within twenty four hours from that time or War would be the inevitabl(e) consequences. The Mex. Gen. went on to say that in case of War he would do all in his power to have the rules and usages of the most civilized warfare observed and hoped that Gen. Taylor would co-opporate with him in so humane an object.—Gen. Ampudia is known to be one of the most inhuman of the Mex. Genls. He has gone so far as to boil the heads of one or two of his prisoners in oil so as to preserve them.—Gen. Taylor made a courtious but decided reply, to the amount that we would not leave but by force. After all this how could we expect anything els but war? Yet evry thing has passed off as before. It is now the opinion of many that our difficulty with Mex. will be settled by negociation and if so hope my dear Julia to hear the 4th Inf.y ordered to the upper Mississippi before the end of warm weather yet. At all events I shall try to get a leave of absence as soon as there ceases to be a probability of difficulties, and then my Dear Julia may I hope to claim you as my partner for life. The Regiments that remain in this country will have beautiful stations but it is not likely that the 4th will be one of them.—I got a letter from Fred. a few days ago. He says he is third for promotion then, but since he wrote there has been vacancies enough to promote him and all the rest of our class and one or two over. He either goes to the 2d Inf.y which is stationed in Michigan or to the 5th which is here, so either you or I will see him soon. Mr. Hazlitt has not got here yet from Corpus Christi. When we left, a number of Officers were left behind to c(ome) around by water, H. Among them.—Do wri(t)e to (me) often Julia while we are separated so far and let us hope, as I (sin)cerely do, that before many months it will not (be nec)essary for us to write inorder to convey our thoug(hts) (to e)ach other. Fred. says in his letter that he hopes (that ne)xt times he sees me to take me by the hand as a <u>Brevet</u> <u>brother</u>. *Give my love to evry one at White Haven. Has John tried to get into one of the new Regiments that are likely to be raised? I have heard that Sarah Walker is engaged, is she married yet? I used to think that Mr. Cloud was waiting for her.—Write as soon as you get this.*

Your Devoted Ulysses

Read these two paragraphs closely. Ulysses' little post script hoping his friends' hope that Miss Julia joins them will come true is cute! Ulysses never misses a chance to ask her to come to him, and maybe he is even a tad jealous of another man paying attention to his <u>Dear</u> <u>Dear</u> <u>Julia</u>, even in a letter. Ulysses has to make sure Julia knows that he (Ulysses) wants Julia to show up even more than his buddy does. This was the first of a long parade of friends of Ulysses in the military who hope Julia comes to him—for increasingly dramatic reasons. All his life, Ulysses' friends in the military would see how desperately he needed her, and someday, they would even go so far as to have houses built just for her. It was the first of a whole history of concerned males, trying to unite Julia with Ulysses. He needed her, and they needed him.

Will Miss Julia accept the compliments of her friend Lt. Wallen I hope the time is not far distant, when I shall welcome her to the 4th Infantry.

Yours truly H. D. W.

P.S. My Dear Julia Mr. Wallen asked me to allow him to put a few lines in my letter and I see he has hoped to see something which one much more concerned in than himself most sincerely hopes that he may not be disappointed and that one is

Your Devoted Ulysses

P.P.S. I have just rec-d another letter from you my Dear Julia of about two weeks later date than the one I got this morning. You dont know how hapy I was at geting two letters in such quick succession from one so dear to me, and such sweet letters as they were too! I know my Dear Julia that you are going to write me very often, and you know how punctual I am in answering. I shall write to you again in one week.

Your devoted Ulysses

This seems like as good a time as any to confront what one lone historian said, suggesting that Ulysses was sexually active in Mexico. Every shred of evidence points the other way. Everyone who ever knew him said he led an austere life in the Army and when not on duty, he kept his thoughts on Julia. Even Ulysses' political enemies in later years admitted there was never any other woman in his life. Secondly, what Ulysses needed was love, and he wouldn't get love from a prostitute. In fact, he had too much love and respect for women as a whole to contribute to the misery of one. It would have gone against all of his values as a "fiercely monogamous" man. Alcohol was a vice that he used as an outlet for sexual frustration many times in his life, because it hurt nobody but himself. He would never have done anything to hurt Julia or any other woman, including a prostitute. In reading over seventy books about Ulysses, this is my definite opinion, and there is no other evidence to the contrary.

CHAPTER FIVE
Ulysses' Engagement

Julia is writing Ulysses more often now, for two reasons. She is back at White Haven, with the social season in St. Louis over. Most importantly, the St. Louis newspapers are filled with the imminent prospect of war with Mexico, and she is becoming more aware of the depth of her love for this soldier.

For Ulysses, the word "engagement" has a whole new meaning. It now means to charge into battle.

"We marched nearly all night the first night and you may depend My Dear Julia that we were all very much fatigued. We start again at 1 o'clock to-day and will probably have an engagement."

Still, he reassures her:

"Don't fear for me My Dear Julia for this is only the active part of our business. It is just what we come here for and the sooner it begins the sooner it will end and probably be the means of my seeing my dear Dear Julia soon."

Point Isabel Texas
May 3d 1846

My Dear Julia
I wrote you a long letter in answer to your last sweet letter a few days ago and intended to bring it with me to this place but when we started I left in such a hurry that I forgot it. I gave you a long account of our difficulties in it and as I now have but a few minuets

to write I will send you the other letter as soon as I get back. At present I can only give you what has happened without any of the circumstances. Col. Cross has been killed by the Mexicans. Cap.t Thornton with three other officers and about fifty Draggoons fell in with a camp of some two thousand Mexicans and of course were taken. One officer and six or seven men were killed and four wounded all the others were taken prisoners. Lt. Porter with twelve men were attacked by a large number of Mexicans and Mr. Porter and one man was killed the rest escaped.—Gen. Taylor left Matamoras with about two thousand troops for this place on the 1st of May intending to give the Mexicans a fight if we fall in with them. We marched nearly all night the first night and you may depend My Dear Julia that we were all very much fatigued. We start again at 1 o'clock to-day and will probably have an engagement. We understand that there is several thousand encamped not far from this place. There was about six hundred troops left in our Fort opposite Matamoras and the presumption is they have been attacked, for we have heard the sound of Artillery from that direction ever since day light this morning. As soon as this is over I will write to you again, that is if I am one of the fortunate individuals who escape. Dont fear for me My Dear Julia for this is only the active part of our business. It is just what we come here for and the sooner it begins the sooner it will end and probably be the means of my seeing my dear Dear Julia soon. You dont know how anxious I am to see you again Julia. Another year certainly cannot roll round before that happy event. I must now bring my letter to a close. I wish I had time to write a much longer one. Give my love to all at White Haven. Write to me soon Julia.

Your Most devoted
U.S. Grant
4th Inf.y

Ulysses survives his first battle, two years after meeting Julia. Notice how he makes note of every detail, including which kind of artillery they used, unknowingly making mental notes for the future.

"When we got in range of their artillery they let us have it right and left. They had I believe 12 pieces. Our guns were then rounded at them and so the battle commenced. Our Artillery amounted to 8 guns of six pound caliber and two eighteen pounders."

Ulysses shows compassion for the victims:

"It was a terrible sight to go over the ground the next day and see the amount of life that had been destroyed."

And as always:

"In the thickest of it I thought of Julia."

Head Quarters Mexican Army
May 11th 1846

My Dear Julia
After two hard fought battles against a force far superior to our own in numbers, Gen. Taylor has got possession of the Enemy's camp and now I am writing on the head of one of the captured drums. I wrote to you from Point Isabel and told you of the march we had and of the suspected attack upon the little force left near Matamoras. About two days after I wrote we left Point Isabel with about 300 waggons loaded with Army supplies. For the first 18 miles our course was uninterupted but at the end of that distance we found the Mexican Army, under the command of General Arista drawn up in line of

battle waiting our approach. Our waggons were immediately parked and Gen. Taylor marched us up towards them. When we got in range of their Artillery they let us have it right and left. They had I believe 12 pieces. Our guns were then rounded at them and so the battle commenced. Our Artillery amounted to 8 guns of six pound calibre and 2 Eighteen pounders. Evry moment we could see the charges from our pieces cut a way through the ranks making a perfect road, but they would close up the interval without showing signs of retreat. Their officers made an attempt to charge upon us but the havoc had been so great that their soldiers could not be made to advance. Some of the prisoners that we have taken say that their officers cut and slashed among them with their Sabres at a dreadful rate to make them advance but it was no use, they would not come. The firing commenced at 1/2 past 2 o'clock and was nearly constant from that until Sun down.

Although the balls were whizing thick and fast about me I did not feel a sensation of fear until nearly the close of the firing a ball struck close by me killing one man instantly, it nocked Capt. Page's under jaw entirely off and broke in the roof of his mouth, and nocked Lt. Wallen and one Sergeant down besides, but they were not much hurt. Capt. Page is still alive. When it become to dark to see the enemy we encamped upon the field of battle and expected to conclude the fight the next morning. Morning come and we found that the enemy had retreated under cover of the night. So ended the battle of the 8th of May. The enemy numbered three to our one besides we had a large waggon train to guard. It was a terrible sight to go over the ground the next day and see the amount of life that had been destroyed. The ground was litterally strewed with the bodies of dead men and horses. The loss of the enemy is variously estimated from about 300 to 500. Our loss was comparitively small. But two officers were badly wounded, two or three slightly. About 12 or 15 of our men were killed and probably 50 wounded. When I can learn the exact amount of loss I will write and correct the statements I have made if they are not right. On the 9th of May about noon we left the field of battle and started on our way to Matamoras. When we advanced about six miles we found that the enemy had taken up a new position in the midst of a dense wood, and as we have learned they had received a reinforcement equal to our whole numbers. Grape shot and musket balls were let fly from both sides making dreadful havoc. Our men (con)tinued to advance and did advance in sp(ite) of (their) shots, to the very mouths of the cannon an(d) killed and took prisoner the Mexicans with them, and drove off with their own teams, taking cannon ammunition and all, to our side. In this way nine of their big guns were taken and their own ammunition turned against them. The Mexicans fought very hard for an hour and a half but seeing their means of war fall from their hands in spite of all their efforts they finally commenced to retreat helter skelter. A great many retreated to the banks of the Rio Grande and without looking for means of crossing plunged into this water and no doubt many of them were dround. Among the prisoners we have taken there are 14 officers and I have no idea how many privates. I understand that General Lavega, who is a prisoner in our camp has said that he fought against several different nations but ours was the first that he ever saw who would charge up to the very mouths of the cannon.

In this last affray we had we had three officers killed and 8 or ten wounded. how many of our men suffered has not yet been learned. The Mexicans were so certain of sucsess that when we took their camp we found their dinners on the fire cooking. After the battle the woods was strued with the dead. Waggons have been engaged drawing the bodies to bury. How many waggon loads have already come in and how many are still left would be hard to guess. I saw 3 large waggon loads at one time myself. We captured, besides prisoners, 9 cannon, with a small amount of ammunition for them, probably 1000 or 1500 stand of fire arms sabres swords &c. Two hundred and fifty mules and pack saddles or harness. Drums, musical instruments camp equipage &c, &c. innumerable. The victory for us has been a very great one. No doubt you will see accounts enough of it in the papers. There is no great sport in having bullets flying about one in evry direction but I find they have less horror when among them than when in anticipation. Now that the war has commenced with such vengence I am in hopes my Dear Julia that we will soon be able to end it. In the thickest of it I thought of Julia. How much I should love to see you now to tell you all that happened. Mr. Hazlitt come out alive and whole. When we have another engagement, if we do have another atall, I will write again; that is if I am not one of the victims. Give my love to all at White Haven and do write soon my Dear Julia. I think you will find history will count the victory just achieved one of the greatest on record. But I do not want to say to much about it until I see the accounts given by others. Don't forget to write soon to your most Devoted

Ulysses

P.S. I forgot to tell you that Fortifications left in charge of Maj. Brown in command of the 7th Inf.y was attacked while we were at Point Isabel and for five days the Mexicans continued to throw in shells. There was but 2 killed, Maj. Brown & one soldier, and 2 wounded.

Ulysses seems energized by the battles, especially the military strategy. Here, he learns the importance of following up a victory.

"We followed up our success by crossing the Rio Grande and driving the remaining four thousand Mex. troops from the city and taking possession our selvs."

Unsure of where he will be ordered next, Lieutenant Ulysses does know one thing:

"Wherever I am I shall continue to write to my Dear Julia very often and hope that the day is not far distant when I shall hold that little hand again in mine."

Ulysses just loves to hold hands! Another hope of Ulysses is haunting, because there will be even more serious separations ahead for him and Julia than this one:

"I feel as if I shall never be contented until I can see you again my Dear Julia, and I hope it will be never to leave you again for so long a time."

Matamoras Mexico
May 24th 1846

My Dear Julia
I recieved your letter of the 5th Ins. about one week ago and would have answered it (as I do all your sweet letters) immediately but I had written to you but a few days before and I wanted to see what mooves we would make next before I wrote again. Since the battles of the 8th & 9th ins. which resulted so disasterously to the Mexicans we have had but little trouble with them. It is pretty well

ascertained now that the loss of the Mexi(cans) in the two days fight amounted to near three thousand from killed wounded and desertion, whilst our force only amounted to two thousand. We followed up our success by crossing the Rio Grande and driving the remaining four thousand Mex. troops from the city and taking possession our selvs. You would be surprised at the difference between an American town and a Mexican one and indeed there is just as much difference between the people. The inhabitants are generally more like Indians in looks and habits than white men. and I think too after so sound a thrashing as our small force gave their large one, we will be able with the assistance of the great number of volunteers that have come to our aid, to bring Mexico to speedy terms. Where the 4th Infy will be when you get this letter is hard to surmise. No doubt Gen. Taylor will take possession of all the towns on or near the river within the next few weeks and I may be at one of them far up the river. Wherever I am I shall continue to write to my Dear Julia very often and hope that the day is not far distant when I shall hold that little hand again in mine. Do not feel alarmed about me my Dear Julia for there is not half the horrors in war that you immagine. One thing though, if we ever get whiped by them we will no doubt meet with cruel treatment. Some of their officers are perfect gentlemen, but it would be impossible for them to restrain the soldiers.

My Dearest Julia does you Pa or Ma ever speak of our engagement, or do they think that time and distance can make us forget each other? I would love to hear you say that you believed they would never make further objections. Dont they know whenever you get a letter from me? I feel as if I shall never be contented until I can see you again my Dear Julia, and I hope it will be never to leave you again for so long a time. I get all your letters, some times though they are a long time on the way. I expect before long to see Fred. down here for I am almost certain he is promoted to one of the Texas (or rather Mexico) Regiments. No doubt he will be very much pleased to come here. If he does come I will get him to ask for a leave of absence at the same time I do. Does Fred. ever say any thing about Miss L.S. in his letters now? I dont believe they correspond. I think it very likely you will see Capt. Morrison in Missouri in a month and then you can hear an account of the battles fought on the borders of Mexico.

He does not say that he will leave but evry one thinks that his family afflictions of late have been so great as to justify him taking a leave of (ab)sence. Has John made application for the Rifle Regiment? I (f)ind that the member of Congress who got me my appointm(ent) as a Cadet is applying to get me into the new Regt. if it is (.....). It is very warm at Matamoras, enough so to have vegitab(les) nearly all winter. I think if I ever get to a good cold (c)lim(ate) once more I will not want to come South again.

Give my love to all at White Haven Julia and write very soon to one who loves you most devotedly.

Ulysses

P.S. The two Flowers you sent me come safe but when I opened your letter the wind blew them away and I could not find them. Before I seal this I will pick a wild flower off of the Bank of the Rio Grande and send you. My Dear Julia do you ever see me anymore in your dreams? How much I wish you could see me in reality! I am certain that you would not know me. I am as badly Sun burnt as it is possible to be, and I have allowed my beard to grow three inches long. Adieu My Dear Dear Julia

Ulysses

It is amazing to hear the sturdy soldier tell of giving the enemy a thrashing, then imagine him wandering around in the desert trying to find two flowers which Julia had sent him. He was so strong, yet so sentimental.

Julia's ardor is heating up, in one of my favorite romantic references to her letters. It is almost risqué for these Victorian times!

"You dont know how proud and how happy it made me feel to hear you say that willingly you would share my tent, or my prison if I should be taken prisoner."

Camp At Matamoras Mexico
June 5th 1846

I received a few days ago My Dearest Julia your sweet letter of the 12th of May. How often I have wished the same thing you there express, namely that we had been united when I was last in Mo. You dont know how proud and how happy it made me feel to hear you say that willingly you would share my tent, or my prison if I should be taken prisoner. As yet my Dearest I am unhurt and free, and our troops are occupying a conquered city. After two hard fought battles against a force three or four times as numerous as our own we have chased the enemy from their homes and I have not the least apprehension that they will ever return here to reconquer the place. But no doubt we will follow them up. I believe the General's plan is to march to Monteray, a beautiful little city just at the foot of the mountains, and about three hundred miles from this place. That taken and we will have possession, or at least in our power the whole of the Mexican territory East of the Mountains and it is to be presumed Mexico will then come to terms. I do not feel my Dear Julia the slightest apprehention as to our success in evry large battle that we may have with the enemy no matter how superior they may be to us in numbers. I expect soon to see Fred. here to join us in the invasion of Mexico. I see that his promotion to the 5th Inf.y was confirmed a month ago at Washington. I have no doubt he will be very glad to get away from Towson(.) Possibly too John Dent may be coming here as a Captain in a new Regiment. Before you get this letter Julia you will probably see or hear of Cap.t Morrison and Lt. Wallens return to the U. States. They have been sent on the recruiting service and will not probably return until next Fall. From the papers we recieve from the States one would judge that there is great excitement about us there, but believe me my Dear Julia you need not feel any alarm for our welfare. The greatest danger is from exposure to the rain sun and dew in a very warm climate. But for my part I am never sick, and I think I have become well acclimated to the South.

My Dearest Julia when you write to me again tell me if your Pa ever says any thing about our engagement and if you think he will make any further objections. I think from what he said to me when I was there last Spring he will not; but he has not written me as he said he would do. But Julia I hope many months more will not pass over before we will be able to talk over this matter without the use of paper. How much I do want to see you again; but I know you would not recognize me, you see me as I was not as I am, for climate has made a change. I mean a change in appearance, but in my love for Julia I am the same, and I know too that she has not change(d) in that respect for she writes me such sweet letters when she does write. In six weeks I have had four letters from you Dear Julia which is much more that I ever recieved in the same time before, wont you continue to write to me often for it gives me so much pleasure to read and answer your letters.

Julia if the 4th Inf.y should be stationed permanantly in the conquered part of Mexico would you be willing to come here or would you want me to resign? I think it probable though that I shall resign as soon as this war is over and make Galena my home. My father is very anxious to have me do so. Speaking of your coming to Mexico dearest I do not intend to hint that it is even probable that the 4th Inf.y will remain (here) for I think it will be one of the first to leave (this) Country.—Give my love to all at White Haven and write very soon and very often to

Ulysses

Julia

CHAPTER SIX
The Dashing Lieutenant

The onset of war has greatly heated up Julia's passion for Ulysses, and made her a much more punctual letter writer. Part of it is surely her girlish crush on the "dashing lieutenant" in battle, but she is concerned for his life, as well. It made her realize how much she cares.

"You say in your letter I must not grow tired of hearing you say how much you love me! Indeed dear Julia nothing you can say sounds sweeter."

The increase of Julia's ardor makes Ulysses more daring and open with her about his fantasies.

"My Dear Julia now that we are so far distant from each other you are my constant thought when alone. When I lay down I think of Julia until I fall asleep hoping that before I wake I may see her in my dreams."

Ulysses reminds Julia of the day she gave him her ring.

"I often take the ring which bears your name, from my finger and think of the day I first wore it. You recollect we were returning from the City."

They must have exchanged rings on the way home from the wedding in the city. Since they first declared their love for each other on the ride *to* the wedding, that must have been quite a ride *home* from the wedding! They surely stopped a dozen times to hug and kiss and be swept away by their newfound passion. That little ride must have been heaven on earth! It is amazing Julia could resist marrying him then and there.

Camp at Matamoras Mex
June 10ᵗʰ 1846

How much gratified I have been my Dearest Julia in recieving another sweet letter from you. Indeed of late you have been so punctual in your answers that it makes up for the long time I was without a letter atal from you. I know if you were aware of the happines(s) it gives me to hear from my Dearest Julia you would continue to write often. You say in your letter I must not grow tired of hearing you say how much you love me! Indeed dear Julia nothing that you can say sounds sweeter. I have written you a great many letters since I have been on the Rio Grande no doubt you have recd them all? The occational mails that we get here shows us how great the excitement in the States is for our wellfare and indeed when I look back at the condition we were in I do not think our danger was much overrated. We were in an enemy's country without a friendly house to retreat to in case of defeat, and surrounded by a well armed force out numbering us three to one, besides evry Mexican citizen would have been ready to have taken our lives as soon as they saw us beaten. But at present my Dearest Julia we are very differently situated. Now our force is three or four times as great as it was and the enemy is no where to be found. Our troops are encamped in the suburbs of one of the largest of Mexican towns, and soon no doubt will start out to continue their conquest.—I would not be surprised if the next letter (but one) I write you dear love should be written on the road from here to Monteray. We are very anxious to push forward for that is our only hope of a speedy peace. How much I should love Julia to walk through Matamoras once with you to let you see the difference between a Mexican town and a Mexican population and that of an American. The Mexican house is low with a flat or thatched roof, with a dirt or brick floor, with but little furnature and in many cases the fire in the middle of the house as if it was a wig-wamb. The majority

*of the inhabitants are Indians. I believe that our present force is
sufficient to keep off any force that Mexico can bring, provided we are
kept in one body.*

*I see that John is not appointed in the new Regiment that has
been raised. Did he apply. I fear Dear Julia that you will not be able
to see Fred this Summer as you have expected, but likely he and I will
be able to get a leave of absence at the same time; then dearest wont
you become mine for ever. Whenever Fred. writes to me he always
asks how our engagement is likely to please your Pa & Ma, or calls
me a Brivet Brother or something of that sort. Fred. has already got
three 2d Lieut's below him in his own Regiment and will probably
have two if not three or four more in the next few Months. Mr. Sykes
has just returned from St. Louis but he did not tell me that he had
seen you.*

*My Dear Julia now that we are so far distant from each other
you are my constant thought when alone. When I lay down I think of
Julia until I fall asleep hoping that before I wake I may see her in my
dreams. I know too Dearest from your letters that I am not forgotten.
The many pleasant hours spent with you often pass in review before
my memory. It certainly cannot be a great while (before) a recurrence
of similar happiness. I often take the ring, which bears your name,
from my finger and think of the day I first wore it. You recollect
we were returning from the City. I dont believe you will be able to
read this letter so I will close it and try and write plainer next time.
Remember me to Ellen & Emmy and all at White Haven and dont
forget Dearest Julia to write soon very soon to you devoted*

Ulysses

Ulysses prepares to stay in camp in Matamoras for a few months, before continuing the fight or, hope against hope, return home to Julia. How Ulysses loves the idea of having a "wife!" He is even shy about writing the word, because it means so much to him. You can feel him blush with pleasure when he dares to write the word "wife."

"I really am very much in hopes that another Spring will not roll around before I will be able to call Julia my own dear, (shall I say wife,)"

Ulysses re-lives over and over, the tantalizing words of his favorite letter from Julia.

"You said that you wished we had been united when I was last in Mo. and how willing you would be to share even a tent with me. Indeed Julia that letter made me feel very happy. How much I ought to love you when you express a willingness to sacrifice so much just for me."

His words about her willingess to sacrifice so much just for him, are haunting. They predict her future.

Matamoras Mexico
July 2d 1846

My Dear Julia
I received last evening your letter of the 10th of June, in which you speak of this Earthly paradise. If it is a Paradise where it rains about four hours a day why then Matamoras is the place. I have no doubt though I should like the place very much if it was only the home of My Dearest Julia, but I know that I shall never be contented until I am with her once more. I am afraid Julia that Matamoras will be

very sickly this Summer. The whole of this country is low and flat and for the last six weeks it has rained almost incessantly so that now the whole country is under water. Our tents are so bad that evry time it rains we get a complete shower-bath. I dont believe that we will leave here for two or three months and then we will either have some hard fighting or bring our difficulties in this quarter to a speedy close. Now that the Oregon boundary is no longer in dispute I think we will soon quiet Mexico and then dearest Julia, if I am not one of the unfortunate who fall, nothing will keep me from seeing you again. I really am very much in hopes that another Spring will not roll around before I will be able to call Julia my own dear, (shall I say wife,) Just think it is now going on three years since we were first engaged! You never will tell me Julia if you think your Pa & Ma will say no. I dont think they can but I would like to hear you say that they will not.—I did not let the flowers in your last letter blow away. When I opened the letter and saw the rose leaves I just thought that only two short weeks ago Julia had them in her own hands and here I am and have not seen her fore more than a year. If I was in Mo. and you were here I know what I would do very soon; I would volunteer to come to Mexico as a private if I could come no other way. But I recollect you did volunteer some time ago, or what showed your willingness to do so, you said that you wished we had been united when I was last in Mo. and how willing you would be to share even a tent with me. Indeed Julia that letter made me feel very happy. How much I ought to love you when you express a willingness to sacrifice so much just for me.—I believe you have burned some of my letters for you say you only have twenty-five of them and it seems to me I have written a great many more; at all events I will write more in the future and you must write often too wont you Julia? So you have read that ridiculous falsehood about the cause of Lt. Deas crossing the river. There was not a word of truth in the whole statement except that he swam the river. It was a strange fancy that struck him at a time when he was not on duty himself. Fred. has not got here yet. I wonder what can keep him? I shall pick a quarrel with him as soon as he gets here for not writing to me. He is a great deal worse than you are about writing; but I ought not to say a word about your writing now for you are so much more punctual than you used to be. I will write to you again in a few days but you must not wait to get another letter before you answer this. I would like to make a bargai(n) for each of us to write, say, evry Sunday (...) then just think I would hear from my Dear love fifty two times in a year. Remember me to all at White Haven.

Your Devoted
Ulysses

.Julia

    It is rather sexy the way Ulysses teases Julia about showing her letters to her brother! There must be things in those letters she doesn't want anyone but Ulysses to read.

P.S. You say that I must not let Fred. read your letters. I know now how to get you to write often. Evry time that two weeks elapse without geting a letter from my Dearest Julia I will just take out one of the old ones and give it to Fred. to read. You had better look out and write often if you dont want him to read them.

U S Grant

P.P.S. Since writing the above I have heard that Fred is in N. Orleans on his way here. I suppose he will be here in two or three days. I'll make him write to you as soon as he comes.

Interesting. The battles have stopped, and so have Julia's letters! Does she only get turned on when Ulysses is fighting? Still, he dreams of Julia becoming his "wife," a word that means so much to him he can't even find the courage to put it in writing. He can only hint to her of his ultimate fantasy.

"A few months more of fatigue and privation, I am much in hopes will bring our difficulties to such a crisis that I will be able to see you again Julia, and then if my wishes prevailed, we would never part again as merely engaged, but as,—you know what I would say."

A humorous side soap opera, is Ulysses waiting for Julia's brother Fred to arrive in Mexico. Fred and his family seem to think he has the makings of a war hero, but months go by before he shows up. Notice Ulysses' jealousy of anyone who might compete for Julia's attention, even her own brother. It's hilarious.

"Fred and me will probably be near each other during the time and between us I am in hopes that I will hear from my Dear Julia evry week, but write oftener to me than to Fred."

Matamoras Mexico
July 25th 1846

My Dearest Julia
*   It must be about two weeks since I have written to you, and as I am determined that a longer time shall never pass with my Dearest hearing from me, whilst I am in an enemie's country, I write to you again, notwithstanding I have not heard from you for some time. Do not understand me though to cast any censure upon you, for you may have written me a dozen letters and me not received one of them yet, for I believe it is about two weeks since we have had a Mail, and there is no telling when we will have another. You must not neglect to*

write often Dearest so that whenever a mail does reach this far-out-of-the-way country I can hear from the one single person who of all others occupies my thoughts. This is my last letter from Matamoras Julia. Already the most of the troops have left for Camargo and a very few days more will see the remainder of us off. Whether we will have much more fighting is a matter of much speculation. At present we are bound for Camargo and from thence to Monteray, where it is reported that there is several thousand Mexican troops engaged in throwing up Fortifications, and there is no doubt either but that Parades has left Mexico at the head of nine thousand more to reinforce them, but the latest news says that he has been obliged to return to the City of Mexico on account of some rupture there. But a few months more will determine what we have to do, and I will be careful to keep my Dear Julia advised of what the army in this quarter is about. Fred. has not arrived here yet but I am looking for him daily. His commission arrived some time ago, and also a letter from St. Louis for him. I have them both in my possession, and wrote to him to hasten on. His Reg.t (the 5th Infantry) is already in Camargo. A few months more of fatigue and privation, I am much in hopes, will bring our difficulties to such a crisis that I will be able to see you again Julia, and then if my wishes prevailed, we would never part again as merely engaged, but as,—you know what I would say. No doubt a hard march awaits us between Camargo and Monteray. The distance is over two hundred miles, and as I have understood, a great part of it without water. But a person cannot expect to make a Campaign without meeting with some privations.

Fred. and me will probably be near each other during the time and between us I am in hopes that I will hear from my Dear Julia evry week, but write oftener to me than to Fred.—Since we have been in Matamoras a great many murders have been committed, and what is strange there seems to be but very week means made use of to prevent frequent repetitions. Some of the volunteers and about all the Texans seem to think it perfectly right to impose upon the people of a conquered City to any extent, and even to murder them where the act can be covered by the dark. And how much they seem to enjoy acts of violence too! I would not pretend to guess the number of murders that have been committed upon the persons of poor Mexicans and our soldiers, since we have been here, but the number would startle you.—Is Ellen married yet? I never hear you mention her name any more. John I suppose is on his way for (the) seat (of) war by this time. If we have to fight (we) may all meet next winter in the City of Mexico.

There is no telling whether it will be as prisoners of war or as a conquering force. From my experience I judge the latter much the most probable.—How pleasant it would be now for me to spend a day with you at White Haven. I envy you all very much, but still hope on that better times are coming. Remember me to all at White Haven and write very soon and very often to

Ulysses

Julia

For the first time, Ulysses scolds Julia for neglecting him. There is something sexy about his desire to "scold" her.

"I have a big bone to pick with you the next time I see you. If I don't get back to Missouri soon I will write to Ellen to give you the scolding I want so much to give myself."

Yet he can't help quickly adding:

"Indeed Julia I would give all the glory to be gained in our battles to see you again now."

Matamoras Mexico
Aug. 4th 1846

My Dearest Julia
I have just received a letter from you, the first for about a month, and you deserve a very short one in answer for not writing sooner. My Regiment is all in Camargo with the exception of two Companies. They went up by water. My comp.y and one other of the 4th Inf.y and two of the 3d Inf.y were retained to escort a battery of Artillery by land through all the mud and water, and you may depend there is no scarsity of it. It will take us about ten days to get there and then I will be so far separated from my Dear Julia that you need not look for a letter for one month after this, but my next will be a long one. It is now after (noon) and I have to go to town yet to (mail) this and for other business so tha(t you) must be satisfied with a very (short) one this time. Fred. has not joined us yet. I have a big bone to pick with you the next time I see you. If I dont get back to Missouri soon I will write to Ellen to give you the scolding I want so much to give myself. Indeed Julia I would give all the glory to be gained in our battles to see you again now. I am very much of the opinion however that there will not be many more battles to fight. No doubt you hope

there will be no more, but if you would believe the volunteers, they are anxious to see as hard fighting as they do hard times. You can see from this letter Julia how we live. Dont you see that the paper has been perfectly saturated with water? This is the way with evry thing else, even to ourselvs. Give my love to evry body at White Haven When I get to Camargo I will answer your letter, for I consider this no answer. But I dont want you to take the (s)ame view of the subject and put (off) writing until you get another.

Adieu My Dearest Julia
Ulysses

Anticipating future battles, Ulysses again shows his compassion:

"Wherever there are battles a great many must suffer, and for the sake of the little glory gained I do not care to see it."

Ulysses and his regiment have just arrived at Camargo, Mexico, a miserable place which makes his previous camp site seem like a "perfect paradice." Still:

"If I could but see and talk to you frequently Julia I would not care to be any place else."

Ulysses constantly dreams of their reunion. Thoughts of Julia are what keep him going.

"How happy we must both be after so long a separation when we meet again. How often I think of our pleasant walks & rides & talks!"

Camargo Mexico
August 14th 1846

My Dearest Julia
After a fatiguing march of over a hundred miles my company has arrived at this place. When we left Matamoras, on the 5th of August, it had been raining a great deal so that the roads were very bad, and as you may well guess, in this low Latitude, the weather was none of the coolest. The troops suffered considerably from heat and thirst. Matamoras is a perfect paradice compared to this place. The recent high waters over-run this place so much as to make the most of the houses untenable, and at present a great many families are

living, or rather staying (for I do not consider that the poorer class of Mexicans live atall) under mere sheds, without any other protection. I might attempt a discription of the Mexican people but then you have your Brother Lewis with you who has been so recently among them and can tell you all about them. Fred. has not joined us yet but I am looking for him now daily. Very soon now the troops at this place will start for Monteray, and then I fear, my Dear Julia, that there will be several months that we will not hear from each other very often. Dont neglect to write very frequently so that when a Mail does come I may hear from <u>my</u> <u>Dearest</u> <u>Julia</u>.

Whether there will be a fight at Monteray or not is a matter about which there are various opinions. It is well known that there is now at Monteray about two thousand Mexican troops, busily engaged in throwing up defences, and the Government too is making her best endeavors to get as great a body together as she can. But it is thought doubtful whether she will be able to get any reinforcement before our arrival, and in that case, it is reported, that the Northern provences intend to refuse to furnish their quota of troops. Upon the whole, taking the expression of opinion here the chances are about equal whether there will be another battle or not. The Volunteers and other troops who have arrived since the battles of the 8th & 9th of May are, of course, very anxious to have another fight, but those who were present those two days are not so particular about it. For my part I believe we are bound to beat the Mexicans whenever and where ever we meet them, no matter how large their numbers. But then wherever there are battles a great many must suffer, and for the sake of the little glory gained I do not care to see it. After the way in which the President has taken to show his feelings for the Army, especially I think we have but little reason to want to see fighting.—Do you recollect that some months ago I told you that now I had got to the far South Western limits of our Territory and the next moove must necessarily take me nearer my Dearest Julia? But at present the prospect is very different. Where this moove is to end there is no telling. All I have to wish, <u>Dear</u> <u>Julia</u>, is that you may feel as contented and as little alarm as I do. If I could but see and talk to you frequently Julia I would not care to be any place else. How happy we must both be after so long a separation, when we meet again. How *often I think of our pleasant walks & rides & talks!—It has been two or three days since I wrote the above. Since that reports continue to reach us which leaves but little doubt that we will have a big fight at Monteray. Fred. is not yet with us but I am expecting him now evry day. How anxious I am to see this affair over that I may go back and be with my Dea(r) Julia again! I will write to you evry opport(unity) I have of Mailing a letter after we leave this, and I shall expect a letter from you Julia by evry Mail that reaches us. Even then I fear I will not hear from you half as often as formerly. I have not been very well for a few days and have been busy in my new duties. I am Quarter Master to the Regiment. Give my love to all at White Haven. Tell Ellen that Mr. Dilworth speaks of her very often. Adieu My Dearest Julia—*

U S Grant

CHAPTER SEVEN
The Persistent Quartermaster

Ulysses is made quartermaster, in charge of keeping the Army supplied with food and ammunition. This shows his Colonel has great faith in him. The job of quartermaster is crucial, but much safer than that of a regular soldier. Most men would be relieved to be out of the line of fire, but not Ulysses. Ulysses prefers to fight! He shows his great courage and patriotism in this letter to his commanding officer.

To Bvt. Col. John Garland

[August, 1846]

I respectfully protest against being assigned to a duty which removes me from sharing in the dangers and honors of service with my company at the front, and respectfully ask to be permitted to resume my place in line. Respectfully submitted.

U.S. Grant
2nd Lt. 4th Inft.

This protest was returned with an endorsement by Bvt. Col. John Garland: *"Lt. Grant is respectfully informed that his protest can not be considered. Lt. Grant was assigned to duty as Quartermaster and Commissary because of his observed ability, skill and persistency in the line of duty. The commanding officer is confident that Lt. Grant can best serve his country in present emergencies under this assignment. Lt. Grant will continue to perform the assigned duties."*

On Aug. 29, 1846, Bvt. Maj. William W.S.Bliss wrote to Garland: *"The Commanding General desires that you will retain Lieut. Grant in his position of QuarterMaster to the 4th Infantry—his services being represented as very useful by Major Allen."*

Colonel Garland and General Taylor were both playing a role in Ulysses' destiny by retaining him as quartermaster. Ulysses was still able to observe military strategy, but at the same time, learn how to keep an Army supplied with food and ammunition. These were crucial to his skill as a General during the Civil War.

Ulysses sees it is necessary to fight to win, that the Mexicans are prolonging the war by avoiding a fight. This will shape Ulysses' determination to be a "fighting general" in the Civil War—the only fighting general on the Union side.

"If these Mexicans were any kind of people they would have given us a chance to whip them enough some time ago and now the difficulty would be over, but I believe they think they will out-do us by keeping us runing over the country after them."

He understands they have to fight to win, but he still feels great compassion for the Mexican people.

"It is a great misery to me how they live."

"If we have to fight I would like to do it all at once and then make friends."

He dreams of a reunion in Gravois County with Julia.

"I know I shall never be willing to leave Gravois again until Julia is mine forever."

He has a bewildering amount of faith she will write him more often.

"Write to me very often Julia"

What makes him think she will write him often? This guy never gives up!

Ponti Agrudo, Mexico
September 6th, 1846

My Dearest Julia
We have left Camargo on our way for Monteray, where it is possible we will have a grand fight. We are now within Six days march of Monteray but it is probable we will not start from here, or from Ser albo, quite a fine city Twelve miles from Ponti Agrudo, for some ten or twelve days yet. When we do start I will write again if an opportunity occurs to send the letter. I am much in hopes my Dearest Julia that after this moove our difficulties will be brought to a close, and I be permitted to visit the North again. If ever I get to the states again it will be but a short time till I will be with you Dearest Julia. If these Mexicans were any kind of people they would have given us a chance to whip them enough some time ago and now the difficulty would be over; but I believe they think they will out-do us by keeping us runing over the country after them. I have traveled from Matamoras here, by land, a distance of two hundred miles. In this distance there is at least fifteen thousand persons, almost evry one a farmer and on the whole road there is not, i dont belive, ten thousand acres of land cultivate(d) On our way, we passed through Reynoso, Old Reynoso Camargo & Mier, all of them old deserted looking places, that is if you only look at the houses, but if you look at the people you will find that there is scarsely an old wall standing that some family does not live behind. It is a great misery to me how they live—Fred. is not with us yet. If he does not make haste he will not have the pleasure

of making himself heard of more than heard from, as you told me he said he would. Have you heard from John since he started with Col. Kearny? No doubt he is hartily tired of soldiering by this time?—I suppose you have heard long ago of the freak Col. Harney took? He is now some place further interior than we are. Whether he and his six hundred men are ever heard of again I think a doubtful matter. So much exposure as the troops have been subjected to has been the cause of a great deel of sickness, especially among the Volunteers. I think about one in five is sick all the time. The regulars stand it some better but there is a great deel of sickness with them too. Gen. Taylor is taking but Six thousand men with him to Monteray. The most of the Volunteers he has left behind.

Julia aint you geting tired of hearing of war, war, war? I am truly tired of it. here it is now five months that we have been at war and as yet but two battles. I do wish this would close. If we have to fight I would like to do it all at once and then make friends.—

It is now about two years that we have been engaged Julia and in all that time I have seen you but once. I know though you have not changed and when I <u>do</u> go back I will see the same Julia I did more than two years ago. I know I shall never be willing to leave Gravois again until Julia is mine forever. How much I regret that we were not united when I visited you more th(an) a year ago. But your Pa would not have heard to anything of the kind at that time. I hope he will make no objections now! Write to me very often Julia, you know how happy I am to read your letters. Mr. Hazlitt is very well. Give my love to all at White Haven. Has Ellen & Ben Farrer made up yet? The time is now geting pretty well up and I am afraid that I may loose my bet—

Ulysses

Ulysses has just survived the Battle of Monterey. What woman wouldn't swoon at these words from her "soldier of love?"

"In the midst of grape and musket shots, my Dearest Julia, and my love for her, are ever in my mind."

Ulysses is *still* unable to write the word which means so much to him, "wife."

"I think before I see another birth day I shall see Julia, and if she says so, be able to call her my own (...) Dear for ever."

Camp Near Monteray, Mex.
Sept. 23d 1846

My Dear Julia
    It is now after night and an opportunity occurs of sending a letter tomorrow to where it can be mailed, and you know my Dear Julia I told you I would not let a single chance escape of writing to you. If I could but see you I could tell you a volume on the subject of our last three days engagement, but as I write this I am laying on the ground with my paper laying along side in a very uneasy position for any one to give a detailed account of battles so you must be satisfied with a simple statement of facts, and the assurance that in the midst of grape and musket shots, my Dearest Julia, and my love for her, are ever in my mind. We have indeed suffered greatly but sucsess seems now certain. Our force is but six thousand that of the enemy is probably much greater, but is not known. The siege of Monteray was commenced on the 20th Ins. but we did not fire our first gun until the morning of the 21st. Monteray is a city of from six to ten thousand inhabitants. The houses are all low and built of stone. In the town and on the commanding points the Mexicans have erected fortifications and seem determined to fight until the last one is taken by shere force.

Already all those on the high points of ground have been taken and many Mexican lives with them. We are now playing upon them with pieces of Artillery and ammunition that we have captured but they still hold their citadel and Artillery enough to man it. Our loss has been very great, particularly in the 3d & 4th Inf.y. The killed and wounded officers runs as follows (leaving out a number of Volunteers who I do not know the names of.)

1st Inf.y Capt. Lamotte an arm off, Lt. Terrett badly wounded and in the hands of the Mexicans, Lt. Dillworth lost a leg. 3d Inf.y Capt. Morris, Capt. Field Maj. Barbour, Lt. Irwin & Lt. Hazlitt killed Maj. Lier severely wounded, the ball passing in at the nose and out at the ear. His recovery doubtful. 4th Inf.y Lt. Hoskins & Lt. Woods killed and Lt. Graham severely wounded. I(n) the other Regt. there was more or less killed or wounded but the loss not so severe. I passed through some severe fireing but as yet have escaped unhurt.

Of course My Dear Julia if I get through (and I think the severest part is now over) I will not let an opportunity of writing to you escape me. I have not had a letter from you since we left Matamoras which was on the 5th of August but I know there must be one or two on the way some place I am geting very tired of this war, and particularly impatient of being separated from one I love so much, but I think before I see another birth day I shall see Julia, and if she says so, be able to call her my own (...) Dear for ever. It is about time for (me) to close writing until Monteray is entirely ours, so give my love to all at White Haven and write very soon to

Ulysses

I cried at the news that Lieutenant Hazlitt had been killed. Bob Hazlitt was Ulysses' roommate at Camp Salubrity, the one who did a summersault off his donkey on the way to a ball.

The Battle of Monterey is over, and Ulysses never mentioned his heroics to his beloved. He volunteered to make a dash on horseback, under a heavy fire, to obtain fresh ammunition for United States troops. Enemy bullets flying in his direction, Ulysses adjusted himself on the side of his horse furthest from the enemy, and with only one foot holding to the cantle of the saddle, and an arm over the neck of the horse exposed, he made his heroic ride. What a perfect chance to impress Miss Julia, especially with her attraction to him as the "Dashing Lieutenant." Yet he says nothing about it. As she matured, Julia would come to cherish Ulysses' humbleness even more than his dashing spirit.

I love Ulysses' sensuous descriptions of Mexico:

"Monteray is so full of Orange and Lime and Pomgranite trees that the houses can scarsly be seen until you get into the town."

Ulysses finally gets his courage up to write his favorite word, "wife."

"Julia is as dear to me to day as she was the day we visited St. Louis together, more than 2 years ago, when I first told her of my love. From that day to this I have loved you constantly and the same and with the hopes too that long before this time I would have been able to call you <u>*Wife.*</u>*"*

His faith in her is unending.

"You have not told me for a long time Julia that you still loved me, but I never thought to doubt it."

Camp Near Monteray Mex.
Oct. 3d 1846

My Dearest Julia

I wrote to you while we were still storming the city of Monteray and told you then that the town was not yet taken but that I thought the worst part was then over. I was right for the next day the Mexicans capitulated and we have been ever since the uninterupted holders of the beautiful city of Monteray. Monteray is a beautiful city enclosed on three sides by the mountains with a pass through them to the right and to the left. There are points around the city which command it and these the Mexicans fortified and armed. The city is built almost entirely of stone with very thick walls. We found all their streets baricaded and the whole place well defended with artillery, and taking together the strength of the place and the means the Mexicans had of defending it it is almost incredible that the American army are now in possession here. But our victory was not gained without loss. 500, or near abouts, brave officers and men fell in the attack. Many of them were only wounded and will recover, but many is the leg or arm that will be buried in this country while the owners will live to relate over and over again the scenes they witnessed during the siege of Monteray. I told you in my last letter the officers that you were acquainted with that suffered, but for fear the letter may not reach you I will inumerate them again. Capt. Morris of the 3d Inf.y Maj. Barbour Capt. Field Lt. Irwin Lt. Hazlitt Lt. Hoskins and Lt. Terrett & Dilworth since dead. Lt. Graham & Maj. Lier dangerously wounded. It is to be hoped that we are done fighting with Mexico for we have shown them now that we can whip them under evry disadvantage. I dont believe that we will ever advance beyond this place, for it is generally believed that Mexico has rec-d our Minister and a few months more will restore us to amity. I hope it may be so for fighting is no longer a pleasure. Fred. has not joined us yet and I think it a great pity too, for his Regiment was engaged at a point where they done the enemy as much harm probably as any other Reg.t but lost but very few men and no officer. Monteray is so full of Orange Lime and Pomgranite trees that the houses can scarsly be *seen until you get into the town. If it was an American city I have no doubt it would be concidered the handsomest one in the Union. The climate is excellent and evry thing might be produced that any one could want. I have written two pages and have not told you that I got a letter a few days ago from my Dear Dear Julia. It has been a long long time since I got one before but I do not say that you have not written often for I can very well conceive of letters loosing their way following us up. What made you ask the question Dearest Julia "if I thought absence could conquer love"? You ought to be just as good a judge as me! I can only answer for myself alone, that Julia is as <u>dear</u> to me to-day as she was the day we visited St. Louis together, more than two years ago, when I first told her of my love. From that day to this I have loved you constantly and the same and with the hope too that long before this time I would have been able to call you <u>Wife</u>. Dearest Julia if you have been just as constant in your love it <u>shall not</u> (....) long until I will be entitled to call you by the (....) affectionate title. You have not told me for a long time Julia that you still loved me, but I never thought to doubt it. Write soon to me and continue to write often. Now that we are going to stay here some time I am in hopes that I will get a number of letters from you. I forgot to tell you that by the terms of capitulation the Mexicans were to retire beyond Linariz within seven days and were not to fight again for eight weeks and we were not to advance for the same time. Fred. certainly will join soon and then I will make him write often. Give my love to all at White Haven*

Ulysses

In his memoirs, Ulysses mentions a journal he kept at
Jefferson Barracks, in which he wrote an account of books he was
reading. It became lost when the regiment moved to Louisiana, and a
friend packed and moved Ulysses' belongings, because Ulysses was
on leave in Ohio. In his memoirs, at the age of sixty-three, when he
was dying, Ulysses still despaired of anyone ever finding the journal,
insisting that if it fell into the hands of someone malicious enough to
print it, it would cause Ulysses great heart-burning. Why, you may
wonder? Why would he be embarrassed if it was only a record of
what he read in his books? From this passage to Julia, it shows the
journal quickly went from being an account of his book-reading, to an
account of his blossoming love for her.

*"Of late I could read but very little for I was so busy riding about and
occationally visiting my friends in the country...who by the way are
becoming very interesting." "That part Julia must have been written
about the time I first found that I loved you so much."*

And a haunting prophecy about his future:

"Without you dearest a paradice would become lonesom."

Camp Near Monteray Mex.
Oct. 20th 1846

My Dear Julia
*How very very lonesome it is here with us now. I have just
been walking through camp and how many faces that were dear to
the most of us are missing now. Just one month ago this night the 4th
Inf.y left this camp not to return again until it had lost three of its
finest officers. (Lt. Graham has since died) I came back to my tent
to drive away, what you call the Blues, I took up some of your old
letters, written a year or so ago and looked them over, I next took up*

a Journal that I kept whilst at Jefferson Barrack and read as far as to where I mentioned "that of late I could read but very little for I was so busy riding about and occationaly visiting my friends in the country—who by the way are becoming very interesting." That part Julia must have been written about the time I first found that I loved you so much. It brought the whole matter to mind and made me think how pleasantly my time passed then. It seems very hard that I should not be able now to spend a few days in the year as I did then evry week. How long this state of things is to continue is yet a problem but it is to be hoped not long. When you walk down the branch to Aunt Fieldings do you ever think of our walks on that road? How very often they come to mind. This is my third letter since the battles to you Julia so that if you dont hear from me often it is not my fault.

We occasionally get reports here that negociations are going or that proposals of the kind have been made by this Government. I hope sincerely that such is the case for I am very anxious to get out of the country. This is the most beautiful spot that it has been my fortune to see in this world, but without you _dearest_ a Paradice would become lonesom.—Fred. is not with us yet and I am now giving up the hope of seeing him here. I have had his commission for a long time and the other day I concluded to send it to him. One or two of the Mails comeing this way from Camargo have been robed lately and the letters sent to Gen. Ampudia and by him to Gen. Santa Ana. Ampudia was polite enough to inform Gen. Taylor of the fact.—Before you get this no doubt there will be great excitement in the states in concequence of the battle of Monteray, and no doubt you will hear many exaggerated accounts of the valorous deeds performed by individuals. I begin to see that luck is a fortune. It is but necessary to get a start in the papers and there will soon be deeds enough of ones performances related. Look at the case of Capt. Walker! The papers have made him a hero of a thousand battles.—Give my love to all at White Haven and write to me very soon. I would like to know Julia if your father ever says or hints a word on the subject of our engagement?

Farewell my Dearest until your next letter which will be in a week or two

Your Devoted
Ulysses

Julia

    P.S. The Mail has not left here since writing the above. All are well except many slight cases of Fever & Ague. Capt. Ridgely of the Artillery, hose name no doubt you have often seen in print, met with a severe accident yesterday, the 26th He was riding through Monteray and his horse fell with him and fractured his skull. His life is despaired of.

U

After the battles, come letters from Julia. Just as surely as day follows night, Julia's letters follow a fight. Their affair is heating up and becoming more adult, though they are united only in their thoughts. Here is their sexiest exchange to date:

"You say in your letter that you wish it was our country that was being invaded instead of Mexico, that you would ask for quarters but doubted if Mr. Grant would grant them. Indeed dearest I am one of the most humane individuals you are acquainted with, and not only would I give quarters to any one who implores them, but if Julia says she will surrender herself my prisoner I will take the first opportunity of making an excursion to Mo. But you must not expect your parole like other prisoners of war for I expect to be the Sentinel that guards you myself."

Ulysses is equally sensuous with his suggestion:

"Dream of me and tell me your dreams."

Camp Near Monteray Mexico
November 7th 1846

My Dear Julia
*   I got one of the sweetest letters from you a few days ago that I have had for a long time and the least I can do in return is to write you at least three pages in, return; even if I have nothing more to write than that I love you, and how very much. I have written very often to you since the battle of Monteray and intend to continue to do so, but still I hope that I may have but few more letters to write you. How happy I should be if I knew that but a very few more letters were to pass between my Dearest Julia and myself,—as mere lovers,— that is to say, how happy I should be if soon Julia was to become mine forever. You say in your letter that you wish it was our country that*

was being invaded instead of Mexico, that you would ask for quarters but doubted if Mr. Grant would <u>grant</u> them. Indeed dearest I am one of the most humane individuals you are acquainted with, and not only would I give quarters to any one who implores them; but if Julia says she will surrender herself my prisoner I will take the first opportunity of making an excursion to Mo. But you must not expect your parole like other prisoners of war for I expect to be the Sentinel that guards you myself. Indeed dearest Julia it cannot be a great while longer that we are to be separated by so many miles space! Very soon now the troops at this place will be on their way for either Tampico or San Louis Potosi at either of which places there will be likely to be a big fight. Some troops will remain here to Garrison the city but who will remain is not known. Before we leave of course I will write again. So many battles must of course result in a final peace and I hope matters will be rushed so as to bring about a speedy settlement of all our difficulties.

November 10th As the Mail only leaves this place once a week I have put off finishing this letter until to-day—Mail day—, Since writing the above orders have been published for the 5th & 8th Infantry and Artillery Battalion, the whole commanded by Gen. Worth, to march upon Saltillo on the 12th Instant. The 7th Inf.y and one comp.y of artillery Garrison Monteray, so it is presumed that before two weeks we will take the field again. I get but few letters from home now and write but very short ones in answer. Some time ago my Father had one of my letters published so hereafter I intend to be careful not to give them any news worth publishing. I have not had a letter from Clara or Virginia for some time. When I write again I will tell Clara that if she will write to you she will get an answer. Clara is very anxious to have me come home and wants me to take Julia with me. Will I have that pleasure <u>dearest</u>? This will be my last Winter in Mexico until I return to the U. States even if I have to resign. I have never yet seen a place where I would as leave be stationed as at Monteray if the population was an American one—and if Julia was here.

The climate is excellent, the soil rich, and the scenery beautiful; Did you understand what I meant in the firs(t) of this letter where I hope but few letters m(ore) would pass between us as mere lovers? Of course though you know that I meant I hoped that it would not be long until I would be with you and then it would not be necessary to write. But in the mean time write very often as I do. I do not know that you get all my letters, but I write very often. Does Sara Walker take the death of Mr. Terret very hard? You say she used to get very long letters from him! Are all well at White Haven? Give them my love and write to me soon. Dream of me and tell me your dreams. When you wrote <u>kiss</u> *on your letter I kissed before I knew whether you had kissed it or not, and frequently after Tell Ellen I will pay her off for trying to play a trick off on me. you say it was her wrote the word on the corner of the sheet of paper. I wrote to Fred. a short time a go and sent him his commision and a letter that I have had for him a long time. Farewell Dearest Julia, I shall write to you again in about one week and my next after that will as likely be from Tampico as any place els*

Ulysses

After displaying heroics in the Battle of Monterey, Ulysses is left to garrison the city following its capture. Julia continues to dream of him. There is something sexy about her dreaming of her once fresh faced young suitor with a full set of manly whiskers.

"I see from your letter that Ellen is as full of mischief as ever, she takes evry opportunity to tease you as she did about your dreaming of seeing me with whiskers!"

Monteray Mexico
December 27th 1846

My Dearest Julia
Again I write you from Monteray. You know I told you that my next letter would probably be written from some place far away. The troops moved as I expected but the 4th Inf.y and one company of Artillery was left to Garrison this city and will probably be here for the ballance of the war. Gen. Worth Gen. Wool & Gen. Butler are all at or near Saltillo with from four to five thousand troops, Gen. Taylor is on his march for Victoria with the greater part of the Army, and I would not wonder if he continued on to Vera Cruz. After Gen. Taylor had been out about three days from this place an Express reached here from Gen. Worth announcing that Santa Ana's army was advancing upon them The Express was forwarded to Gen. Taylor and he returned but finding that the danger ahead was not so great as was threatened he has again taken up his line of march for Victoria. There is but little doubt but that Santa Ana is at San Luis Potosi with an army of from 20 to 30 thousand but I do not believe that he intends advancing but will wait for us to go to him. The citizens of this place have become very much allarmed at the threats of the Mexican General and have nearly all left the town, but I think in a few weeks they will find that Santa Ana is not coming as fast as he says, and the inhabitants will return. A report reached here a day or two since that the Mexican congress has passed a resolution to admit a Minister from the U. States to treat. I hope it may be true.

You say Julia that your Pa said as soon as he heard that I was QuarterMaster that he pronounced me safe for Qr. Mrs. did not have to go into battle; that is very true but on the 21st of September I voluntarily went along with the Regiment and when Mr. Hoskins was killed I was appointed acting adjutant to take his place and in that capacity continued through the fight.

I have written you two pages my Dearest Julia without telling you that I had recieved your sweet letter of the 7th of November. I feel very happy when I can get such long letters from you Dearest and then this one has some such good news in it! You say your Pa often asks about me and then he named me when you were counting apple seeds? When I read this I felt as though I was just geting his concent to our long long engagement. How long it does seem since I saw you last! You ask when my next birth day will be On the 27th of April I will be 25 years old. Just think when we were first engaged I was but twenty two and I thought then that long before one year passed Julia would have been mine forever. I regret very much that such was not the case. I see from your letter that Ellen is as full of mischief as ever, she takes evry opportunity to tease you as she did about your dreaming of seeing me with whiskers! I expect when I see her she wont be satisfied with teasing me about them but will pull them and to show you that they are long enough to be pulled I will send you a lock of them.

Julia (w)hy did you not tell me some of your drea(ms) you say you frequently do dream of me now? I (think) a great deel about my dear Julia but of late I but seldom dream. You must write very often to me Julia and tell me if you got a letter containing a check for Mrs. Porter. In your last letter you did not say whether Mrs. P. is still at the Barracks or not? Give my love to all at White Haven and kiss Emmy for me. Do ask your Pa to write to me some time and say that he will give me Julia. Fred has not written to me for a long time. I bid you good by Dear Julia hoping that before a great while I will be able to see you.

Ulysses

Julia

P.S. I have got Emmy's kiss and the hundred you send. Recollect I am going to collect them all when I see you next, besides paying you the hundred I send you in return.

U.

Two hundred kisses! That must have been a happy reunion.

In his letter to an unknown friend, Ulysses expresses his frustration at not being allowed to fight and get the war over with.

To An Unknown Friend

[Dec., 1846]

Here we are, playing war a thousand miles from home, making show and parades, but not doing enough fighting to much amuse either the enemy or ourselves, consuming rations enough to have carried us to the capital of Mexico. If our mission is to occupy the enemy's country, it is a success, for we are inertly here; but if to conquer, it seems to some of us who have no control that we might as well be performing the job with greater energy. While the authorities at Washington are at sea as to who shall lead the army, the enterprise ought and could be accomplished.

Ulysses has just joined General Winfield Scott's command. Ulysses sends kisses to all the Dent girls, but it's clear where his real passion lies. This is the very first time Ulysses sends Julia "a thousand kisses."

"Give my love to the whole family and a kiss to Misses Ellen and Emmy and a Thousand for Miss Julia."

Camp Palo Alto Texas
Feb. 1st 1846 (1847)

My Dearest Julia

From the heading of my letter you will see that since my last the 4th Inf.y has materially changed its Position. Two days before we left Monteray we thought we were stationary for some time to come but as soon as Gen. Scott took command evrything was changed and now here we are prepairing to embark, I believe, for a small Island laying between Tampico and Vera Cruze no doubt to make a decent upon the City of Vera Cruze. As soon as we are stationary I will write again. I am afraid Julia that you do not get all my letters for I see that at home they get none of them. Evry few weeks I get a letter from there beging me to write. They say they have not had a letter from me since the troops went to Monteray. Of course I have written a number. At Vera Cruze we will probably have a desperate fight but our little Army goes so much better prepaired than it has ever done before that there is no doubt as to the result. I fear though that there is so much pride in the Mexican character that they will not give up even if we should take evry town in the Republic. Since we left Monteray I have been very far from well and now I could remain behind if I would but I think by the time our sea voyage is completed I will be well and while I am in the country I want to see as much of it as possible. Evry letter I get from home begs of me to leave Mexico and I think if Mr. Polk does the Army another such insult as he did in officering the Rifle Reg.t I will leave.—My Dear Julia you cannot know the anxiety I feel to see you I would almost be willing to be sick enough to leave the country just to get back to Gravois once more. This is a very pretty country to look at but I am geting so thoroughly tired of it that I begin to think like one of our Captains who said that if he was the government he would whip Mexico until they would concent to take the Sabine for their boundary and he would make them take the Texans with it. When we leave here I think I shall give up Quarter Mastering and go back to my Company. Fred never writes to me any more. Is he still at Baton Rouge? His Reg.t is encamped here with us and will sail with us—I heard from some one that Fanny Higgins is engaged to be married. Is it so? What do the people in the States think about peace? Do they think there ever will be peace again between the U. States and Mexico? Tell Fred. when you write to him not to think of applying to be relieved from where he is, for he would soon find that he did not know when he was well off. How was John and Lewis the last time you heard from them?

I have nothing left to write dearest Julia except how much I love you and how very anxious I am to see you again and all that you know for I have told it to you with the utmost candor a thousand times. Give my love to the whole family and a kiss to Misses Ellen & Emmy and a Thousand for Miss Julia. How often I take the ring from my finger just to see the sweet name engraved in it! Write very often to me Julia and I will promise more than an equal number.

Ulysses

Julia

P.S. Dearest Julia since writing the above I rec'd a letter from Mrs. Porter. It was sealed with black wax and the direction did not seem to be in your hand. This allarmed me a little but you cannot immagine my allarm when I saw your brother's name was signed to the last page. But the sweet note from your dear self restored me to confidence of my dearest Julias health. You must not neglect to write as your pa advises you for all your letters reach me. Two or three months ago I sent Mrs. Porter a check on Col. Cummings enclosed in a letter to you. Did you ever get the letter? If you did not Mrs. Porter will not loose the money for no one els could draw it but will take

some time for me to find out if you got it and to send another. write
Dearest Julia

U

CHAPTER EIGHT
The Torrid Zone

Ulysses is at sea, heading for the attack on Vera Cruz. He faces dangers such as small pox and yellow fever. But he is sustained by ever more vivid dreams of uniting with Julia.

"I have dreamed of you twice since my last letter. All my dreams agree in one particular, that is in our marriage, either that the day is set or the seremony is being performed."

The steamy tropics intensify Ulysses' hunger for love.

"You must recollect we are now in the Torrid Zone."

Ship North Carolina
Island of Lobos Mexico
Feb.y 25th 1847

My Dearest Julia
 There is now laying at this Island over thirty transports ready to fall down to Anton Lizardo as soon as the remainder of the Army joins us which will probably be in the course of six or seven days. Lobos is a small Island about one mile in circumference and ten miles from the main land. It is covered with the India rubber tree (You must recollect we are now in the Torrid zone) which like some others of the Tropical trees has a number of different trunks. The limbs bend over until they touch the ground and there take root and grow as large as the parent tree. On the ship North Carolina we have over four hundred troops. A great part of the time we have had a very heavy sea and often you would think the ship would capsize. It rocks so much now that I am afraid I will not sucseed in writing so that you can read it. I have not been troubled with sea sickness

but have almost recovered from my former illness. There has been several cases of small Pox here among the volunteers and one Reg.t, the Mississippi Reg.t has lost in the last few weeks about one hundred men. Their sickness has resulted principally from being crouded and not keeping up a strick Police. We have lost no one aboard our vessel. The general opinion now is that we will have a fight when we attempt to disembark and a big one at Vera Cruz. It is hoped that it will be the last! There is a report here that Gen. Taylor has had a fight with Santa Ana some place beyond Monteray and repulsed him but it is not generally believed. We will all have to get out of this part of Mexico soon or we will be caught by the yellow fever which I am ten to one more afraid of than of the Mexicans. Gen. Scott will have with him about twelve thousand land troops and a large Naval force. Fred's Reg.t is here. I should like to see him here but if I was in his place I never would make application to come to Mexico. I have long since been tired enough of this country but I suppose I will have to see the war out. In my next no doubt I will have news of a great battle to relate. If we are likely to be stationary for several months after the battle I will apply for a leave of absence for a few months. If I should sucseed in geting a leave I will make my way for St. Louis as fast as possible. My anxiety to see you my Dearest Julia increases with the space which separates us. Vera Cruz is 20 degrees south of Jeff. Bks. I have dreamed of you twice since my last letter. All my dreams agree in one particular, that is in our marriage, either that the day is set or the seremony is being performed.

Feb. 27th Having no opportunity of Mailing this I left one page blank to fill up when an opportunity did occur. To-morrow a mail leaves here and I can not fail to improve it. My Dearest Julia time can not suffice to make my absence from you more bearable. I begin to believe like some author has said,—that there are just two places in this world—One is where a person's intended is, and the other is where she is not. At one of these places I was always happy and hope ere long to return, at the other I feel much discontent. Dont you think Julia a soldiers life is insupportable? Just think in all this time there has been but three battles fought towards conquering a peace. If we have to fight I would like to see it all done at once. Julia you must write to me often and when I get off (the) rocking ocean I will write a long letter; that will probably be from Vera Cruz.—Give my love to all at White Haven and dream of me yourself dearest. At least I have the pleasure of dreaming of you some times but not half so often as I would like. My love a thousand times over to you dearest Julia and twice as many kisses. Adieu

Ulysses

If I remember my math, that's two thousand kisses this time! Wow!

Ulysses' regiment has successfully conquered the city of Vera Cruz. I *love* this line of Ulysses' to Julia about his duties. His honesty and self deprecating sense of humor is so endearing.

"I am doing the duties of Commissary and Quarter Master so that during the siege I had but little to do except to see to having the Pork and Beans rolled about."

Ulysses tries to be philosophical about their long separation.

"Julia ain't it a hard case that this Mexican war should keep me two long years as it has done from seeing one that I love so much. But <u>*time*</u> *only strengthens and proves the reality of their being such a thing as love."*

Camp at Vera Cruz Mex.
April 3d 1847

My Dearest Julia
It has been longer since I wrote you last than I have ever before gone without writing, but I wanted to wait until the Siege of Vera Cruz was completed and the fighting over. You will no doubt read flaming accounts of the taking of this City and the Castle San Juan de Ulloa. Yesterday I visited the Castle and find that its strength has never been exagirated. The City is a solid compact place the houses generally built of stone and two or three stories high, the churches like most Catholic churches are very much ornamented. The whole place is enclosed by a stone wall of about fifteen feet in hight and four or five feet thick. Taking into account all the out works of the place it seems as if it would be impossible for any enemy in the world to come and drive us away. Fred. is here and well. I see him evry day. I will leave the discription of the battle here to him. I am doing the duties of Commissary and Quarter Master so that during the

siege I had but little to do except to see to having the Pork and Beans rolled about. It is not known when the troops will leave here but they will move some place soon, before the sickly season. How much my Dearest Julia I would be pleased to hear that Mexico has agreed to treat. I think they must do so soon for Gen. Taylor at his end of the line of opporations has routed Santa Ana and totally disorganized his army. Here Gen Scott has taken the key to their whole country and the force that Garrisoned this place are all prisoners of war on their Parole not to fight during the war.—Do you recollect Dearest about six months ago I told you that another Birth day certainly would not roll round before I would be with you. Well here it is near the time and I have not started yet. I have always been so much in hopes that the war would soon end that I have not followed the desire of my Father to resign. He insists that evry officer of the Regular army ought to resign after the appointments that have been made. I believe he is right and if there is no prospect soon of the War closing I will go any how. I rec'd one of the sweetest letters from you about ten days ago! You speak of Captain Gardenier in it, is there not a report that he and Mrs. Porter are to be married. I have heard so. Remember me to Mrs. P. and don't forget to send me the poetry you promised. We have a very pretty encamping ground here and though the Sun is very hot yet the sea brease makes it quite comfortable. It is a great pity that people compose the Mexican soldiery should be made the tools for some proud and ambitious General to work out his advancement with. Julia aint it a hard case that this Mexican war should keep me two long years as it has done from seeing one that I love so much. But _time_ only strengthens and proves the reality of their (being) such a thing as love—If I could but see you and have a long talk I could then serve out this war with some degree of contentment, but as it is I am very impatient. Fred was in here a while ago and no doubt would have had some message if he knew who I was writing to. Fred. knows of our engagement and has spoken of you to me once or twice.—I often take the ring you put on my finger off and look at the sweet name in it. Give my love to your Pa Ma Ellen Emmy &c. Write very often my Dearest Julia to

Ulysses

In the battle of Cerro Gordo Ulysses learns the value of attacking the enemy's rear, and that with the correct military strategy, no enemy is impregnable. He also reveals a secret, something deep in his heart which means more to him than life itself: that his love for Julia is returned. This is what keeps him going, what he longs for, the incredible sensations, in the flesh, of his love being returned, a pleasure he has never before experienced.

"Just think Julia it is now three long years that we have been engaged. Do you think I could endure another years separation loving you as I do now and believing my love returned?"

Castle of Perote Mexico
April 24th, 1847

My Dear Julia
You see from the above that the great and long talked of Castle of Perote is at last in the hands of the Americans. On the 13th of this month the rear Division of Gen. Scott's army left Vera Cruz to drive Santa Anna and his army from the strong mountain passes which they had fortified, with the determination of driving back the Barbarians of the North, at all hazards. On the morning of the 17th our army met them at a pass called Cierra Gorda a mountain pass which to look at one would suppose impregnable. The road passes between mountains of rock the tops of which were all fortified and well armed with artillery. The road was Barricaded by a strong work with five pieces of artillery. Behind this was a peak of the mountains much higher than all the others and commanded them so that the Enemy calculated that even if the Americans should succeed in taking all the other hights, from this one they could fire upon us and be out of reach themselves. But they were disappointed. Gen. Twiggs' Division worked its way around with a great deel of laibor and made the attack in the rear. With some loss on our side and great loss on the part of the Enemy this highest point was taken and soon the White flag of the enemy was seen to float. Of Generals and other officers and soldiers

*some Six thousand surrendered prisoners of war Their Artillery ammunition supplies and most of their small arms were captured. As soon as Santa Ana saw that the day was lost he made his escape with a portion of his army but he was pursued so closely that his carriage, a splendid affair, was taken and in it was his cork leg and some Thirty thousand dollars in gold. The pursuit was so close that the Mexicans could not establish themselvs in another strong pass which they had already fortified, and when they got to the strong Castle of Perote they passed on leaving it too with all of its artillery to fall into our hands. After so many victories on our part and so much defeat on the part of the Mexicans they certainly will agree to treat. For my part I do not believe there will be another fight unless we should pursue with a very small force.—From Vera Cruz to this place it is an almost constant rize Perote being about Eight thousand feet above the ocean. Around us are mountains covered with eternal snow and greatly the influance is felt too. Although we are in the Torrid zone it is never so warm as to be uncomfortable nor so cold as to make a fire necessary. From Vera Cruz to this place the road is one of the best and one that cost more laibor probably than any other in the world. It was made a great many years ago when Mexico was a province of Spain. On the road there are a great many specimens of beautiful table land and a decided improvement in the appearance of the people and the stile of building over any thing I had seen before in Mexico. Jalapa is decidedly the most beautiful place I ever saw in my life. From its low Latitude and great elevation it is never hot nor never cold. The climate is said to be the best in the world and from what I saw I would be willing to make Jalapa my home for life with only one condition and that would be that I should be permitted to go and bring my Dearest Julia.
—The 5th Inf.y, Fred's Reg.t was was not present at the fight of Cierra Gorda. A few days before we left Vera Cruz the 5th Inf.y was ordered down the coast to Alvarado to procure horses and mules for the use of the army, and when we left they had not returned. My Dearest Julia how very long it seems since we were together and still our march is onward. In a few days no doubt we will start for Puebla and then we will be within from Eighty to a Hundred miles of the City of Mexico; there the march must end. Three years now the 4th Inf.y has been*

(on) the tented field and I think it is high time t(hat) I should have a leave of absence. Just think Julia it is now three long years that we have been engaged. Do you think I could endure another years separation loving you as I do now and believing my love returned? At least commission and all will go in less time or I will be permitted to see the one I have loved so much for three long years. My Dearest dont you think a soldiers life a hard one! But after a storm there must be a calm. This war must end some time and the army scattered to occupy different places and I will be satisfied with any place wher I can have you with me. Would you be willing to go with me to some out-of-the-way post Dearest? But I know you would for you have said so so often.—Your next letter will probably reach me in Puebla the 3d city in size in the Republic of Mexico. Write to me often Julia I always get your letters. I will write again as soon as the army makes another halt. Has your pa ever said anything more about our engagement? You know in one of your sweet letters you told me something he had said which argued that his consent would be given. Remember me affectionately to you father and mother Miss Ellen & Emmy.

Ulysses

Julia

P.S. Among the wounded on our side was Lt. Dana very dangerously. In the Rifle Reg.t one officer, Lt. Ewell, was killed Mr. Maury lost his hand Mason and Davis a leg each. A great many Volunteer officers were killed and wounded. I have not had a letter from you since the one I answered from Vera Cruz but there have been but few mails arrived since. I hope to get one soon.

U

Ulysses expresses his disappointment at not being allowed to fight. One can feel his heart break, almost like a child who is not allowed to attend a party.

To An Unknown Friend

April 24, 1847

It was war pyrotechnics of the most serious and brilliant character. While it was a most inspiring sight, it was a painful one to me. I stood there watching the brigade slowly climbing those ragged heights, each minute nearer and nearer the works of the enemy with our missiles flying over their heads, while white puffs of smoke spitefully flashed out in rapid succession along the enemy's line and I knew that every discharge sent death into our ranks. As our men finally swept over and into the works, my heart was sad at the fate that held me from sharing in that brave and brilliant assault. But our batteries did their duty, and no doubt helped in achieving the glorious result.

Jalapa is the most beautiful part of Mexico we have seen. I suppose we move on toward the Capital at once.

Again, Ulysses bravely demands to be allowed to fight. This is amazing, since his position as Quartermaster gives him a much better chance of going home to Julia alive. His sense of duty, and love of fighting, is an instinct so powerful he cannot suppress it, even out of love for a woman. It is his destiny calling, and he must answer.

Resignation Endorsement

(April, 1847)

I should be permitted to resign the position of Quartermaster and Commissary. Why should I be required to resign my position in the Army in order to escape this duty: I must and will accompany my regiment in battle, and I am amenable to courtmartial should any loss occur to the public property in my charge by reason of my absence while in action.

Again, his higher ups refuse to remove Ulysses from his safer position as Quartermaster. They did not realize, they were playing a role in this great man's destiny. By denying him his desire in the short term, they were keeping him alive, to live and fight another day, at the head of the Union Army in the Civil War.

Ulysses' letter resigning his quartermaster post was returned to him by his superior, Brevet Colonel John Garland, with the following endorsement:

I. The resignation of Lieutenant Grant is not accepted, and Lieutenant Grant is informed that the duty of Quartermaster and Commissary is an assigned duty, and not an office that can be resigned. As this duty was imposed by a military order from a superior officer, the duty cannot be evaded except by a like order relieving Lieutenant Grant from duty.

II. The good of the service requires that Lieutenant Grant continue to perform the duties of Quartermaster and Commissary in the Fourth Infantry. However valuable his services might be, and certainly would be, in <u>line</u>, his services in his present assigned duties cannot be dispensed with, and Lieutenant Grant will continue in their discharge.

CHAPTER NINE
Kisses and Flowers

Ulysses longs for Julia when he is taken ill with chills and fever. In this reference to a kiss she sent him, we see that Julia herself is quite talented at the art of romance.

"I rec'd the two flowers you kissed and sent me. It is very pleasant my Dearest to get a kiss from you even on a flower that has to travel two thousand miles to reach me but how much more pleasant it would be if I could be with you to steal a real one!"

No (1)
Puebla Mexico
May 17th 1847

My Dearest Julia
I rec'd your sweet letter marked No (1) at Tepeyahualco the evening before we left there and would have answered it that night but I was very sick with the chills and fever. In that letter you spoke of what a good nurse you are. How much I wished then I could be with you! We started the next morning for this place and I was sick all the way but I am well now. At a little town about ten miles from here our troops had a small fight but no one on our side was hurt. A few of the Mexicans were killed. Santa Ana is said to be ten or twelve miles in our advance fortifying a Bridge but I suppose we will not go there for a few weeks to molest him. Puebla is much the largest city we have yet seen in Mexico. It contains from 80 to 90 thousand inhabitants. The houses are large and well built. It surpasses St. Louis by far both in appearance and size the mass of the people are the same beings that we have seen all over the country. At a certain ring of the church bell or when the senior Priest of the place passes you might see them on their nees in the streets all over the city. Although we are now within a few days march of the capittal of the Mexican Republic I do not see that the chances for peace brighten in the least. The people are proud

and subject to the will of a few and they have no government to act for them.—The 5th Inf.y is now with us. I see Fred frequently. Of course we are the best friends in the world and I will do as you request, keep him out of mischief. How much my Dearest Julia I regret that I had not taken my Father's advice and resigned long ago. Now no doubt I would have been comfortably in business and been always near one of whom I am always thinking and whom I love better than all the world besides. The night after I rec'd your last letter I dreamed that I had been ordered on the recruiting service and was near where you were. In my dream, I said now I have often dreamed of being near my dear Julia but this time it is no dream for here are houses that I recollect well and it is only two days travel to St. Louis; but when I woke up in the morning and found that it was but a dream after all how disappointed I was! My Dearest how much I wish I could see you here for one day to see all the grand churches, the beautiful public walks &c. &c. They are far superior to anything you expect. The churches of the city are very numerous and extravigantly furnished. We are now quartered in a Convent. This place from its elevation is very healthy and much more pleasant both in summer and winter, so far as climate is concerned, than Jeff. Bks. You ask if Fred. is in earnest about his attachment for Miss Cross. I believe he is but you must not tell him that I told you so. He recieves letters from her. My Dearest Julia if this war is to continue for years yet as it may possibly do (but I do not think it will) can I stay here and be separated from you (whom I love so much) all the time? I have no intention of anything of the kind. In the course of a few months more I will see you again if it costs me my commission which by the way I value very low for I have been a very long time ballancing in my mind whether I would resign or not. At one time about two years ago or near that, I was offered a professorship in a College in a very pretty town in Ohio and now I regret that I did not go there. I often think how pleasantly I would have been settled now had I gone. No doubt you would have been with me dearest and I have always been happy when I was near you. My Dearest Julia before now I would have applied for a leave of absence and insisted upon geting it had your father and mother given their consent to our engagement. I do not doubt but they will give it, but when I go to Mo. I would like you to become mine forever my dearest, and if I am to stay in the army I would come back myself and see the war out. May 23rd My Dearest Julia I have had no opportunity of mailing this since we have been here. I am now perfectly recovered from the chills and fever of which I had an attack. There is but little news here. Santa Ana is taking a position between here and the City of Mexico but the people of the country seem to be disatisfied with him and there are very many of them who would be glad to hear of his death either by violance or otherwise.—Fred is well. You must remember me and him to Mr. Elting. Give my love to all at White Haven. Ask Ellen if I have won that bet. I bet that her and Ben Farrer would make friends in two years.—You must write to me often dearest for I get all your letters. Number them and I will tell you if I loose any. I intend writing to you very often so that if any letters should be lost you will hear still often enough to know how much I love you and whether I am sick or well.—I have not heard from Mr. Dana lately but the last I heard he was improving. He is in Jalapa. I rec'd the two flowers you kissed and sent me. It is very pleasant my Dearest to get a kiss from you even on a flower that has to travel two thousand miles to reach me but how much more pleasant it would be if I could be with you to steal a real one! I think I will be entitled to several when I get back to Mo.—When you write to John and Lewis remember me to them. Tell them they must whip the Mexicans badly at their end of Mexico, we have whiped them so often here that we are geting tired. Write often very often Dearest

*to Your affectionate
Ulysses*

Describing the charms of Mexico, Ulysses reveals his yearning for the warmth Julia has always given to him since he became a lonely soldier.

"The climate is delightful but yet I long very much to be back to my old home and particularly to the first home I had after entering the army."

No. 2
Puebla Mexico
May 26th 1847

My Dearest Julia
I wrote you a long letter a few days ago and marked it No 1 and now I will write you again believing that it is doubtful if the other ever reaches. There are no troops going from here to Vera Cruze and the road is so infested with Mexican armed men that a mail stands but a small chance of reaching there, but coming this way they are well guarded with the new troops that are constantly arriving. I cannot venture to write you as I otherwise would lest some day my letter might be in the hands of the enemy. I am very well and so is Fred. I saw him this morning. As I told you in my other letter, Puebla is a beautiful, large, and well built city, surpassing anything we had seen before in Mexico. The climate is delightful but yet I long very much to be back to my old home and particularly to the first home I had after entering the army. You must write me long letters my Dearest Julia and expect short ones for a short time until the line from here to the sea coast is more safe. Remember me to all at White Haven and wish for my speedy return to the states. I will closeing this hoping that you may recieve my other letter yet fearing that you will not.

My Dearest Julia Adieu
Ulysses

After three long years, Colonel Dent finally gives his daughter consent to marry Ulysses. It seems that she finally became determined enough about it to get her way. At the onset of their romance, she seemed unsure, and wrote infrequently. Once the battles began, her feelings for Ulysses deepened, and once she was sure of what she wanted, him, she laid down the law to papa.

"You know how often I have asked you if your Pa could give his concent to our engagement. I know now that he will and I am happy."

But the Colonel wasn't happy, as eye witnesses saw him sobbing at their wedding! This exchange is curious. It sounds like someone was spreading a false rumor about Ulysses' honor. If Julia was concerned about it, the rumor might have been that he was seeing another woman. But she says she is satisfied that the rumor was false, and Ulysses is relieved by her letter.

"It not only assured me that you were satisfied falsity of the report you mentioned in your previous one (why did you not tell me my Dearest the Object the man could have in perpetrating such a falsehood.)

Puebla Mexico
August 4th 1847

My Dearest Julia
    A few days ago I wrote you a short letter in answer to yours telling me of the report you had heard, hearing at that time that a privat express was going to Vera Cruz, but after writing it I found that the express had left before I had as much as heard that one was to leave.—You must not attribute you geting but a few and but short letters from me to any disinclination on my part in writing them. No my dearest I would be willing to write you a whole sheet evry day if

you could but get my letters. I have told you before, but I will now repeat it, that but few Mails go from here to Vera Cruz and those are in great danger of being captured as several of them have been. Mails coming in this direction are much safer from the fact that troops are constantly joining the army from that direction.—I recieved another letter from you by some troops that come in last evening and one too that gave me more happiness than any previous one that I have ever recieved. It not only assured me that you were satisfied falsity of the report you mentioned in your previous one (why did you not tell me my Dearest the object the man could have had in perpetrating such a falshood.) but it set me at rest on another subject. You know how often I have asked you if your Pa would give his concent to our engagement. I know now that he will and I am happy. My greatest trouble now is how I am to get back and when. I think certainly by Fall. If I thought another year was to pass over first I would be miserable. The same mail that brought your letter brought (me) several from home. My sister Virginia said in her's that of all persons in the world except myself she wants most to see you and she wants to see us both in Bethel soon. I sincerely hope Dear Julia that her wish may be gratified. This waring in a foreign country does very well for a while but a person who has attachments at home will get tired of it in much less time than I have been at it. I believe I have told you before that of all the countries and all the climates on Earth no other people are so blessed by Nature as the inhabitants of this part of Mexico. The church has all the power, all the wealth. I think I would be safe in saying that three fourths of the expence of building Puebla has been in churches and church property.—When we will move towards Mexico is not known unless it is by the Commanding-General. We hear a great many reports of there being a strong peace party in the city of Mexico who are only waiting our approach to come out boldly but I do not know how true it is. I have not seen Fred. for a day or two but I know he is well. Give my love to all at White Haven. I will close this with a P.S. when I find I can mail it.

Yours most Devotedly
Ulysses

Julia

August 8th P.S. I have not yet had an opportunity of mailing this letter and do not know when I will have.—Tomorrow we start for the City of Mexico where no doubt we will have another big fight. Rest assured my Dearest Julia I will not let an opportunity of geting out of Mexico escape me after I have once seen the Capittal.

Fighting his way toward Mexico City, General Scott conquers Churubusco, and young Ulysses is a part of it. Again, Ulysses shows his compassion:

"The slaughter of our men is greater than ever before, and worse than death is the awful suffering of the torn and wounded on both sides."

"Too much blood has been shed."

Ulysses already shows himself to be more astute at military strategy than even the Commanding General, Winfield Scott.

"I have tried to study the plan of campaign which the army has pursued since we entered the Valley of Mexico, and in view of the great strength of the positions we have encountered and carried by storm, I am wondering whether there is not some other route by which the city could be captured, without meeting such formidable obstructions and at such great losses. If I should criticise, it would be contrary to military ethics, therefore I do not."

To An Unknown Friend

[Aug 22, 1847]

I wondered what must be the emotions of General Scott, thus surrounded by the plaudits of his army. The ovation was genuine, and from the hearts of his men. This has been the greatest battle of all, and it looks now as if the city would yield without another. May heaven grant it, for the slaughter of our men is greater than ever before, and worse than death is the awful suffering of the torn and wounded on both sides.

While the cheers were going up for General Scott, General Rincon, one of the captured Mexican prisoners confined in the church, was standing at a window leaning out; he uncovered his head, and his countenance lighted up, and his eyes sparkled with every manifestation of delight. I have no doubt but the old veteran, animated with the chivalrous instincts of the true soldier, when he heard the plaudits which the General received from the brave men he had so recently led to victory, forgot that he was the defeated and a prisoner, and for the moment entered into the enthusiasm of the occasion.

Too much blood has been shed. Is it ended, or will hostilities be resumed? We are prepared for either event. I have tried to study the plan of campaign which the army has pursued since we entered the Valley of Mexico, and in view of the great strength of the positions we have encountered and carried by storm, I am wondering whether there is not some other route by which the city could be captured, without meeting such formidable obstructions, and at such great losses. If I should criticise, it would be contrary to military ethics, therefore I do not. There is no force in Mexico that can resist this army. To fight is to conquer. The Mexicans fight well for awhile, but they do not hold out. They fight and simply quit. Poor fellows; if they were well drilled, well fed and well paid, no doubt they would fight and persist in it; but, as it is, they are put to the slaughter without avail.

Ulysses gives an even more detailed account of what he considers to be mistakes made by the high command in the Mexican War, which resulted in unnecessary deaths. He's sounding less like a lowly lieutenant and more like a Supreme Commander, which is what he has always been inside.

To An Unknown Friend

[Sept. 12, 1847]

You will thus see the difficult and brilliant work our army has been doing. If Santa Ana does not surrender the city, or peace be negotiated, much more hard fighting may be expected, as I foresee, before the city is captured. My observations convince me that we have other strong works to reduce before we can enter the city. Our position is such that we cannot avoid these. From my map and all the information I acquired while the army was halted at Puebla, I was then, and am now more than ever, convinced that the army could have approached the city by passing around north of it, and reached the northwest side, and avoided all the fortified positions, until we reached the gates of the city at their weakest and most indefensible, as well as most approachable points. The roads and defenses I had carefully noted on my map, and I had communicated the knowledge I had acquired from Mexican scouts in our camp, and others I met at Puebla who were familiar with the ground, to such of my superiors as it seemed proper, but I know not whether General Scott was put in possession of the information. It is to be presumed, however, that the commanding General had possessed himself of all the facts.

It seems to me the northwest side of the city could have been approached without attacking a single fort or redoubt, we would have been on solid ground instead of floundering through morass and ditches, and fighting our way over elevated roads, flanked by water where it is generally impossible to deploy forces.

What I say is entirely confidential, and I am willing to believe that the opinion of a lieutenant, where it differs from that of his

Commanding General, <u>must</u> be founded on <u>ignorance</u> of the situation, and you will consider my criticisms accordingly.

After fighting two more ferocious battles, Ulysses is still learning lessons in generalship, like the need to take away the enemy's artillery, cut off their supplies and sea ports. Among other acts of heroism for which he never takes credit, Ulysses placed Julia's wounded brother, Frederick, on top of a wall so he would receive medical attention. Yet, he never even mentions this kind act to the wounded man's own sister, which should have greatly impressed her! Ulysses is modest beyond belief. He is also unbelievably honest. I was always impressed with the following lines, which I believe no other long absent lover would convey:

"Exposure to weather and a Tropicle Sun has added ten years to my apparent age. At this rate I will soon be old."

How many men would tell their lover "I will soon be old?" Just about everyone I know, including me, wouldn't do it! You want the girl to wait for you, don't you? But to Ulysses, honesty was the path to true love.

Here, he expresses his frustration, longing to get out of Mexico.

"If you were here and me in the United States my anxiety would be just as great to come to Mexico as it is now to get out."

Ulysses dreams of seeing the Gravois Creek. What happy memories it holds, what an important part it played in the *drama* that was their romance! It nurtured their spirits—then separated them the night he came to propose, by turning into a raging torrent.

"Pray that the time may not be far distant when we may take our walks again up and down the banks of the Gravois. Truly it will be a happy time for me when I see that stram again."

City of Mexico
September 1847

My Dearest Julia

Because you have not heard from me for so long a time you must not think that I have neglected to write or in the least forgotten one who is so ever dear to me. For several months no mail has gone to Vera Cruz expect such as Editors of papers send by some Mexican they hire and these generally fall into the hands of the enemy who infest the wole line from here to the sea coast. Since my last letter to you four of the hardest fougt battles that the world has ever witnessed have taken place, and the most astonishing victories have crowned the American arms. But dearly have they paid for it! The loss of officers and men killed and wounded is frightful. Among the wounded you will find Fred's name but he is now walking and in the course of two weeks more will be entirely well. I saw Fred. a moment after he received his wound but escaped myself untouched. It is to be hoped that such fights it will not be our misfortune to witness again during the war, and how can be? The whole Mexican army is destroyed or disbursed, they have lost nearly all their artillery and other munitions of war; we are occupying the rich and populace valley from which the great part of their revenues are collected and all their sea ports are cut off from them. Evry thing looks as if peace should be established soon; but perhaps my anxiety to get back to see again my Dearest Julia makes me argue thus. The idea of staying longer in this country is to me insupportable. Just think of the three long years that have passed since we met. My health has always been good, but exposure to weather and a Tropicle Sun has added ten years to my apparent age. At this rate I will soon be old.—Out of all the officers that left Jefferson Barracks with us, besides this four or five who joined since, are gone. Poor Sidney Smith was the last one killed. He was shot from one of the houses after we entered the city.

Mexico is one of the most beautiful cities in the world and being the capital no wonder that the Mexicans should have fought desperately to save it. But they deserve no credit. They fought us with evry advantage on their side. They doubled us in numbers, doubled us and more in artillery, they behind strong Breast-works had evry advantage and then they were fighting for their homes. It truly a great country. No country was ever so blessed by nature. There is no fruit nor no grain that cant be raised here nor no temperature that cant be found at any season. You have only to choose the degree of elevation to find perpetual snow or the hotest summer. But with all these advantages how anxious I am to get out of Mexico. You can readily solve the problem of my discontent Julia. If you were but here and me in the United States my anxiety would be just as great to come to Mexico as it is now to get out.

Oct. 25th At last a mail is to leave here for the U States I am glad at finally having an opportunity of leting you hear from me. A train is going to Vera Cruz and with it many of the wounded officers and men. Fred. is geting too well to be one of them. I am almost sorry that I was not one of the unfortunates so that now I could be going back. It is hoped that in the future mails will be much more frequent though in fact it is generally believed that as soon as congress meets the whole army will be ordered from this valey of Mexico. There is no use of my teling you any more that I will take the first opportunity of geting back to Mo. for I have told you that so often, and yet no chance has occured. At present Gen. Scott will let no officer leave who is able for duty not even if he tenders his resignation. So you see it is not so easy to get out of the wars as it is to get into them.—Write to me often dearest Julia so if I cant have the pleasure of sending letters often to you let me at least enjoy the receipt of one from you by evry Mail coming this way.—No doubt before this the papers are teaming with accounts of the different battles and the courage and science shown by individuals. Even here one hears of individual exploits (which were never performed) sufficient to account for the taking of Mexico throwing out about four fifths of the army to do nothing. One bit of credit need not be given to accounts that are given except those taken from the reports of the different commanders.

Remember me my Dearest Julia to you father & mother and the rest of the family and pray that the time may not be far distant when we may take our walks again up and down the banks of the Gravois. Truly it will be a happy time for me when I see that stram again.

Farewell My Dearest Julia
U S Grant

CHAPTER TEN
Waiting and Wanting

Ulysses impatiently waits for a peace treaty to be signed between the United States and Mexico, so he can finally go home to Julia. He feels pity for the plight of most Mexicans.

"The rich keep down the poor with a hardness of heart that is incredible."

And his longing to be with Julia almost reaches the breaking point.

"...it is scarsely suportible for me to be separated from you so long my dearest Julia."

Tacabaya Mexico
January 9ᵗʰ 1848

My Dear Julia

Since I wrote to you last one Brigade has moved to this place which is about four miles from the City of Mexico and from being so much higher than the City is much more healthy. One Brigade has gone to Toluca and it is rumored that before a great while we will move to some distant part, either Queretero, Zacetucus, San Louis Potosi or Guernivaca unless there is a strong probability of peace. It is now however strongly believed that peace will be established before many months. I hope it may be so for it is scarsely suportible for me to be separated from you so long my dearest Julia. A few weeks ago I went to the commanding officer of my Regiment and represented to him that when the 4th Inf.y left Jefferson Barracks, three years ago last May, I was engaged, and that I thought it high time that I should have a leave of absence to go back. He told me that he would approve it but found that it would be impossible to get the Comd.g Gen. to give the leave so I never made the application. I have strong hopes though of going back in a few months. If peace is not made it is at all events about my turn to go on recruiting service. As to geting a sick leave that is out of the question for I am never sick a day. Mexico is a very pleasant place to live because it is never hot nor never cold, but I believe evry one is hartily tired of the war. There is no amusements except the Theatre and as the actors and actresses are Spanish but few of the officers can understand them. The better class of Mexicans dare not visit the Theatre or associate with the Americans lest they should be assassinated by their own people or banished by their Government as soon as we leave. A few weeks ago a Benefit was given to a favorite actress and the Governor of Queretero hearing of it sent secret spies to take the names of such Mexicans as might be caught in indulging in amusements with the Americans for the purpose of banishing them as soon as the Magnanimous Mexican Republic should drive away the Barbarians of the North. I pity poor Mexico. With a soil and climate scaresely equaled in the world she has more poor and starving subjects who are willing and able to work than any country in the world. The rich keep down the poor with a hardness of heart that is incredible. Walk through the streets of Mexico for one day and you will see hundreds of begars, but you never see them ask for alms of their own people, it is always of the Americans that they expect to recieve. I wish you could be here for one short day then I should be doubly gratified. Gratified at seeing you my dearest Julia, and gratified that you might see too the manners and customs of these people. You would see what you never dreamed of nor can you form a correct idea from reading. All gamble Priests & civilians, male & female and particularly do on Sundays.—But I will tell you all that I know about Mexico and the Mexicans when I see you which I do hope will not be a great while now. Fred. is in the same Brigade with me. I see him evry day. He like myself is in excellent health and has no prospect of getting out of the country on the plea of sickness.—I have one chance of geting out of Mexico soon besides going on recruiting service. Gen. Scott will grant leaves of absence to officers where there is over two to a Company. In my Reg.t there (are three) or four vacancies which will be fi(lled) soon (....)h and will give an opportunity for (one) or two now here to go out. Give my love to all at White Haven and do not fail to write often dearest Julia. I write but seldom myself but it is because a mail seldom goes from here to the sea coast. Coming this way it is different for the Volunteers are constantly arriving.

When you write next tell me if Mrs. Porter and Mrs. Higgins are married or likely to be.

Adieu My Dearest Julia
Ulysses

With the fall of Mexico City, there are no more battles to be fought. But peacetime is much tougher on Ulysses than war time, because there is nothing to occupy his restless spirit. The young soldier reveals his struggle with loneliness.

"We are now stationed in the little Village of Tacabaya about four miles from the City of Mexico and you dont know how lonesom it is. But I ride into town allmost evry day to pass an hour or two."

Here, the battle-toughened fighter, the soldier who heroically braved enemy fire to gallop off for ammunition, blushes when questioned about his engagement. So cute!

"I saw Captain Gardinier in town a few days ago. The first thing he asked me was about you. He told me that I need not blush for he knew all about our engagement, that you used to make rather a confident of him. I used to think so from the way you spoke of him sometimes in your letters."

The shy soldier reveals a touch of jealousy and possessiveness regarding Julia's relationship with Captain Gardinier. Watch for more on this later!

Tacabaya Mexico
Feb.y 4th 1848

My Dearest Julia
I recieved a few days ago your long sweet letter enclosing one from my father. By the same Mail I got another from home directed to Gen. Worth en(quiring) of the Gen.l my fate if I was dead, or if al(ive) my whereabouts: by the same Mail I also got o(ne) from my sister Clara anouncing that they had at last, after waiting six months,

recieved a letter from me. She says that they had recived a letter from Wren. a few days before and that you had desired to be remembered, and she begs me to come home soon and take Julia along. How happy I should be to do so and I hope it will not be long before I may claim that privilege. There are several vacancies in the 4th Inf.y for 2d Lieutenants and as soon as they are filled some two officers will be sent on the recruiting service and I am certain that the commanding officer will send me for one.—We are now stationed in the little Village of Tacabaya about four miles from the City of Mexico and you dont know how lonesom it is. But I ride into town allmost evry day to pass away an hour or two. I do hope that if the Mexicans dont make peace soon that our Government will decide upon occupying this whole country then the married officers would bring their families here and with the society we would then have I would not want a better station, except I would never be satisfied unless you are here too, my Dearest Julia. Would you come to Mexico? I look forward to the time for my going back to Missouri with a great anxiety and dont you think it too bad that I have never got leave to go! Fred. is here in Tacabaya and is very well.—I asked him why he had not written to you and he says he has written by evry mail. There was a time when no mail went from here to the U. States for about five months and it was in consequence of this that they never heard from me at home. I never let an opportunity of sending a letter pass without writing. Feb.y 13th A train starts for Vera Cruz in a day or two and I will now close this letter. Peace news is stronger than ever. Commissioners have agreed upon terms of peace and if Congress confirms their conditions it is thought that we will all be on our way in sixty days from this time. If I was certain that in this time we were going how long the time would appear—How strange it will be for you to see the 4th Inf.y again and how sad too. When we left Jefferson Barracks I was a Brevet 2d Lieutenant and the youngest officer in the Regiment now there are some fifteen Lieutenants below me all new faces in the Reg.t. One after another has fallen until but few of the old ones are left. Dont you recollect Cap.t Alvord & Lt. Gore? They are both here and the proudest men now that they are married. They both speak frequently of you. I saw Cap.t Gardinier in town a few days ago. The first thing he asked me was about you. He told me that I need not blush for he knew all about our engagement, that (you) used to make rather a confident of him. I used to think so from the way you spoke of him sometimes in your letters.—I should like to see Fanny Higgins very much to see the alteration it makes in her having her eyes straitened. I have not yet delivered the message that Ellen sent to Jarvis but I will take it in the greatest earnest too. Tell Miss Ellen that I cannot give up that I have lost that bet that we made some years ago but on the contrary she is the loser. Give my love to your Pa & Ma and the rest of)the family and write dearest Julia very often. If (a) Mail does not start for a few days I will try and write to Wrenshall. You say that I must send back the letter you sent me from my home but I do not know what I have done with it. The letters I get from you I keep with me generally about a week so that I can read them over and over again when ever I am by my self—then I put them (in) my chest. Julia wont you send me your Daguerotype? How very much I would like to have it to look at since I must be deprived of seeing the original.

Write my Dear Julia as often as you can to one who loves you so much

Ulysses

SIGH. Does this guy know how to end a letter, or what?

In this next letter from Tacubaya, Julia accuses Ulysses of neglecting her. Her longing for him is increasing, at last beginning to match his own.

"You say in your sweet letter that you would be happy to come to me! How happy I should be if such a thing were possible. If you were here I should never wish to leave Mexico. But as it is I am nearly crazy to get away."

Here, Ulysses reveals, in a subtle way, he is still jealous that Captain Gardinier is Julia's confidant. You can feel in his words, a small dart of pain. So cute! And so funny.

"I have not seen Captain Gardinier, who says he is your confidant, for some time but he is in town and I know wants to be remembered to you."

Tacabaya Mexico
March 22d 1848

My Dearest Julia
 I recieved a day or two ago your sweet letter, sweeter because it had been so long since I had recieved one before. Two Mails come to the City of Mexico without bringing a letter from you. I never let a Mail go from here without writing to you still you accuse me of neglect and say that you had determined to not write again until you had recieved an answer to some of your last letters. You must not make any such resolutions as this dear Julia for as I have told you a thousand times before I am never so happy as when I hear from you and I could not neglect you. You say in your sweet letter that you would be happy to come to me! How happy I should be if such a thing were possible. If you were here I should never wish to leave Mexico. But as it is I am nearly crazy to get away. I applied for leave of

absence a few weeks ago but Gen. Butler refused to give it. The only chance at present is for peace to be made which we are very sanguine will be made, but you know more on this subject than we do here. I see that you and my sister have commenced a correspondence. I hope it may prove interesting but unless Clara takes more pains in writing to you than she does writing to me I fear that her letters will fail to interest you. I have not seen Fred. for more than a week but as a mail starts from here to-day I suppose he will write to you.—Tacubaya is a very healthy place but it is so dull here. It is about four miles to the City and as I have several horses at my disposal I generally gallop into town evry day and spend an hour or two. I wish you could be here to take one of these rides with me and see the beautiful Valley of Mexico. The whole Valley is spread out to the view covered with numerous lakes, green fields, and little Villages and to all appearance it would be a short ride to go around the whole valley in a day, but you would find that it would take a week. It is always spring here the winter months being the most pleasant.—Herr Alexander, the great Jugler, has been amusing the people of Mexico for the last ten days. A great many respectable Mexicans male and female attend which argues well that these people at least believe that we will have pease. Before the armistice and treaty were entered into the Mexican people could not visit a place of amusement which was attended by the Americans. Their own people would not allow them.

I have no news to tell you Dearest Julia. Those officers who, you know are generally well. I have not seen Cap.t Gardinier, who says he is your confidant, for some time, but he is in town and I know he wants to be remembered to you.—I dont intend to make any more bets with Miss Ellen for I see that she would claim the wager, win or loose. I will forgive the debt this time. Give my love to all of the family and to my acq(uain)tances. From your letter I suppose Georgia (M.) is married before this? Remember me to Misses Geo(rgia) and Fanny.—Write often dearest Julia to one who always thinks but one who unhappily cannot dream of you often. If I could only always see you and talk with you in my dreams whenever I closed my eyes to sleep, I should be much better satisfied. Adieu my dearest Julia

Ulysses

Ulysses mourns another long, two month period of not hearing from his lover.

"What must I think of you. Just think two long months without hearing from one that I love so much. Well I do not blame you so long as you dont forget me and love me as you say you do."

You can almost hear Ulysses sigh over the cruelty of fate which has kept them apart. But they're about to make up for lost time!

"It is too bad ain't it? Just think we have been engaged almost four years and have met but once in that time, that was three years ago."

Tacubaya Mexico
May 7th 1848

Dearest Julia
I have not recieved a letter from you for two months or more until two days ago, but when one did come it was most welcom. It has been a good while since I wrote to you but I can easily explain the reason. On the 3d of April I started with a party to go to the top of Popocatapetl the highest mountain in North America. From the mountain a portion of us went across into the Valley of Cuernavaca to visit the great mammoth cave of Mexico. On this trip I was absent from Mexico sixteen days and in the mean time a mail went off. The day after my return another mail started but I did not hear of it until I saw it leaving, so you see my dearest Julia you cannot attach any criminality to my apparent neglect. What must I think of you. Just think two long months without hearing from one that I love so much. Well I do not blame you so long as you dont forget me and love me as you say you do.
There is a great deal of talk of peace here now. The knowing ones say that the Mexican Congress will ratify the terms proposed

and that the advance of the American Army will be on its way for Vera Cruz in three weeks. I at least hope dear Julia that it will not be long before I can see you again. It is too bad aint it? Just think we have been engaged almost four years and have met but once in that time, that was three years ago.

I see Fred almost evry day. I told him what you desired me to. Fred read me a little of Miss Ellen's letter.

The trip to the snow mountain and to the cave was very pleasant and would have been more so had we succeeded in geting to the top, but the weather was so unfavorable that all failed. The day that we arrived at the foot of the mountain we ascended about one half of the way to the top and there encamped for the night. We had been there but a short time when it began to blow rain, hale & snow most terrificaly and of course we were in bad plight next morning for ascending a mountain which is difficult at best Next morning however we started through a snow storm which had continued from the night before and the wind blowing hard enough almost to carry a person away. The snow on the mountain drifted so rapidly that it was impossible to see over thirty or forty yards in any direction so we lost the view that we would have had of the surrounding valleys. We ploded on for several hours through all these difficulties when all found that it was perfect madness to attempt to go farther, so we turned back when about 1000 feet below the Crater. That night about the time we were going to lay down, first one person would complain of his eyes hurting him then another and by 9 o'clock evry one was suffering the most excrusiating pain in the eyes. There was but little sleeping done by the party that night. Next morning nine of the officers were blind so that they were obliged to have their horses led One day however restored evry one so far that it was determined not to give up the expediti(on) We then divided, a portion waiting for a favorable (day) succeeded in reaching the top of the Mountain, the rest of us passing over a low ridge commenced descending and after twenty miles of gradual descent arrive in tierra Calliente, or hot county, Here we were halted by some Mexican officers who forbid our entring the place. The commander said that the place was occupied by Mexican troops and by the terms of the Armistice we were obliged to content our selvs out side of town that night. We met troops at three other places before we reached the cave. They showed no hostile feeling but were very punctillious in their observance of the armistace. The fact is they wanted to annoy us by making us go around without seeing their towns. Traveling through tierra Calliente is a beautiful and strange sight to a Northerner. All seasons of the year you will find vegetation in full bloom. We passed some of the most beautiful sugar Plantations in the world and finest buildings in the world. They beat any in Louisiana. Evry one has on it fine coffe fields and orchards of Tropical fruits such as oranges Bananas and twenty kinds of fruit that I never heard of until I came to Mexico. I have written so long that I must close with telling you that after six days travel from the snow Mountain through this beautiful valley we arrive at the great cave of Mexico and explored it to a considerable distance. The cave is exceedingly large and like the Mammoth cave of Kentucky its extent has never been found out. Some of the formations are very singular. One would think that they were works of art. We had with us torches and rocketts and the effect of them in that place of total darkness was beautiful.

　　　　Give my love to all at home. Dont forget to write often. Two months is too long to wait for a letter from one that I love so much.

　　　　　　　　Adieu My Dear Dear Julia
　　　　　　　　Ulysses

P.S. I would take another sheet and give you a more minute description of my trip but there is an officer waiting, very impatiently for me to get through and go to town where I am obliged to. Dont neglect to write very soon and very often Dearest Julia.

The peace treaty has been signed, and it is now only a matter of time before Ulysses and his love are reunited. They only courted for two months before he left for military duty, only seeing each other once in four years, for two weeks. The bond they formed was indeed powerful, to have lasted so long with only letters to touch each others' hearts. And what is Ulysses dreaming of? Why, kissing, of course!

"So my dear Julia I think by July at farthest I shall be able to claim some of the kisses that you have sent me in your letters."

And this haunting premonition of their dramatic future together on the world stage.

"If the 4th go to Calafornia will you go with me? But I know you will. You have often told me that you were willing to go with me any place."

Tacubaya Mexico
May 22d 1848

My Dearest Julia
I have just recieved your sweet letter of the 17th of April and hasten to answer it. I have no doubt but this will be my last letter from Mexico. Peace is certain and already evry preparation is being made to move the troops to Vera Cruz. I think by the 1st of June there will not be an American soldier in the City of Mexico and by the last of June probably not on Mexican soil. What will be our destination it is hard to guess but we will have some perminant station and I am determined to have a leave of absence. So my dear Julia I think by July at farthest I shall be able to claim some of the kisses that you have sent me in your letters. No doubt many troops will be sent on the Rio Grande and others to Calafornia but whenever they go officers who have families will take them along. If the 4th go to Calafornia will you go with me? But I know you will. You have often told me that

you were willing to go with me any place. I am happy at the idea of geting away from Mexico at last because I will be able to see my dear dear Julia again and I hope not to separate. But for this I would be contented to remain in Mexico for ever.

Our commissioners left the City this morning for Caratro and no doubt will give us full news of the confirmation of the Treaty by the Mexican Government in the course of a week. By that time all will be ready to start and away we will go for our homes, many of us with lighter hearts than we started here with.

Even on the extreme borders of our Territory, with the society that a Garrison will necessarily make, and with you there too, I shall be very happy.

Fred has recieved his sword. I see him evry day is quite well. I told him that you were going to write to him in the next week. I send you this letter by Cap.t Morris who is going out of the country on a sick.leave.

I suppose you have read of the attempt to rob a large house in the City of Mexico and in which several officers were concerned? The officers are Lt. Tilden 2d Inf.y & Lts. Dutton & Hare Pa. Volunteers. They have been tried and their guilt established and on Thirsday next are to be hung. Tilden was a Cadet one year with Fred and me. I will write you but a short letter this time but with the firm belief that I shall be the bearer of the next one myself.

Give my love to your family. I will make Fred write before we leave the City of Mexico.

> *Yours devotedly,*
> *Ulysses*

Ulysses will be leaving Mexico soon, but even a few more weeks without Julia seems like an eternity to him. Here he reveals his suseptibility to depression without her, even at the tender age of twenty-six.

"The thought of seeing you so soon is a happy one dearest Julia but I am so impatient that I have the <u>blues</u> all the time."

Now, watch closely as a drama unfolds.

"General Terrace of the Mexican army lives here in Tacubaya with his family. He has five daughter young ladies who are very sociable with the officers of the U.S. Army. A few weeks ago an Aide-de-Camp of General Velasco threatened to mark their faces as soon as we left."

Many, many years later, following Ulysses' presidency, Mr. and Mrs. Grant visited Tacubaya. In her memoirs, Julia revealed: "We saw the beautiful town of Tacubaya, where Lieutenant Grant was quartered so long and where, no doubt, his loyalty to one at home was severely tested, although he did not say so. Oh, no! But I had my thoughts."

After reading all of Ulysses letters from Tacubaya, it is easy to put two and two together. He was lonely, there were five Spanish daughters socializing with the U.S. officers. Do you think Julia was justifiably worried about his fidelity?

Tacubaya Mexico
June 4th 1848

My Dearest Julia
    I wrote you a letter about two weeks ago saying that I should not probably ever write to you again from this part of Mexico. But as

there is a Mail going in a few days, and it will probably go faster than the troops will march, I will write to you again and for the last time, from here. Peace is at last concluded and the most of the troops are on their way to Vera Cruz. On Thursday next the last of the troops in the Valley of Mexico will leave and I think by the 25th or 30th of July I may count on being in St. Louis. The thought of seeing you so soon is a happy one dearest Julia but I am so impatient that I have the <u>Blues</u> all the time. A great many of the business people, in fact nearly all of them, want to see us remain in their country. Already a revolution is looked for as soon as our backs are turned. People who have associated with the Americans are threatened with having their ears & noses cut off as soon as their protectors leave. Gen. Terrace of the Mexican army lives here in Tacubaya with his family. He has five daughter young ladies who are very sociable with officers of the U.S. Army. A few weeks ago an Aid-de-Camp of Gen. Velasco threatened to mark their faces as soon as we left. The threat reached the ears of one of the officers who was in the habit of visiting the young ladies and he gave the valient A.D.C. who was going to make war against innocent females, a good thrashing in a public place, and much to the amusement of the by-standers. Already some barbarites have been commited such as shaving the heads of females, and I believe in one or two cases they cut their ears off. Yesterday an officer had his horse saddle and bridle stolen in broad day light and from the very dencest part of the city. Such thefts are very common. I most hartily rejoice at the prospect of geting out of Mexico though I prefer the country and climate to any I have ever yet seen.

I am going to write you but a short letter dearest Julia because I start at the same time this does. Our march to Vera Cruz I fear will be attended with much fatigue and sickness. Already the rainy season is begining to set in and at Vera Cruz there has been several cases of Yellow fever. Evry precaution will be taken to keep the troops from geting sick however.

We are all to halt and encamp before we get to the coast and as fast as transportation is ready the troops will be marched aboard at night and push off immediately.

Give my love to all. Fred. is well. Write to me again as soon as you recieve this and direct as usual. Wherever a Mail meets us it will be stoped and we will get our letter.

> *Adieu but for a short time*
> *Ulysses*

Well, what do you think? Was Ulysses flirting and making love to the Mexican General's daughters, as Julia suspected? Of course not! I feel sad to think she couldn't believe him when he told her he'd been faithful. Some factors include documentation by fellow officers, after Ulysses became famous, that there was never any woman but Julia in his life, and that he led a very austere life in Mexico. She did not have access to any of that information. Would he have risked venereal disease and illegitimate children? Surely not. He was shy and awkward around women, and "as modest as a schoolgirl." And he was always described as "fiercely monogamous." What is monogamous? Since that describes me, I will tell you. Monogamous does not mean we have superior willpower. It means we don't *want* but the one love. We want the real thing, or nothing. We want love, romance, sex and giving that one beloved our entire lives, or it is a desecration of everything we hold dear. That is how I know Ulysses was faithful to Julia, because he was so much like me. And he would never have lied to her. Hamilton Fish, of Ulysses' presidential cabinet said, "Grant couldn't lie if he wrote it down on a piece of paper." How, then, could he ever lie to his wife? Impossible. Inside, she must have known this about his character. Why, then, would she doubt him? Because she still didn't realize how much she was loved by him, even after he was gone. If she were here right now, I would say, don't you *get* it, girlfriend? You were the only woman in his life! Can't you just accept it? Perhaps it was hard for her to accept such magnificent love—as he described it, "a love so pure." Maybe she just didn't feel—worthy. But he found her worthy. Julia, sometimes I think I understand Ulysses better than you do! I wish I could see you to tell you this.

The previous letter, which unfortunately left a lifetime of doubt in Julia's mind about Ulysses' loyalty, was his last love letter from Mexico.

Ulysses and Julia no doubt experienced a rapturous reunion in St. Louis. One can almost feel Julia blush as she later recalled, "I was enchanted when Captain Grant returned home."

Julia's sister, Emmy, recalls that Ulysses was bronzed from exposure to the sun and more reserved than previously. His four years in battle had matured him, though Julia remained about the same.

Some authors have decried Julia during this period, pointing out that while Ulysses had matured, she had not grown up, staying about as she was when he left home. But for Ulysses, that was a good thing. He didn't want her to change. He needed her to be the one stable thing in his life. He needed her to stay his sweet, youthful, carefree Southern belle who kept his mind off the bloody miseries of war. This was to be a theme through-out all of their lives together.

This love letter, written on a visit to Ulysses' home, following his reunion with Julia, is one of my favorites. It shows a man who went through every deprivation of war, but can't go a few days without the warmth of his woman without brooding.

"I felt as unhappy Dear Julia after leaving you as I did happy upon seeing you first."

The poor grammar in this sentence makes it all the more poignant.

"The whole way I done nothing but think of you..."

August 7th 1848
Bethel Ohio

Monday evening
My Dearest Julia
I have just arrived at home and find all my family in good health. They had not recieved my letter written from the mouth of the Ohio so I took them all by surprise. About seven miles from home a young lady took passage in the same stage with (me) and hearing that my name was Grant enquired if I was not a brother of Virginia Grant's. She said that she had been at the same boarding-school with my sister and would call and see her while the stages were changing. From this we got into conversation and rode quietly up to my fathers house where I was quite attentive in assisting the young lady out and looking after her baggage. They all thought as much as could be that it was Julia that I had brought home, and infact upon making some calls an hour or two afterwards I was told that she had understood that I had brought Mrs. Grant home with me. See how easy it is in a country vilage to give a report circulation!

I felt as unhappy Dear Julia after leaving you as I did happy upon seeing you first. The whole way, I done nothing but think of you, and of how happy I should be at our next meeting. But then you know how very much I love you and how could we part without my grieving. I will leave here on Thursday and reach St. Louis Sunday night or Monday morning. One of my Sisters will accompany me only they say they cannot get ready by the time I want to start.

After my arrival Dear Julia I hope we shall never be so long separated again. My feelings since I left you the last time convinc

It's a real shame this letter was cut off, because Ulysses had a real good line of mush going. Isn't it wonderful? We women so rarely see into the hearts of men. It's a thing of beauty, isn't it? Why, he's actually talking about feelings! *"My feelings since I left you the last time convinc"*

I think he cut off the letter in mid-sentence, and never mailed it, because he realized he had spoken of paying attention to another lady, and it might make Julia feel jealous. Julia's fragile feelings were as important to Ulysses as were his own. My husband, Tedd, thinks Ulysses *was* trying to make Julia jealous at first, then caught himself being disingenuous, and decided against mailing the letter. Whatever his reasons, someone in Bethel saved the letter, thank goodness, and we are indebted to them, for it reveals a bridegroom so ardent, so tender, so devoted, one can't help but feel Julia Dent was one lucky little bride.

CHAPTER ELEVEN
Heavenly Wedding

Ulysses returned home from the war in July, 1848. This time, he would advance as quickly as possible! Ulysses quietly urged Julia to set an early wedding date. This time, she did not resist. August 22 was selected for their union, and the young war hero went home to visit his parents, probably thinking he would bring them back to St. Louis with him.

Ulysses' own family refused to attend his wedding. This must have hurt him terribly. They said it was because her family were slave owners, and Ulysses' mother was too shy to appear in company. But it just fits the pattern of their emotional distance from their sensitive son, unwilling to share with him the joy of what was surely the happiest day of his life. It only serves to point out how desperately he needed someone loving in his life like Julia.

After four long years, the waiting was over. August 22, 1848 had finally arrived. It was Julia and Ulysses' wedding day.

They planned to be married in the Dents' townhouse in St. Louis. Julia and her family were all staying there, for the big event.

The wedding was scheduled for 8:00 that night. Julia intended to spend the day dreamily getting ready, with her sisters and bridesmaids attending her. As is the tradition, she didn't expect to see her handsome bridegroom until the moment she descended the staircase in her wedding gown.

But first thing that morning, who should come to call but Captain Grant?

Nelly and Emmy, Julia's sisters, shrieked and giggled and tried to shoo him away. "Oh, Captain Grant! It's bad luck for the bride and groom to see each other before the wedding, on their wedding day!" they scolded. But the Captain wouldn't leave.

Ulysses was staying nearby at the Planters hotel, and he did not want to spend his wedding day alone in his hotel room. He wanted to be with Julia, to warm himself with her love.

It is telling that Ulysses cared nothing for traditions, and even though they were to be wed that evening, he couldn't bear to stay away from Julia a moment longer. It also shows his stubborn streak.

He certainly didn't let other people's criticisms or differences of opinion change his course of action, not even the disapproval of the family of his bride-to-be.

Ulysses was too poor to give his bride a gift of jewels on their wedding day, which was then a custom. Instead, he gave her something much more intimate and meaningful, a wristlet with a little picture of her bridegroom inside. Julia wore it for the rest of her life.

Ulysses finally went back to his hotel room to prepare for the wedding. He had decided to wear his dress uniform.

At this same hour, Julia prepared to don a fairytale wedding gown given to her by her friend, Caroline O' Fallon, whom Julia called, "the beautiful angel of my childhood."

8:00 P.M., the hour of their wedding had arrived. Ulysses stood at the bottom of the stairs in his dress uniform, shiny sword dangling at his side.

It was fitting Ulysses wore his uniform, for this was a great conquest.

The room was filled with banks of candles, their soft light flickering across the faces of young women in hoop skirts and officers in uniform. James Longstreet, Julia's cousin and Ulysses' best friend, towered over Ulysses as his best man. Colonel Dent sagged as though at a funeral, not a wedding.

But the scorn of the Colonel meant nothing to Ulysses on this day. The only thing that mattered was that at long last, sweet Miss Julia would be his and his alone. As he waited at the bottom of the stairs for the arrival of his bride, what was he thinking? After four long years, she would finally be his. At last, as he wrote in his love letters, "the consequence (matrimony) of a love so pure."

Julia appeared at the top of the stairs in her wedding gown, a creamy costume of tulle and jasmine. She was surely the most beautiful sight Ulysses had ever seen.

And to Julia, gazing through her bridal veil "blusher," which turns all one sees into an ethereal fairy tale, Ulysses must have looked like her handsome prince, waiting for his princess. Julia was radiant in her love, Ulysses was quiet and serious. She let her happiness pour forth, his burned quietly within. Guests remembered he was the "perfect embodiment of a soldier, dignified and brown." And that he was "as cool under the questions of the preacher as he was under fire during the Mexican war." He clasped her soft little hand in his, and guests recalled they had never seen a couple who seemed to fit together so perfectly, who were so destined for a happy married life.

Emmy and her girlfriends maneuvered themselves to the prime position to "get the best view of the groom's face." And Colonel Dent wept when his favorite daughter took her vows. These were no tears of joy, for Colonel Dent hated his future Yankee son-in-law with a passion. Captain Grant was taking his favorite daughter away, and he could do nothing but stand there and watch. For Julia was determined to marry him, no matter what.

He had probably tried to talk to her, tried to reason with her, to no avail, just as Ulysses' parents had surely tried to talk to him. What was the point of her going to finishing school, the Colonel inwardly fumed. Julia studied music, and her bridegroom was tone deaf. She learned to dance, and he had two left feet. She was trained to be a great Southern lady, and he was a Yankee. He had bred his daughter to be the mistress of a sprawling Southern plantation, and now she was destined to live in a tiny Army Barracks! For what? For love! Oh, the agony for Colonel Dent. His hopes of passing his dream on to his daughter, shattered.

He did have one bit of revenge. Rather than have his daughter's wedding and reception at White Haven, which would have made it the social event of the county, he had it in their small townhouse in the city.

In Julia's memoirs, she recounts, "We did not go to the country that summer. I do not know why." It is obvious. Had they gone there, Colonel Dent would have been forced to have the wedding and reception at White Haven. He would have had to have an orchestra and a sumptuous wedding feast. Instead, he had a small table in the back room of the apartment, with fruit and ices. Julia defends her beloved Papa, recalling that the table was set with "all Papa's good taste could provide." She always saw the best in him. Surely, if his daughter would have married someone of whom he approved, say, a wealthy Southerner, Colonel Dent would have put on the proverbial dog. But he was miserable about her selection of husband, and having the wedding in a cramped apartment was one way of expressing his unhappiness.

But by this time, Julia and Ulysses were in a dream world of their own. It had been raining that evening, but when it stopped, the windows were opened to let in the refreshing night air. The smell of rain filled the room along with the sensual scent of jasmine, Julia's favorite flower. After the exchange of vows, a violinist played romantic tunes, and a Spanish dancer performed, in honor of the bridegroom's service in the Mexican War.

It was a gay party, but Ulysses was probably in great suspense for it to end. When the final guest said farewell and disappeared into the night, the moment finally arrived.

After four long years, Ulysses finally got the woman he loved. At last, they were man and wife. At last, they were all alone. Well, not exactly all alone.

The bride and groom spent their long awaited wedding night in Colonel Dent's townhouse. It's kind of strange. One would hope the Colonel and his clan had the good graces to leave for the night, or at least sleep on the other side of the house!

Perhaps Julia wanted it that way. She was so attached to her family. But whatever the reason, the very next day, Ulysses spirited his bride away on a steamboat and left the scowling Colonel Dent as far away downriver as possible.

In the Southern tradition, the couple's friends tossed bouquets of flowers into the water after them, as they waved good-bye. Off they floated down the Mississippi River, where all the pleasures of married life awaited them like shiny Christmas packages waiting to be opened.

Ulysses and Julia were now in a state of total bliss. Julia was such a warm and giving bride, Ulysses had never felt so loved in his entire life.

Julia recalled it all had a dreamlike quality.

"I enjoyed sitting alone with Ulys," she recalled. "This was very very pleasant. He asked me to sing to him, something sweet and low and I did as he requested."

How sweet, that Ulysses disliked music, except from the voice of his own beloved Julia.

Julia says neither her husband nor she ever forgot it. They had "waited four long years for this event" and it's fair to say their honeymoon was everything they dreamed it would be.

After dreaming of her for so long, how Ulysses must have delighted in his young and tender bride.

On their honeymoon, Julia recalls that her husband took special delight in her enjoyment of seeing new sights. Except for finishing school, which was only a few miles from White Haven, Julia had never been away from home. From the start, Ulysses enjoyed expanding his Southern sweetheart's horizons.

As always, this aspect of their romance is a poignant parallel to his role as destroyer of the Old South. The South as a whole was leading an isolated life. They did not keep pace with progress. Following the war, and their re-entry into the Union, the horizons of most Southerners were greatly expanded, as were Julia's horizons tenderly expanded by him.

Julia and Ulysses Grant were mesmerized by each other. As Julia recalled, "I don't remember any of the other passengers on the ship." Recalling their honeymoon daze, she said, "It was always like a dream to me, and very, very pleasant."

Recalling his lonely days in Mexico, their honeymoon was surely a fantasy come true to Ulysses.

Following their two week honeymoon on the steamboat, Julia and Ulysses arrived in Ohio to visit his parents. According to Julia, the newlywed pair "saw everything through magic glasses." Julia met all his friends, heard all his nicknames, and saw that everybody liked him. But Julia witnessed first hand his polite but unemotional mother, and the shallow, conditional attentions of his bragging father. She experienced first hand the lack of warmth that had hurt her sensitive husband, and left him so vulnerable and so in need of her love.

While visiting his well-to-do cousins in Louisville, Julia recalls that, "my dear husband intimated very modestly that if he saw any chance for a business opening he would be glad to resign, and although these gentlemen had large business connections at New Orleans, New York, Liverpool, and, I think, Paris, not one of them offered even to introduce him to any businessman."

Wealthier, flashier people may have mistaken his shyness for dullness, his modest ways for simple-mindedness, his slow, calm manner for lack of ambition.

But Julia saw the warmth and nobleness of his heart. She knew of his courage and his willingness to work hard.

From now on, when others hurt him, she hurt, too.

But any pangs of disappointment were soothed by the balm of his new bride's love. With her soft little hand in his, Ulysses could face anything.

The new Mrs. Grant lavished her husband with the love he had craved all his life. To most men, the honeymoon period is a state of bliss, but for Ulysses, being hugged and kissed and petted by a woman for the very first time, marriage was a state of euphoria.

As the late Lloyd Lewis, in his book "Captain Sam Grant" recalls, "In Julia, the bridegroom was finding a warmth of affection he had never known. He grew uxorious." ("Uxorious" is a seldom used word, but it is *always* used when referring to Ulysses S. Grant! Uxorious means foolishly or excessively in love with one's wife.)

"Where he had always shrunk from nicknames, he purred at "Dudy" from the warm lips of Julia, she of the beautiful skin and amorous figure."

After their marriage, Julia playfully started calling Ulysses "Dudy."

It is poignant how much Ulysses loved the word "wife," even as a single young man. He wrote Julia from Mexico, *"How happy I should be if I knew that but a very few more letters were to pass between my Dearest Julia and myself, as mere lovers"* He greatly preferred the *"affectionate title"* of *"wife."*

His attitude was surprising. To many of us, the word "lover" sounds much more exciting and romantic than "wife." But to Ulysses S. Grant, the idea of a "wife" was one he cherished since boyhood, and continued to cherish into old age.

We know that Ulysses could barely contain himself every time he so much as stole a peek at his new bride. But how did the bride feel about her bridegroom?

Julia wistfully recalled, "General Grant was the very nicest and handsomest man I ever saw."

In her memoirs, she always refers to him as "my dear husband" and "my beloved husband." She says, "It was always sunshine when he was near."

Ulysses S. Grant was not a perfect man. He was shy, smoked too much, was a terrible dancer, a terrible card player, and in time, would reveal a slew of other soon-to-be famous flaws. But to Julia, he was her prince.

Julia was by no means perfect. She was spoiled, extravagant, and as she herself admitted, often "childish and unreasonable." But in each other's eyes, the two giddy lovers saw the true beauty of each other's hearts and souls.

Prior to his wedding, Ulysses had applied for a two month leave of absence to spend with his bride.

In one of my favorite quotes from Lloyd Lewis' "Captain Sam Grant," Mr. Lewis writes, "The change from the armed camp to the love bed was so marked, that at the end of his leave, Ulysses applied for another two months leave of absence." This gave him a grand total of four months to devote to cuddling and lovemaking.

When Ulysses' four month leave came to a close, he received orders to report for duty at a post on the Great Lakes. He was sorry to see his honeymoon end, but looked forward to setting up housekeeping with his new bride.

Before proceeding to the Army Barracks, the brand new Mr. and Mrs. Grant returned to White Haven to say good-bye to Julia's family.

There, the lure of White Haven and its easy, pampered life still called to Julia like a siren song.

For Ulysses' Southern sweetheart, the moment of Unconditional Surrender was still not at hand.

Julia recollects: "We returned home about the middle of October, when my struggle at parting with my father began. My heart was well-nigh broken when the time approached to say farewell. This parting, I felt, was to sever my bonds with home. My first journey with Ulys was only a short one of two or three months and I knew I was to return again, but now I was to leave my dear home and make one among strangers—and then parting with Papa! I could not, could not, think of it without bursting into a flood of tears and weeping and sobbing as if my heart would break."

"Papa came into the sitting room where Ulys and I were. Ulys was telling me how troubled he was, and that for four years he had been anticipating how pleasant it would be for us to spend our days together, and here at the end of the first two months I was relenting. My father said: "Grant, I can arrange it all for you. You join your regiment and leave Julia with us. You can get a leave of absence once or twice a year and run on here and spend a week or two with us."

His heart torn to pieces, Colonel Dent probably cried, "Our princess can't live with the army!"

This surely brought another round of wracking sobs from Julia, and everyone else in the traumatized house.

Ulysses took action.

"Ulys's arm was around me, and he bent his head and whispered, "Would you like this, Julia? Would you like to remain with your father and let me go alone?"

"No, no, no, Ulys," she protested, taking one step closer to unconditional surrender. "I could not, would not, think of that for a moment."

"Then," he said, "dry your tears and do not weep again. It makes me unhappy."

Ulysses ushered his wife out the door, leaving Colonel Dent to wonder what just happened. Ulysses' coolness in the midst of chaos had won another victory against the South. For him, a more important victory than that at Appomattox!

And so, Julia Dent, petted and waited on all her life, gave it all up to live in an Army Barracks at Sacket's Harbor. It consisted of two small rooms. The tiny kitchen was too hot to bear in summer, and the only room warm enough to stand in winter. There was snow up to the window panes, and frozen bottles of water. Ulysses himself described it as "a dull little hole." But they'd never been happier. They quite literally had their love to keep them warm.

How cozy they must have been in bed under a warm blanket, in front of the fire, in their army barracks bedroom.

Julia was without slaves for the first time in her life. But the newlyweds had fun playing house. After the harshness and austerity of his former life, Ulysses was in heaven watching his little bride flit about, beautifying the barracks.

In her memoirs, Julia prattles on, "I must say just a word as to my pretty table appointments. I had some very pretty silver given me both by the Captain's family and my own, and a very pretty set of China decorated with gay flowers. These were my especial joy, and my table was simply delightful with the beautiful china and the handsome tea and coffee set of Sheffield plate. Our pretty silver spoons and forks and all were so bright and new. The carpets were bright and beautiful, soft and warm, and their selection was the occasion of more than one happy, gay ride up to Watertown behind the Captain's fleet steed. The curtains for my two or three rooms I brought from my home. They were a dark, rich crimson of some soft woolen material and very pretty over ivory-tinted embroidered muslin, and with the pretty little trinkets and souvenirs I brought from my dear home made our rooms look very pleasant indeed.

We were very happy at Madison Barracks. The officers seemed to think a great deal of Captain Grant and when they visited us would say, as they looked around our pretty quarters: "Grant, you look so happy and comfortable here, that we are almost tempted to get married ourselves."

It is sad that Ulysses S. Grant is so often remembered as a "butcher" and a "remorseless killer." He was actually a warm-hearted, romantic man who loved to listen to his wife chatter on about china and silverware. Luckily for the country, he was also the only man who knew how to win the Civil War.

Because Julia knew nothing about cooking, Ulysses hired a girl to cook for them.

Julia admits "That first year, I nearly bankrupted my dear husband with my experiments." But her "dear husband" didn't care. Ulysses did not marry Julia for her housekeeping abilities, but for her love and kisses.

Ulysses was bored with his desk job in the Army at this time. But cuddling at home with Julia was as delightful as sipping a julep on Colonel Dent's front porch.

After a lifetime of emotional indifference from his parents, he actually had someone who cared about him. Besides pampering him with her affection, Julia fussed over the young soldier like nobody ever had before. He once wrote to her, when she was visiting White Haven, in regards to his upcoming fishing trip, *"Don't be allarmed about my fishing—I will take good care of myself and not get my feet wet as you fear."* What might have seemed a trifle to someone else, such as his wife worrying about him getting his feet wet, was simply heaven for the love-hungry Ulysses.

CHAPTER TWELVE
Newlyweds

Ulysses was ordered to serve on a general court martial at Fort Ontario, Oswego, N.Y., by district orders 10, February 22, 1849. On that short trip he sent his new wife three poignant letters.

This is absolutely my favorite love letter from Ulysses to Julia. It is the first one written to her after they were married. The reason it is my favorite is that it is the first time he signed his letter, "A thousand kisses," and it contains my favorite line from any of his letters, the ultra-romantic:

"I find that I love you just the same in Adams that I did in Sackets Harbor."

Adams N.Y.
Feb. 27th, 1849

My Dearest Julia
    With a very bad pen, bad ink, and a sheet of Fools Cap paper, furnished by the same Frost that we stoped with when we passed through Adams, I pen you these lines—We are thus far on our journey without difficulty or accident.
    How often I thought of you I can not say but it was a number of times. We found no sleighing and to-morrow will have, no doubt, a tedious trip in the stage. As soon as I arrive at Oswego I will write to you, but as we will be on the road until after night you will probably miss a day recieving letters.
    We didnot come on the same road that you and Clara & I took, and therefore did not see the old house in which we spent such an unpleasant night. When you write to me dont forget to tell me of any news that you may get in letter whilst I am gone.—
    I find that I love you just the same in Adams that I did in Sackets Harbor. A thousand kisses and much love to you.
        U.

In this, his second letter as a married man, Ulysses refers to a note stuck to the top of his valise by his loving wife. She must have asked him to dream of her, as he replies:

"Although I may not dream of you I think of you <u>very</u> <u>very</u> often and of how much I love you."

Julia must have been worried lest he fall ill when away from her care, a sentiment which surely tasted sweet to him. Julia's fussing over him in her gracious, Southern style was heaven to Yankee Ulysses, especially in light of accounts that his mother was unconcerned about him when he was sick.

"If I am the least bit sick I certainly will tell you."

Oswego N.Y.
Feb.y 28th 1849

My Dearest Julia
It is 11 O'Clock at night and Mr. Hunt and myself have just arrived and had time to get our suppers. You see how punctual I am in writing to you. I found your note stuck to the top of the valise and read it with the greatest pleasure. Although I may not dream of you I think of you <u>very</u> <u>very</u> often and of how much I love you.
All the officers of the Court Martial are here and we think that we will not be detained more than two or three days.
Our ride to-day was very fatiguing. All the seats were taken and Mr. Hunt and myself were obliged to take a passage on top of the stage. Bad roads compelled the stage to travel abo(u)t as slow as a person would walk. I think you may look for me home on Monday. If I am the least bit sick I certainly will tell you.
To-morrow when I am rested I will write you a longer letter.

Adieu My dear dear Julia,
U

Ulysses' love for his wife is a constant theme in all of his letters.

"I can not tell you anything except how very very much I love you and how often I think of you."

This is the first time Ulysses calls Julia "Juje." It must have been one of those affectionate newlywed nicknames. After their marriage, he called her "Juje" and she called him "Dudy," revealing a great warmth of affection and deepening intimacy between them.

"A thousand kisses and much love to you my dearest Juje"

Oswego N.Y.
March 1st, 1849

My Dearest Julia
We are through the Court Martial and will start home day-after-tomorrow. We meet again to-morrow too read over the proceedings and will be too late for the stage so that Saturday is the day that we will start. Either Saturday night or Sunday night, about 1 O'Clock at night, you may look for me. I can not tell you anything except how very very much I love you and how often I think of you. It is possible that we will go by the way of Syracuse if it causes no detention, and I think it will not.
I am affraid that from our late arrival at this place that my letter may not have got in the Mail so that, although I have written daily, you may miss two days in geting letters. To-morrow I shall look for a letter from you. This is the last letter you need look for from me. The first stage that starts after the one that carries this will carry me so there is no object in writing again.
I am very well. A thousand kisses and much love to you my dearest Juje.
U.

In early spring, the new Mr. And Mrs. Grant were transferred to a barracks in Detroit, Michigan. There were more social activities here, which delighted the vivacious Mrs. Grant. There were many dances held at the National Hotel, and Julia and Ulysses attended with all the other officers and their wives.

To please Julia, Ulysses escorted her to all the cotillions, but he still felt clumsy and embarrassed on the dance floor. And so Ulysses S. Grant, future victor of the Civil War, future president of the United States, "held down a seat all evening" while his wife danced the night away. Mrs. Tripler, the Army surgeon's wife, recalled the shy Captain Grant stood around "with his hands behind his back, like a schoolboy who had not learned his lesson." But the Captain "was always very tender and devoted to his wife." Colonel James Pitman, a fellow officer, remembered that "Grant was very attached, almost, I would say, overly attached to his wife."

Ulysses S. Grant seemed unremarkable in every way except his devotion to his wife, which was always noticed.

In April of 1849, Julia went for a visit to White Haven, leaving her ardent bridegroom behind. Following are several letters from Ulysses to Julia during her absence.

In this first letter, there are a few indications he is unhappy about her absence, especially his opening remark:

"This you know is my Birth day and I doubt if you will think of it once."

Ulysses reveals a theme which will haunt him the rest of his life:

"I find Detroit very dull as yet but I hope that it will appear better when I get better acquainted and you know dearest without <u>you</u> no place, or home, can be very pleasant to me."

Through-out his letters, the concept of "housekeeping" seems pleasurable to Ulysses, like a domestic art form with Julia at its center, although she neither cooked nor cleaned!

"Now that we are fixed to go to hous keeping I will be after you sooner than we expected when you left."

Detroit Michigan
April 27th 1849

My Dearest Julia
I recieved your Telegraphic dispach yesterday morning from which I see that you are on your way to St. Louis. I hope you may find all at home well, and get this soon after your arrival. This you know is my Birth day and I doubt if you will think of it once.—I have a room and am staying at present with Mr. Wallen. Wallen and family are as well as can be expected under present circumstances.
I have rented a neat little house in the same neighborhood with Wallen and Gore In the lower part of the house there is a neat double parlour, a dining room, one small bedroom and kitchen. There is a nice upstares and a garden filled with the best kind of fruit. There is a long arbour grown over with vines that will bear fine grapes in abundance for us and to give away. There are currents and plum & peach trees and infact evrything that the place could want to make it comfortable.
I will have a soldier at work in the garden next week so that by the time you get here evrything will be in the nicest order. I find Detroit very dull as yet but I hope that it will appear better when I get better acquainted and you know dearest without <u>you</u> no place, or home, can be very pleasant to me. Now that we are fixed to go to hous keeping I will be after you sooner than we expected when you left. I think about the 1st of June you may look for me. Very likely Ellen will come along and spend the Summer with us.—I hope dearest that you had a very pleasant trip. I know that you have thought of me very often. I have dreamed of you several times since we parted.

I have nothing atal to do here. I have no company and consequently do not go on Guard or to Drills. Mr. Gore and myself are to commence fishing in a day or two and if sucsessful we will spend a great many pleasant hours in that way.

When I commence housekeeping I will probably get a soldier to cook for me, but in the mean time if any good girl offers I will engage her to come when you return.

Dearest I nothing more to write except to tell you how very dear you are to me and how much I think of you. Give my love to all at home and write to me very soon and often. Yours devotedly

Ulys

This is the first time he signs his name "Ulys." Another sign of their growing intimacy.

P.S. I recieved two letters here for you which I opened and read; the one from Annie Walker I forwarded to you at Bethel. One from Elen I did not send inasmuch as you would be home so soon. Give my love to Sallie and Annie.

U

The following seems to be an innocuous order for a new Military frock coat and new vest. This order has previously been published in books to show Ulysses' apparent lack of concern about his appearance, saying simply to make it, "about 1/2 inch shorter than Capt. Gore's." But look closely, and its obvious he is ordering the new uniform to look good for his rendezvous with his wife in St. Louis. Ulysses' mind and heart was never far from romance.

Detroit Michigan
May 3d 1849

Mr. Earl
Dear Sir
 Please send me one Military frock coat (Infantry) made to the measure of Capt. J.H. Gore 4th Inf.y but about 1/2 an inch shorter in the waist than his. Also one dark vest.—I should like to recieve the above articles before the end of this month, if possible, inasmuch as I expect to make a visit to St. Louis for a few days in the Month of June, leaving here on the 1st proxim(o)
 Capt. Gore & Lieut Collins, both of the 4th Inf.y, have requested me to say that they would like to have the clothing ordered by them, forwarded as soon as possible.
 Please send me, in addition to the above articles, a Cap bugle with the figure four

I am Sir
Your Obt. Svt
U.S. Grant
1st Lt. 4th Inf.y

In this next letter, notice the ongoing struggle between Ulysses and his parents-in-law for possession of his wife. You can feel his pain and disappointment in this line:

"Dr. And Mrs. DeCamp brought the latest news from St. Louis. They say that you were very well and half inclined to come with them but your mother vetoed it."

But how sweet and gentle he is with her, always referring to her as "dearest." Another gem: her concern that he doesn't get his feet wet on a fishing trip. To Ulysses, this kind of female nurturing, so foreign to him before meeting Julia, was like manna from heaven.

"Don't be allarmed about my fishing—I will take good care of myself and not get my feet wet as you fear."

Detroit Michigan
May 20th 1849

My Dearest Julia

I received your long sweet letter by yesterdays Mail and you know with what pleasure I read it. It is the second recieved since your arrival. Dr. & Mrs. DeCamp brought the latest news from St. Louis. They say that you were very well and half inclined to come with them but your Mother vetoed it.

But in ten days from now dearest I will start after you. If Ellen is comeing with you you might telegraph me and let me know exactly the day you would start and I could meet you at Chicago. But it will probably be better if I should go all the way to St. Louis. I want to see them all there.

I recieved a long lecture from Clara yesterday. Virginia is sick so that the Dr. has to attend to her twice each day. The rest are all well and I am glad that Father is trying to sell his Bethel property or exchange it for City property. They have not heard from you since you left Louisville.—Clara has just written Mrs. Lee a long letter.

I have moved into our house and will get it in the best order I can before I start for you. The owner of the house furnishes the materials for the repairs that are wanted and the soldiers do the work. I will have the house thoroughly whitewashed and painted. Gregorio is living with me and a soldier is cooking for me at present, but I will not keep him after I start to get you.

I have no horse yet but if I can get a good one in St. Louis without paying too much I will bring one along from there.

We heard of the dreadful fire in St. Louis the same afternoon that it was raging so. Is it possible that it was as distructive as it is represented to have been? The fire may drive off the Cholera but it will be at a fearful expense to many citizens. I will send this letter by Col. Bainbridge who is going immediately to St. Louis and will deliver it at least five days sooner than it would go by Mail. One letter next Sunday will be the last I shall write. Any after that would not get to you as soon as I will myself. I will not stay in St. Louis more than a day or two if the Cholera is raging, but if it is not I will stay eight or ten days.

Dont be allarmed about my fishing—I will take good care of myself and not get my feet wet as you fear.

I have not become acquainted with many of the people of Detroit yet and have not visited any of the young ladies. You know I told you that I would be quite a gallant while you (are) absent, but as I see no one that I like half as well as my own dear Julia I have given up the notion

There has not been a single case of the Cholera here yet and the city authorities are doing all they can, in the way of having the streets and yards cleaned and limed, to keep it off.

Why dont Ellen write to me some time. I have written to her! But I know how (it) is, She is too lazy even to keep up the correspondence with her dear little Mc. What has become of Elting? Write to me as soon as you get this and then you need not write again. Give my love to all at home and a thousand kisses for yourself.

Your devoted
Ulis

The first paragraph of this letter is like a plaintive wail. I love the way he says:

"I know now how dearly I love you, and will never give my consent to your making another long visit without me..."

Lay down the law, Ulysses!

Detroit Michigan
May 26th 1849

My Dear Dear Julia
I write to you dearest for the last time until it happens that we are again separated, which I sincerely hope will never take place. I know now how dearly I love you, and will never give my consent to your making another long visit without me, unless it should be absolutely necessary.

By another year I can get a leave of absence for four months and I do not know but that I could at this time if I wanted it. I watch the papers regularly to see how the Cholera is at St. Louis and it distresses me, not a little, to see such unfavorable accounts. Dearest I do wish that you was away from there. Both of us would be uneasy about dear friends I know, who would still be in the midst of the disease, but I hope that by this time it is quiting the City.—If I am not unfortunate I will be in St. Louis on the 4th or 5th of June at the outside and if the Cholera is bad I think we will start back in a day or two after. Should there be no danger I will remain a week or ten days at home.

I am geting along very well with our house. A soldier has been at work for several days white washing and painting. The place looks very different now from what it did when I wrote to you before. Mrs. Wallen, Mrs. Gore and all the rest here are very well. They seem anxious to see you. Our quiet town is very healthy and there seems to be but little apprehension about the Cholera. I am going to write you

but a short letter because you will not recieve more than a day or two
before I see you myself dearest Julia and I doubt if I do not beat it to
St. Louis.

Give my love to all at home and tell Wrenny that he will now
be relieved of his trouble as Carrier. You know he says in your letter
"Devil take the P. Office I'm Carrier." Ten kisses to all except yourself
dearest, those due you I will pay in kind very soon.

Yours affectionately
Ulis

P.S. I will write in the next page a few lines in reply to the note Ellen
wrote in your last letter

U

Kiss

Notice the difference between the tender tone he displays in
all letters to his wife, and his much harsher, sarcastically playful tone
to his sister-in-law. Interesting, since Ellen Dent was rumored to have
been much more outwardly beautiful than her older sister, Julia. Julia
alone holds the place of honor in Ulysses' heart and he always treats
her with what has been described as "a delicacy that would make more
sophisticated men blush."

Dear Sister, or Miss Vanity I Should Say.
Dont you know that you are as vain as you can be and all just
because some silly fellows, not knowing any other way to keep up
conversation, have flattered you. But you did'nt understand them and
as I think a goodeal of you myself, I will forgive it all.

Now I can tell you that if I did get the "old maid of the family,"
as you say, I got the very one I wanted, and the only one I wanted,
and very much too to the disappointment of her Sister (Nellie I mean)
and another lady spoken of in your note. Besides you (had) better look

out or this same Sister Nellie (will) be a much "Older Maid" before she finds one with all the qualifications, (that she can get). However be ready to come here with us to Detroit and we may be able to find you a beaux inasmuch as you are a stranger and people may not have time to find you out. But you must not look your "Uglyest" for if you should you will loose so by contrast with "Sis" that evrybody would be at dagers ponts with me for showing such good taste in my selection (you know how disappointed when you found that it was not you I was going to see) that none of the beaux would look at you. Give my love to evrybody. I sent you ten kisses in the other part of my letter but as I expect to be in St. Louis so soon and dont know but that you might claim them all I will take nine of them back and have them distributed among the little girls across the way.

Your affectionate brother
Ulis

CHAPTER THIRTEEN
The Lonely Lieutenant

In the summer of 1849, Ulysses discovered that his dear Julia was pregnant. How happy he must have been! But his joy was soon dulled by Julia's announcement that she was going home to White Haven, to have their baby. In her memoirs, she insists she was following doctor's orders. But babies were delivered comfortably all the time in Detroit.

Julia was probably frightened at the prospect of childbirth and sought the comforts of White Haven, Papa, and her slaves to attend her, sadly depriving her husband, Captain Grant, of the experience of caring for his wife in pregnancy, watching his baby grow in her beloved belly. He also missed the birth, and by the time he arrived to meet his infant son, it had been named after Julia's papa, Frederick Dent, rather than after its own papa. Score one for Colonel Dent. Note that when their second baby was due, Ulysses was on his way to California but wrote to tell Julia in no uncertain terms, that this time, if it was a boy, he desired their baby would be named after him.

No letters exist from Ulysses to Julia during the time she spent at White Haven, during her pregnancy. He may have been expressing his disappointment to her at being left out of the pregnancy of his first child. Right before she left for White Haven, Julia tells of an incident which seems trivial, but reveals a young husband who was quick to jealousy and in a bad mood about his wife's departure.

"The day before I left, all the friends I knew called to say good-bye. I was quite worn out with this company, and as I bade one of the young officers adieu, quite late in the afternoon, he said, "You must not stay long, Mrs. Grant, we shall miss you." I was very tired and nervous and broke into a flood of tears, almost sobs, when the young gentleman said: "Oh! Madame! I will see you on the boat."

When Julia told her husband this, he was amused "but annoyed."

"He is vain enough to think it was his adieux that caused the tears." Ulysses grumpily noted.

Ulysses had a right to be down in the Detroit dumps. He was going to miss out on one of the most beautiful experiences of a man's life, watching his baby grow inside of his wife. How he would have loved to take care of them both! How gallant he would have been to Julia. How could she want to leave her husband at this time? How could she not want to share this with him? Julia's papa was surely pressuring her to come home. Perhaps he frightened her with stories of childbirth, and used this circumstance to get her to come home. And once there, the lure of White Haven pulled her securely into its arms. Ulysses spent a lonely winter, all by himself, during what should have been one of the happiest, most exciting periods in his life. And the crowning insult was how Julia named the baby after papa and not Ulysses.

To Bvt. Maj. Oscar F. Winship

Detroit Michigan
June 14ᵗʰ 1850

Maj.
 I have the honor to apply for a leave of absence for four months for the purpose of visiting my friends in Missouri and the state of Ohio.
 I am induced to make this application at this time for the reason that my services can probably be better dispensed with at present than at any future time, there being at this Post, with one comp.y, a Commanding officer, Adjutant and three Company officers besides myself. Urgent family reasons also induce me to respectfully submit this application.

   I am Maj.
   Very Respectfully
   Your Obt. Svt.
   U.S. Grant
   1st Lt. 4th Inf.y

To Maj. O. F. Winship
A.A. Gen. East.n Div.

When the baby was born, Ulysses forgave his wife, as he had done before, and would do, countless times in the future. He hastened to St. Louis where no doubt his happiness at seeing her again, and the pleasure of holding his first son, healed his hurt feelings. Ulysses got his feelings hurt easily, and you can bet Julia's preference for Papa at this time, both his presence and naming the baby after him, hurt Ulysses terribly. But he loved her so much, he forgave her everything. Papa had won a few battles, but Ulysses was still determined to win the war. Julia departed with him, probably with great reluctance, and left the Colonel plotting to get her back once more, as soon as he could manage it.

Back in Detroit, Ulysses and Julia were happy again. Julia warmly describes their little love nest by saying, "Everything was very snug and convenient."

But there are hints of Ulysses' drinking problem popping up. Ulysses sued Zachariah Chandler, an up and coming citizen of Detroit, for not sweeping snow from his sidewalk. The future mayor of Detroit accused Ulysses of slipping because he was drunk, declaring, "If you soldiers would keep sober, perhaps you would not fall on people's pavements and hurt your legs." The jury found for Ulysses, fining Mr. Chandler a grand total of six cents.

The miniscule fine may reflect there was some truth in Chandler's assertion that Ulysses had been drinking. Never-the-less, when Ulysses became President of the United States, he and Chandler had many a laugh over the comically dramatic incident.

Had Ulysses started drinking to chase away the "blues" during Julia's absence? Possibly. It sounds like that winter, when he slipped on the sidewalk, he had not shaken the habit, despite Julia's return to him.

Still, this was a happy time.

Fatherhood coaxed Ulysses even further out of his shy shell. He had found the cure for his inherent loneliness. Surely he was in heaven, with his sweet little wife and baby cuddled up beside him.

It is humorous to note a quote from Ulysses S. Grant's memoirs, regarding this rich period of his life. He leaves much to the imagination. "On the 22d of August, 1848, I was married to Miss Julia Dent, the lady of whom I have before spoken. We visited my parents and relations in Ohio, and, at the end of my leave, proceeded to my post at Sackett's Harbor, New York. In April following I was ordered to Detroit, Michigan, where the next two years were spent with but few important incidents." (Except I was deliriously happy, became a father and purred whenever my wife called me "Dudy." But this information would not be in keeping with the restrained tone of the General's book. We'll just have to read between the lines!)

Though a new mother, Julia continued to be as vivacious and fun-loving as ever, and a constant source of pleasure and amusement to her husband. That winter, Julia and some of her girlfriends planned a costume ball. They decorated their home up like the inside of a sultan's court. Ulysses was very involved planning Julia's costume, and even selected and purchased her tambourine himself. (That is just so sweet!) However, Ulysses refused to wear a costume himself. Instead, he wore his uniform and went to the ball as a "Brevet Captain in the Fourth Infantry." Like everything about Ulysses, this is slightly mysterious. When he was in the Army in Corpus Christi, Texas, on the way to the Mexican war, Ulysses dressed up like "Desdemona" and tried out for a play with his brother officers, because there were no women to play the parts. But now, perhaps he was afraid of looking foolish in front of his wife.

Julia took girlish pleasure in their party, and as always Ulysses took great pleasure in her. For a long time after, he called her "my little Tambourina." He loved to see her enjoying herself.

That spring, Julia took baby Frederick home to White Haven for what was supposed to be a short visit, leaving Ulysses alone at the Army Barracks. He was so used to the comforts and joys of his "delightfully feminine" little bride, their cozy love nest seemed bleak and barren without her.

Ulysses' correspondence with his wife at this time is heart-rending. He starts out trying to sound cheerful, begins pining for more letters from her, and soon deteriorates completely into a desperately lonely figure.

Ulysses was having a terrible time getting his wife to come home. The lure of White Haven, its gracious, easy ways, its sweet, winding honeysuckle vines, the "comforts of slavery" removing the weight of motherhood from her small shoulders, had seduced "Miss

Julia" in its soothing embrace once again. One can almost see Colonel Dent smile, if he stole a peek at one of Ulysses' pleading, lovesick letters. Perhaps Colonel Dent and the genteel life of the Old South would defeat Ulysses S. Grant after all?

Following are letters from Ulysses to Julia after she left him for a supposedly short trip to White Haven:

Here, Ulysses pines for his son, who is only one year old. It's the first time he affectionately calls Fred, "the little dog."

"You must write me a greatdeel about the little dog. Is he walking yet?"

Ulysses missed seeing his son walk for the first time! Heartbreaking.

Ulysses tries to get Julia to come home by telling her how much the neighbors miss her, rather than how much *he* misses her. A "flanking" maneuver!

"Mrs. Gore sends a great deel of love to you. She says that she has no idea that she would miss you so much."

Detroit Michigan
May 21st Wednesday (1851)

Dearest Julia
	As I promised you I write on this day, and for the last time to Bethel. Since you have been gone I have been a little lonesome but have got along very well. I generally visit Mrs. Gore and Mrs. Grayson evry day and occationally take a ride.

Mrs. Grayson's horse run off with their buggy a day or two after you left and tore it to pieces. The very next day she run off with Maj. Gore's and scarsely left enough of it to get mended.

Mrs. Gore has not been sick yet but from the Maj. staying so close to his room I would not be surprised to hear of her being taken at any time.—I like the place I am boarding at, very well. Col. Grayson and Clarke are going there too so we will just four at our table.

I have no news to write you dearest Julia except I would like to see you and Brink. very much. You must write me a greatdeel about the little dog. Is he walking yet?

Your scarf got here last Sunday. I will send it to you at St. Louis so as to be there by the time you arrive.

Last Sunday night, at Church, I lost the ring you gave me so long ago off of my finger and could not find it. I am in hopes the sexton will find it and give it to me by next Sunday. It distresses me very much to think it is gone and at first I had a notion not to tell you of it but to get one just like it, with your name in it, and wear that.

Mr. Hunt has been spending several days here. He is looking very bad and is almost as bald as Dr. Tripler. He says Harritt Camp is to be married this Summer shure enough. All our acquaintances at Sackets Harbor are well.

Mrs. Gore sends a greatdeel of love to you. She says she has no idea that she would miss you so much. Capt. Brent will be here in a day or two and relieve me. I will then make a visit to Grosse Isle and likely to Fort Gratoit.

Give my love to all at home and to our friends around. Write to me often and long letters dearest Julia. I am looking for a letter from you this evening.—Mr. Kercheval and Miss Allicve were at the Broadway house at the same time you was but they did not find (it) out that you were there until after you had started.

Good buy dearest.
Ulyss

In this next letter, Julia is still being seduced by White Haven, and Ulysses finds out he is going to be sent back to Sackets Harbor. He looks forward to returning to their original love nest, and hopes this may entice his bride to come home. Again, he waxes dreamily about the pleasures of housekeeping with Julia. But he won't even put furniture into the house until she is there to make it a home.

"I anticipate pleasant housekeeping for the next year or two. I shall provide nothing in the way of furnature until you arrive except a carpet for one room."

Detroit Michigan
Wednesday 28ᵗʰ May 1851

Dearest Julia

 You will no doubt be astonished to learn that we have all been ordered away from Detroit. Maj. Gore goes with his company to Fort Niagara; but as there are not sufficient quarters there he has represented the matter to Washington and no doubt our destination will be changed to Sacket's Harbor. Wont this be pleasant. I will write to you again before we leave here and tell you all about it. Dr. Tripler goes with us and Capt. McDowell goes to Jefferson Barracks. I will send your scarf by him.

 Mrs. Gore is thoroughly disgusted at the idea of going to Gratiot. She seems really distressed at the idea of being separated from you. She starts to-day so as to be there before her troubles come on.

 I think now I will send for you sooner than you expected to return when you left. When you come I will meet you at Detroit and we will spend a week here and at Fort Gratioit. If Ellen is not to be married this Fall get her to come with you and spend this Winter.

 There is no possible news in Detroit. Evry thing is about as when you left. People all pretend to regret our departure very much and I presume some of them are sincere. For my part I am glad to go to Sackets Harbor. I anticipate pleasant housekeeping for the next year or two. I shall provide nothing in the way of furnature until you arrive except a carpet for one room.

I hope dearest Julia you have not been as unfortunate about getting letters this time as you was the last time you left me. I have had but one from you yet but I am expecting another now evry day.

(A great mystery has just been solved! Judging from the above paragraph, Ulysses *did* write to Julia when she was last at White Haven, having their baby! He says he hopes she is not so unfortunate about getting his letters this time, as she was the last time she left him. I always thought he was too much of a gentleman to not write to his dearest at this time. Hooray!)

You have none idea dearest how much I miss little Fred. I think I can see the little dog todeling along by himself and looking up and laughing as though it was something smart. Aint he walking? I know they will all dislike to see him leave Bethel.

Write to me very soon dearest and tell me all about what kind of a trip you had from Cincinnati, how you found all in St. Louis &c. &c.

Give my love to all of them and kiss them for me. Kiss Freddy and learn him to say papa before he comes back. Dont let him learn to say any b(ad) words.—Mrs. Gore says Jim is learning to talk but I guess he talks about as he did when you left.

Good buy dearest Julia and dont forget to write very often. I will write punctually evry week as I promised.

Ulysses

P.S. I am about selling my horse and if I do I will send you $50.00 by my next letter.

U

The pull of White Haven must have been strong. With the kind of love at home she got from her husband, to keep leaving him and staying away for so long, the lure of the easy life of the Old South was awfully potent. Mixed in was the love of Daddy and being his little princess, although it seems it would have been much more fun to be treated like her husband's princess. Yet, the lure of White Haven was the lure of a dream world, versus a life of reality. In the end, she made her unconditional surrender to him, but it took a long time for her to surrender once and for all. And with her own surrender, came the surrender of the entire South as a civilization. He needed her desperately—to help him destroy her own world. Only the extreme love she had for Ulysses would have made her do it.

In this next letter, Ulysses responds to Julia's concern about the possibility of unsavory "boarders" in the boarding house where Ulysses is staying. Notice the delicacy with which he treats her in the following two lines. Her happiness means everything to him. I sense that he just loves to refer to him and Julia as "we."

"When you come we will get evry thing nice and nothing but just what you want. The few things we have I will pack up carefully and have them shipped."

Detroit Michigan
June 4th 1851

Dearest Julia.
I wrote you in my last that we had all been ordered away from here and that it was uncertain whether we would go to Sacket's Harbor or to Fort Niagara. We are still in suspense but I suppose this evenings mail will decide. Maj. Gore's Comp.y left for Gratoit last Friday. The Maj. And Mrs. Gore are still here. Mrs. Gore has a very fine daughter.
Day after to-morrow is the time set for our departure but I presume I shall not leave for several days after.
The Biddle house opened this morning and I commenced with them. Your letter from Bethel got here in due time and in answer to your fears relative to boarders let me tell you that there was no boarders but Col. Grayson Clarke a clerk and myself. I have the room I took over Mr. Rood's Book store yet and find it quite as pleasant as it would be at the hotel.
Capt. McDowell leaves to-day or to-morrow for Jeff. Bcks. I gave the Capt. your scarf. Mrs. McDowell will give you all the news from Detroit. Dont neglect to call upon her soon after her arrival.
Mrs. Whistler & Louisa came strait for Detroit as soon as they heard that we were to be moved. I am very glad they were away when the order arrived. McConnell got the Col. to apply to have our destination changed to Sackets Harbor and the old lady dislikes it

very much. You know then as a matter of course that if she had been here the Col. would never have dared apply for the change.

There is no news of importance in Detroit. Col. Chapman of the 5th Inf.y is here on his way to join his Regt. I sent some word to Fred. by him.

Dearest Julia I miss you very much and little Fred. too. You dont tell me whether he walks yet or not. Why dont you write more about him. I think I can see the little dog making faces and trying to talk. Was he not a great favorite at our house? I know they hated to see him leave very much.

I have not written home since the order for our change. When you write tell them.

I have been very busy for a few days turning over quarter Master property to Capt. Brent, geting the Comp.y baggage moved to Gratoit and recieving provisions for the next year. I do not visit any except at Mrs. Gore's, and not there now, so the only amusement I have is to take a long ride on horse back evry day. We have had the most terrible weather since you left. The whole country is flooded and it is quite cold enough for overcoats. It seems as if summer never would come.

I will close this letter my dearest Julia and write you another in a few days. You need not answer this until you hear from me again. As soon as I know where we are going I will let you know where to direct.

Kiss all of them at home for me and tell Freddy that he is comeing to see his pa before a great while. I told you I believe dearest that I should buy no furnature except carpeting for one room. When you come we will get evry thing nice and nothing but just what you want. The few things we have I will pack up carefully and have them shiped.

Good buy dearest and kiss all of them for me again.

Your affectionate husband
Ulys

It always warms my heart and puts a smile on my face to read his letters. Her happiness is so important to him, he promises to buy "nothing but just what you want." He even promises to pack up the few things they have "very carefully." He is just so sweet to her it always makes me sigh and makes me feel good. It also makes me wonder why she'd ever want to leave someone who was such a sweetheart. I think most people would give anything for a love like that. But the lure of the Southern life led many people to do even crazier things. It was a seduction of the most powerful kind. It made people do things that made no sense at all, barbaric things. It was the fantasy of living like Kings and Queens. A lovely illusion with a vise-like grip on Julia, and the entire South, that even an ardent lover like Ulysses had trouble breaking. It was Ulysses versus the South right from the moment they met.

But reality was coming—coming in the form of a handsome lieutenant on horseback with a loving heart—destined to become the grim "iron man" of a general who would crush the dream of the South with the reality of his awe inspiring army.

He slowly, tenderly pried her fingers away from the fantasy world to which she was clinging.

TO Bvt. Maj. Gen. Roger Jones

Detroit Michigan
June 7th 1851

Gen.
  I have the honor of acknowledging the receipt of my
Commissions as Brevet 1st Lieut. & Captain in the 4th U.S. Infantry.

      I am Gen.
      Very Respectfully
      Your Obt. Svt.
      U.S. Grant
      1st Lt. & Bvt. Capt. 4th Infy

Just the way he calls her "dearest" all the time would make any woman melt!

"I know you will write as soon as you get this wont you dearest?"

Detroit Michigan
June 7th 1851

Dearest Wife.

    We have just recieved the order changing our destination to Sackets Harbor and I hasten to write to you so that you can write to me soon. I know you will write as soon as you get this wont you dearest?

    Maj. Gore is ordered to Saut St. Marie. Col. Whistler has gone to Kentucky so McConnell and myself will have the old lady, with all her traps, on our hands for the journey.

    I know you will be delighted, as I am with the prospect of getting back to Sacket's. My hope is that they will let us remain there long enough to enjoy it.

    Mrs. Gore is doing very well and so is her little girl. She has not yet given her a name. Mrs. Grayson wants her named after her and I can see plainly that she is quite peaqued that Mrs. Gore will not do it. She talks of calling her Bell.

    There is no news of importance in Detroit. I have sold my horse for $110.00 since I wrote to you last, so now I am deprived of those long rides I have been taking evry evening. We leave here however next Tuesday (this is Saturday) so that I shall not want him much more.

    I hope dearest Julia you had a pleasant trip from Bethel to St. Louis and that dear little Freddy has been well all the time. You dont know how anxious I am to see him. I never dreamed that I should miss the little rascle so much. I know they were all delighted to see him in St. Louis. You must write me a greatdeel about him as soon as you get this. I have not had a letter from you since the second one. I suppose you wrote again from Bethel. The Arrow is not yet in but when she comes I shall expect to find a letter from you.

I have not heard from home since you wrote to me nor have I written to let them know that we have been ordered to Sackets Harbor. I will write in a day or two.

Give my love to all our friends and kiss them all at home for me. Let Fred. kiss his Grandma and Aunts for me. Dont they think the world and all of the littl(e) dog? If he is as good as he used to be I know they must. Be sure and write me long and frequent letters and I will continue as punctual as I have been in writing to you.

I send you with this letter a check for $50.00 made payable to you father. I think likely this will be the last money I will send you for I expect that you will come back sooner than you expected when you started. I told you that I would meet you here when you returned. This is in case you do not travel in company with some one going all the way.

Adieu dear dear Julia. A thousand kisses to you and Fred.

Ulysses

On his way back to Sackets Harbor, Ulysses searches for gentle, almost indirect ways to suggest Julia return to him, and to write to him more often.

"I think dearest Julia if you know any one traveling this way next month you had better come back."

"You must write to me more punctually wont you dearest?"

In his closing salutation, Ulysses uses the word "dearest" twice in the same sentence! What a sweetheart.

"I have no more time to write dearest so good buy dearest."

Niagara Falls
New York
June 11th 1851

Dearest Julia
    I am at the above place on my way to Sacket's Harbor and as I have a half hour to spare it cannot be better employed than in writing to you dearest. I wrote to you as soon as we learned where we were going and inclosed you a check for $50.00 I hope you got it all safe. Mrs. Whistler and Louisa are along but they stop just below here. We have had the most terrible weather since you left. There has been scarsely a dry day and it is cold enough for overcoats and big fires.— All the Detroit people seemed to regret our leaving them very much and think they intend to get up some representation to get us back.—I believe I told you Maj. Gore was going to Saut St. Marie!
    I think dearest Julia if you know any one traveling this way next month you had better come back. I want to see you and Fred.

very much and as we are going to where there are good quarters there is no difficulty in the way of our keeping house comfortably.

I have not had a letter from you since the one in which you told me you would leave Bethel on the next Wednesday. You must write to me more punctually wont you dearest? Did you get home without any trouble? And was dear little Fred. well all the way. I feel so anxious all the time lest he should have another attack like the two he had before you left.

There was nothing new in Detroit when I left. Mrs. Gore is doing very well but I have not seen her since she was confined. I believe she is satisfied with going to the Saut. Mrs. Grayson has been very kind to her through all her sickness.

I boarded at the new hotel from the time it was opened until I left and so enough to show me that we would not be comfortable nor satisfied. Col. Dibble is evidently too close to get along with boarders, or with the hotel, after the other hotel is completed.

I have no more time to write dearest so good buy dearest. Give my love to all at home and kiss little Freddy for me. Remember me to all our friends. Adieu again.

Ulysses

P.S. Tell your pa to have the direction of my paper changed when he is in town some time, (I presume you are in the country) and finds it convenient. Dont forget to tell me if you got the money I sent you all safe.

Ulys.

In the above letter, he used the word "dearest" five times. It may be a record. Now, let's count how many ways he tries to entice her to come back. I find this one hint so poignant. He refuses to even try to make his house into a home without her. The thought of the lonely soldier living in an unfurnished house, waiting for his wife to come back, is heartbreakingly sad.

"I shall make no preparation for housekeeping until you come on. A bed-room carpet will be the extent of my purchases."

Another poignant attempt to entice her home.

"I have been to see some of our old acquaintances and they all seem anxious to see you back again."

Sacket's Harbor
June 16th 1851

Dearest Julia

You will see from the above that we are already at Sacket's Harbor. I wrote to you from Niagara Falls last Wednesday to let you know that we were on the way. Sacket's Harbor is just the same place it was when we were here before. There are no new faces to be seen and but few of the old inhabitants have left. The garrison however will be more pleasant than when we were here before. Besides the Col's family and ourselvs there are in garrison three other families. Dr. Christie of the Navy Lieut. Stevens' Navy and Dr. Bailey of the Army. I have been to see some of our old acquaintances and they all seem anxious to see you back again. I was at Mrs. Kirby a few days ago. Mrs. Kirby and her second daughter are absent, and have been, all winter. I shall make no preparation for housekeeping until you come on. A bed-room carpet will be the extent of my purchases. I think you will be here dearest Julia in July or August at the out side. I am geting quite uneasy about you and Fred. I have not had the scratch of a pen from you since about a week after you left. Wont you write often?

Miss Harriet Camp is to be married soon. She admitted the fact to me her self. Mr. Sternes and Mr. Barbour have both been married since we saw them. Sackett's Harbor is as dull a place as can be immagined. There is no building and no improvements going on of any sort. The place must look up now however. They have their rail *road completed to within seventeen miles of here and the ballance is nearly graded and will be completed by October. Sackets Harbor is now within about fourteen hours of travel of N. York City.*

A few of the ladies of Watertown have adopted the new Turkish dress. I saw a lady here in the street with it on a day or two ago. The dress is really beautiful. It is a very great improvement on the old stile, but at the same time I should regret exceedingly to see or hear of any friend of mine wearing it until the dress has been fully adopted and has seased to attract attention. I suppose you see it occationally at St. Louis!

Dearest you have no idea how uneasy I feel not hearing from you. Had it not been that Fred. was so sick just before leaving Detroit I should feel no alarm. As it is I am in constant dred lest I may hear bad new from the dear little dog. I am very anxious to see him and his ma. K(iss) him for me. I suppose he is runing ab(out) now. I tell evry body who inquires about him that he is.—Since you left I have been as well as it is possible for a person to be all the time. I hope dearest that I will soon hear that you and Fred. have been just as well.

Give my love to all at your house and kiss them for me. Tell me if Ellen is to be married in the Fall. Remember me to all our friends and write soon. Dont neglect to call on Mrs. McDowell soon. Adieu dearest Julia.

Ulysses

(Kiss)

Why does he go on and on about a new "Turkish dress style?" It seems he wants Julia to think he is noticing other women and what they're wearing, and come home as soon as possible. But she knows she's got him wrapped around her little finger, so neither the new, beautiful but seemingly scandalous Turkish Dress, nor the beautiful women wearing them bring her running back, nor the "old acquaintances anxious to see you" nor the prospect of furnishing the new house nor the mention of the bed-room carpet, a reminder of the bedroom and who is waiting there, nor the fact he misses her, nor the fact he's missing out on seeing his son walk and run for the first time, nor the people inquiring about their baby and probably wondering why he isn't there, and not even the kiss at the end of the page. Heartbreaking. But if there's one thing you can say about U.S. Grant, even as an abandoned young husband, he doesn't give up.

But in this next letter, notice the hurt way he refers to "since you left me," rather than simply "since you left."

Ulysses moves in to the garrison at Madison Barracks, Sackets Harbor, New York, and prepares to spend the 4th of July by himself. He is becoming increasingly depressed.

"I am beginning to be like you was when you said you did not care a cent for any of them at home for you had no friends."

Sackets Harbor N.Y.
June 22d 1851

Dearest Julia

Here it is the 22d of June and yet I have not heard a word from you. I am really geting quite uneasy lest something is the matter. I have written you some six weeks since I have heard a word and in one of the letters inclosed you a check. I do not hear if you got it, if you are at home or anything from you. Dearest why dont you write? You know how you scold when I neglect writing more than a week. I am begining to be like you was when you said you did not care a cent for any of them at home for you had no friends. Your not writing keeps me in constant suspense lest poor little Freddy may be sick again. Write to me as soon as you get this and dont neglect in future to write at least once evry week. I have not gone an entire week without writing to you but once since you left me.

All our things arrived from Detroit, and I moved into Garrison, yesterday. The Col. has not arrived yet but we look for him this week.

I have selected for my quarters the rooms Col. Smith formerly occupied, on the opposite side of the sally port from where we lived before. Evrything looks much better about the Barracks than they did when we were here before. The fences have been put up and the place repaired.

Since I have been here I have visited Watertown and Brownville each twice and taken an occational ride into the country. Things look just as they did evry where except in Watertown. That you know was burned down about two years ago. It has been built up however better than it was before and evry thing looks flourishing.

In a few weeks they will have their Rail road completed. New York City and Watertown then will be within about twelve hours travel of eachother.

The people in Sacket's Harbor are making great preparations for celebrating the 4th of July. Having the 4th Infantry Band here is such a treat to them that they expect extra doings this year from formerly.

I have got no news to write you and, as it has been so long since I heard from you, no questions to answer. I think I must hear this week and then no doubt will find enough to fill a sheet just in replying to what you have to say.

If Ellen is not to be married this Fall bring her on here to spend the Winter with us. I know she will be delighted to come. I have said in some of my former letters that you had better return soon if you find a good opportunity of coming. Write to me about the time you expect to start and I will meet you on the road. If you find some one of your acquaintances visiting N. York you can come with them as far as Syracuse and I will meet you there. Let me know if the girl you have got is comeing with you so that if she is not I may look out and engage one before you get here.

Do write soon and often dearest Julia. Kiss all of them at home and kiss dear little Fred. evry night for his pa. Has he improved much since he left? If the little dog had not been so sick before he left Detroit I would not feel the least uneasiness, but as it is I feel a constant dread lest I shall hear bad news. I know I shall be afraid to open the first letter I get from you. Tell me if you have got all my letters, that is to say about two letters per week, or at least three letters evry two weeks. Adieu dearest Julia. A thousand kisses for you. Dream of me.

Ulys.

It seems he is still "laying siege" to Julia and somewhat emoting into a void. If he had not kept up his attentiveness and insistence that she come back to him, he just may not have ever heard from her again.

This letter probably contains more hopeful enticements to come back than any other. He even entices her with thoughts of how wonderful it would be for her sister! (Who would accompany Julia, of course.) It is also painful to realize he's never heard his son call him "Pa." He is really missing out. When Julia spent her whole pregnancy and childbirth with Papa, he missed out on that, too. Colonel Dent got to share it with Julia, instead. Score one for Colonel Dent. (Her pregnancy.) Surely he purposefully kept her distracted from letter writing and thoughts of her husband, hoping to just will Ulysses away into oblivion, into the frozen little hole in the wall of reality from whence he came.

Ulysses "scolds" Julia for the first time over her neglect, which seems sexy, somehow. Here are a few of the most poignant of Ulysses' attempts to lure her to Sackets Harbor.

"The people are very clever and there are several very pleasant families in the garrison."

"Evry few days the ladies get up a picknick and take a sail."

Sackets Harbor N.Y.
June 29th 1851

Dearest Julia
After a lapse of more than one month I at length recieved a letter from you yesterday. I do not see that you had any excuse whatever for not writing before. It seems that you had stayed in the city some days and then moved to the country and remained there some time before writing. My dearest dont you know that I must have been very uneasy all that time? I knew that you had left Bethel, alone, and that dear little Fred. had been sick and was so liable to be so again. Do not neglect to write for so long a time again. I have written

to you very often and I suppose you think all is well so long as you hear from me. But I shant scold you any more until you neglect me again.

I am highly delighted with Sacket's Harbor and only hope that we may remain here for a long time to come. The people are very clever and there are several very pleasant families in the garrison. We all amuse ourselvs by riding over the country fishing, sailing &c. Evry few days the ladies get up a picknick and take a sail. At Sacket's Harbor we are within half a day of Niagar Falls the same time from N. York City and within a day of Montreal or Boston. Next week I am going down to Montreal and Quebeck Canada to spend a few days. My next letter will probably be from Quebec. If I see anything interesting to write about I will give you a full account If Ellen was here now she would have a fine opportunity of seeing the finest cities in Canada.

Col. Whistler and family are here. They are all well and the same as ever. The old woman knows the price of eggs and chickens here as well as the oldest inhabitants though she has not commenced keeping house. Mr. Hunt is not very well. McConnell made up his mind to be disgusted with Sacket's Harbor so he is not now willing to see anything good about the place.

I think you had better not start for Sacket' Harbor during the month of July nor August if it is sickly on the river, but if it is not sickly come in August by all means. I will meet you in Detroit when you do come if you have not got company further. If you find company going to N. York City you can travel with them as far as Rome N.Y. and I can meet you there. In fact so far as economy goes you might go to N. York City better than for me to go all the way to Detroit, and then you would get to see that great city.

Dearest you must take good care of l(ittle) Fred. and learn him to say pa before he gets (here.) Do you think he recollects me? Has he any more teeth? You don't tell me anything about him. Have you seen Mrs. McDowell and Maj. Morrisons family. Remember me to all of them. I suppose that by the end of this week I will get some letters from you in answer to my skolding ones. I know you wont make it necessary for me to schold any more.

Give my love and kiss all at home for me. A thousand kisses for you and Freddy. Tell me if Bridget will come with you to Sacket's Harbor. Adieu dearest Julia.

Ulysses

Ulysses' penchant for organization is endearing in his promise to "keep a memorandum of all that I see" so he can share it with Julia, though she barely accounts any of her experiences to him. He is rather like a sad clown, trying to lure her back with a new carpet, furniture, scenery, nice weather—and heartbreaking how he begs her to make sure his toddler son doesn't forget him. Revealing his longing for his baby boy, Ulysses writes:

"Don't let him forget his pa..."

"I want to see him so badly that I can hardly wait."

His obvious delight in housekeeping shows his homey, domestic side, as he finally gives up waiting for his wife to return to furnish their house. All of his efforts to bring her back can be condensed in this plaintive appeal:

"Summer is the time to enjoy Sackets Harbor..."

Sacket's Harbor N.Y.
July 3d 1851

My Dearest Julia
 To-day I start for Montreal and Quebec. It is but a little over half a days travel to the former place and a little over a day to the latter. I will keep a memorandum of all that I see and if there is any thing worth relating I will tell you in my next. When I got a letter from you I expected to recieve another very soon but none has come yet, I think however when I come back there will be two or three for me. Dont you feel the least uneasiness about me dearest. I will take just as good care of myself as if you were along. I regret though that you are

not along. The scenery on the St. Lawrence is said to be magnificent, and Quebec is said to be entirely foreign in appearance, customs and evry thing els. But we will see and tell you more about it in a day or two.

Mrs. Whistler, Louisa and myself went to Watertown a few days ago and Mrs. W. and I got a carpet each, both off of the same piece. I think it is a very nice one and I have no doubt you will think so too. We have a soldier here who is an eligant cabinet maker and I have got him at work making us a fine center table, two handsome parlor chairs and lounges.

The weather here is delightful. Summer is the time to enjoy Sackets Harbor to advantage so you must come before it entirely passes away. I am delighted that you are not in the city for I see that the cholera is raging there to a considerable extent. I have nothing in particular to write you dearest Julia except to take good care of our dear little boy. Dont let him forget his pa and when you write write a greatdeel about him. I want to see him so badly that I can hardly wait. I expect if he should stay there long his Aunt Ell. would learn him more badness than he would unlearn in five years. Kiss him evry day for me dearest Julia.

In your letter you did not say anything about how many letters you had recieved from me. As you did not complain I presume you had recieved all that I had written. You did not tell me if Ellen was to be married in the Fall. I told you in one of mine to ask her to come here and spend the winter if she was not to be married, or at least come and make us a visit.

Give my love to all at home and kiss them all for me. A thousand kisses for your self dearest Julia. Do not fail to write very of(ten) to your affectionate husband.

Ulyss

His continuing request for Julia's sister to make a visit, masks the hope Julia herself, will visit as well!

Ulysses, the humble officer, writes Julia from West Point, where he is making a visit to his alma mater. He says this will be the last time he sees West Point for years. Note that the next time he returns, it will be as the hero of the Civil War, and the most famous man in America, if not the world. And that upon his death, every cadet from West Point will turn out to do him honor. Not in the humble Ulysses' wildest dreams...

Camp Brady
West Point N.Y.
July 13th 1851

My Dearest Julia

 I wrote to you last from Quebec on last Sunday. In that letter I gave you a little discription of the place and my travels. From there I returned to Montreal and thence up lake Champlagne. My trip has been a very pleasant one and I really felt very glad to get back to the old place where I spent, what then seemed to me, an interminable four years. Evry thing looks as natural as can be, and although I only got here yesterday evry thing seems like home. I should really like very much to be stationed here. Most of the officers are persons who were cadets with me In passing up Lake Champlagne the boat stoped for a few minuets at Plattsburg, but I did not see Capt. Wallen or any of the officers stationed there.

 I shall leave here to-morrow, probably not to visit the place again—for years. When I get back to Sacket's Harbor I shall remain there until I am ordered away or go to meet you. I suppose I will find a letter at the Harbor from you in which you will say something about when you expect to return. I want to see you and Freddy very much, now particularly, since we are where we can keep house. I will get evrything as comfortable as I can as soon as I go back so that when you come back there will not be much but some furnature, crockery &c. to get to commence.

 I occationally see accounts from St. Louis stating that there has been so many deaths, from Cholera, in the city for the last week. These accounts distress me a goodeal. But knowing that you are in the country is a great relief. I hope you and Freddy are quite well. Does the little dog run about yet? I know he must, and try to talk, too. I expect he wont know me when he sees me again. His grandma and pa will be sorry to see the little fellow leave them I know, but they wont miss him like I do. By next Summer he will be big enough for me to take him out riding and walking. Who does he like best at his grandpas? I know it is not his Aunt Ell. Give my love to all at home dearest Julia and write to me very often. I have but little to write about at present but I will write you a long letter in about one week. I am just as well as it is possible to be. (......) The President that is to be, (I mean Gen. Scott) is here at present. He is looking very well. His wife and daughter are stoping here at the hotel on the Point. The General stops at the hotel about two miles below here. There are a great many visitors here now attending the Cadets parties which take place evry other evening. I should like to attend one of them again but I do not k(now) that I can. Next summer if we are st(ill) at Sacket's Harbor I will get a leave for a week and bring you here. It is one of the most beautiful places to spend a few days you ever saw. Adieu dear dear Julia, kiss Fred. and all of them at home for me. Come back to me as soon as you think it is safe to travel with Fred.

> *Your affectionate husband*
> *Ulys.*

It is so sweet how he asks her to "come back to me." How can she resist? Well, she does. While he is relying on the sympathetic company of other men's wives, Julia has "got off among the beaux again." In this next letter, Ulysses expresses his most acute pain yet over her abandoning him for the easy charms of White Haven.

"Mrs. Whistler says that you care nothing about me, that you have got off among the beaux now and are playing the young lady again."

These few lines break my heart:

"I wish you were here; the Summers are so pleasant and there are several pleasant families in garrison."

"I have a horse and buggy and all to-gether you would enjoy yourself very much."

Sacket's Harbor N.Y.
July 27th 1851

Dearest Julia
I got a sweet letter from you yesterday, but like all your others you had but a few moments to write, nor did you acknowledge the receipt of any letter. I wrote to you from Quebec and from West Point but I cannot tell if you ever recieved either of the letters. In fact I have seen nothing from you that shows whether you know that I have ever taken a trip since comeing to Sacket's Harbor. Mrs. Whistler says that you care nothing about me, that you have got off among the beaux now and are playing the young lady again. I do not believe it though. It seems that you have been dreaming about me which is an evidence that you have not forgotten me entirely. I wish you were here; the Summers are so pleasant and there are several pleasant families in garrison. I have a horse and buggy and all to-gether you would enjoy yourself very much When you write to me I don't believe you ever think of my letters. I have asked you so many questions which you never answer. I wanted to know if Ellen was to be married this Fall and if she was not if she would'nt come here with you and spend the Winter. I want to know if Bridget will come with you and a great many other questions I have asked.
Yesterday afternoon Mrs. Whistler, Louisa and myself went to Watertown and Brownville. I called at Col. Bradleys. They enquired very particularly after you, as in fact all your old acquaintances have done. You speak of comeing on here in September if I recommend it. I would recommend your coming as soon as you have an opportunity if you think it safe for Fred. How many teeth has the little dog got?

And does he have any more attacks of sickness? I want to see the little rascal so bad I can hardly wait until September. Elijah Camp talks of going near St. Louis next month and if he does I think you had better come with him. If he goes I will write to you in time for you to get ready and meet him.

If you have an opportunity of traveling with anyone with whom you are acquainted who is visiting New York you had better come with them as far as Syracuse and let me know so that I may meet you there. I should think you would find families traveling in that direction all the time. Will they miss Fred. much from your house? I know they will. Does he try to talk yet?—I found your ring the other day. I suppose in taking my handkerchief out of my pocket the ring sliped off and it has laid there ever since, and although I have worn the coat a great deel, and had my hand in the pocket a hundred times, since, I never found the ring until a f(ew) days ago.

Give my love to you pa, ma, sisters and all of them at home and dont dearest Julia neglect to write to me often and let me know what letters you get from me. Kiss little Fred. and all of them for me. There is nothing new to write about from here. I am enjoying excellent health as I always do. Good buy dearest Julia and dont forget the scolding I have given you in this, and try not to deserve it again.

Your affectionate husband,
Ulys

It would be interesting to note how many times in their relationship he tells her to be sure to write often! He never gives up hope! Julia seems to be scatterbrained, easily distracted, spoiled, etc,—but he always forgives her because he loves and needs the good side of her so much: her warmth and affection, her sensuality, her sense of humor, her outgoing fun-loving ways which save him from his shyness, seriousness and hyper-sensitivity.

Notice in his next letter how Ulysses tells Julia to promise her parents that someday, little Frederick will come back and visit them again—when he is old enough to travel *by himself.* (In other words, *without Julia!*)

"Does Fred continue well? Tell his Grandpa and ma that when he gets big enough to travel by himself he may go and stay with them for six months."

Sacket's Harbor N.Y.
August 3d 1851

Dearest Julia
    I got another, and a long sweet letter from you the last week. If you would write to me as regularly as the two or three last letters I would be perfectly satisfied and see how easy it would be. I do not think you had better wait until September to come here but you should start the first good opportunity, unless by waiting a few weeks you can be present at Nelly's wedding. When you come give me notice so that I may meet you on the road some place. The best place would be Rome N. York if you should be with company going to N. York City. I am very well and enjoy myself as well as could be expected when away from you and Fred. Does the little dog understand all that is said to him? I expect him and his pa will be taking a ride evry evening when he comes here, and often he will let his ma go along. There are several nice families living in Garrison and plenty of children for Fred. to play with.
    Sackets Harbor is as dull a little hole as you ever saw but the people are very clever as you know very well and all together we could not have a more pleasant station. I presume however it will not be our luck to remain here long. We will be much more comfortably fixed than we have ever been before and it usually happens in such cases with the Army that they are moved as soon as they are comfortable.
    You have never told me whether you have recieved your crepe shawl! I sent it by Capt. McDowell whose lady you should have called upon. You have before this I know.—Does Fred continue well? Tell

his Grandpa & ma that when he gets big enough to travel by himself he may go and stay with them for six months. Does he give much trouble? I expect now that he is runing about it takes one person all the time looking after him to keep him out of mischief.

I got a letter from Maj. Gore a few days ago. He writes that they are all well and as contented as people could expect to be at the Saut. Mrs. Gore and Jim send love to you and Fred.

The only amusement we have here is fishing, sailing and riding about the country. I have an eligant horse and buggy to take you and Fred. out with evry day. I hope dearest Julia that you and Fred. enjoy good health and are having a pleasant visit. I wish very much that I could be with you but I have been on leave of absence so much in the last three years that I cannot think of asking again for several years to come. Tell Fred. that he must be a good boy and not let grandpa & grandma say that he is naughty and that they are tired of him. I see dearest t(hat) you have been suffering again with the neu(ral) gia. Dont you think you might muster courage enough to have the tooth pulled that causes all that pain? I think you might. The pain of extracting it is but for a moment while the pain it gives you is for years.

Give my love to all at home and kiss Fred. for me. Remember me to Maj. Morrison's family and to Capt. McDowell's. Write soon to me dearest Julia and very often.

Your affectionate husband
Ulys

Ulysses continues to pine away for his wife and son. He asks her questions like how many teeth Fred has, but she never takes time to answer. No doubt Colonel Dent is keeping them busy. While the other couples at Madison Barracks enjoy the delightful weather and summer activities together, Ulysses can only dream of sharing it with the ones he loves.

"I am so sorry that you are not here now. Sacket's Harbor is one of the most pleasant places in the country to spend a summer."

"There are several pleasant families in garrison and the parade ground would be such a nice place for Fred. to run."

He speaks wistfully again of "going to housekeeping." And he's always so considerate about making her happy.

"All that we want now to go to housekeeping is the table furnature. That I will not buy until you come on lest I should not please you."

Sacket's Harbor N.Y.
August 10th 1851

My Dearest Julia
My regular day for writing has come again but this time I have no letter of yours to answer. I am looking for a long letter now evry day. I am so sorry that you are not here now. Sacket's Harbor is one of the most pleasant places in the country to spend a summer. It is always cool and healthy. There are several pleasant families in garrison and the parade ground would be such a nice place for Fred. to run. I want to see the little dog very much. You will start now very soon will you not? Evry letter I get now I shall expect to hear that you

are geting ready to start. I have not got a particle of news to write you only that I am well and want to see Fred. and you very much.

I have had some very nice furnature made in garrison and otherwise our quarters look very nice. All that we want now to go to housekeeping is the table furnature. That I will not buy until you come on lest I should not please you. The furnature made in garrison is nicer than I could buy in Watertown and more substantial. It consists of lounges, chairs and a center table.

I know dearest Julia you will dislike very much to leave home, and I know that they will miss you and Fred. very much; but you know that you must come after while and you might just as well leave soon as late. Write to Virginia and see if she will not come with you if you come that way. I have told you to ask Nelly two or three times but you never say anything about whether she can come or whether she is to be married this fall or anything about it. I suppose however from your always sending your letters by McKeever to the post office that she is to be married to him soon.—What news do the boys send from California? Are they doing as well as formerly? I suppose they say nothing more about comeing home now.

Col. Whistler confidantly expects to be ordered away from here in the spring. What leads him to think we will go I dont know. I hope his prediction may not prove true.

Tell Fred. to be a good boy and not annoy his grandpa & ma. Is he geting big enough to whip when he is a bad boy? I expect his Aunt Ell. annoys him so as to make him act bad evry day. When he comes here I will get him his dog and little wagon so that he can ride about the garrison all day. You dont tell me, though I have asked so often, how many teeth he has.

I have not heard from home now for a long time, and to tell the truth I have not written since I was at Quebec.

I hope all are well at your house. Give my love to them all and write soon.

Dont forget to avail yourself of the first good opportunity to come on here.

Adieu dearest Julia. A thousand kisses to you and Fred.

Ulys.

The fact that old Colonel and Mrs. Whistler want Julia to hurry back to Sacket's Harbor seems the funniest enticement yet to get Julia to come back.

"Col. & Mrs. Whistler wish to be remembered to you and say for you to hurry home."

The "scoldings" sound like a much more fun reason to return. This sounds rather sexy, and seems almost like some sort of code word!

"...if it was not that you are comeing here so soon I would give you a good skolding."

> *Sackets Harbor N.Y.*
> *August 17th 1851*

My Dearest Julia.
*   I got a letter from you a day or so since and if it was not that you are comeing here so soon I would give you a good skolding. Notwithstanding all that I have said to you about neglecting to answer my letters here comes another without one word in reference to any thing that I had written*
*   But as you are comeing so soon I shall say no more about it.*
*   I got a letter from Clara yesterday. She complains of your not writing more frequently. They are very anxious to have you go by Bethel.*
*   I have got all the furnature and evrything nice for housekeeping except the table ware and that you know can be got in a few hours. I shall look for you early next month and infact I dont see why you should not start immediately. You can come to Detroit and there stay until the Steamer Ocean, Capt. Willoughby commanding, comes out and Capt. W. will see you safe(ly) aboard the Lake Ontario*

Steamer which will land you safely at Sackets Harbor. I will write to Capt. W to see you safely along. This will obviate the necessity of my going to Buffalo perhaps to wait four or five days and then come back without you. The time is so short now until you start that I shall not write again so look for no more letters, nor no more skoldings, from me. Tell Fred. that he must promise to write often to his grandpa and ma. Write as soon as you get this and tell me as near as you can what day you will start, whether Bridget will come with you &c. &c. so that I may know how to provide. There is no difficulty about geting girls here, but if Bridget suits you it will be much better to bring her than to run the risk of get a poor one.

Col. & Mrs. Whistler wish to be remembered to you and say for you to hurry home. I have nothing special to write about so I will close this, my last letter, by sending my love to all at home. Remember me to Capt. & Mrs. McDowell and to Maj. Morrison and family. Adieu dearest Julia, don't forget to write immediately upon the receipt of this.

Your affectionate husband
Ulys.

I love it when he says, "your affectionate husband." Sigh. Is there anything sweeter to a woman than an affectionate husband?

Julia finally returned home to Ulysses in September. After a five month separation, his empty, lonely quarters was full of love again. No doubt, he forgave her for clinging to White Haven. All that mattered was that now, they could finally go to housekeeping.

CHAPTER FOURTEEN
Housekeeping Honeymoon

Reunited in their cramped Army Barracks, Ulysses was overjoyed to have his "Jujy" back. She was glad to see her sweet soldier once again. But part of Julia's heart still clung to White Haven, to the effortless old, Southern way of life she held so dear.

"Miss Julia's" Unconditional Surrender was not complete.

But their reunion was a happy one, and soon after, Ulysses' sweet little Southern wife became pregnant again.

As a young father, Ulysses still indulged his vices, like smoking too much, losing at "loo," (a card game much like Euchre) and he raced horses down the street at a breakneck pace. But he also did something which showed he was taking fatherhood seriously. He joined the "Sons of Temperance," another name for "Alcoholics Anonymous." Why? There is no record of Ulysses being intoxicated in public at this time. Did he just want to help others live a pure, clean life, as he obviously desired to do? Or did the lonely soldier drink by himself when Julia was at White Haven? Ulysses' reasons for joining the Sons of Temperance remain a mystery. He not only joined, but he became the moving spirit behind the group, serving as its president, carefully keeping the whole thing organized, keeping the hall clean, like everything he did in life, making a wholehearted, painstaking commitment. In one of his letters to Julia from Camp Salubrity, Ulysses mentions someone selling whiskey at a picnic, but crosses this reference out. Ulysses seemed hauntingly driven to disassociate himself from the use or even the mention of liquor. Perhaps because he knew it was his weakness. Perhaps because he feared it was his downfall.

Whatever the reasons, Julia supported her husband's efforts by proudly displaying his "Sons of Temperance" certificate on the wall of their little home.

In this letter to Colonel Grayson, we see Ulysses' love for horses, gambling and the fact Sacket's Harbor is frozen solid. Most interesting is that he still receives the Detroit newspaper, though he lives in Sacket's Harbor. From another comment, earlier, it seems he also still receives the St. Louis Newspaper. Ulysses kept up with current events all over the country this way—leading all the way up to the Civil War, where knowledge like his, gained by his voracious appetite for reading the newspapers, made a big difference.

To Bvt. Lt. Col. J.B. Grayson

Sackets Harbor N.Y.
November 12th 1851

Col.,

I take the liberty of addressing you this note to enquire if the stock holders in the Detroit & Saline, and in the Plymouth roads have been assessed since I left Detroit, and if so, how much? I would like also to know what dividends these roads will likely pay on the 1st of January. I have sold my stock to Callender, the sale to take effect after the January assessments have been paid and the dividends called in.

I see from my Detroit paper that sporting is on the ascendent in your place and that some of the nags make good time. I should like very much to change back again to Detroit.

We are all quite well at this post but frozen up. Give my regards to Mrs. Grayson and John and to all my friends in your City.

Yours Truly
U.S. Grant

To Col. J.B. Grayson U.S.A.

Detroit Michigan

In the above letter, Ulysses yearned to return with his family to the milder climate and other pleasures of Detroit. Sadly, the very next letter reveals this wish will never be.

To Bvt. Maj. Gen. Thomas S. Jesup

Sackets Harbor N.Y.
May 26th 1852

Gen.
The 4th Infantry having recieved orders to repair to Fort Columbus N.Y. preparitory to a move for the Pacific Division, I would respectfully request instructions as to what I shall do with the public property, pertaining to the Quarter Master's Department, at this place.
I would respectfully recommend that the horses, and the forage, on hand be sold.

I am Gen.
Very Respectfully
Your Obt. Svt.
U.S. Grant
Bvt. Capt. & R.Q.M. 4th Infy

To Gen. T.S. Jesup
Qr. Mr. Gen. U S A
Washington D.C.

To Bvt. Maj. Gen. Thomas S. Jesup

Sackets Harbor N.Y.
May 31st 1852

Gen.

Having been directed to provide transportation, to Governor's Island, for the three companies of the 4th Infantry, stationed at Forts Niagara & Ontario and this place, I would respectfully report; that I have not got the means of paying for such transportation, and doubt the propriety of entering into any contract that will depend upon the action of Congress, (the passage of the defiency bill) to comply with.

I would respectfully request instructions.

I am Gen.
Very Respectfully
Your Obt. Svt.
U.S. Grant
Bvt. Capt. & R.Q.M. 4th Inf.y

To Maj. Gen. T.S. Jesup
Qr. Mr. Gen. U.S.A.
Washington D.C.

CHAPTER FIFTEEN
Disaster

In 1852, Ulysses S. Grant seemed an ordinary fellow with an extraordinarily happy marriage.

He gambled, smoked and "was a restless, energetic man who needed occupation, and plenty of it, for his own good." But he was an "amiable, good fellow" who was devoted to his growing family.

And then, disaster struck.

Ulysses was transferred to the Pacific Coast. It would mean an arduous passage by ship to Panama and a difficult crossing of the Isthmus which was all jungle. And Julia, who was "in the family way," could not accompany him. Nor could their two year old son.

For Ulysses, it was the worst thing that could have happened.

Ulysses and Julia were now inseparable, and Julia, eight months pregnant, became desperate and irrational about accompanying him.

"When we were almost ready to ship, my dear husband quietly and calmly told me that he had been all the time thinking it over and he had come to the conclusion that it would be impossible for me to go with him in my condition. Of course, I was indignant at this and said I would go, I would, I would, for him to hush; that I should not listen to him; that he knew nothing whatever about the matter; and that I would go, etc., etc., And of course, I shed tears. This he could not stand and begged me not to grieve about it, and as the doctor and all advised that I should not go now. He said: "You know how loath I am to leave you, but crossing Panama is an undertaking for one in robust health." Ulys asked me to think it over, and if on the morrow I felt as I then did, I should go with him anyway, as he could not bear to see my distress; that he thought it would be running a great risk, both with my life and that of our boy, but that he would not insist on my remaining at home if I still continued opposed to it. So I slept well and did conclude that it would be a great deal better to remain with our friends until this, the greatest of woman's ordeals, was over, but I expected, hoped, to yet accompany my dear husband to California. In this I was disappointed. He sailed July 5, my second son, Ulysses, was born on July 22."

Ulysses first sailed for New York, where the regiment stayed awaiting the arrival of another ship to take them to Panama.

Endowed with such a romantic heart, Ulysses likes to chat about weddings and other people's romances, in this first letter to Julia as he optimistically embarks on what will prove to be a disastrous two year separation. Still, he can't help but already pine for his family.

"Kiss Fred. for me. Does he talk about his pa."

Governor's Island N.Y.
June 20th 1852

Dear Julia.,
We are all now pretty well settled in camp with the usual comforts; that is, a chest and trunk for seats and a bunk to sleep in. The ladies have come over from the city and are living in a few vacant rooms that are not required by the company of Artillery stationed on the island.
The weather has been exceedingly warm for the last few days and very unpleasant for the camp. The great difficulty in living in camp is that persons are so much exposed to the weather. A warm day is much more felt, in a tent, than in the sun; and a tent is but little protection against the cold.
I have been doing nothing but to busy myself making arrangements for the comfort of the camp. I have all to do in making preparation for our departure and I now begin to fear that I shall be so busy as to prevent my going to Washington. I spoke to Col. Bonneville on the subject this morning and he seems to think that it will be out of the question for me to go. If I cannot go I want father to write to our member of congress and have one set of my papers, on the subject of the stolen money, saved. It is very important that they should not be lost.
Governor's Island is situated in the Harbor of N. York City and about one & a half miles from Castle Garden landing. We can go

to the city almost all hours of the day in small boats belonging to the Government, and which ply regularly for the convenience of us all. But while it keeps so warm there is but little pleasure in visiting the city. Most of the day we get the benefit of the sea breeze here while in the city we would get but little of it.

How did you and Fred. get along? I am begining to grow impatient to hear now as the time approach(es) when I should hear. Were they all delighted to see Fred.? And how has he behaved? Did Clara get my letter in time to go to the city to meet you? Write soon and answer all these questions.

the ladies that are here are Mrs. Gore, Mrs. Haller, Mrs. Wallen, Mrs. Maloney and Mrs. Collins. Mr. Forsythe was married to a young lady living somewhere about Rochester, but whose name I did not learn, on last Thursday. He has arrived in the city with his bride and will probably be here with her to-morrow. Mr. Jones too will be married this week. He sent invitations for us all to attend his weding to-morrow evening I believe. He is to marry Miss Whitney of Rochester. I never thought she would have him.

Two companies of our Regiment go round the Cape, Cape Horn, in a sail vessel, and Mr. Hunt goes with them. The Compa(nies) selected to go are Maj. Larnard's and (Maj.) Haller's. They will take their lad(ies) with) them.

It is impossible to tell anything abou(t) when we will start.

Give my love to all at home and be sure and write soon and often. I will write again about Wednesday. Kiss Fred. for me. Does he talk about his pa.

Your affectionate husband.
Ulys.

This next letter reveals something which will make a difference later on: Army wives in California cannot afford servants. And it being a free state, there are no slaves. Without coming out and saying it, yet, Ulysses knows this will be a problem for his pampered wife.

"I think on the whole it is a dangerous experiment for the ladies to go to Calafornia. There is one thing certain they make up their minds before they start to get along with their work without assistance."

Ulysses' instincts also tell him he is in for a rough time confronting his old personal demon: loneliness.

"I do not feel as if I can be a great while without seeing you and Fred."

Fort Columbus, Governor's Island, N.Y.
June 24th 1852

My Dearest Julia.
It is time now to write my second letter for this week but I must confess that there is but little to write about. I generally go to the city evry day but as I have business with the Quarter Master there I do not get to see much of the city. The other evening I went to see the trained animals you heard me reading about before you left Sackets Harbor. Their performances are truly wonderfull. The monkeys are dressed like men & women, set up and take tea like other persons, with monkeys to wait on the table; they go riding on horseback and in a coach with dogs for horses, a monkey driving and another acting as footman. During their drive a wheel comes off the carriage and they have an upset. The driver immediately rushes for the dog's heads,—who act as if they were making desperate efforts to run away—and seizes each by the bit and holds them while the

footman gets the wheel that come off and brings it to the carriage to be put on again. All this and many other tricks sufficient to fill up an evening they do apparently understanding all the time what they are about. I forgot to say in the beginning that I recieved youre note from Cincinnati punctually when due. I was very glad to hear that you had got through without accident to yourself or Fred. and without loss of baggage. Did Clara meet you at the Broadway house? I expect she did not get my letter until you got there. There has been no letter come here for you since you left. I have been expecting a letter from St. Louis, and indeed I am anxious to hear from them before we leave. I shall write to them in the course of a few days. What do they say of your arrangement of spending the summer in Ohio? Dont you think you have taken the wisest course?

It seems now more than probable that we will leave here about the 10th of next month, or as soon after that as transportation can be provided. Maj. Larnard's and Maj. Haller's Companies sail by the way of Cape Horn. It will probably take them from five to six months to go round. I should like the trip by the ports that the vessel will necessarily put in too for water &c. Mr. Hunt goes with them for benefit of his health.—Now as the time approaches for going I am anxious to be off. The later in the season we put off going the worse it will be crossing the Isthmus.

Did you get a letter from Mrs. Gore? She wrote one to you and I want you to be sure and answer it soon. Her brother accompanies her to California. I think on the whole it is a dangerous experiment for the ladies to go to Calafornia. There is one thing certain they make up their minds before they start to get along with their work without assistance. Some of the ladies of the 2d Infantry who went with their husbands in 1848 have returned and do not intend going back again I believe.

How does little Fred. behave? He has got acquainted well enough I suppose to behave as cuning as he did before he left Sackets Harbor? Does he ever talk about his pa? You must write a greatdeel about the littl(e) dog. I want to see him very much. I do n(ot) feel as if I can be a great while without seeing you and Fred. I did not know but I would get a leave of absence for a short time and go home but I do not believe it possible. All preparation for starting devolvs on me so that out of all the Regiment I am the only one that cannot get a leave of absence. I am going to Washington next week, however, and I may find out something there about the time we will start and if there is time I will go on to Ohio and see you. Adieu my dearest Julia. Give my love to all at home. Kiss Fred. for me. Write soon.

> *Your affectionate husband*
> *Ulyss.*
> *Over*

I forgot to say that I found yours and Freds l(e)tter enclosing a lock of each of your hair. I put them away and will take good care of them. I am looking for a letter from you now evry day. Have you rec'd one from St. Louis yet?

> *U.*

In this next letter, notice how sweet he is, always sending her presents. He also seems to worry a bit obsessively about debts— something which, because of his poor head for business, would dog him for the rest of his life, even as he became the most famous man in the world.

"I thought this an eligant opportunity of sending you something nice and accordingly you may look out for a very pretty present within three days after getting this letter."

It's kind of cute and old-fashioned the way he refers to her having his baby as "your troubles."

"When you have our other little one be sure and have some one to write to me immediately, dearest. I hope we will not sail until I hear you are all well over your troubles and I do not think we can sail before that."

Fort Columbus, Governor's Island, N.Y.
June 28th 1852

My Dearest Julia;
I was highly delighted at recieving a letter from you, so soon, written in Bethel. It relieved me from all apprehension for your safety. You have had so much experience traveling alone that you can get along as well as any lady by yourself, but having Fred. to take care of I felt uneasy until I heard that you had arrived safely. The little dog no doubt is taken care of without giving you any trouble. I miss him very much.
We still have no idea when we are to sail. The Regiment has to get two hundred more recruits before they can go; but that number they will have by the 10th of next month. What is to detain us more than ten days after that time I dont know.

You want to know what I am doing? It is hard to tell. We are on the Island about one or one & a half miles from the main shore where all the officers except myself have to attend two or three drills per day, and attend four or five roll calls in addition. Between times we get together and talk over matters relating to our move &c. Evry body is highly delighted with going and wants to be off.

Since I have been here I have met a great many persons that I new before, some from Detroit and some from evry place that I had ever been. Among them was Capt. Johnston from Georgetown. I thought this an eligant opportunity of sending you something nice and accordingly you may look out for a very pretty present within three days after getting this letter. The present I send to Fred. I thought very appropriate; the one I send to you is the best I could think of. I intended to send something to Clara, Gennie and Mary at the same time, but I could not think what to get so I thought it better to let you buy them a present.

I send you Capt. Calender's note by this letter. He has paid my tailors bill so that I have not got a debt against me in the United States, that I know of, except my public debt, and that I shall go to Washington on Wednesday and try and have settled. I met Marshall, member of Congress from Calafornia who I knew very well in Mexico, and he promises me to take the matter up as soon as he goes back to Washington. When ever Capt. Calander makes any payment get some one to credit him with the amount on the back of his note and send him a receipt for the amount. He will not pay you anything before next March, but as the note bears interest that makes no matter. I will send you $100.00 by my next letter. I would send it by this but having Capt. Calender's note in it the letter will be so bungling that it might attract suspicion that would lead to its being opened. What money you have and what I will send you will answer you until I can send again from Calafornia.

There seems to be no doubt but we will get the two dollars per day additional pay that has been allowed heretofore to persons serving on the Pacific. If we do get it I will try and save the whole of my pay.

Does Fred. talk and gesticulate as much as he did? Does he go much with his grandpa? I know they are all very much pleased with him and delighted at having him at home. When you have your other little one be sure and have some one to write to me immediately dearest. I hope we will not sail until I hear you are all well over your troubles and I do not think we can sail before that. Mrs. Gore is very well and sends love to you. It is by no means a certain matter that she will go to Calafornia. I think it is very foolish in the Major going. His health is such that he can get a sick leave by asking in a minuet. Give my love to all at home. Kiss Fred. for me. Write to me when you get your presents and tell me how you like them. Remember me to Aunt Polly and family, Aunt Ann & family and Uncle Samuel and family.

Has your box from Sackets Harbor reached you yet? It is time now that you had got it. All here that you know are quite well. Capt. Mc goes in a day or two to see his sister.

Adieu dearest Julia; Don't forget to write soon and often tell me all about yourself and Fred. Tell me what new words Fred. learns to say. I presume in a month or so he will be talking quite plainly.

> *Adieu again*
> *Your affectionate husband*
> *Ulys.*

A side drama: Ulysses thinks Major Gore's health is not up to the trip to California, and that he should not go. Watch for more on this later.

Even though Julia is currently staying with Ulysses' family, to await the birth of their baby, Ulysses assumes full financial responsibility for their care. It is believed she went to his parents' home, instead of her own, because there was some danger in St. Louis, possibly the cholera. Earlier, Ulysses refers to her going to Bethel as "the wisest course."

Pay Master's Office, New York, N.Y.
June 28th 1852

Dearest Julia,
Immediately after completing my letter to you this morning I come to the city on business and while here I thought best to get the check of one hundred dollars to send you. Dont neglect to acknowledge the receipt of it as soon as possible.

Your affectionate husband
U.S.

Kiss Fred. for me again. A thousand kisses to yourself.

U.

I have got this check made payable to father so that you can get him to draw the money for you the first time he goes to the city.

U.

This discovery is awesome. Ulysses is staying at Willard's Hotel as a nobody, who can't get anyone to help him with his debt worries. In less than twelve years he will make a triumphant return to the Willard as Supreme Commander of the Union Army, and will be mobbed by the entire contingent in the Willard Hotel. Yet, his demeanor will remain as shy and modest as it was when he wrote this letter.

Willards Hotel, Washington D.C.
July 1st 1852

My Dearest Julia;

You will see from the above that I have at last got to Washington to attend to my pecuniary matters. The run from New York here is but a matter of a few hours. I left N. York last evening and arrived here at six o'clock this morning. I have not yet seen Mr. Barrere, or any one els on the subject for which I am visiting here. To-day all places of business are closed and the buildings dressed in mourning for Mr. Clay, whos funeral took place but a few hours since. This evening I shall visit Mr. Barrere and to-morrow, if possible, go before the Military Committee and make affadavit of my losses and try to get them to report favorably on the matter. As soon as this is done I will go back to New York. My leave is only for three days.

The weather is so warm here compared to what I have been accustomed to that I feel as if I would melt away.

I know some ten or twelve members of the two houses of Congress, and officers of the Army who will introduce me to any one els that it may be necessary for me to know, so that on the score of acquaintances to attend to my business I cannot fail. In the morning I will call upon Mr. Cass and Mr. Shields and present my business to them and urge action on the ground that I am now leaving the vicinity of Washington and might not be able to attend to it hereafter.

I was very much disappointed in the appearance of things about Washington. The place seems small and scattering and the character of the buildings poor. The public buildings are ornimental and the grounds about them highly improved. I have only taken a short stroll around the city so I am not prepared to say much about it.

Nothing has transpired, relative to our move, since I last wrote to you. It is now thought that the Regiment will be filled up in two weeks from this time, and then the Colonel will report his readiness to move. It will probably be some two weeks more after that before vessels can be chartered and us get off. Have you ever got the box shipped to you from Sackets Harbor? I want you to keep me advised on this subject so that I may write to Mr. Hooker if you do not get it in time.

I was looking for a letter from you when I left Governor's Island but it was most to soon to expect one. When I get back I suppose I will find one and no doubt I will hear of many of Fred's tricks that he has been playing off of late. Has he got so that he makes himself at home yet? How much I want to see the little dog. Dont forget to write me a greatdeel about him dearest!—Have you got your presents yet? And the money I sent you? I suppose so without doubt.

Give my love to all at home and kiss Fred. for me. Remember me to all our friends. A thousand kisses for yourself dearest Julia.

> *Your affectionate husband*
> *Ulys.*

Do you hear often from home and what do they say about your being in Ohio? Write soon.

> *U.*

In his last letter, Ulysses mentions the rundown state of Washington D.C. It's fun to know that as president of the United States, fifteen years later, he will do more than any other president to make Washington the beautiful city it is today. He appropriated funds to complete construction on the Washington Monument, which had been abandoned. He paved the streets, made improvements to George Washington University and the Library of Congress and began a sweeping campaign to make Washington the capital of the nation, with appropriately beautiful monuments, seats of culture and of education. As he writes now, however, it is as a young man of age thirty who is obviously being ignored in Washington.

It's so sad toward the end of Ulysses' next letter when he speaks of imagining seeing his wife and son on the train, when he is alone. He is already starting to break down, and hasn't even left for California yet. I love the way he inquires about the little presents he sent her, "How were you pleased with my selection?" He's so sweet and thoughtful, but also needs to hear about what pleasure he has given her. She seems the only one who can make him feel important, as he is pretty much treated like a nobody everywhere he goes. But he always seeks out womanly nurturing, as with the three "old maids" who surely were glad to fuss over Ulysses, because he so obviously needed it.

"There was a cunning little rascal, about Fred's age, seting a few seats in front of me comeing from Baltimore last night, who was all the time busy, lifting the window and puting it down again. I thought I could see you and Fred. as you were going along in the cars."

"I presume before this you have got the little presents I sent you and Fred.? How were you pleased with my selection?"

Girard House, Philadelphia Pa.
Sunday, July 4th 1852

Dearest Julia;

    I am this far on my way back to New York and having a half an hour I will devote it to writing you a short letter.—I found that Mr. Barriere, who I most wanted to see, had left Washington and would not be back for some ten days. So my mission proved partially a failure. I saw several other member however who promised to give the matter their support when ever it was brought up. Among others General Tailor, from the Zainsville District, told me that if I would write to him he would do all for me in his power. The first day in Washington I could do nothing nor see any one. It was the day of Mr. Clay's funeral and consequently evry house in the city was closed and evry body at the funeral. Judging from appearances, and from the voice of the press, Mr. Clay's death produced a feeling of regret that could hardly be felt for any other man.

    Among other things my object in going to Washington was to go before the Military Committee and state all the particulars in my case. But I found that that Committee held no meeting before Tuesday evening, and I could not wait until that time.

    I got in here this morning and it being Sunday I had to remain until 5 O'Clock P.M. before there was a train starting for New York; so I took a stroll around and found three old maids, cousins of mother's, who I staid and took dinner with. They were delighted to see me and say that I look just as I did nine years ago when they last saw me. They had a great many enquiries to make after all our friends in Ohio, and also after you dearest and little Fred. of whom they have frequently heard. There was a cunning little rascal, about Fred's age, seting a few seats in front of me comeing from Baltimore last night, who was all the time busy, lifting the window and puting it down again. I thought I could see you and Fred. as you were going along in the cars.

    I have but a moment more til I must close. I expect to find at least one letter awaiting me dearest when I get home.—I presume before this you have got the little presents I sent you and Fred.? How were you pleased with my selection?

Give my love to all at home and write soon and often. Dont get mad because this is not four pages, for I have no more time. A thousand kisses for yourself and Fred. Adieu dearest Julia.

Your affectionate husband
Ulysses

It gave me chills when I read, in the above letter, Ulysses' description of sadness over the death of Mr. Clay. Ulysses wrote, *"Judging from appearances, and from the voice of the press, Mr. Clay's death produced a feeling of regret that could hardly be felt for any other man."*

The outpouring of grief at the death of a different man surpassed all sorrow yet experienced across the nation. It was the death, thirty-three years later, of Ulysses himself. How shocked he would have been now to see into the future.

Ulysses hoped their stay in New York might last long enough that Julia would have the baby and be able to come to New York to say good-bye. But his regiment suddenly, unexpectedly received word they would sail in the morning. Before leaving, Ulysses hastily wrote Julia.

One can feel Ulysses' heart pumping with adrenalin as he suddenly receives word of an imminent departure for California. His heart is full, as he realizes for the first time what this transfer really means.

"I never knew how much it was to part from you and Fred. until it come to the time for leaving."

"You must be a dear good girl and learn Fred. to be a good boy."

And these haunting words:

"Our separation will not be a long one anyway. At least lets hope so."

[July 5, 1852]

Dear Dear Julia
We sail directly for the Isthmus. I never knew how much it was to part from you and Fred. until it come to the time for leaving. Several of the ladies will be left behind by this sudden move. Mrs. Montgomery is probably on her way here, Mrs. Rains is left, and Mrs. Judah will probably be confined this week.
You must be a dear good girl and learn Fred. to be a good boy. I think there will be an opportunity for you to join me in the course of next Winter in company with the other ladies of the Regiment left behind.—I will write to you from evry place we put in shore. You must write to me soon and direct as I have told father.

It distresses me dearest to think that this news has to be broken to you just at this time. But bear it with fortitude. Our separation will not be a long one anyway. At least lets hope so. Good buy dear dear Julia. Kiss Fred. a thousand times. A thousand kisses for you dearest Julia.

And then, he was gone.

After three happy years of marriage, he had been ripped from his lover's arms. The other officers had their families along, and they chattered and nuzzled as they gazed out to sea. But Captain Grant had no one with whom to share his adventure. He stared out at the blackness of night all alone.

As the Southern constellations rose in the sky, Ulysses longed for his wife. There was the Southern Cross Julia had wanted to see. Oh, how he wished she was there beside him, saying, "Oh, Ulys! How delightful!" like she did on their honeymoon ride on the steamboat.

Passengers on the ship remembered Ulysses as pacing the deck all alone, smoking incessantly. For the first time, he became seasick. Yet, he didn't want to worry his family, and wrote Julia optimistic letters, to cheer her.

In this next letter, notice how Ulysses always puts an optimistic spin on things for Julia's sake. Ulysses says he is "very well," although seasick. I doubt most people who were seasick would cheerfully say they were very well in the same breath. Notice how he wants to make sure Julia names their son after *him* this time. She gave that honor to her own father, "Colonel" Frederick Dent, with their first son, also in Ulysses' absence. But even in a touchy matter like this, Ulysses is always so gentle and loving when addressing his wife.

"If it is a girl name it what you like, but if a boy name it after me. I know you will do this Julia of your own choise but I want you to know it will please me too."

Ulysses tries to sound hopeful about accomplishing something with this move to the Pacific Coast.

"My dearest Julia if I could only hear from you daily for the next (...) days I would have nothing to regret in this move. I expect by it to do something for myself."

Steamer Ohio
July 15th 1852

My Dearest Julia;
What would I not give to know that you are well at this time? This is about the date when you expected to be sick and my being so far away I am afraid may afflict you. I am very well, only sea-sick, and so are all the passengers, notwithstanding we are in latitude 10 degrees North. We have been blessed with remarkably fine weather from the begining; a very fortunate thing for a vessel coming to this latitude in July, with 1100 persons on board.
You see dearest Julia how bad it would have been had you accompanied me to New York. The Regiment had but two days

*notice before sailing and I had but a few hours. You know I wrote
to you Sunday afternoon from Philadelphia when I knew nothing,
nor suspected nothing, of the move. The orders to sail were sent by
Telegraph and obeyed before there was time to correspond.*

*There is no insident of the voyage to relate that would interest
you much, and then dearest I do not know how this letter will find
you. I hope for the best of course, but cannot help fearing the worst.
When I get on land and hear that you are all over your troubles I
will write you some long letters. I cannot say when you may look for
another letter from me. This goes to New York by the vessel we come
out upon. To-morrow we commence crossing the Isthmus and I write
you this to-day because then I may not have an opportunity. I write
this on deck standing up, because in the cabin it is so insufferably hot
that no one can stay there.*

*The vessel on the Pacific puts in at Acapulco, Mexico, and I
may find an opportunity of mailing a letter from there. If I do you will
hear from me again in about three weeks or less.*

*Before recieving this dearest I (hope) the little one will be
born. If it is a girl name it what you like, but if a boy name it after me.
I know you will do this Julia of your own choise but then I want you to
know it will please me too.*

*Dear little Fred. how is he now? I want to see him very much.
I imagine that he is beginning to talk quite well. Is he not? I know he
is a great favorite with his Grandpa & ma and his Aunts. Does he like
them all? Kiss the little rascal for me.*

*My dearest Julia if I could onl(y) hear from you daily for the
next (...)days I would have nothing to regret in this move. I expect by it
to do something for myself.*

*The only ladies with us are Mrs. Gore, Mrs. Wallen, Mrs.
Slaughter, Mrs. Collins & Mrs. Underwood. The poor things I fear
will regret it before twenty four hours. It is now in the midst of the
rainy season and we have to cross the mountains on mules, through
passes which are too narrow for two abreast, and the ascent and
descent to precipitate for any other animal. Give my love to all at
home dearest Julia. I hope you recieved the check for one hundred
that I sent you. I have one hundred & fifty dollars in the hands of Col.
Swords, Qr. Master in New York which I will direct him to send you.*

Adieu Dearest, A thousand kisses for yourself, Fred. and our other little one. I will let no opportunity of mailing a letter pass unimproved. Write often dearest to your affectionate husband

Ulyss

CHAPTER SIXTEEN
Ulysses, the Hero

Ulysses was a sad, solitary figure on shipboard, but it did not hinder the fulfillment of his duties as Quartermaster. Everyone remembered him as being kind. "He looked at everyone as if he was truly interested in you," a shipmate recalled. Others aboard the steamship Ohio came to him if there was any sort of dispute, for the quiet Ulysses showed such good common sense. "Let's ask long-headed Sam," they'd say, "He'll know what to do."

Ulysses' leadership style changed suddenly from competent to heroic when cholera broke out.

Cholera! The word struck fear in the bravest heart, because of the swiftness with which it brought death.

Ulysses had just disembarked with his troops and their families in Aspinwall, Panama, a sweltering jungle awash in mud, where torrential rain alternated with a blazing sun. Ulysses was leading his charges through slippery mud and tangled vines, across the Isthmus of Panama, heading for Panama City. From there, they would finally catch the ship which would take them on to California.

As they waded through flooded, winding jungle paths toward the exotic village of Cruces, Panama, word quickly spread that the cholera was there, awaiting them. Caused by drinking fever-laden water, and highly contagious, cholera swept swiftly through the ranks, killing men, women and children by the hour.

Ulysses' stricken wards writhed with the death cramps, dropping to their deaths in the mud. But Ulysses stayed calm. Ulysses ordered the healthy on to Panama City, while he stayed behind with the sick and those who had families.

When Ulysses and his sickly group reached Panama City, the cholera victims were herded onto a barge in Flamingo Bay, called the "Death Ship." While petrified orderlies on the ship refused to care for the afflicted passengers, Ulysses did not run. He took charge of the dying men, women and children, day and night, with no thought of his own safety. For two weeks, Ulysses administered compassion, soup and medicine, and when his patients died, he, as Quartermaster, furnished the sacking and cannon balls with which the dead were lowered into the bay.

Ulysses had made one of his wisest decisions in not allowing Julia and his two year old boy to make the trip. For when it was over, every child on that ship had died.

Arriving in San Francisco, grateful survivors told anyone who would listen, "Captain Grant was like a ministering angel to us all."

Unassuming, young Ulysses had amazed all with his coolness and courage. With his mother's quiet confidence, her common sense, Ulysses was born to take command of just such dire situations.

Yet out West, he still had to face a demon that for him, was far more life-threatening than cholera: loneliness.

Ulysses tried to make the best of it.

Missing the womanly presence of Julia, Ulysses asked a Mrs. Sheffield and her husband to move in with him. Mrs. Sheffield remembered:

"Oftentimes while reading letters from his wife, his eyes would fill with tears, he would look up with a start and say, "Mrs. Sheffield, I have the dearest little wife in the world, and I want to resign the army and live with my family."

Sergeant Eckerson, posted at the same garrison, remembered the day he received a letter stating that he was appointed agent of the Ordinance Department, a position that Ulysses had helped him obtain. Ulysses came in to say, "Congratulations," then confided, "I, too, had a letter last night." He showed the last page of his letter, which contained a penciled outline of a baby's hand. Ulysses stood silently, trembling, with tears in his eyes. Then he went away.

"He seemed to be always sad," the Sergeant remembered.

In the evenings, the lonely Captain Grant sat with Mrs. Sheffield and her husband and, as Mrs. Sheffield recalled, "told me of his wife and children and how he missed them."

Meanwhile, Julia was relaxing in the lap of luxury again at White Haven, to the great joy of Colonel Dent. With his favorite daughter and two grandsons by his side, all waited on by slaves, his dream of Southern aristocracy was alive and well. Colonel Dent had never been happier, while his Yankee son-in-law had never been more miserable.

Ulysses sent optimistic letters to Julia at first, *"I am, so far a Calafornian in taste..."* he assured her, but the upbeat façade began to crack. *"I wish you were here, but servants are not allowed, and you could not live without servants, could you, dearest?"*

His pay in the Army was so small, Ulysses' only hope of affording to bring his family to him was to make money in some other way. Thus began one of the longest, most heartbreaking losing streaks in history.

It broke my heart to read Ulysses' love letters to his wife, from the Pacific Coast. Following are his love letters, in their entirety, from his two lonely years in exile, without Julia.

In Panama, the Grants' good friend, Major Gore, was one of the cholera victims. As Ulysses predicted, Gore was foolish to make the trip. Ulysses says nothing of his own heroic efforts to his wife. In fact, he downplays the whole catastrophe so she will not be alarmed. But he does assure her she did the right thing by staying behind.

"My dearest you could never have crossed the Isthmus at this season, for the first time, let alone the second. The horrors of the road, in the rainy season, are beyond description."

Being unsure if she has delivered their baby yet, he does not want to distress her.

"You must not give yourself any uneasiness about me now dearest for the time has passed for danger."

Steamer Golden Gate
Near Acapulco, Mexico, Aug. 9th 1852

My Dearest Julia;
I wish I could only know that you, and our dear little ones were as well as I am. Although we have had terrible sickness among the troops, and have lost one hundred persons, counting men, women & children, yet I have enjoyed good health. It has been the province of my place as Quarter Master to be exposed to the weather and climate on the Isthmus, while most of the others were quietly aboard ship, but to that very activity probably may be ascribed my good health. It no doubt will be a relief to you to know that we have been out from Panama over four days and no sickness has broken out aboard. All are healthy and evry minuet brings us towards a better climate.
Among the deaths was that of poor Maj. Gore. The Maj. was taken before daylight in the morning and in the afternoon was dead. Mrs. Gore took his death very hard and then to think too of the trip

she had to undergo crossing the Isthmus again! My dearest you could never have crossed the Isthmus at this season, for the first time, let alone the second. The horrors of the road, in the rainy season, are beyond description.—Mrs. Gore will be at home, if she is so fortunate as to stand the trip, before you get this. I hope father and Gennie will go and see her soon. Lieut. Macfeely, 2d Lt. Of Maj. Gore's Comp.y, accompanied Mrs. Gore and may go to our house to see you. He promised me that he would. I gave him an order on the Qr. Mr. in New York for $150 00 Mr. Hooker owes me which he gets he will send you.

Mrs. Wallen and the other ladies along are tollerably well, but a goodeal reduced. Mrs. Wallens weight when she got across the Isthmus was 84 lbs. Her children, Harry Nanny & Eddy look quite differently from what they did when they left New York. But thank fortune we are fas approaching a better climate. The Golden Gate takes us nearly 300 miles per day.

We have seen from a Calafornia paper our destination. All but one company goes to Oregon. Head Quarters (and of course me with it) goes to Columbia Barracks, Fort Van Couver, Oregon. In consequence of one company of the Reg.t, and all the sick being left at the Island Flamingo, near Panama, to follow on an other steamer, we will remain at Benecia Cal. for probably a month. Benecia is within a days travels of where John is and of course I shall see him.

You must not give yourself any uneasine(ss) about me now dearest for the time has passed for danger. I know you have borrowed a goodeal of trouble and from the exagerated accounts which the papers will give you could not help it. From Mrs. Gore however you can get the facts which are terrible enough.

I have not given you any discription of any part of our journey, and as I told you in all my letters dearest, I will not until I hear of your being well. I say however that there is a great accountability some where for the loss which we have sustained.—Out of the troops at Sackets Harbor some twelve or fifteen are dead, none that you would recollect however except O'Maley, and Sgt. Knox, the one you thought looked so much like Maloney.

Elijah Camp is with us. He goes as sutler, probably with Head Quarters.

Give my love to all at home dearest and kiss our dear little ones for me. Fred, the little dog I know talks quite well by this time. Is he not a great pet? You must not let them spoil him dearest. A thousand kisses for yourself dear Julia. Dont forget to write often and direct, HdQrs. 4th Inf.y Columbia Barracks Fort Van Couver, Oregon.

> *Adieu dear wife,*
> *Your affectionate husband*
> *Ulys.*

P.S. You may be anxious to hear from Maggy. She looks wors than ever. She has been sea-sick ever since she started. She regrets very much that she had not staid with you.

Mrs. Wallen was going to write to you from Panama but Maj. Gore's taking sick prevented.

> *Again adieu dear dear wife.*
> *U.*

This entire letter burns with Ulysses' love for his family. This line could sum up Ulysses and Julia's entire relationship:

"How I long to hear from you dearest Julia!"

And this line sums up his entire catastrophic time on the Pacific Coast:

"My dearest what is there that I would not give, or undergo, to see you and our two dear little ones now!"

Steamer Golden Gate
Between San Diego & Sanfransico Ca(l)
August 16th 1852

My Dearest Julia;
    There is a bare chance that we may meet a steemer to-day from San fransisco and if we do the Captain intends to send the passenger's letter's aboard. If we do meet the steamer you will get this letter by the same mail as the one I wrote from near Acapulco, and therefore I can only add that my health still prevails on board, and that I am perfectly well. My greatest anxiety to write is to let you know that a rumor which you will probably see in the papers is without foundation; namely that the Golden Gate, with all her passengers, was lost off Monteray Calafornia. While in at San Diego this morning we recieved Sanfransisco papers up to the latest dates and saw a rumor to the above effect, and although the paper did not credit the report I knew it would distress you until you heard a positive contradiction.
    We will get into San Francisco to-morrow night and in the course of a few weeks proceed to Oregon. In the mean time I shall visit John. As soon as I can get my papers off after our arrival at Benecia (which is within two or three hours of San Franciso) I will

apply for a seven days leave and go to Knights Ferry. The distance is only one days travel.

You dont know dearest Julia how fortunate it is that you are not along at present. How we will be situated is as yet all in the dark. It may be that we will have to tramp over the country looking for Indians for months, or it may be that we will be quiet, but in tents, without a single comfort. As soon as we are atal perminent it is our intention to have one of the officers who have left their wives behind go, at the mutual expense of all, and bring out all the ladies. It may be Maj. Alvord or it may be me who will go, or it may be that Col. Buchanan will be comeing with his wife at that time and arrangements can be made for all to come with him.

Our voyage on the Golden Gate has been a very pleasant one, only a little sea sickness. We are not atal crowded, yet there are enough to make it pleasant.

How I long to hear from you dearest Julia! Yet I cannot hope to hear for a month yet. If I told you to direct your letters to Benecia instead of San Diego I might hope to hear sooner. Now you had better direct as I told you in my letter from Panama: that is to Columbia Barracks, Fort Van Couver, Oregon. I presume your letters from San Diego will be forwarded, but the Mail from there is only semi-monthly also, and if they are you will hear from me evry two weeks.

In my last I told you of two or three from Sackets Harbor, who you would probably remember, that died on the road. Besides those I told you of, there was the Band Master and O'Maley and the Drummer, Herman.

My dearest what is there that I would not give, or undergo, to see you and our two dear little ones now! If I could only know that you three are well I would be perfectly satisfied with my position. We are going to a fine country, and a new one, with a prospect of years of quiet, when once settled. Chances must arrise, merely from the location of land if in no other way, to make something which if should not benefit us soon will at least be something for our children.

I write to you dearest Julia as if I knew that you were perfectly well and able to enter into all these calculations. I would that I did know so. I can't think otherwise but what a satisfaction it would be to know, possitively know, that you were.

I wrote to Ellen from Acapulco and told her that she must send you my letter as soon as she read it. Although you would get no later news by it I wanted you to get as many letters as possible.

Give my love to all at home and all our friends. Tell me all about Fred. and our other little one. Who it looks like! its name &c. Fred. must talk very well! Often I set upon the deck of the vessel and wish I could see the little dog runing about. Does he ever say anything about his Pa? Dont let him forget me dearest Julia. Kiss him and the babe for me a thousand times, dearest.

Adieu dear dear Julia
Your affectionate husband
Ulys.

This is the first time since he left her that Ulysses begins a letter longingly using his favorite word, "wife." In this simple salutation you can tell how much it means to him to have his very own wife, simply by the addition of the unnecessary, but to him so meaningful, word "My." I just love the way he calls her: *"My Dear Wife."*

Benecia Calafornia
August 20th 1852

My Dear Wife.

    We have arrived, all safely, at this place where we will remain, probably, for some three weeks. When we leave here it will be for Fort Van Couver as I have told you in all my previous letters from Panama up to this place.—Benecia is a nice healthy place where our troops will pick up what they lost on the Isthmus in a very short time. I can assure you it was no little that all lost in the way of flesh. Capt. McConnell and myself when we got across were in prime order for riding a race or doing anything where a light weight was required. I have not been sick but the degree of prostation that I felt could not be produced in any other latitude except that of the tropics, and near the equator at that.

    I should not write you now because there is no Mail going for several days but I am going up to the Stanislands, to-morrow, to see John and before I get back the Mail may leave, and I can assure you dearest Julia that I shall never allow a Mail to leave here without carrying a letter to you.

    I am staying with Fred. Steel, a class-mate of mine, who was at our wedding, and when I told him we had a little boy named Fred. he was very much elated. McConnell, Russell and Underwood all joined in telling what a nice boy Fred. is. I really believe Fred. was much more of a favorite with the officers than we thought.

    I spent an hour or two with Mrs. Stevens in San Francisco, and she would have come up with us only Stevens was sick. They will be here in a day or two and make this their home. Mrs. Stevens seemed very much disappointed at not seeing you and Mrs. Gore. She sayd that she had heard you say so much about Mrs. Gore that she felt almost like she was an old acquaintance.

I have seen enough of Calafornia to know that it is a different country from any thing a person in the states could imagine in their wildes dreams. There is no reason why an active energetic person should not make a fortune evry year. For my part I feel that I could quit the Army to-day and in one year go home with enough to make us comfortable, on Gravois, all our life. Of course I do not contemplate doing any thing of the sort, because what I have is a certainty, and what I might expect to do, might prove a dream.

Jim. de Camp come aboard at San Francisco to see Mrs. Wallen and he told her that John was making one hundred dollars per day. This is Friday night and on Sunday night I expect to be with John and then I will write to you, and make him write also, and it is more than probable that you will get the letters at the same time as you get this.

I wish dearest Julia that I could hear from you.—I cannot hope to hear from, after your confinement, for at least a month yet. It distresses me very much. If I could only know that you and our little ones were well I would be perfectly satisfied. Kiss them both for me d(e)arest and dont let Fred. forget his pa. No person can know the attachment that exists between parent and child until they have been separated for some time. I am almost crazy sometimes to see Fred. I cannot be separated from him and his Ma for a long time.

Dearest I hope you have been well taken care of and contented at our house. I know they would do evrything to make you comfortable. I have often feared that you would fret and give yourself trouble because I was not there.

Give my love to all at home dear and kiss our little ones for their pa. Write me all about both of them.

Adieu dear dear Julia,

> *Your affectionate husband*
> *Ulyss.*

Ulysses goes to lots of trouble to go visit Julia's brothers in California, just so he can feel some connection to her. Notice Ulysses' spelling of the word "ants" as "Aunts" and how it gives the event he is describing his usual cry for womanly attention!

"We then went to bed together, and got probably little more than an hours sleep when I got awake finding myself covered with a meriad of Aunts."

Another gem: Ulysses' occasional bursts of poor grammar, which are always so poignant.

"Kiss our dear little ones for me dearest Julia. You don't know how anxious I am to see them. Dear little Fred, I know, talks quite well! Dont he dear?"

Benicia, California
August 30th 1852

I have just returned from the Stanislaus, bringing John with me. I find that there is a mail just being made up for the states and as I told you in my last letter, (which you will recieve at the same time as this) I now hasten to give you the account of my visit.—I started from here in the evening, by steamboat, for Stocton where I arrived before morning. At Stockton I got a mule and rode over to your brothers, d(is)tant about forty miles. I was very much surprised to find houses almost evry mile, and the road very much more crouded with teams than almost any in the Atlantic States. These teams mostly cross your brother's ferry and are carrying provisions, goods &c. for Miners in the Diggings. I was very much pleased with the prospect at Knight's Ferry. There are three stages per day, each way, crossing at the ferry, generally come loaded with from eight to twelve passengers each. All these stop at the hotel, which is kept in connection with their other business, and dine. Lewis can tell you all about their business of course but you will be glad to know what they are doing from me. Their ferry, which is managed by two persons, is drawn across a little river about one hundred & fifty feet wide, by ropes attached to both shores. It takes about one minuet from the time they leave one shore until they reach the other. For this they now charge two dollars which is much less than they formerly got. In connection with this is their tavern, or as it is called, "The Knigt Ferry house" where the passengers by stage, and many teamsters stop and get a dinner at one dollar. They have stables which the stage companies pay them about two hundred dollars per month rent for, and board all their men (w)ith them at ten dollars per week. They have a traiding house where they get pretty much all the dust the Indians, and some Miners, dig. They have a Ranch where they have several hundred cattle and numerous horses, all worth about thribble what they would be in the Atlantic States. So much for their business, that is the nature of it, as to the profits they are clearing from fifty to one hundred dollars daily.

I found dearest immediately upon my arrival a letter from you encl(os)ing one from Wrenny, and one from Ellen. But they were both written before you had heard of our being ordered from Governor's Island. It was with great pleasure I recieved them but it did not afford me the relief it would to have got one of a later date. Just think dearest I have not had one word from you since you got the news of our departure from Governor's Island.

Our regiment is now in Camp at this place where we will remain probably two or three weeks when we proceed, by sail vessel, for Columbia Barrack(s) Fort Van Couver. It is detestable going in this way because it will take so long. The way the winds are now prevailing we may be three weeks going about six hundred miles. But there is no danger for it is the dry season and there are no storms.— On account of the Mail closing so soon and wanting to answer Ellen's letter too I cannot write you all the particulars that I will hereafter. I feel somewhat tired too for I started, on horseback, yesterday from John's and rode to Stockton, 40 miles, before 3 o'clock leaving John's a little befor (8) o'clock. I had then come immediately aboard the steamer and was told that we would arrive at Benicia at 12 o'clock and as the boat only merly touches here for less that two minuets of course I could not sleep. Well it was nearly morning before we arrived hence the loss of one nights sleep after a hard day's ride. The night befor was almost like it. John had no idea at night of comeing down with me, so we set up until we almost fell asleep talking. We then went to bed, togethe(r), and got probably little more than an hours sleep when I got awake finding myself covered with a meriad of Aunts. We had of course to change our quarters and I could sleep but little more.

Kiss our dear little ones for me dearest Julia. You do not know how anxious I am to see them. Dear little Fred I know, talks quite well! Dont he dear? Is he not a great favorite with all at home? He could not be otherwise. John is very anxious to see him and likes to hear the officers who know him speak of him. Adieu dear dear Julia. Give my love to all at home and be sure to write often. Your affectionate husband

Ulys

P.S. I forgot to say that I am as well as can be and so is John. Mrs. Stevens is here with us and is well and so are all the children. Mrs. Stevens says she has written to you three times but has always directed to Sackets Harbor.

U.

Ulysses' stopover in California is at an end, and he is proceeding by steamer toward his post in Fort Vancouver, Oregon. Ulysses loves California, but something is missing.

"Altogether I am, so far, a Calafornian in taste, wanting but one thing. That dearest is to have you and our little ones with us."

Julia is also back to her poor letter writing habits, having not sent one letter since before he left Governor's Island. Their second baby, Ulysses Jr. was born a month ago, but she has still not written to him about it.

"One line telling me that you was well and that our dear little ones were well too would make me perfectly happy."

Steamer Columbia
Sept. 14th 1852

My Dearest Julia;
We have left Benicia for our station at Fort Van Couver where we will arrive, probably, in about four days. We are aboard of a nice little steamer that is perfectly sea-worthy, but from the present movements I know that I am bound to be sea sick all the way up. I feel it already and would not write only that there is a mail just going to the states. You know dearest Julia that I will never allow a Mail to go without bearing a letter to you?
I have had no letter from you since we left except one written before you knew that we had left Governor's Island. One line telling me that you was well and that our dear little ones were well too would make me perfectly happy. I know dearest that you have written often, but your letters going to San Diego keeps them back half a month. I am in good health, as usual, and see nothing in this country to induce sickness. From my little experience I think it a peculiarly favored

country. Of course I have seen but a small portion of the country and cannot judge of the whole, but from what I have seen the clima(te) is unequaled. Up on the Stanislaus, where John is, it is very warm, at this season, but there is no change from warm to cold, from rain to dry &c. as there is with us, or with people who live up on the lakes. Alltogether I am, so far, a Calafornian in taste, wanting but one thing. That dearest is to have you and our little ones with us. There is not a more pleasant country in the world, and where I go it is said to be equal to anything, or any place, in this country. Oregon I used to think I would prefer to Calafornia but now that it has come to the pinch I would rather remain here. I only hope that I will be as much pleased with Van Couver as I am with the portion of Calafornia that I have visited. So much dearest for Calafornia: we are now geting close to San Francisco where this letter has to be mailed.

Mrs. Wallen, Mrs. Slaughter (a very nice lady by the way) and Mrs. Collins go with us. They are all sea-sick now however and not visable. Mrs. Stevens I have had the pleasure of seeing frequently. She is very well and so are all the children. She was quite anxious to get Maggy to live with her, and as Getz only has one year to serve I recommended her to go. Mrs. Stevens proposed giving her seventy dollars per month but she says she would prefer going with me, if you are comeing here, for ten dollars.

Capt. McConnell and Mr. Russell are both very well. Mr. Russell has a strong inclination to go into copartnership with Stevens in a Ranch, as termed here, a farm in the Atlantic States. At the present rate of vegitables one crop would make a farmer rich. Capt. Wallen has also had an offer of $600.00 per month, with two rooms and board, for himself & family, if he would stop in San Francisco and take charge of a Hotel. If he does it it will make me (a) Capt. My post however would not be (changed) by the promotion.

Remember me to all our friends, give my love to all at home and kiss our dear little ones a thousand times for their papa. When I get one line from you dearest saying that you are well and through your troubles I can write much better. Adieu dear dear Julia.

Your affectionate husband
U.S.G.

I cannot help always tying Julia's fate to that of the Union, and see from reading the following letter, how fortunate it was that she was pregnant and unable to make the voyage with Ulysses. She and their son may very well have died. It would have destroyed Ulysses, and it is doubtful he would have ever become the victorious General Grant without her by his side.

In this next letter, the final paragraph is especially heartbreaking. In Mexico he dreamed of Julia, now he dreams of her and the children they've had together.

"Night-before-last I dreamed that I got home and found you, Fred. and a beautiful little girl, all asleep. Fred. woke up and we had a long conversation and he spoke as plainly as one of ten years old. Is my dream true, with the exception of my being there?"

On board Steamer Columbia
Astoria Oregon
September 19th 1852

I have written you one letter from aboard this Steamer since we left Benicia and as she returns with a mail, the only one that will leave Oregon for two weeks, I write again. It is now 9 o'clock at night and in a few minuets we will be on our way for Columbia Barracks where we will arrive about breakfast to-morrow. As the Steamer only stops there long enough to land us there will be no time to give you any impressions that I may form of the place. There are however many passengers aboard who are well acquainted with the place and they all coincide in saying that it is as pleasant a place as there is in the country. The country is certainly delightful and very different from the same latitude in the Atlantic States. Here, I am told, ice scarsely ever forms to a greater thickness than one inch although we are about one degree North of Sacket Harbor.

Astoria—a place that we see on maps, and read about,—is a town made up of some thirty houses, (I did not count them) situated on the side of a hill covered with tall trees, looking like pines, with about two acres cleared to give way for the houses. There is nothing about the place to support it only that it is near the outlet of the Columbia river and they have a custom house, distributing post office for the Territory, and a few pilots for vessels coming into the mouth of the river. Boats anchoring in the stream (they have no wharf) gives occupation for a few boatmen to carry passengers ashore to see the town that they read about in their young days. So much for Astoria.— Our trip from San Francisco has been the roughest that I have ever experienced. All the passengers, and some of the officers of the boat, have been sea-sick. The wind blew for three days most terrifically, but now it is mild and we are in the river.

My dearest Julia had it not been for your situation you would have come with me. Seeing what you would have suffered I do not regret that you could not come along. I would give a great deel if you were here now, but I do not believe that you could have stoo(d) the trip at this season of the year with all the detintions consequent upon having troops along.

I have no doubt but I shall like Oregon very much. Evry one speaks well of the climate and the growing prospects of the country. It has timber and agricultural land, and the best market in the world for all they can produce. Evry article of produce can be raised here that can be in the states; and with much less labor, and finds a ready cash market at four times the value the same article would bring at home. Dearest I know you do not care about hearing this but would like to hear more about myself. Well! Whilst we were in Benicia I devoted myself, as much as possible, to seeing Calafornia. I spent some days (as I told you before) with John, and was highly delighted with evry thing I saw. I afterwords spent a few days in San Francisco and must say that I consider that city the wonder of the world. It is a place of but a few years groth and contains a wealthy population of probably fifty thousand persons. It has been burned down three times and rebuilt each time better than before. The ground where the houses are build have either been filled in or els the hills dug away, and that too at an expense of not less than five dollars per day for labor.—After seeing San Francisco I spent my days galloping over the country in the neighborhood of our post, visiting Vilijo, the Capitol of the state, and looking at the resources of the country.—The whole country from Benecia to the southern limits of the state, where not cultivated, abounds with wild oats, in a luxurious groath, which only differs from our oats in becoming degenerate in the size of the grain, from not being replanted.

Dearest I could give you chapters upon what I have seen and thought upon our Pacific possessions, but I have not recieved a line from you since your confinement. I know that letters have been mailed to me regularly, but being directed to SanDiego we do not get them for a month after we would had we known where we were going from the start. I expect however, by the mail which is now in San Francisco, that I shall get several.—Night-before-last I dreamed that I got home and found you, Fred. and a beautiful little girl, all asleep. Fred. woke up and we had a long conversation and he spoke as plainly as one of ten years old. Is my dream true, with the exception of my being there? Give my love to all at home and kiss our little ones for me.

Your affectionate husband
Ulys.

a kiss for you

Ulysses always kissed the spot where he wrote "kiss," intending Julia to kiss it, too.

Their baby had been a boy, Ulysses S.Grant Jr. born July 22, 1852.

In this letter, Ulysses reveals the first of a long string of admittedly foolish business dealings, efforts to raise money to afford bringing his wife and family to him. And revealing a pang of hurt feelings, he suggests she may be as happy at White Haven as she would be with him. He knows her, and knows how attached she is to her home and way of life, suggesting perhaps she still loves it as much as she loves him.

"I expect dearest that you are in St. Louis enjoying yourself quite as well as though you were here."

And he is painfully honest about his business failings:

"I was very foolish..."

> *Columbia Bks. Fort Vancouver O.T.*
> *October 7th 1852*

My Dearest Julia;
> *Another mail has arrived and not one word have I got from you. I have not heard a single word from you since about the 1st of July. I know though dearest that you have written often but your letters being directed to other parts of the country I do not get them. I am in hopes the next mail will bring me several letters. I am very anxious to hear from our little ones and from you dear dear Julia.*
> *I am very much pleased with Vancouver. This is about the best and most populous portion of Oregon. Living is expensive but money can be made. I have made on one speculation fifteen hundred dollars since I have been here and I have evry confidence that I shall make more than five thousand within the year.*
> *The population of Oregon is much less than I supposed. There is not over 15000 inhabitants in the whole territory Emmigrants are comeing in however very rapidly. The poor people have suffered very*

much this year. A great many widows have arrived penniless having lost their husbands on the road and spent all they had to get this far. They will now have a long winter to worry through and in a country where everything is sold at exorbitant rates, and where no simpathy is shown.

I wish dearest that you were here. I think now that I shall be promoted this winter and when I am promoted I shall apply for orders to go to Washington to settle my accounts. If I am not promoted by spring I will resign my Quarter Master appointment and make the application. This is supposing that your brother does not return this winter and bring you with him.

I have written a long letter home so that be where you may you will hear from me as soon as the mail can take a letter.—I have dreamed of you and our little ones two or three times lately. I always see you and them perfectly well. I wish I could know that my dream was true—

You cannot tell dearest how anxious I am to hear from you.

Did Lieut. Macfeely give you $150 00 that I loaned him when he went back with Mrs. Gore? Have you seen poor Mrs. Gore since she went home? I have heard that she lost evry thing she had except just what she had on her back.

I expect dearest that you are in St. Louis enjoying yourself quite as well as though you were here. If I could only be there to spend the winter I should be too happy.—Tell Ellen that I got her letter at Benica and wrote a very brief reply. I shall write her a long letter by the next mail.

You will no doubt wonder what speculation I made? I will tell you I went into partnership with Elish Camp and enabled him to buy, on credit, the house and a few goods where he keeps store. The business proved so profitable that I got $1500 00 to leave the concern. I was very foolish for taking it because my share of the profits would not have been less than three thousand per year.

Give my love to all at your house. Dont fail to write often and tell me all about our dear little ones. Fred. no doubt talks as plainly now as any body. Does he ever ask after his pa? Did you get the presents I sent you and him? I know you were pleased with them. I have a very handsom watch and chain that John gave me to send to you. I will send it by the first opportunity.

Is Fred. a good boy or has his aunt Ell learnt him to be bad? Pinch him for me. Kiss our little one for me. A thousand kisses for yourself dearest.

Adieu dear Julia until the next mail. I am in hopes then to have some letters from you to answer.

> *Good buy*
> *Ulys.*

Poor Ulysses! His misspelling of "good bye," as "good buy," makes him sound like a sad clown, in light of his pathetic attempts to make money.

Ulysses bemoans the lack of communication with Julia.

"Just think, our youngest is at this moment probably over three months of age, and yet I have never heard a word from it, or you, in that time."

Here is one of the most heartbreaking passages in any of his letters to Julia. Ulysses' hopeful "plans" led him to nothing but financial ruin, and a dead end in his desperate attempts to raise money to bring his family to him. One can feel his fragile hopes and tender dreams in his words:

"I have made something dearest for us, (including our children,) and have got the plans laid, and being carried out, by which I hope to make much more."

Fort Vancouver O.T.
October 26th 1852

My Dearest Wife;
Another mail has arrived and not one word do I get from you either directly or indirectly. It makes me restless dearest, and much more so because now I know that I must wait over two weeks before I can possibly hear. I can write you nothing until I hear from you and learn that you, and our dear little ones, are well. Just think, our youngest is at this moment probably over three months of age, and yet I have never heard a word from it, or you, in that time. I have my health perfectly and could enjoy myself here as well as at any place that I have ever been stationed at if only you were here. It is true that my pay would not much more than pay the expenses at table; yet I think, judging from what has taken place, that the expens could be born here better than the ordinary expenses in the Atlantic States. I have made something dearest for us, (including our

children,) already, and have got the plans laid, and being carried out, by which I hope to make much more. I have been up to the Dalles of the Columbia, where the Immigrants generally first stop upon their arrival in Oregon, comeing by the overland route. I there made arrangements for the purchase of quite a number of oxen and cows, and for having them taken care of during the winter. If I should loose one fourth of my cattle I would then clear at least one hundred per cent, if I should loose all I would have the consolation of knowing that I was still better off than when I first come to this country. I have in addition to cattle some hogs from which I expect a large increase soon, and have also bought a horse upon which I have been offered and advance of more than one hundred dollars.

You have probably seen dearest Julia a publication reflecting upon the officers of the 4th Inf.y whilst crossing the Isthmus. You will soon see in the papers a very flat contradiction, with the actual facts given. It is stated that even Capt. Grant ran off, and left the men to take care of themselves. The facts are that the troops with the exception of a guard under the command of Lt. Withers, and a large portion of the camp women, and Capt. Wallen's company, disembarked at Gorgona N.G. whilst the rest were sent further up the river (Chagress) to Cruses. The next day after Capt. Wallen marched through to Panama, which left Mr. Withers and his guard, Dr. Tripler and myself at Cruses and all of us remained until I had got evry one started, (where they were unwell, on mules or in litters) excepting one or two who were so low with the cholera that they could not be carried.) These persons were removed to to comfortable quarters, the services of a Doctor employed, and arrangements made for their transmission through to Panama as soon as they should recover sufficently. If I had time I would like to write several sheets from which I would request extracts made by one of your brothers for publication. But in consequence of having attended an indignation meeting "of the officers of the Regiment," on the subject that I have just been writing about, it is now after the hour when the mail is to close. I can however send this by an officer who is just starting for San Francisco who will see that it goes by the steamer from there.

Give my love dearest to all your brothers, sisters, and our acquaintances, giving my very best love to your pa & ma. Kiss our dear little ones a thousand times for their pa, who is far away from them, and retain for yourself love and many kisses.

Your affectionate husband bids you adieu dearest until the next steamer arrives.

Adieu
Ulys.

CHAPTER SEVENTEEN
The Joy of Letters

In this next letter, Ulysses is overjoyed at news of the birth of his second son and receipt of four letters from Julia, but he is obviously concerned his children are being brought up by the cantankerous Colonel Dent, and is worried lest they grow up to be "rood," presumably like their arrogant, slave-holding grandpa. Ulysses starts in with "enticements" to hopefully attract his wife to him in Oregon, such as the promised pony for little Frederick. Between that and his labor to earn money, Ulysses spends half his life trying to unite himself with his flighty but desirable Southern belle wife. It is a theme that runs through-out their romance, all the way to her ultimate surrender.

"Your letters, and Clara's too, said so much about dear little Fred. and Ulys. You have no idea how happy it made me feel."

"I am so glad too, dear Julia, to hear that our other little one is such a fine healthy boy! You must take good care of them and not let them grow rood. I have but a few minuets to write so I cannot say all I intended on this subject."

"Tell Fred. that Mr. Brooke, a gentleman who I have long known, has presented him with a pony which he will have just as soon as he gets here."

Columbia Bks. Fort Vancouver O.T.
December 3d 1852

My Dear Dear Wife.
You can scarsely concieve how this Mails arrival has made me. It not only brought me a letter from you, but four letters, and two

more from Clara written dearest at your request. I will not have time to answer your letters this time because the Mail closes in less than an hour. Now that I have got letters however I can prepare letter(s) before the arrival of the different Mails and then add a Post Script informing of what I may have recieved.

Your letters, and Clara's too, said so much about dear little Fred. and Ulys. You have no idea how happy it made me feel. If I could hear Fred. talking it would do me a great deel of good. I know from the way he used to attempt to talk he must have a great deel to say. I am so glad, too, dear Julia, to hear that our other little one is such a fine healthy boy! You must take good care of them and not let them grow rood. I have but a few minuets to write so I cannot say all I intended on this subject. Tell Fred. however that Mr. Brooke, a gentleman who I have long known, has presented him with a pony which he will have just as soon as he gets here. I am glad to hear that Jenny is with you in St. Louis, or rather at White Haven farm. How do your family like her? I know not otherwise than well. Jenny is so good and affectionate that no one could dislike her. Give her my love and tell her to write to Clara that I have recieved her two letters, but have no time to answer them this mail.

Now about myself. I am in perfect health except I have suffered terribly of late from cramps. I have suffered so much that I walk like an old man of eighty. It is probably the effect of a terrible cold which I have scarsely recovered from. A week in the house will cure me and that I am going to take.

About pecuniary matters dear Julia I am better off than ever before, if I collect all that is due me, and there is about eighteen hundred dollars that there is but little doubt about. There is two hundred which I loaned a few weeks since which I do not expect to get. The person has already sacrificed his word, and as I had no note I may safely set it down as lost. I have got a farm of about one hundred acres, all cleared and enclosed, about one mile from here which I am going to cultivate in company with Captains Brent Wallen and McConnell. I have leased it in my own name but there is four times as much of it as I could possibly buy seed for. We expect to rais some thirty acres of potatoes which may safely be put down at one dollars & fifty cents per bushel, and may be twice that, and the yeald *in this country is tremendious The ballance we will put oats in. The labor we all expect to assist in. It is necessary in this country that a person should help themselvs because it takes a great deel to live. I could not possibly keep house here for less than about one hundred & fifty dollars per month aside from all expenses of clothing &c. Capt. McConnell & Wallen, the only officers here that you know are both well. Mc desired me particularly to remember him and Miss Kate to you Fred. & Ulys. Mrs. Wallen asks most particularly after you when ever she sees me.*

Give my love to all at your house Congratulate Fred. Dent for me and kiss his bride. I must now close for I am after the hour for closing the Mail. Maggy and Getz are still with me, and for having such servants I am envied by evry body that comes to the house. You have no idea of the interest they both take in you and Fred. When I got these letters they fairly jumped with joy.

Write to me often dearest. Kiss Fred. & Ulys a thousand times for me. Make them good boys. As many kisses for you dear wife.

Adieu. It will be a month I understand before another Mail leaves here.

Your affectionate husband
Ulys.

One can feel Julia cringe when reading of her husband losing two hundred dollars on a bad loan he made, without getting a note in writing. She must have realized her husband has a good heart, but a very bad head for business.

If my husband was "suffering terribly from cramps," as Ulysses says in this next letter, I think I would do anything to get to him and take care of him. But I know it is easier said than done, what with the horrendous boat trip necessary for Julia to get to her husband. It is easy to judge Julia harshly for not doing anything to get to Ulysses, but she also had her children's' well being to think of—as well as the safety and comfort of White Haven holding her snugly in place like a magnet to metal. His love demanded so much of her, and as yet, she was not physically or emotionally capable of surrendering to it.

One can feel the loneliness as a sickly Ulysses attempts to nurture himself.

"I am now intending to spend one or two weeks indoors, on toast and tea, only going out once per day to see if the supply of wood is kept complete."

He continues to long for his family.

"If I could see Fred. and hear him talk and see little Ulys. I could be contented provided their mother was with them."

"Learn them to be good boys and think of their Pa."

"Kiss Fred. and Ulys. for their Pa and tell them to kiss their Ma for me."

Columbia Bks. Fort Vancouver O.T.
December 19th 1852

My Dear Wife:

The Mail Steamer very unexpectedly arrived this morning before I had half my correspondence completed. It brings no Mail however to this point but leaves it at Astoria to be brought up by the river steamer. As the Mail Steamer starts back before we will get the last Mail I cannot tell you whether I will recieve any letters or not; but I am very sure that there are letters for me.

I am, and have been, perfectly well in body since our arrival at Vancouver, but for the last few weeks I have suffered terribly from cramp in my feet and legs, and in one hand. You know I have always been subject to this affliction. I would recover from it entirely in a very short time if I could keep in the house and remain dry. My duties however have kept me out of doors a great deel, and as this is the rainy season I must necessarily suffer from wet and cold. I am now intending to spend one or two weeks indoors, on toast and tea, only going out once per day to see if the supply of wood is kept complete.

This is said by the old inhabitants of Origon to be a most terrible winter; the snow is now some ten inches in depth, and still snowing more, with a strong probability of much more falling. The Thermometer has been from Eigteen to twenty two degrees for several days. Ice has formed in the river to such an extent that it is extremly doubtful whether the Mail Steamer can get back here to take off the Mail by which I have been hoping to send this. You must know the Steamer comes here first, and then goes down to Columbia about four miles, to the mouth of the Willamett river, and up that some fifteen miles to Portland, the largest town in the Territory, though an insignificant little place of but a few hundred inhabitants. I do not know enough of this country to give you the account of it I would like to, having a desire to say nothing that is calculated to mislead others in their opinions of it, but this I can say; so far as I have seen it it opens the richest chances for poor persons who are willing, and able, to work, either in cuting wood, saw logs, raising vegitables, poultry or stock of any kind, of any place I have ever seen. Timber stands close to the banks of the river free for all. Wood is worth five dollars per cord for steamers. The soil produces almost double it does any place I have been before with the finest market in the world for it after it is raised. For instance beef gets fat without feeding and is worth at the door from seventy to one hundred dollars per head, chickens one dollar each, butter one dol(l)ar per pound, milk twenty five cents per quart, wh(e)at five dollars a bushel, oats two dollars, onions four dollars, potatoes two dollars and evry thing in the same proportion. You can see from this that mess bills amount to something to speak of. I could not mess alone for less than one hundred dollars per month, but by living as we do, five or six together it does not cost probably much over fifty. I have nearly filled this sheet dear Julia without saying one word about our dear little ones about whom I think so much. If I could see Fred. and hear him talk and see little Ulys. I could then be contented for a month provided their mother was with them. Learn them to be good boys and (to) think of their Pa. If your brother does not come out there is no telling when I am to see them and you. It cannot be a great while however because I would prefer sacrifising my commission and try something to continuing this seperation. My hope is to get promotion and then orders to go to washington to settle my accounts. If you, Fred. and Ulys. were only here I would n(o)t care to ever go back only to visit our f(r)iends. Remember me most affectionately to all of them. Kiss Fred. and Ulys. for their Pa and tell them to kiss their ma for me. Maggy and Getz enquire a greatdeel after you and Fred. They evidently think the world and all of him. I h(o)pe he is a favorite with his grandpa and all his Uncles and Aunts. I have no dought though the little rascal bothers them enough. When you write to me again dear Julia say a goodeal about Fred. and Ulys. You don't kn(o)w what pleasure it gave me to read yours and Clara's account of them.

Has Jennie left yet? I suppose so however. How did they like her at your house? Adieu dear dear wife; think of me and dream of me often. I but seldom dream myself but I think of you none the less often.

Your affectionate husband
Ulys. to his dear wife Julia.

I love the way he signs this letter, "Ulys to his dear wife Julia."

Without Julia and his children by his side, letters became Ulysses' lifeline. Unfortunately, Julia was a terrible letter writer.

Ulysses still assumes Julia cares about him, however, assuring his wife not to worry lest he fall through the ice crossing the frozen river. He projects wifely feelings on her, though by now, he must feel he is talking into a void. His hunger to see his two sons is painful, especially when he says,

"The dear little dogs how much I wish I could see them."

Still, he seems more concerned for her than for himself when he consoles her,

"Do not fret dear Julia about me."

Columbia Barracks O.T.
January 3d 1853

I wrote a letter two weeks ago upon the arrival of the Mail Steamer at this place and told you that I had no doubt but that I would find letters. I was disappointed.

The weather has been very cold here and what is most unusual, the Colum(bia) river has been frozen over. Captain Ingalls and myself were the first to cross on it. It is now open however so you need not feel any alarm about my falling through. It either rains or snows here all the time at this place so I scarsely ever get a mile from home, and half the time I do not go out of the house during the day. I am situated quite as comfortable as any body here, or in the Territory. The house I am living in is probably the best one in Oregon. Capt. Brent and Ingalls and their two clerks Mr. Bomford & myself live to gether and Maggy cooks for us and Getz assists about the house. Evry one says they are the best servants in the whole Territory. With Getz's pay, the sale of his rations, the wages we give and Maggy's washing, they get about 75 dollars per month. Living together as we do I suppose board, washing, and servant hire does not cost us over 61 dollars per month each, but alone it would require economy to get along inside of near twice that amount. For instance flour is 42 dollars per barrel and evry thing is proportionally dear. I expect to go to San Francisco in two or four weeks now, under orders to bring up public funds, and if I do I shall stay over one trip of the Steamer and go up and spend ten days with John and Wrenshall. You need not be atall surprised if my next letter should be from San Francisco.

I promised you to tell you all about Oregon, but I have seen so little of it that I know nothing that I have not told you. The country is very new but almost doubling its population yearly. The soil is generally very fertile but then there is but a very small proportion of it that can be cultivated.

My dearest I wish, if I am to be separated from you, and our little ones, that I could at least be where it did not take two months to get a letter. Just think, you write to me and tell me all Fred's pranks and how finely Ulyss. is coming on all of which interests me exceedingly, but then I think what improvements must have taken place since the letter was written. I suppose that Ulys will be seting alone by the time you get this. Is Fred. very patronising towards him? I expect he wants to nurse him? The dear little dogs how much I wish I could see them. Is Fred. as fond of riding as he was in Bethel? How was Jennie pleased with her visit? And how were they all pleased with her? As a matter of course she had left before you will get this. Fred. and his bride no doubt have gone too. Does your brother Lewis intend remaining in Missouri? or will he return to Calafornia? I have never recieved a line from your brother John since my arrival at Van-Couver although I wrote to him soon after we got here.

All the ladies here are quite well and the gentlemen also. Mrs. Wallen stays at home all the time and in fact she could not well do otherwise. She always enquires very particularly after you evry mail.

Give my love dearest Julia to your Pa & Ma and all the rest of the family. Tell Fred. to be a good boy and recollect his pa and mind evry thing his grand pa & ma tells him. Kiss him and Ulys for me and write a great deel about them. I will close here for the present hoping that before the Mail closes we will get the mail which has just come up and then I can let you know if I get anything.

> *Adieu dear wife*
> *Ulys.*

It breaks my heart to read Ulysses eagerly promise her, *"And then I can let you know if I get anything."* Meaning if he gets any letters from her. The hope of getting letters from her is the only ray of warmth he's got in his cold, lonely room.

P.S. There is not a particle of hope of geting the Mail that come up in time to add anything to this If the mail should come in time to give me five minuets I will write you another letter if it is only to tell you whether or not I have heard from you. Do not fret dear Julia about me. I am perfectly well and have entirely recovered from those attacks of cramp which I had a few weeks since. They amounted to nothing except they were painful. Adieu again dear dear Julia.

> *Your affectionate husband*
> *Ulys*

You will see in the above letter that Ulysses is rooming with Rufus Ingalls, an old roommate from West Point and a good friend in the Mexican War. Rufus becomes a first hand witness to Ulysses' longing for his wife and how it destroys him. Rufus will play an integral part in Julia's ultimate surrender.

For comfort, Ulysses continues to cling to letters and dreams.

"I had a long dream about Fred. last night. I thought I was at home playing with him."

> *Columbia Barracks O.T.*
> *January 4th 1853*

Dear Wife;

The mail has arrived and brought me a long letter from you in which you give me a long account of our dear little ones. How much I should like to see them! I had a long dream about Fred. last night. I thought I was at home and playing with him. He talked so plain that he astonished me, then too his remarks were so sensible. I cannot recollect what I thought he said. Do you think Ulys. is going to be as smart as Fred? I am glad to hear that you are all well at your house. So Jennie has gone! And Fred. and his wife too! You do not say how they liked Jennie at your house, nor how she was pleased with her visit. I know though that it must have been satisfactory all round.

Capt. McConnell has just been reading me a portion of a long letter from his sister. She had just arrived at home. From New York to Charlston she went alone and as she expected to be very sea sick she shut herself up in her State room and did not come out the whole trip, but astonishing (to say) was not sick for an instant. She says that in the course of her travels she did not meet with any who she like half so well as you. She enquires particularly after Fred.

You enquire about my quarters! I have told you in the letter which will go by the same mail as this. The Plan is very much the same as yours only a little larger with higher sealings, and a piaza on thre sides, upstairs and down. As I told you it is probably the best dwelling house in Oregon at present. But you must not think that the ballance of the quarters are like this; far from it. They are what are called temporary buildings having been put up in great haste with round and green logs, floors of rough green plank. They are very cold at present but they will be made comfortable next summer. I live where I do in consequence of being Commissary & Qr. Master.

I have written this in a very great hurry on account of having many public papers to get into the office.

Kiss our little ones for their Pa. Write often to your affectionate husband

Ulys.

Ulysses rejoices over long letters from Julia and his sister about his two sons. Notice the way he caresses the words, "my dear wife." You can feel how much it means to him to have a wife, even though she is so far away.

"It made tears almost start in my eyes, with joy, to hear so much about them by one mail. I only wish dearest that I could be there to look upon them now, and to see my dear wife again."

Columbia Bks. Fort Vancouver O.T.
Jan.y 29th 1853

My Dearest Wife;
There will be another Mail leaving here now very soon. Since I last wrote I have enjoyed excellent health and am larger than I have ever been before. I believe the usual effect of an Oregon climate is to make a person grow stout; at least I should judge so from the appearance of evry body that I see here and new before they came. The climate of Oregon is evidently delightful. Here we are North of 45 degrees and though the oldest inhabitants say it has been about the most severe winter they have ever known here, yet it would surprize persons even as far south as St. Louis to be here now and witness our pleasant days. Farmers are ploughing and some sorts of vegitables have been growing all Winter, and will continue to grow. Such a thing as feeding cattle, except those that work is not dreamed of at any season. The farm that I have is a part of it already ploughed and I hope to have the whole of it finished in the course of a couple of weeks. All here are living very pleasantly only it requires very close watching to keep within our means. For instance; yesterday I was obliged to purchase some flour, for Government, and I could not get it under forty dollars per barrel; and that was about twelve dollars less than it could have been purchased for a week ago. All other articles, of food, are in about the same proportion.—There has been great suffering among the immigrants this year in consequence of the very

high prices they have been compelled to pay for evrything they got, and then too from loosing their stock, and their all, in the mountains.

I have now written enough, for once, on these subjects dearest Julia; I will now notice your sweet letter. It was one of the most interesting letters I have recieved, because it told so much about our dear little ones; then too I got letters from Jennie and Orvil in which our two boys are spoken of in such high terms as a mother could speak of them. It made tears almost start in my eyes, with joy, to hear so much about them by one Mail. I only wish dearest that I could be there to look upon them now, and to see my dear wife again. Whilst speaking of seeing you and our two little boys let me tell you of the last plan I have hit upon for your geting out here. I am first for promotion to a (.......) full Captaincy; Capt. Alden it is said intends to resign in a few months; (Brevet) Colonel Buchanan is near the head of Captains of Infantry and when either of these go I will get my promotion. I will then have to give up my present position as Regimental Quarter Master and join my Company wherever it may be. I shall then apply for orders to go to Washington to settle my accounts as disbursing officer, and when I return bring you with me.

January 31st the Mail has just come in but brought no letter from you. I left this portion of my letter in order to answer anything that I might recieve from you. I know at so great a distance as we are separated letters of different dates may arrive together, and then a Mail come without bringing anything. I however always feel much disappointed when I do not get letters from you. Write evry ten days and I will be almost sure to hear then by evry Mail.

Maggy and Gates have given me a little present for Fred. which I enclose with this. They appear to think a great deal of him and never fail to enquire, the first thing after arrival of the Steamer (and before the Mail is opened) how you and Fred. are.

We are somewhat in hope that Col. Whistler will join us here. He writes that he is determined to come and asks advice as to whether he had better bring his family with him. The advice will likely be (the Colonels letter was to the Adjutant) a short description of this post; its conveniences & its inconveniences. It is undoubtedly the best station in Oregon and the Colonel would not probably subject to a change for four or five years. The policy seems to be to transfer the enlisted *men, when their time is near out, to some Regiment that has been but a short time in this country, and order the officers home to recruit new men. Give my love to all at home, kiss our little ones for me, and dream often of me. Dont fail to write as often as I told you.*

> *Adieu dear dear wife*
> *Your affectionate husband*
> *Ulys.*

Ulysses is pinning all his hopes on getting orders to Washington to settle his "accounts," the theft of $1,000 under his care during the Mexican War, as a way to get back to the East Coast and get Julia and his children to come back with him. This hope is what keeps him going.

Also, note that he does not credit the wisdom of Julia not accompanying him for himself, but to the lucky fact that she "could not come." (Because she was pregnant) When in fact it was his decision. Ulysses rarely took credit for anything, because of his innate modesty. He certainly was not the type to ever say, "I told you so!"

Another telling comment from Ulysses, his playful way of teasing Julia about her girlfriends' comments:

"If anyone attempts to teaze you again about my making love to Spanish girls at Vancouver you can tell them that they must be desperately ignorant of the history of their own country not to know there was probably never a Mexican or Spaniard in this part of Oregon."

His wry joke tells Julia, his fidelity goes without saying.

Ulysses is always noticing "rations" and adding up the cost of everything, like growing "vegitables." So cute! This habit seems quirky, now, but will be a huge advantage to him as Supreme Commander in the Civil War. He dreams of growing and selling enough "vegitables" to bring his family to him, and works hard to make his dream come true. Ulysses continues to be foolish about money, however, loaning $200 to an officer who disappeared, and admitting:

"He has not paid and from what has transpired I know he never will. I wish to gracious you had that."

This is one of my favorite lines from any of his letters. Though he is struggling to raise money and sacrificing every penny he can for his own pleasure, he can deny her nothing.

"If you want the pearl handled knives you speak of buy them dearest."

Columbia Barracks O.T.
February 15th 1853.

Dear Julia:
The Mail Steamer will be here to-day and I must fill up three pages for you, in advance, leaving the fourth to answer anything I may get from you. Since my last I have been very well. My opinion of Vancouver still remains unchanged. My hope is that I may be promoted to a company stationed at this post. The probablities however are that I shall have to go to Humbolt Bay. Col. Buchanan is there at present, I believe, establishing the post. There are no buildings at present. But you know when my promotion comes I intend applying for orders to go to Washington to settle my accounts.
We have had since the middle of Jan.y as pleasant weather as one could desire, this too at a place nearly two degrees North of Sackets Harbor. A great drawback to Oregon is that the land is so heavily timbered that it would take almost a life time to clear up a farm. People here dont however cultivate large farms as they do in the states. In this part but few cultivate more than from six to ten acres, and, where they are industrious and prudent, get rich at that. They will raise three or four acres of potatoes and usually get from 4 to 600 bushels per acre, and these generally bring $2.00 per bushel. On the ballance they can raise all other kinds of vegitables for their own use and to sell. Their bread they buy. Their cattle & hogs run out the year round and keep fat all the time.

16th of Feb.y

  The mail is in and brought with her your long sweet letter of the 7th & 8th of December/52. You do not know how delighted I was to hear so much about our little boys. I am now so glad that you could not come along. As it is Fred. is a strong healthy boy. Had you come he no doubt would be in his grave. I believe there was some twenty or more children of his age, and younger, come across the Isthmus with us. Out of that number seventeen died on the Isthmus and all the others contracted disease so that I believe there is not a single one left. Mrs. Wallen's little boy that she lost a few weeks ago, I believe, was the last survivor. You see now why I am glad that you did not come.

  If any one attempts to teaze you again about my making love to Spanish girls at Vancouver you can tell them that they must be desperately ignorant of the history of their own country not to know that there was probably never a Mexican or Spaniard in this part of Oregon.

  Fred. I expect is a very good boy, at least if he has not been spoiled he must be, and does not give his ma much trouble. How I should like to have the little dog with me for a few days! Who does Ulys. look like? your family or mine? I hope he will grow up as good a boy as Fred. If Ulys. wont sleep of mornings I would keep him awake an hour or two past the usual time for a few nights. That would bring him too.—Your watch & chain are very pretty and I now have the opportunity of sending them to the states. You may look for them at "Wells & Fargo's American Express Company's Office, St. Louis," in about ten days after you get this. It requires repairs but they can be made in St. Louis. You speak of sending Mrs. Gore a present. I should like you to do so very much, and a handsome one too, but I do not want, unless it is absolutely necessary, to send you any money for some time yet. I am using evry dollar that I can raise. Potatoes for seed cost $2.00 per bushel and I shall plant 200 bushels, besides twenty acres of oats, and then raise a vegitable garden. I loaned $200 00 to an officer, who was going to San Francisco some two months since, on the solemn promise that he would return it by the next Mail.

He has not paid and from what has transpired since I know he never will. I wish to gracious you had that. Has Capt. Calender commenced paying you yet? If he has not I must, notwithstanding my necessities here, send you money. Mr. Camp owes me $150 00 on a note that I hold against him, but it is not due for some time yet. If he lives and continues as prosperous as at present I would not give sixpence to have it secured. Do as you please with your money dearest Julia, I know you are always prudent with expenditures.—Did you ever get a letter from Mrs. Stevens? She has written to you and you must write to her whether you ever got hers or not. If you want the pearl handled knives you speak of buy them dearest. All the gentlemen and ladies here are very well (Mrs. Wallen & Mrs. Collins are the only ladies,) Capt. McConnell, Wallen & Lt. Collins are the only gentlemen you know. Mrs. Slaughter has gone to Steilacoom, on Pugets Sound to be stationed there.—Col. Whistler writes that he is very anxious to join, but I am sorry to say that I very much fear he will not be permitted to do so.—I think dearest your letters will come regularly now.—I was disappointed in my trip to San Francisco. The Commissary there thought it was not necessary for me to go after funds, but directed me to draw drafts on him when ever I required money. As the passage alone here & back is $150 00 it is not likely that I shall see that city soon. Give my love to all at your house kiss our dear little boys for thier papa. A thousand for yourself dear Julia.

I forgot to say that I think you had better make a visit to Bethel for three or four months this Summer coming. Dont you think so? If you will write them the time you will start some one will meet you.

Ulys.

Another thought about Ulysses' generosity to his wife, telling her, *"If you want the pearl-handled knives you speak of, buy them, dearest."* It shows something funny about Julia, at that time of her life. Though her husband was lonely and struggling desperately to save money to bring her to him, she tells him she yearns for some "pearl handled knives." She rarely wrote to him, yet she bothers to tell him she covets some pearl handled knives! It shows she was still spoiled, pampered, and really had no idea how much her husband was suffering. Yet, Ulysses derived pleasure from giving her pleasure. The fact that his flighty little wife wanted pearl handled knives, and he could give them to her, made him feel warm inside and helped him forget the grimness of his own life. It would always be this way for Ulysses. She got his mind off the seriousness that forever pervaded his mind.

Ulysses' sister-in-law, Ellen, who was in love with him when he first came to White Haven, reveals a hint of why Ulysses chose Julia instead of her. His response to Ellen's letter reveals she has a temper. Julia was widely reported to have a sweet, cheerful, nurturing spirit, which was just what love-starved Ulysses craved. Calm, quiet Ulysses wisely shied away from a temperamental mate. It was not what he needed.

"Ellen says Ulys. looks like her and bids fair to have her temper and wants to know if I am not delighted."

Ulysses Junior was extremely good looking. If Ellen looked like Ulys, Ellen must have been very beautiful—on the outside, anyway.

Ulysses longs to share the pleasures of the Pacific Coast with his wife—pleasures he could enjoy if only she were there.

"I wish you could be here dearest to enjoy the fine climate we have and the wild scenery."

Columbia Barracks, O.T.
March 4th 1853

My Dear Wife:
I had the pleasure of reading a sweet letter from you and Ellen last evening and was delighted to hear so much about our dear little ones, and to hear too that you and them are so well and are enjoying youselvs as much as you do. I got a letter from father also in which he has a greatdeel to say about Fred. He says that Fred. went with him to Georgetown and Felicity and evrybody thought him a great boy.—Ellen says Ulys. looks like her and bids fair to have her temper

and wants to know if I am not delighted. Tell her that the boy had better keep his temper to himself when I get home. I am very tired and sore this evening. You know that I am farming extensively and I work myself as hard as any body. I have just finished puting in barley and I am glad to say that I put in evry grain with my own hands. By the end of the coming week myself and partners will have planted twenty acres of potatoes and an acre of onions. In a week or two more we will plant a few acres of corn. If I can only manage to keep up until next fall I hope to be well enough off for the future. At present however I am cramped all the time. I have a large quantity of wood cut for which I had to pay and but little of it will be sold for three months yet. I have been obliged to buy horses, a wagon, harnass, farming utensils, garden seed &c. I have too over two thousand dollars due me but little of which will I get for six or eight months yet, and, I regret to say, some of it never.

There is considerable excitement here just at this time in consequence of the rumor of the discovery of gold high up on the Columbia river and at the Grand Rondi in this Territory. If the rumors should prove true it will cause a great influx of people to this part of Oregon. The fact is my dear wife if you and our little boys were here I should not want to leave here for some years to come. My fears now however are that I may be promoted to some company away from here before I am ready to go. I wish you could be here dearest to enjoy the fine climate we have and the wild scenery. Since the middle of January there has not been scaresely a day when an overcoat was required, yet people who have been here the longest say that it has been an unprecidented severe Winter.—The Mail which brought your letter brought me a piece of unwelcom news. It brought orders for the Qr. Master here, Capt. Brent, to proceed to Fort Hall, and for me to perform the duties of that office in addition to those of the Commissary. This is a great nusance because evry thing that is shipped to other posts, or to this, have to be done by the quarter master here. All purchases are made by him and all buildings are put up by him. It is not like doing the same duty in the States because there communication from place to place is easy. Here I will be obliged to superintend, (with one clerk,) a blacksmith shop, Tin shop, sadlers shop, Carpenter's shop and some two hundred pack and harnass mules, all without additional compensation.

I recieved a long letter by this Mail from Charles Ford. He says that evry body who is any body, has left Sackets. Improvements however are going on. They have got their Rail Road track laid and it has stimulated people there so evry body is as busy as a bee. He says that he had a call from half the village to see and read my letter to which his is an answer.

Capt. Brent intends applying for permission to continue on from Fort Hall to the United States, and if he gets it he will probably return next Winter with Mrs. B. I think this might prove a good opportunity for you to come on here. I will know his arrangements however in time to let you know what to do.

Give my love to all at your house and kiss Fred. & Ulys for me. I got a specimen of Freds. writing that his Aunt Nelly enclosed in your last letter you must not let Fred's grand pa spoil him. Can Fred. say every thing he wants too? and does he understand all that is said? Does he gisticulate like he used to do before he could say many words? Whenever the mail arrives Maggy always enquires most particularly after you and Fred. but she never enquires after Ulys. How I would like to see the dear little dogs. Tell Fred. that Mr. Brooke has given him a pony that he can have to ride as soon as he gets here. Does Fred. know his letters yet? If he was here I would learn him to read before he was four years old. You know that he knew nearly all his letters before he could pronounce many of them. What does he call his Grandpa & ma? And his Uncles and Aunts? Adieu dear dear wife. Dream of me often.

Your affectionate husband.
Ulys.

Don't forget to let me know as soon as you get your watch from Wells & Fargo's Express office. I have forgotten whether or not you ever told me if (y)ou got the presents I sent you from New York City or not. Did you get them. Has Capt. Calender ever paid you anything on the note which you hold against him? It is time now that he commenced paying up. Adieu again dear Julia.

It is sad that Julia never mentioned the presents Ulysses sent her from New York City! The *"pretty little presents"* which he so eagerly waited to hear, *"and how were you pleased with my selection?"* I just don't think she understood how he doted on every word from her.

Very sexy!

"I see from your letter that you have been dreaming of me, but had me associated with wild horses."

Columbia Barracks O.T.
March 19th 1853

My Dear Julia:
I have just recieved a long letter from you of the 20th of January from which I am happy to hear that you and our dear little boys, as well as all our friends, are quite well. How much I should like to see Fred. and Ulys.! I have no doubt but Fred. must have become very interesting by this time; and Ulysses too will be standing alone and attempting to talk. If there was any prospect of my being promoted to one of the companies at this place how much I would be delighted to have you here. There is not a more delightful place in the whole country and it has never been your fortune to witness any thing like such scenery. Evry body presents a perfect picture of health. I have grown out of my clothes entirely and am still geting larger. I take a great deel of exercise, and, I flatter myself, to some purpose. I have in the ground a field of barley evry grain of which I sewed with my own hands. The ground is already broken for twenty acres of potatos, and a few acres for onions and other vegitables. I shall do all the ploughing myself all summer. You know besides my farming operation I have a large quantity of Steamboat wood cut for which I get $2 50 per cord more than it cost me to get it cut. It has to be howled but a short distance and that is done with my own private horses and wagon. Besides these speculations Capts. Wallen, McConnell and myself are starting two drays which we think will bring in from $10 to 15 dollars per day each.—If I am atal fortunate next fall will bring me in a good return which will make me easy for the future, for then I will never permit myself to get the least in debt.
I see that you must be geting near out of means. Has Capt. Calender not commenced sending you money on the notes you hold

against him? I think it was March I told him to commence sending you fifty dollars evry alternate month. Be sure and let me know as soon as you get this if necessary I will then send you a hundred or two dollars.

I am glad to hear that Fred. is growing up a good boy and that his Aunt Ellen is not learning him any mischief.

Do you intend on going to Bethel this Summer? I think you had better make a visit there. If you go get Mrs. Gore to go with you. Maggy and Getz are still with me. They always enquire particularly after you and Fred. Maggy told me the other day that she and Getz had save four hundred and fifty dollars since they have been at Vancouver. Maggy gets twenty five dollars per month for cooking and two dollars per dozen for washing. Besides this there is Getz's pay and he sells his ration for twelve dollars per month and lives himself in the kitchen.

I am very sorry to hear that you have been suffering from weak eyes again! Take good care of them.

The money you got from Mr. Mackfeely was the hundred & fifty dollars left with the Quarter Master in New York.—Have you got the watch yet? It must have reached Wells & Fargo's Express office before this.

I see from your letter that you have been dreaming of me, but had me associated with wild horses. It is true that I have had the handsomest and probably most spirited horse in Oregon until lately, but I have sold him and have now two of the most sedate fellows you ever saw. Two besides Fred's poney I mean. By the way I must get Fred's poney up and ride him this Summer. Does Fred. talk any about his poney?

Mrs. Wallen and family are quite well. Capt. McConnell. Mrs. Wallen sends you a great deel of love. She will be left entirely alone this summer as far as lady's society goes. The Company that Mr. Slaughter belongs too has gone to Puget's Sound. The one Collins belongs too starts soon for Scott's Valley, California. This is the Company that I belong too. I believe I told you that my promotion would in all probability take me to Humbolt Bay, California? I know nothing of the place except that I believe there are no quarters there.—You charge me to be cautious about riding out alone lest

*the Indians should get me. Those about here are the most harmless
people you ever saw. It is really my opinion that the whole race would
be harmless and peaceable if they were not put upon by the whites.*

*Give my love to all at home and continue to write often. Does
Fred. know his letters? He will now soon be three years old and he
ought to read by the time he is four. Kiss him and Ulys for me. A
thousand kisses for yourself Dear Julia.*

> *Your affectionate husband*
> *Ulys.*

P.S. I sent Mrs. Bailey the ring Mrs. Stevens sent her.

> *U.*

I love the way Ulysses always signs his letters, "Your
affectionate husband."

Ulysses enjoys farming, because he has high hopes of earning enough money to bring his family to him. Everything he does is connected to uniting with Julia. But he is unhappy about Julia's dream that she will never join him on the coast. It seems Julia was psychic, because her dreams and premonitions always came true. Ulysses tries valiantly to keep his hopes alive and assures his wife:

"I am doing all I can to put up a penny not only to enable you and our dear little boys to get here comfortably, but to enable you to be comfortable after you do get here."

"I never worked before with so much pleasure, because now I feel sure that evry day will bring a large reward."

Columbia Barracks
Washington Territory
March 31st 1853

My Dearest Wife;
The Mail has just arrived bringing me a very short and very unsatisfactory letter. You speak of not joining me on this coast in a manner that would indicate that you have been reflecting upon a dream which you say you have had until you really imagine that it is true. Do not write so any more dearest. It is hard enough for us to be separated so far without borrowing immaginary troubles. You know that it was entirely out of the question for you to have come with me at the time I had to come. I am doing all I can to put up a penny not only to enable you and our dear little boys to get here comfortably, but to enable you to be comfortable after you do get here.
You ask why I do not live with the bachilors? I do: that is there are two "messes" and I am in one. Capt.s Brent & Ingalls, Mr. Bomford, Brooke and Eastman are in the same mess that I am. If it is economy you think I should consult all I have to say is that my expenses are about twenty dollars per month less than if I was in the

other. We all live and eat in the same house so that Maggy & Getz wash for us and wait upon us; and besides Maggy wastes nothing. The other "mess" is separated from evry officer so that all expenses of servant hire &c. is surplus.

I am farming now in good earnest. All the ploughing and furrowing I do myself. There are two things that I have found out by working myself. One is that I can do as much, and do it better, than I can hire it done. The other is that by working myself those that are hired do a third more than if left alone.

I was surprised to find out that I could run as strait a furrow now as I could fifteen years ago and work all day quite as well. I never worked before with so much pleasure either, because now I feel sure that evry day will bring a large reward.

I believe I told you that I have to do that detestable Quarter Master business this Summer? I dislike it very much. Mr. Camp become very much dissatisfied here and sold out. He was making money much faster than he will ever do again. Notwithstanding his bad luck having his store blown up he has cleared in the few months he has been here more than six thousand dollars, this without two thousand capital to start with.

Mrs. Wallen is quite well and so are all the officers. Capt. McConnell is here. Mr. Hunt is at Humbolt Bay, Russell at Fort Reading Calafornia. All were well when last heard from. Capt. Wallen met with a serious accident a few days since. He was riding in a wagon and the horse commenced kicking so to save himself he jumped out and fell throughing his right rist entirely out of joint. He will probably be lame in it all Summer.

You can tell your brother that we have had the news all the time that long beards were allowed, at least, on this coast. I have not shaved since I left Calafornia consequently my beard is several inches long. Why did you not tell me some more about our dear little boys? I would like to hear some of Fred's sayings. I wish I could have him and his brother here. What does Fred. call Ulys.? What does the S stand for in Ulys.'s name? in mine you know it does not stand for anything! Give my love to all at your house. When you write again dearest write in better spirits.

Does Fred. and his Aunt Ellen get on harmoniously together? I expect she teases him. Cant you have your Dagueriotype taken with Fred. & Ulys. along? if you can send it by Adam's and Co('s) Express, to Portland, O.T. I presume you have recieved your watch ere this? I have no opportunity of buying any pretty presents here to send you.

Adieu dear dear wife. I shall hope to get a long sweet letter from you next Mail. Kiss our little boys for their pa. A thousand kisses for yourself dear wife.

Your affectionate husband.
Ulys.

Ulysses' spirits are sinking. He is obsessed with the need to make money.

"My dear wife it is very hard to be seperated from you so long but until I am better off it cannot be helped. If I can get together a few thousand dollars I shall most certainly go home however."

20th 1853
San Francisco, Cal.
May

Dear Wife,

I got here yesterday morning and astonishing to say was not atal sea sick by the way. I leave here again to-day for Knights Ferry where I shall have the pleasure of dining, with your brothers, to-morrow. I shall remain there about five or six days.

I have been trying to think what I could get pretty, that could be sent by mail, for Fred. and Ulys. but I can think of nothing.—I paid Mrs. Stevens a long call yesterday. Her and the children are well. Mr. Stevens has been sick a good deal since they come out here. He is off from here now and probably will be absent most of the summer. Mrs. S. says she wrote you a very long letter when she first come out here but she has never got a word in reply. Stevens is rich.

I saw young Dodge, Gladwin and Mrs. Gladwin, all of Sackets Harbor, yesterday. They are doing a good business here.

I have been ordered here as a witness on Lieut. Scott's trial, but yesterday he sent in his resignation which will stop all proceedings against him.

I have but little to write you dear Julia only that I am still in the same robust health that I have been in ever since we come out here. Mrs. Stevens did not know me I have grown so stout, and so with several other persons. I am much more fleshy than I ever expected to be. Hard work, and the climate, agrees with me.—Kiss our little boys for me and tell them that their pa wanted to send them a present but he could find nothing to send. When you go to town you must get something for them and tell them it was their pa sent it, or the money to buy it.

I send you with this deed for the land located with my land warrant for you to sign before a Commissioner. Dont neglect to attend to this the first time you go to St. Louis and have it mailed to Preston Brady, Detroit, as soon as possible.—When I get back from your Brothers I will write you a long letter, and another as soon as I get to Columbia Barracks. Give my love to all of them at home. You will get another letter from me by the same mail as takes this in which I have told you all the inconveniences that the Ladies of the Regiment have had to undergo.—Tell Ellen and Emmy to write to me as well as yourself. Emmy I know will however. Dont neglect to write to Mrs. Stevens.

My dear wife it is very hard to be seperated from you so long but until I am better off it cannot be helped. If I can get together a few thousand dollars I shall most certainly go home however.

Kiss our dear little boys for me. A thousand kisses for yourself dear wife.

Your affectionate husband
Ulys.

In this next letter, Ulysses has bad luck and sounds depressed, as when he says "to write more about myself, as you so often request me to do, I do not know how." He was probably beginning to drink heavily.

The surveying party Ulysses outfitted was commanded by Bvt. Captain George Brinton McClellan of Pennsylvania. It was reported that McClellan found Ulysses drunk on duty and never forgave him. McClellan later became Commander in Chief of the Union Army during the Civil War—ultimately to be replaced by none other than General Ulysses S. Grant.

This point in the young Ulysses' life is summed up in his sad confession:

"I have been very unfortunate lately."

Columbia Barracks W.T.
June 15th 1853

I have just returned from Calafornia and found three long sweet letters from you; one of March, (no date) April 10th and 25th In all of them you speak so highly of our dear little boys, as in fact all the letters I get from my home. I got one from Jenny and Molly in which they speak almost as much of them as you do. They say that father has gone to Galena and will stop to see Fred. That he thinks the country does not afford another like him.—When they wrote father had not yet returned and of course I heard nothing of the proposition to have me resign that you spoke of. I shall weigh the matter well before I act. If I could only remain here it would be hard to get me to leave the army. Whilst in Cal. I made arrangements as would enable me to do a conciderable business, in a commission way, if I could but stay.

I have been quite unfortunate lately. The Columbia is now far over its banks, and has destroyed all the grain, onions, corn and about half the potatoes upon which I had expended so much money and labor. The wood which I had on the bank of the river had all to be removed, at an expense, and will all have to be put back again at an expense.

You ask about Mr. Camp. Poor fellow he could not stand prosperity. He was making over $1000 00 per month and it put him beside himself. From being generous he grew parsimonious and finally so close that apparently he could not bear to let money go to keep up his stock of goods. He quit and went home with about $8000.00 decieving me as to the money he had and owing me about $800 00. I am going to make out his account and send it to Chas. Ford for collection. I will some day tell you all the particulars of this transaction. I do not like to put it upon paper.

I got the lock of Ulys.s' hair you send and kissed it. I dreamed of seeing you, Fred. and Ulys. night before last. I thought Fred. & Ulys. were exactly alike, but not what Fred. was when I saw him last. They looked puny and not near so good looking as Fred. was. Did Fred. recognize his grandpa Grant? I sent you and the two boys presents from San Francisco. I hope you got them.

I told you in my letter from San Francisco that I am promoted! I go to Fort Reading in Calafornia. It is not probable however that I shall leave here before October. I got a letter from Mr. Hunt but a short time since. He was quite well but hartily tired of Humboldt Bay, or rather with the commanding officer there. In my other letters which you have not yet recieved I have answered all your questions about others of our Regiment.—Dr. Baily was not at Governor's Island when I got there but had gone to Mackinac. I sent the thimble presented by Mrs. Stevens but never heard whether it was recieved or not.

I am very busy now being both Depot Qr. Master and Depot Commissary and having two expeditions to fit out for the great Pacific Rail Road Surveying party under Governor Stevens. They require a large number of pack animals and many articles besides that have to be purchased, all of which has to be done by me.

I am very well dear Julia but to write more about myself, as you so often request me to do, I do not know how.

Give my love to all at your house and kiss our dear little boys for me. Does Ulys. walk yet? From the progress he appears to be making I suppose he must. Continue dear Julia to write me as you do *about the boys. I like to hear of Fred's sayings. If he talks as he used to try to do he must be very interesting.*

    People are waiting for me with a drove of horses so I must close. A thousand kisses for you dear dear Julia.

        Adieu from your affectionate husband.
        Ulys.

There is something sad about the way he says, *"...to write more about myself, as you so often request me to do, I do not know how."*

CHAPTER EIGHTEEN
Ulysses' Despair

The failures of Ulysses' crops, timber and everything else, including the reprimand from McClellan, are weighing on him. Though he does not come out and say so, one can tell it from his physical illness and from his sad plea for more letters from his wife. He feels abandoned by the Gods of fortune and by his own family. Does Julia's lack of letters express disappointment and exasperation over the money Ulysses has been losing in his disastrous financial speculations? She seemed to write when he seemed hopeful about the future, her letters stop when his luck runs south. He receives many letters from his parents at this time, so the mail was getting through. Julia just wasn't writing.

Ulysses' endless financial speculations reveal his attempts to make money to bring his family to him, as well as an addiction to the excitement of gambling. Quiet though he appears, he needs drama in his life. It is also telling that he is so honest with Julia about his failures. If I had lost money like he did, I think I'd try to hide it from my husband. He hid nothing from her. This way, he knew she was truly loving him and accepting him for himself, faults and all. This was a cornerstone of their honest, loving relationship. One hundred percent honesty like this would seem like a painful challenge! But it brought such beautiful rewards.

"I have lost from dishonesty of others, a number of hundreds of dollars which, if you had would educate our dear little boys."

Columbia Bks. W.T.
June 28th 1853

By this Mail I recieved no letter from you, nor from any one at your house. Where Mails come but twice per month it does seem as though I might expect news from you and our dear little boys.
I cannot say that I have been atal well since my return from California. I have had a very sever cold and have been, necessarily,

very busily engaged fitting out the expedition going out to meet Major Stevens of the Rail Road surveying party, and another party going into the Cascade range of mountains for the purpose of exploring are to be fitted out also. I have purchased for them within a few days some two hundred horses besides other property and have still more to get. The present state of the Columbia makes transportation very difficult so I have to get Indians to pack, on their backs, all the provisions of one of these parties, over the portage at the Cascades, about forty five miles above here. The two companies of Infantry that come around Cape Horn have arrived, and with them, four families. Maj. Rains & lady & children, Mrs. Haller and two children, Mrs. Maloney and Mrs. Forsyth. Forsyth was detained, on duty, at San Francisco and very soon after leaving there Mrs. Forsyth who was within a few weeks of her confinement, was taken sick and went into convulsions. By the time they arrived here she had had a great many and was supposed to be beyond recovery. Soon after being got ashore however she was delivered of a child which had probably been dead for several days, and there is hopes of her recovery. As has been the fate of all the ladies who come out with us all these ladies are destined to the greates annoyance. Maj. Rains, and Hallers Co. goes to the Dalles. There are no quarters for them and as Maloney and Forsyth belong to the same co. they will all four families have to remain here while their husbands, though but ninety miles from them, will be more remote than if one was in Main and the other in Louisiana.—Maj. Larnard and lady, I forgot to say have also arrived They go to Pugets Sound.

I will now speak of myself and affairs. Evry thing that I have undertaken, as a speculation, has proven profitable. I have though been unfortunate in some respects. I believe I explained in my last letter the result of the high waters! I have now had a chance of looking at matters and I find that we will have a crop of several thousand potatoes, and according to the opinion of old setlers they will bring from three to five dollars per bushel. This is in consequence of so many being drowned out. While in California I purchased a quantity of pork, its being low ther(e,) and knowing the price here, I made in partnership with another gentleman, about four hundred dollars upon it. I have still another lot to arrive and the article having risen we will clear about six hundred. Then another speculation which I have entered into is this. I made arrangements below for the sale of pigs and hogs. I have out now a man buying them and I am confident of clearing, for my share, a thousand dollars in the next four weeks. I told you in my last that if I could remain here that i would be able to do a handsom business in the Commission way! It is in this way. While in San Francisco a large business firm, from I have purchased flour &c. wanted me to watch the markets here, (they are very changeable) and when any article was, in my opinion, a speculation to inform them. They would furnish the capital, me make the sales and divide the profits. This dear Julia is the bright side. On the other hand I have lost from dishonesty of others, a number of hundreds of dollars which if you had would educate our dear little boys. The debt of eight hundred dollars against Camp I am going to sue for. You will be much surprized when I have an opportunity of explaining his whole conduct. He is I fear slightly deranged, and in that state of penuriousness, and dishonesty, of the whole family broke out. Enough. Give my love to all at your house, kiss our dear little ones for their Pa. I get a great many letters from home now. They all say as much of Fred. & Ulys. as you do. I got a long letter from father this time. He has explained his whole business. The family will move to Covington, or Newport, Ky. and

The rest of this letter cannot be found.

In this next letter, I love the way Julia sends Ulysses leaves which she has kissed. Their romance continues, although one can see and hear Colonel Dent smugly boasting that Julia's children will be living with him at White Haven all their lives—which means that Julia will always be his princess of White Haven, as well. Yes, Ulysses' absence suits Colonel Dent just fine.

"I dreamed of you last night but not either of our dear little boys. I mearly saw you for a minuet without having an opportunity of speaking to you and you were gone."

"My dear julia I have spoken of speculations so much that the subject is becoming painful."

"My dear Julia I have said nothing about the pink leaves upon each of which you say you presed a sweet kiss. I cannot, in this, return the favor on flowers but you may rest assured I will imprint them when we first meet upon your lips and those of our dear babes."

Columbia Bks. W.T.
July 13th 1853

My Dearest Julia;
It is about 12 o'clock at night, but as the Mail is to leave here early in the morning I must write to-night.—I got your long sweet letter giving an account of our dear little boys at the picnic where Fred. started behind his Grand ma, but wanted her to ride behinde him before he got through. You know before he could talk he would always persist in having his hands in front of mine when driving. The loose end of the lines never satisfied him.
My dear Julia if you could see the letters they write from my home about our dear little boys it would make you as proud as it does me. I am sure there never was one of my own brothers or sisters

who have been more thought of than Fred. & Ulys. In the long letter
I got from my father he speaks of him as something more than boys
of his age. You understand though that I can make allowances for
his prejudices either in favor or against; where prejudices are strong
pred(il)ections are generally right, so I must conclude that Fred. &
Ulys. are more than I ever dreamed they were. I dreamed of you last
night but not of either of our dear little boys. I mearly saw you for
a minuet without having an opportunity of speaking to you and you
were gone.

My dear julia I have spoken of speculations so much that the
subject is becoming painful, but yet I know you feel interested in what
I am doing.—In a former letter I told you, for the first time, of the
downs of all I had done. (Before I had never met with a _down_.) Since
that I have made several hundreds in speculations of various sorts. In
groceries which I do not sell, and which are not retailed. I have now
a large quantity of pork on hand which is worth to-day ten dollars pr.
barrel more than I gave for it at the very place where it was bought.
All this will help to buy dresses for Fred. & Ulys. but what interests
me most is to know how it is to let their pa see them wear them, and
their ma put them on to advantage.

I wrote you that Scott was appointed Inspector General
and that it would take me to Fort Reading.—It turns out that he
has not been appointed so I must await my place either for Alden's
resignation, or for Col. Buchanan's promotion. The first would take
me to Fort Jones, of which I have spoken, in former letters; the latter
to a detestible place where the mails reach occationaly. I should
however have command of the post, with double rations and two
companies. Wallen is going to San Francisco before you recieve this
letter with the intention of setting up a Dairy, Pigery, and market
Garden, if practicable,. He will go on leave for a few months and
then, if successful, strike out for himself.

You ask how many children Laura has? Before this you know.
She has but two; Harry who is a healthy & smart boy, and Nancy who
has always, until lately, been healthy.

My dear Julia I have said nothing about the pink leaves
upon each of which you say you presed a sweet kiss. I cannot, in
this, return the favor on flowers but you may rest assured that I will

imprint them when we first meet upon your lips and those of our dear babes.

How can your pa & ma think that they are going to keep Fred. & Ulys. always with them? I am growing impatient to see them myself.—Tell Fred. to say <u>Ugly</u> <u>Aunt</u> <u>Ell</u> I wont let you learn me anything. So Fred. might say the same to his Uncle. If you cant go your self send him to his other Grandpa's for tuition for a few months.—Indeed dear Julia you must either go with the children or make a very good excuse. They want to see you so much. If you have not got means enough I have still some in N.Y. I shall never draw it so long as I remain in this country except in your favor. I hope you got the hundred which I sent you, and also the begining of what Calender was to send you. Give my love to all at your house. I got the pink leaves that you kissed. A thousand kisses for our little boys and yourself.

Adieu dear julia. The Steamer is in sight that is to take this.

Your affectionate husband
Ulys.

Before being transferred to the even more lonely Fort Humboldt, Ulysses writes a recommendation for his cleaning lady.

Columbia Bks. W.T.
July 19th 1853

The bearer, Margaret Getz, has lived with me over two years, on the Atlantic and Pacific Coast. I can recommend her most highly as a good family servant. She is a washer, ironer, plain cook and in evry way qualified to undertake the entire work of a small family.

Getz is a sober, industrious, and capable, man. He is a practicle gardner, a good man with horses, and no doubt would prove a good porter in a store.

U.S. Grant
Bvt. Capt. & R.Q.M. 4th Inf.y

Grasping at any means for a reunion with his wife, Ulysses tries to get orders to go to Washington D.C. to settle an old account, not surprisingly, money having been stolen from him in the Mexican War. He had hoped to go to Washington, then fetch his wife from White Haven and bring her back to California with him. His request was denied.

To Bvt. Maj. Gen. Thomas S. Jesup

Qr. Mr's Office
Fort Vancounver, W.T.
September 8th 1853

Gen.
Having resigned my appointment as Regimental Quarter Master, and having unsettle(d) accounts for years back, I would, most respectfully request orders to go to Washington for the purpose of settling my accounts.

I am particularly anxious to be present in Washington for the reason that I had public funds stolen from me during the Mexican war, and for which I have been petitioning Congress ever since, but without being able to get any action on my claim.

At the same time I forward this I forward a similar claim to the Commissary General.

I am Gen.
Very Respectfully
Your Obt. Svt.
U.S. Grant
1st Lt. & R.Q.M. 4th Infantry
Bvt. Capt. U.S.A.

To Bvt. Maj. Gen. George Gibson

Office of Com.y of Subs
Fort Vancouver, W.T.
Sept. 8th 1853

Gen.
        Being relieved as Ass. Com.y of Subs. I have the honor respectfully to request orders to repair to Washington for the purpose of setling my public accounts.
        I am making a similar application to the Quartermaster General.

I am Gen.
Very respectfully
Your Obt. Svt.
U.S. Grant
1st Lt. & A.A.C.S. 4th Infantry
Bvt. Capt. U.S.A.

To Bvt. Maj. Gen. Geo. Gibson
Com.y Gen. U.S.A.
Washington D.C.

To Bvt. Maj. E.D. Townsend

San Francisco, Cal.
October 12th 1853

Maj.
   Finding that an application for orders to repair to Washington, D.C. to settling my accounts as a disbursing officer in the Quarter Master's & Commissary's Departments has not passed throu(h) Division Head Quarters I would respectfully submit the enclosed renewed application.
   My former application was approved by Col. Bonneville, Comd.g 4th Inf.y.

                    I am Maj.
                    Very Respectfully
                    Your Obt. Svt.
                    U.S. Grant
                    Capt. 4th Inf.y

TO Maj. E.D. Townsend
Asst. Adj. Gen. P.D.
San Francisco, Cal.

To Bvt. Maj. Gen. Thomas Jesup

> *Fort Humboldt, Humboldt Bay Cal.*
> *February 3rd 1854—*

Gen:—

Enclosed please find my Statement of allowances to officers for 2d & 3d Qrs 1853—Voucher No 1. 2. & 3. To abstract "B" 4th Qr. same year—

Mr. Eastman, who was my clerk, informs me that I have been reported for nonrendition of my accounts for 2d Qr. 1853—Within the time prescribed by law—They were mailed on the 1st & 2d of November, which owing to my absence was the earlyest I could possibly get them off

> *I am Gen*
> *Very Respectfully*
> *Your Obt Svt*
> *U.S. Grant*
> *Capt. 4th Inf.y*
> *Late R.Q.M.*

To Maj. Gen. T.S. Jesup
Qr. Mr. Gen. U.S.A.
Washington, D.C.

The first time Jefferson Davis, future president of the Confederacy, ever heard of U.S. Grant, was when the lonely, faltering young Captain Grant was tardy handing in some military records.

On Oct. 31, 1853, Secretary of War Jefferson Davis wrote to Ulysses: *"Pursuant to the provisions of an Act approved January 31, 1823, of which I hereto append an extract, you have this day been reported to the President as having failed to render within the period prescribed by law, your accounts for the quarter ending June 30 1853.*

On the receipt of this communication, you will forthwith forward your accounts to the proper office for settlement, and address to this Department such explanation as you may desire to make, in order to relieve yourself from the penalty of the Act above cited." Copies of this letter were sent to seven other officers. On Jan. 12, 1854, Bvt. Maj. Gen. Thomas S. Jesup wrote to Davis. *"I have the honor to report the reception of the money and property accounts of Captain U.S. Grant, Regimental Quarter Master 4th Infantry, for the 2d and 3d Quarters 1853. He was reported on the 5th instant for the non-rendition of these accounts."*

Ulysses has forgotten what year it is, dating his letters 1853 when it is actually 1854.

While Julia is safe and warm at White Haven, an unhappy Ulysses arrives at Fort Humboldt, a military post far more remote than his previous one. He gives her a description of his lonely new residence.

"Imagine a place closed in by the sea having thrown up two tongues of land, closed in a bay that can be entered only with certain winds."

Ulysses' misspelling of "California" seems poignant to me.

"Give my love to all at your house and kiss them for me. Our two dear little boys give a dozen extra for their Pa, in Calafornia."

Fort Humboldt Cal.
Jan. 18th 1853 (1854)

My Dear Wife.
After a long and tedious voyage, from San Francisco to this place, I have arrived in safety. I cannot say much in favor of the place. It is about what I expected before my arrival. You know what my opinions of it were. Imagine a place closed in by the sea having thrown up two tongues of land, closed in a bay that can be entered only with certain winds.
In geting here, a distance of but a little more than 250 mile, we were two (days) in coming. There is no mail going but Mr. Hunt is just about starting for S. Francisco and I must avail myself of this occation of geting a letter to where it can be mailed.
Hunt is making application for promotion in a new Regiment, should any be raised this Winter, and any assistance that could be given by your father, or brother Lewis, in the way of writing to Col. Benton he would gladly recieve, and, appreciate. In a few days I hope

to have an opportunity of sending you a letter, and of having a steel pen instead of an old quil one, to write with.

Give my love to all at your house and kiss them for me. Our two dear little boys give a dozen extra for their Pa, in Calafornia.

Adieu dear wife
Ulys.

P.S. Mr. Hunt wants me to mention that his application is for a Captaincy. I hope that this matter will be attended to wishing him success.

U.S.G.

By far, Ulysses' saddest love letter away from home. It begins
with the haunting:

"You do not know how forsaken I feel here!"

Fort Humboldt,
Humboldt Bay, Cal.
February 2d 1853 (1854)

My Dear Wife.
*You do not know how forsaken I feel here! The place is good
enough but I have interests at others which I cannot help thinking
about day and night; then to it is a long time since I made application
for orders to go to Washington to settle my accounts but not a word
in reply do I get. Then I feel again as if I had been separated from
you. and Fred. long enough and as to Ulys. I have never seen him. He
must by this time be talking about as Fred. did when I saw him last.
How very much I want to see all of you. I have made up my mind what
Ulys. looks like and I am anxious to see if my presentiment is correct.
Does he advance rapidly? Tell me a great deel about him and Fred.
and Freds pranks with his Grandpa. How does he get along with his
Uncle Lewis?*
*I do nothing here but set in my room and occationally take
a short ride on one of the public horses. There is game here such
as ducks, geese &c. which some of the officers amuse themselvs by
shooting but I have not entered into the sport. Within eight or ten
miles Deer and occationally Elk and black Bear are found. Further
back the Grisley Bear are quite numerous. I do not know if I told you
what officers are at this post? Col. Buchanan, Hunt, Collins, Dr. Potts
and Lt. Latimer to join. Expected soon. Col. B expects promotion by
evry Mail which, if he gets, will bring Montgomery in command of
the post. Mrs. Collins is the only lady at the post. Dr. Potts however
will have his wife here in a short time. The quarters are comfortable
frame buildings, backed by a dense forest of immense trees. In front is
the Bay. We are on a bluff which gives us one of the most commanding*

*views that can be had from almost any point on the whole Bay.
Besides having a view of the Bay itself we can look out to sea as far
as the eye can extend. There are four villeges on the Bay. One at the
outlet, Humbolt Point is the name, where there are probably not more
than 50 inhabitants. What they depend upon for support I do'nt know.
They are probably persons who supposed that it would be the point
for a City and they would realize a California fortune by the rise
of lots. Three miles up the Bay is Bucksport and this garrison Here
geting out lumber is the occupation, and as it finds a ready market
in San Francisco this is a flourishing little place of about 200. Three
miles further up is Euricka with a population of about 50(0) with
the same resourses. The mills in these two villeges have, for the last
year, loaded an average of 19 vessels per month with lumber, and
as they are building several additional mills they will load a greater
number this year. Twelve miles further up, and at the head of the Bay,
is Union, the larges and best built town of the whole. From there they
pack provisions to the gold mines, and return with the dust. Taking
all of these villeges together there are about enough ladies to get up a
small sized Ball. There has been several of them this winter.*

*I got one letter from you since I have been here but it was
some three months old. I fear very much that I shall loose some
before they get in the regular way of coming. There is no regular mail
between here and San Francisco so the only way we have of geting
letters off is to give them to some Captain of a vessel to mail them
after he gets down. In the same way mails are recieved. This makes it
very uncertain as to the time a letter may be on the way. Sometimes,
owing to adverse winds, vessels are 40 and even 60 days making
the passage, while at others they make it in less than two days. So
you need not be surprised if sometimes you would be a great while
without a letter and then likely enough get three or four at once. I
hope the next mail we get to have several from you. Be particular to
pay postage on yours for otherwise they may refuse to deliver them at
the San Francisco Post Office. I cant pay the postage here having no
stamps and not being able to get them. I have sent below however for
some.*

*I must finish by sending you a great deel of love t(o) all of
you, your Pa. Ma. brother and sisters, niece and nephews. I have*

not yet fulfilled my promise to Emmy to write her a long letter from Humboldt.

Kiss our little ones for me. A thousand kisses for yourself dear Julia.

Your affectionate husband
Ulys

I notice Ulysses tells Julia that he actually lives with Colonel Buchanan, who it is always said, hated Ulysses. If he hated him so much, why did they live together? This bears more investigating. Perhaps he actually cut the young Captain extra slack, instead of being the villain always described!

Ulysses' loneliness is driving him to the breaking point.

"The state of suspense that I am in is scarsely bearable. I think I have been from my family quite long enough and sometimes I feel as though I could almost go home "nolens volens." (The book, "The Trial of U.S. Grant" says *"nolens volens"* means "with or without permission.")

Poor Ulysses is also being tortured by a toothache.

"I have been suffering for the last few days most terribly."

Fort Humboldt
Humboldt Bay, Cal.
Feb. 6th 1854.

My Dear Wife;
A mail come in this evening but brought me no news from you nor nothing in reply to my application for orders to go home. I cannot concieve what is the cause of the delay. The state of suspense that I am in is scarsely bearable. I think I have been from my family quite long enough and sometimes I feel as though I could almost go home "nolens volens." I presume, under ordinary circumstances, Humboldt would be a good enough place but the suspense I am in would make paradice form a bad picture. There is but one thing to console; misery loves company and there are a number in just the same fix with

myself, and, with other Regiments, some who have been separated much longer from their families than I have been.

It has only been a few days since I wrote to you but it will not do to let an opportunity pass of geting a letter into the San Francisco Post Office, and there is a vessel to leave here tomorrow. It is not all the vessels that it will do to entrust letters with. A few that come take the trouble, and expense, of going to the Post Office in San Francisco and geting all the mail directed to this bay and bring it without my remuneration either from the Post Office Department, or from individuals.

I have been suffering for the last few days most terribly. I am certain that if you were to see me now you would not know me. That tooth I had set in Wattertown (You remember how much I suffered at the time) has been giving me the same trouble over again. Last evening I had it drawn and it was much harder to get out than any other tooth would have been. My face is swollen until it is as round as an apple and so tender that I do not feel as if I could shave, so, looking at the glass, I think I could pass readily for a person of forty five. Otherwise I am very well. You know what it is to suffer with teeth.

I am very much pleased with my company. All the men I have are old soldiers and very neat in their appearance. The contrast between them and the other company here is acknowledged as very great by the officers of the other company. The reason is that all my men are old soldiers while the other were recruits when they come here. I have however less than one third of the complement allowed by law and all of them will be discharged about the same time. I wish their times were out now so that I could go on recruiting service if no other way.

My dear wife you do not tell me whether you are contented or not! I hope you enjoy yourself very much.—Has Capt. Calender continued to send you money? Some three or four months since I bought two land warrants, one of which I want to send you but when I got to San Francisco I found that they were not negociable on account of not having on the transfer the Seal of the County Clerk. I sent them back to Vancouver to have this fixed and when I get them I will send you one. They are worth about forty dollars more there than I gave for them.

Do you think of going to Ohio this Spring? I hope you will go. They want to see you very much. Evry letter I get from home they speak of it.

In my letter written a few days ago I told you what officers we had here, the amusements, etc. So I have nothing more on that head. Living here is extravigantly high besides being very poor. Col. Buchanan, the Dr. and myself live together at an expense of about $50 per month including servant hire and washing. Mr. Hunt lives by himself. Give my love to all at home. Write me a great deel about our little boys. Tell me all their pranks. I suppose Ulys. speaks a great many words distinctly? Kiss both of them for me.—I believe I told you that Mrs. Wallen had lost another child. I do not think Wallen will ever raise either of his children. Harry & Nan(n)y are large fat children but they do not look right and they are forever sick. If Wallen was out of the Army and had to pay his Doctor's bill it would amount to about as much as our entire living.—Kiss Fred. and Ulys. for their pa. A great many kisses for you dear wife.

Your affectionate husband
Ulys.

This letter is the most conflict-ridden of any ever written by Ulysses S. Grant. He wants to go home, but fears losing the meager pay he can count upon to send his family.

"Whenever I get to thinking upon the subject...<u>poverty</u>, <u>poverty</u> begins to stare me in the face and then I think what would I do if you and our little ones should want for the necessities of life."

When Ulysses speaks of how Julia could never join him at Fort Humboldt because she could not have a servant, he sounds very hurt. He could not afford the kind of servants to which she is accustomed, and slavery is not allowed in California. This is the real root of the reason why she has not come. The whole tone of his second paragraph sounds very wounded. He admits his pain that she is more attached to her way of life at White Haven, than she is to him.

"I could be contented at Humboldt if it was possible to have you here but it is not. You could not do without a servant and a servant you could not have. This is too bad is it not? But you never complain of being lonesome so I infer that you are quite contented."

Ulysses' dream reveals his fear he has been forgotten by his wife.

"I dreamed of you and our little boys the other night the first time for a long time I thought you were at a party when I arrived and before paying any attention to my arrival you said you must go you were engaged for that dance."

Fort Humboldt
Humboldt Bay, Cal.
March 6th 1854

My Dear Wife;
        I have only had one letter from you in three months and that
had been a long time on the way so you may know how anxious I am
to hear from you. I know there are letters for me in the Post Office
department, someplace, but when shall I get them. I sometimes get
so anxious to see you, and our little boys, that I am tempted to resign
and trust to Providence, and my own exertions, for a living where I
can have you and them with me. It would only require the certainty
of a moderate competency to make me take the step. Whenever I get
to thinking upon the subject however <u>poverty</u>, <u>poverty</u>, begins to stare
me in the face and then I think what would I do if you and our little
ones should want for the necessities of life.
        I could be contented at Humboldt if it was possible to have you
here but it is not. You could not do without a servant and a servant
you could not have. This is to bad is it not? But you never complain
of being lonesome so I infer that you are quite contented. I dreamed
of you and our little boys the other night the first time for a long time
i thought you were at a party when I arrived and before paying any
attention to my arrival you said you must go you were engaged for
that dance. Fred. and Ulys. did not seem half so large as I expected
to see them. If I should see you it would not be as I dreamed, would it
dearest? I know it would not.
        I am geting to be as great a hand for staying in the house now
as I used to be to run about. I have not been a hundred yards from my
door but once in the last two weeks. I get so tired and out of patience
with the loneliness of this place that I feel like volunteering for the
first service that offers. It is likely a party will have to go from here
for Cape Mendeceno in the course of a week and if so I shall try and
make an exkursion out into the mines and in the fall another out on
the immigrant trail. This will help to pass off so much of the time.
        This seems to be a very healthy place; all here are enjoying
excellent health. The post has been occupied now for about fourteen

months, by two Companies, and I believe there has been but two deaths. One by accidentally shooting himself and the other by a limb from a tree falling on a man.

Wallen has made up his mind to resign. Mrs. W. declared she would not go back to Vancouver that if he went he would go without her. W. has gone into the coal business.—Stevens is going ahead at a rapid stride. A recent decission of the Courts in a land case made him one hundred thousand dollars better off than before. Mrs. Stevens and husband intended to have gone home last January but S. could not find time to go. Mrs. S. will soon be confined again. You recollect what she said at Sackets Harbor?

Mr. Hunt has just recently returned from San Francisco. While there he met John looking well.—There is no news here only occationally a disater at sea. A few days since a steamer went down just inside the Columbia river bar; vessel with all aboard except one lost. I am in a great hurry to get this ready for the Mail so I must bid you all good buy for the present. Give my love to your pa, ma, sisters and brother. Kiss our little boys for me. Talk to them a great deel about their pa. A thousand kisses for yourself dearest.

I have some land warrants one of which I want to send you but I am afraid to trust it to the mail. I will send it by the first favorable opportunity. They are worth about $180 00 in N. York; I do not know what you will be able to get in St. Louis.

Adieu dear wife.
Ulys

Ulysses certainly sounded glum, recounting stories of people dying and disasters at sea. His former optimism is gone, and the fact this usually adventurous, energetic man has withdrawn into his room most of the time draws me to the conclusion that he was headed toward a nervous breakdown.

In this next letter, Ulysses has reached the breaking point, missing Julia and yet fearing she does not love him as much as he loves her. He clearly feels abandoned by her, and lashes out at her for neglecting him.

"I cannot believe that you have neglected to write me all this time..."

"Do write me long letters and don't put off writing until just as "Pa" or "Brother Lewis" are just going to town as you nearly always assign as an excuse for cuting your letters short."

"How very anxious I am to get home once again. I do not feel as if it was possible to endure this separation much longer. But how do I know that you are thinking as much of me as I of you? I do not get letters to tell me so."

Fort Humboldt
Humboldt Bay, Cal.
March 25th 1854

I have had just one solitary letter from you since I arrived at this place and that was written about October of last year. I cannot believe that you have neglected to write me all this time but it does seem hard that I should not hear from you. I am afraid too that many of my letters do not reach you. The only way of mailing them is to give them to a Captain of a vessel to put them in the Post Office at San Francisco, which, if he does, they are all safe, but I have no doubt but that many times they never spend a second thought about letters entrusted to them.

April 3d After geting as far as I have done in this letter I was interupted by the entrance of some officers, from continuing for the evning and as the bar at the outlet of the bay was so rough as to prevent vessels from going out for some days I have not taken it up until now. There has been no vessel going out since. The irregularity of mails is an annoyance which can only be appreciated by those who suffer from it. We here however do not suffer from it so much as at two or three stations in this (by government) neglected country. It is very much to be feared that even this last place is to be abandoned for another in the interior where none, or but very poor quarters, will be found. The best we can expect is to go to fort Jones where the buildings were hastily run up by the soldiers. They are just rough log penns, covered over, with places for a door & window but left without these luxuries as well as without floors. Mrs. Collins was there for two or three months where she says she had to live in one of these penns cooking, eating, sleeping and recciving calls from officers, all in but one of these small apartments. Here we are better off having each two comfortable rooms, plastered and with a brick chimney, to each. Mr. Hunt and myself live together and I think will be able to bring our mess bills down to a moderate rate.

How very anxious I am to get home once again. I do not feel as if it was possible to endure this separation much longer. But how do I know that you are thinking as much of me as I of you? I do not get letters to tell me so. But you write I am certain and some day I will get a big batch all at once. Just think; by the time you recieve this Ulys. will be nearly two years old and no doubt talking as plainly as Fred. did his few words when I saw him last. Dear little boys what a comfort it would be to see and play with them a few hours evry day! I like to have you write me a great deel about them. Do write me long letters and don't put off writing until just as "Pa" or "Brother Lewis" are just going to town as you nearly always assign as an excuse for cuting your letters short. You told me to direct your letters to Sappington Post Office: why cant you finish those for me and mail at the same office? I have been wanting to send you a land warrant for some time as the best means of transmitting money; but I am afraid to entrust one to the Mail. As soon as the Pay Master makes his appearance however I will see if I cannot get a check on the east to send you.

Evrything to see or write about at Humboldt Bay can be taken in at a glance. I have not been a quarter of a mile from my room for about one week, and I am in excellent health too. Except an occational ride of a few miles on horseback none of us go out at present, this not being game season.

Do you ever hear anything from Ohio? I have not had a letter from there written since last October.

I am enjoying good health but growing more lazy evry day for want of something to do. When the mountain streams dry up a little more however I will find something to do for if we do not move to the interior I, at least, have to go there with a party of men which will take one month. This will be clear gain.

Give my love to all at your house. Kiss our dear little boys for their pa who thinks so much about them. I have to close dear julia for want of something more to write about. A thousand kisses for you dear wife. Write to me soon and tell me all about evry body at home.

> *Your affectionate husband*
> *Ulys.*

In the last part of this letter, it is important to note Ulysses' mention of the upcoming arrival of the Pay Master. Why? Because it was while Ulysses was handing out pay at the pay table, that he was found to be under the influence of alcohol, which led to his resignation from the Army. This has been a point of much debate, but his anticipation of the Pay Master's arrival certainly supports the story.

"As soon as the Pay Master makes his appearance...I will see if I cannot get a check on the east to send you."

Back in Sacket's Harbor, the Sons of Temperance were missing Ulysses. No one else gave energy to their cause the way he did. Without his leadership, the Sons of Temperance fell into disrepair and decay, and finally closed down altogether.

Sadly, the same thing was happening to Ulysses.

"Without the warm presence of his family," writes Lloyd Lewis, "The Son of Temperance broke his fraternal vows."

Fort Humboldt, Cal.
April 11th 1854

Col.

I have the honor to acknowledge the receipt of my Commission as Captain in the 4th Infantry and my acceptance of the same.

I am Col.
Very Respectfully
Your Obt. Svt.
U.S. Grant
Capt. 4th Inf.y

To Col. S. Cooper
Adj. Gen. U.S.A.
Washington, D.C.

Fort Humboldt,
Humboldt Bay, Cal.
April 11th 1854

Col:

I very respectfully tender my resignation of my commission as an officer of the Army, and request that it may take effect from the 31st July next.

I am Col.
Very Respectfully
Your Obt. Svt.
U.S. Grant
Capt. 4th Inf.y

To Col. S. Cooper
Adj. Gen. U.S.A.
Washington D.C.

Endorsements read:

Respectfully forwarded, with the recommendation that it be accepted.

> Robt. C. Buchanan
> Bvt. Lt. Col. Capt. 4th Inf Commdg

>> Head Quarters, Detacht 4th Inf
>> Fort Humboldt, Cal. Apl 11th 1854

*Hd. Qrs. Dept. Of the Pacific
San Francisco, April 22/54*

Approved and respectfully forwarded.

> John E. Wool
> Major General

*Head Qrs. of the Army N.Y. 26. May 1854
Respectfully forwarded By command of Maj. Gen. Scott.*

> Irvin McDowell
> Asst. Adjt. Genl.

It is respectfully recommended that Capt. Grant's resignation be accepted, to take effect as tendered July 31, 1854. The enclosed paper, dated May 29th, shows the state of Capt. G's accounts with the Treasury.

A.G. Office   *S. Cooper*
May 30/54   *Adj. Genl.*

Accepted as tendered.

> Jeffn Davis
> Sec. Of War

To 1st Lt. Joseph B. Collins
Post Adj.t

Fort Humboldt,
Humboldt Bay, Cal.
April 11th 1854.

Sir:
I would respectfully request a leave of absence for <u>sixty</u> <u>days</u> with permission to apply for an extension until the 31st of July, 1854 at which date I have requested my resignation as an officer of the Army to take effect.

I am Sir
Very Respectfully
Your Obt. Svt.
U.S. Grant
Capt. 4th Infy

There has been much debate about U.S. Grant's resignation from the Army. Theories range from one extreme to another, from being a completely innocent decision, to being asked to resign or face a court martial. The two most touching, informative quotes I found were from Ulysses' friends at this time, then young Lieutenant Henry Hodges and Captain Rufe Ingalls.

According to Lieutenant Hodges: "It seems that one day while his company was being paid off, Captain Grant was at the pay table, slightly under the influence of liquor. This came to the knowledge of Colonel Buchanan; he gave Grant the option of resigning or having charges preferred against him. Grant resigned at once. In my opinion the regiment always thought Col. Buchanan was unnecessarily harsh and severe—he knew that Grant was liked and highly respected in the regiment and it seemed as though he might have overlooked this first small offense at his (Buchanan's) post."

Rufus Ingalls, who was a close friend of Ulysses from West Point all the way to Appomattox, later described the sad scene:

"Grant, finding himself in dreary surroundings, without his family, and with but little to occupy his attention, fell into dissipated habits, and was found, one day, too much under the influence of liquor to properly perform his duties. For this offense Colonel Buchanan demanded that he should resign, or stand trial. Grant's friends at the time urged him to stand trial, and were confident of his acquittal; but, actuated by a noble spirit, he said he would not for all the world have his wife know that he had been tried on such a charge. He therefore resigned his commission, and returned to civil life."

Reading this account makes me want to cry! Poor Ulysses, always thinking of his wife.

In studying his own letters, I believe that Ulysses resigned abruptly because of the ultimatum given by Buchanan regarding his drinking for this reason: Ulysses did not communicate with Julia on the matter. He was always so open with her, he surely would have written to her about what he was thinking and planning, after spending two years away from her, and communicating to her all his ideas about how to reunite with her. He never consults her or communicates with her, just the terse letter after the fact, where he sounds defensive about his resignation, almost mocking himself with the way he refers to his "leave of absence" in quotes, as if it is not really a normal leave of absence. In his letters from Mexico, he never put the quotes around that term: leave of absence. When he does so now, he makes a mockery of the term, in his dry, understated way. His attitude is defensive and hurt. He seems unsure of her response. In her own memoirs, Julia reveals that after returning home, Ulysses turned to her and said, "You know I couldn't leave New York until I heard from you." Also, if he had been letting her know he was going to resign so they could be reunited, his letter now would have a joyful tone to it, anticipating a reunion at last. Instead, it has a sad, defensive tone, not joyful at all. And so tight-lipped and uncommunicative about something he's been hoping for for so long. What should have been a happy occasion for him, does not sound like a happy occasion at all. Why? Because it was forced on him under shameful, embarrassing, unhappy circumstances. He also clearly fears a reproach from her over the whole affair, or it would have had the tone of: "My dearest Julia, I am coming home to you!" He gives no explanation of the most important decision of his whole two years away, yet he went into great detail about all his other ideas: pigs, timber, potatoes, etc... To give no explanation or communication on such an important subject, with such enormous ramifications for them both, is suspicious. The decision to resign was made under duress and he does not want to talk about it. Something has hurt him terribly.

It's possible he feels so abandoned by her, so hurt, due to her lack of letters, that he feels he owes her no explanation for his resigning. But there is a tone of hurt pride in the letter too intense— there is something hanging in the air which he is not talking about.

There is no discussion of how he arrived at this decision, and no sense of joy that they will soon be reunited. The tone is defensive, hurt, grim, ashamed, self mocking on the mention of a "leave of absence." Unsure of her response. He never refers to his drinking in writing, which was wise. It left historians to ponder over it for all eternity. As well, it was reported that he said he wouldn't, for all the world, let his wife know he was brought up on such a charge, (drinking) so of course, he wouldn't bring it up to her. Never-the-less, there is a tone that expresses his fear she may have heard about it anyway, and he fears she may be ashamed of him and he may be unwelcome back home.

Fort Humboldt
May 2d 1854

Dear Wife;
I do not propose writing you but a few lines. I have not yet recieved a letter from you and as I have a "leave of absence" and will be away from here in a few days do not expect to. After recieving this you may discontinue writing because before I could get a reply I shall be on my way home. You might write directing to the City of New York.
It will require my presence in Calafornia for some four or six weeks to make all arrangements, public & private, before starting. I may have to go to Oregon before leaving; I will not go however unless I get an order to cover my transportation. On my way I shall spend a

week or ten days with John Dent.—My love to all at home. Kiss our little boys for their pa. love to you dear Julia.

Your affectionate husbd.
Ulys.

Captain U.S. Grant was relieved of command on May 1.

I just noticed, though he resigned on April 11, Ulysses wrote to Julia the day *after* he was relieved of his command. Only after his resignation had been accepted, did he face the sad task of communicating with her what he had done. He faced the whole situation alone, without including her in his thought process at all. How lonely for him.

Hearing of his son's resignation, Ulysses' father was so upset, he wrote to the Secretary of War, and tried frantically to undo it. On June 21, 1854, Jesse Grant desperately wrote the following letter:

"Your letter of the 7th inst announcing the acceptance of the resignation of my son Capt U.S. Grant, was recd a few days ago through Hon. A. Ellison. That was the first intimation I had of his intention to resign If it is consistant with your powers & the good of the servis I would be much gratifyed if you would reconsider & withdraw the acceptance of his resignation—and grant him a six months leave, that he may come home & see his family.

I never wished him to leave the servis. I think after spending so much time to qualify himself for the Army & spending so many years in the servis, he will be poorly qualifyed for the pursuits of privet life.

He has been eleven years an officer, was in all the battles of Gen Taylor & Scott except Buenavista, never absent from his post during the Mexican war, & has never had a leave of six months— Would it then be asking too much for him, to have such a leave, that he may come home & make arrangements for taking his family with him to his post

I will remark that he has not seen his family for over two years, & has a son nearly two years old he has never seen. I suppose in his great anxiety to see his family he has been induced to quit the servis.

    Please write me & let me know the results of this request.

Jefferson Davis sent Jesse a heartbreaking, and swift reply:

Washington, June 28, 1854

Sir. In reply to your letter of the 21 instant asking that the acceptance of the resignation of your son, Captain U.S. Grant may be withdrawn and he be allowed six months leave of absence, I have to inform you that Captain Grant tendered his resignation but assigned no reasons why he desired to quit the service and the motives which influenced him are not known to the Department. He only asked that his resignation should take affect on the 31st July next and it was accepted accordingly on the 2nd instant and the same day announced to the army. The acceptance is therefore complete and cannot be reconsidered.

               Very Respectfully,
               Yr. Obt. Svt.
               Jeffn Davis
               Secretary of War

Ulysses was given $250 in back pay, which he received in the form of ten gold coins. On his voyage home across the Isthmus, he gave most of the coins away to travelers in trouble, who touched him with their sad stories. By the time he reached New York City, Ulysses' money was almost gone, and he had no way to get home to St. Louis.

One of Ulysses' Southern pals from West Point, Simon Bolivar Buckner, was stationed on Governor's Island. The Kentucky born gentleman later told of how Ulysses came to see him, downcast and penniless, and had asked his old friend to pay his hotel bill until Ulysses' father could send money from Ohio. The manager of the Astor House Hotel in New York was fed up with Ulysses' inability to pay. Rather than give his friend cash, which always had a way of slipping through Ulysses' fingers, Buckner guaranteed his bills at the Astor House hotel and "took charge" of the down and out Captain Grant, possibly letting him sleep on Governor's Island, until his father's help arrived.

Jesse Grant finally sent his errant son the money to come home. Ulysses thanked Buckner, who had been an angel. Standing on the grounds of Governor's Island, Captain Buckner watched Ulysses go, and silently wished him well.

Ulysses' ordeal on the Pacific Coast began and ended on Governor's Island.

CHAPTER NINETEEN
Going Home

Julia did not know the day or the hour her beloved one would return. She kept trying to pretty herself up in anticipation of that moment. It had been two years. Would he still think her beautiful? Would the same magic transpire between them?

In late August of 1854, Ulysses was on his way to White Haven in a horse drawn buggy. Every clop of the horse's hooves brought his tired body and sagging spirit closer to his love.

At last, Ulysses reached the rolling hills of White Haven, splashed with the golden hues of summer. The bridle path lay open before him as it had the first time he arrived there, ten years before.

But oh, how different this was from his first arrival at White Haven! Then, he had been the handsome young soldier, "as pretty as a little doll," the "little prince" come to conquer the hearts of all the ladies fair.

Now he was the vanquished. A broken soul, no longer "pretty," no longer a soldier, his handsome face worn from suffering, his graceful body dissipated from too much liquor and lonely nights. In the eyes of the world, he was a failure.

He paused at the entrance to White Haven, wondering how he would be received. Then, mustering up his courage, Ulysses rode on up to the house.

One of the Dents' slaves saw him first.

"For the Lord's sake!" she cried. "Here is Marss Grant!"

Starved for affection, the broken Ulysses fell into Julia's arms.

Julia's two sisters, Emmy and Nelly, had been jealous when Ulysses married Julia. Seeing him now, a shell of a man, they were relieved he had not turned his haunting eyes in their direction.

But Julia welcomed him as before, just like she did the first time they met. In her arms, the sufferings and disappointments of the last two years fell away like fragile flower petals.

Welcome, always welcome.

Just as she made him feel welcome in her parlor in their early courting days, so she welcomed him now, softly closing the door behind them on the stares and whispers of the outside world.

Julia's Southern hospitality was the same as if Ulysses had returned a general. He remembered with pleasure why he loved her so much.

Ulysses' boys had been frightened when they first saw him, a shabby, bearded stranger dragging himself up to their pristine front porch. But once they realized he was their "Pa," they soon warmed up to him.

Julia later recalled, "We wanted for no other happiness."

With the soothing nourishment of Julia's love and care, Ulysses began to recuperate.

They spent the last lazy days of the fading summer billing and cooing around White Haven. Julia became pregnant right away. It was like their honeymoon all over again. Only this time, Colonel Dent was there.

While Ulysses' health was improving, Colonel Dent's dream was crumbling. Their fortunes always seemed to be at odds.

The Colonel's dream of Southern aristocracy did not include an unemployed son-in-law who had allegedly been kicked out of the Army.

Colonel Dent, the pillar of Gravois society, knew his neighbors were whispering. And it mortified him.

It was bad enough when his princess moved out and married a Yankee. Now, that Yankee was living right under his roof, sleeping late, spoiling the Colonel's grandsons and smooching his favorite daughter right in front of him. It was intolerable.

Ulysses wanted to work. He offered to help Colonel Dent with the work around White Haven, but Colonel Dent refused. There were slaves for such labor.

And so, Ulysses S. Grant, West Point graduate, Mexican War hero, took to chopping wood and selling it on street corners.

Wearing his fading old Army jacket and a slouchy, battered hat, he sold cord wood to Colonel Dent's neighbors. This caused a new round of gossip, especially because Ulysses allegedly "slept in" and got a later start than the other wood peddlers. This only fanned the fires of the gossip surrounding Julia's husband, that he was a lowlife and a loser.

Ulysses was never bothered about the neighbors' gossip. "I gained my sleep, and lost nothing in the price," he quietly explained. "They lost their sleep and gained nothing in the price."

Still, Ulysses' downtrodden appearance gave the whole county something to snicker about.

Julia's brothers and sisters had married much better than she did. Her brothers had married Southern socialites. Nelly was married to a successful doctor. And Julia, the belle of White Haven, was married to a disgraced firewood salesman. How awful for her, the neighbors whispered, though Julia's husband certainly worked hard.

Despite what anyone else thought of her husband, Julia always treated him like a king. When he returned at night from selling firewood, she greeted him with a hug and a kiss. And he treated her so tenderly, his devotion to Julia was remembered by every witness to those difficult days, friends and enemies alike.

Nourished and strengthened by Julia's love, Ulysses now felt strong enough to move on. She had helped him gather up the tatters of his dignity to begin a new life.

Ulysses decided they would move out of White Haven. He would build them their own home, with his own hands.

Their new baby was due soon. The baby's proud "Pa" wanted his family to have a home of their own. He set to work with courage and determination, clearing trees and preparing the timber.

This was a new test for the pampered Julia. The easy life of White Haven suited her just fine. But her husband had a stubborn independent streak. He wanted them to have something of their own. As she watched her obstinate husband digging in the dirt, her belly growing bigger with his child, Julia couldn't help feeling pangs of uncertainty about their future.

Julia and Ulysses' baby was born into poverty on the Fourth of July. It was their first and only daughter, who they named Ellen (Nelly) after Julia's mother. Julia and Ulysses were now occupying her brother's house, an "elegant villa," as Julia described it, known as "Wish-ton-wish." Julia would have liked to stay there, but her husband was determined to have his own place.

When the house was finished and the Grants moved in, Julia recalled: "I did not like it at all." She and Ulysses referred to the rough hewn log cabin as, "Hardscrabble."

Did Julia ever regret marrying Ulysses? She never showed it. But she must have done a lot of soul searching. Had her Papa been right about Ulysses?

Once, Colonel Dent visited their new home, and Julia tried hard to put on a good front for him. As Colonel Dent rode up to Hardscrabble on horseback, Julia was holding up a jar of homemade jelly.

"How is my Queen bee, today?" her Papa called.

Julia answered cheerfully, "The Queen bee is gathering honey for her hive!"

"The Queen bee doesn't gather honey," Colonel Dent cruelly snapped, inferring that Julia no longer lived like a Queen.

This hurt Julia terribly. She was her father's favorite, and now he was, in so many words, accusing her of being "poor white trash."

Lying awake in their bed at night, in their "crude, rough house," with no prospects ahead, it would have been natural to think back about the life of ease she abandoned to follow her heart. She probably choked back tears so her exhausted, sleeping husband couldn't hear.

Ulysses worked as hard as he could to make it as a farmer. But it was brutal, having not a cent to his name upon his inglorious homecoming from California. In a series of painful letters, Ulysses asked his penny-pinching father for help.

His father's help was not forthcoming. For Jesse Grant, the perceived failure of his son Ulysses was a source of great shame. Following the Mexican War, Jesse Grant had been in braggadocio heaven, stopping people on street corners to boast about "my Ulysses." Now, with the rumor spreading that Ulysses had been forced to resign from the Army in disgrace, the bright, shining pedestal on which Jesse Grant had set his son came crashing down about his ears.

Jesse was so humiliated, he actually moved to another town to avoid the mocking, knowing smirks of the neighbors. In Jesse's mind, he had done all he could for his son: sent him to the best private elementary schools, got him the appointment at West Point, exalted him as a war hero when he came home. And now, his favorite son had let him down.

Jesse Grant complained to the neighbors: "I'll have to remake Ulysses all over again." But a neighbor also keenly observed: "U.S. is the only one with any soul."

Jesse had recently opened a new leather store, in the bustling, lead-mining town of Galena, Illinois.

Shortly after his return home, Ulysses got his courage up to visit his father and ask for help in person, in the form of a job. He brought Julia with him. But Jesse replied that the only way he would give his son a job, would be if he left his wife and family down South, at White Haven, and moved north, to Galena—by himself. This rejection of all he held dear stung Ulysses to the core.

There was no way Ulysses would separate himself from Julia again, even to feed his family. Hurt and indignant, the disgraced soldier accompanied his wife back to Missouri.

Julia suffered greatly, seeing her Ulysses suffer. She alone seemed to see his true inner value.

As a couple, Julia and Ulysses tried to stay optimistic. This is revealed in Ulysses many letters to his father, trying in vain to cover his inner desperation with an outward layer of cheer, with cheerful statements such as, "I like farming more and more."

It is poignant to note that though physically and financially these times were much harder on Ulysses than his days in California, yet now there is a tone of hopefulness, because Julia is by his side.

Though he was well-fed in California, the work was light and his pay check assured, his letters are gut-wrenchingly sad and gloomy. In the Hardscrabble days, though he is frowned down upon, breaking his neck, stricken with malaria, with the wolf at the door, his letters are much more upbeat. Even when he writes of them both being ill, there is a note of contentment when he mentions Julia. If she is near, he feels whole and at peace.

Following are some heart-rending letters from Ulysses during his days of struggle. Most of them are to his father. I include these letters because reading them, just made me love Ulysses all the more.

Ulysses sounds like his old, optimistic self again, because he is back with Julia. However, you can practically feel his father's skepticism as he reads this letter from his fallen son. He must remember Ulysses' optimism about all his failed business ventures in California, all of which struck the same positive tone—just before they spiraled into disaster.

"Evry day I like farming better and I do not doubt that money is to be made at it."

Ulysses subtly indicates his father's help would have made a big difference. But his father did not help.

"This year if I could have bought seed I should have made out still better than I did. I wanted to plant sixty or seventy bushels of potatoes but had not the money to buy them."

Ulysses continues to figure and to plan, listing amounts of vegetables he hopes to plant. His hopefulness is heartbreaking. Then he gets to the real point of the letter, which I am sure was excruciating for him to write:

"If I had an opportunity of getting about $500 for a year at 10 pr. cent I have no doubt but it would be of great advantage to me."

Ulysses' relatives, including his own sister, are avoiding him.

"Mary makes no acknowledgement of having recieved a letter from me!"

Sappington P.O.
St. Louis Co. Mo.
December 28th 1856.

Dear Father:
Your's & Mary's letter inclosing Land Warrant was recieved a few days since.
Evry day I like farming better and I do not doubt that money is to be made at it. So far I have been laboring under great disadvantages but now that I am on my own place, and shall not have to build next summer I think I shall be able to do much better. This year if I could have bought seed I should have made out still better than I did. I wanted to plant sixty or seventy bushels of potatoes, but I had not the money to buy them. I planted twenty however and have sold 225 bushels and have about 125 on hand, besides all that I have used. Next summer I shall plant what is left of them and buy about fifty bushels of choise seed besides. I have in some twenty five acres of what that looks better, or did before the cold weather, than any in the neighborhood. My intention is to raise about twenty acres of Irish potatoes, on new ground, five acres of sweet potatoes, about the same of early corn, five or six acres cabbage, beets, cucumber pickles & mellons and keep a wagon going to market evry day. This last year my place was not half tended because I had but one span of horses, and one hand, and we had to do all the work on the place, living at a distance too, all the hawling for my building, and take wood to the city for the support of the family. Since the 1st of April my teams have earned me about fifty dollars per month independent of doing my own work. This year I presume I shall be compelled to neglect my farm some to make a living in the mean time, but by next year I hope to be independent. If I had an opportunity of geting about $500 for a year at 10 pr. cent I have no doubt but it would be of great advantage to me.

Julia and the children are all very well. Mrs. Dent has been at the point of death for the last two weeks, but is now much better and will recover.

Mary makes no acknowledgement of having recieved a letter from me! Did she not get an answer to hers written shortly after you were here? I wrote in answer.

Some three weeks since I went into the Planter's House and saw registered "J.R. Grant, Ky." on the book. Making enquiry I found that J.R.G. had just taking the Pacific R.R. cars. I made shure it was you and that I should find you when I got home. Was it you?

Remember me to all at home. Tell Molly to write to me again. Write soon.

Yours Truly
U.S. Grant

To J. R. Grant, Esq.
Covington Ky.

P.S. In view of the Land Warrant having to go to such a distance, and likely, after reaching Washington Territory being obliged to pass through the hands of so many strangers, I have filled the assignment to J.R. Grant. It will be better for you to assign it again than that it should be endangered.

U.S.G.

In this heartbreaking letter, Ulysses makes "the last appeal" to his father for help, indicating all of his other appeals have been rejected.

"It is always usual for parents to give their children assistince in begining life (and I am only begining though thirty-five years of age, nearly) and what I ask is not much."

This personalization of Ulysses' struggle touched my heart. It also points out how the once pampered Julia is now living a Spartan life.

"My expenses for my family have been nothing scarsely for the last two years. Fifty dollars, I believe, would pay all that I have laid out for their clothing."

I read and re-read this next line, trying to understand it, and finally realized what Ulysses meant when he wrote:

"I have worked hard and got but little and expect to go on in the same way until I am perfectly independent; and then too most likely."

I think it means Ulysses expects to "work hard and get but little" for the rest of his life.

Sappington P.O.
St. Louis Co. Mo.
Feb.y 7th 1857.

Dear Father;

    Spring is now approaching when farmers require not only to till the soil, but to have the wherewith to till it, and to seed it. For two years I have been compelled to farm without either of these facilities, confining my attention therefore principally to oats and corn; two crops which can never pay; for if they bear a high price it is because the farmer has raised scarsely enough for his own use. If they abundent they will scarsely bear transportation. I want to vary the crop a little and also to have implements to cultivate with. To this end I am going to make the last appeal to you. I do this because, when I was in Ky. you voluntarily offered to give me a Thousand dollars, to commence with, and because there is no one els to whom I could, with the same propriety, apply. It is always usual for parents to give their children assistince in begining life (and I am only begining, though thirty-five years of age, nearly) and what I ask is not much. I do not ask you to give me anything. But what I do ask is that you lend, or borrow for, me Five hundred dollars, for two years, with interest at 10 pr. cent payable anually, or semmi anually if you choose, and with this if I do not go on prosperously I shall ask no more from you. With this sum I can go on and cultivate my ground for marketing and raise no more grain than is necessary for my own use. I have now in the ground twenty five acres of wheat with the view of geting in that much meadow; but this ground I shall not probably have for another year as it is not on my part of the place, and is for sale. I am geting some ten or twelve acres more cleared this winter which will turn off about 300 cords of wood that will be valuable next summer and winter; but the choping has to be paid for now.

    The fact is, without means, it is useless for me to go on farming, and I will have to do what Mr. Dent has given me permission to do; sell the farm and invest elswhere. For two years now I have been compelled to neglect my farm to go off and make a few dollars to buy little necessities, sugar, coffee, &c. or pay hired men. As a proof of this I will state that since the 2d day of April last I have kept a strict account of evry load of wood taken to the City, or Coal Banks, by my team and it has amounted, up to Ja.y 1st, to a fraction over 48 dollars per month. Now do not understand from this that if I had what I ask for my exertions wood sease; but that they would be directed to a more profitable end. I regard evry load of wood taken, when the services of both myself and team are required on the farm, is a direct loss of more than the value of the load.

My expenses for my family have been nothing scaresly for the last two years. Fifty dollars, I believe, would pay all that I have laid out for their clothing. I have worked hard and got but little and expect to go on in the same way until I am perfectly independent; and then too most likely.

All of Mr. Dent's family, now here, and Julia are suffering from unusual colds. Dr. Sharp has purchased a house in Lincoln Co. this State and will move their soon; was to have gone several days ago, in fact, but recieving a Telegraphic Dispach a few days ago that his father was very low he started immediately home, taking his wife and child with him.—Mrs. Dent died on the 14th of Jan.y after an illness of about a month. That leaves Mr. Dent, and one daughter, alone.

Julia wishes to be remembered. Please answer soon.

Yours Truly
U.S. Grant.

As Ulysses continues to struggle, Julia keeps on loving him, and soon, is "in the family way" again.

Ulysses writes to his sister. He tries to strike an optimistic tone, but this line reveals he's in the middle of his losing streak.

"My wheat which would have produced from four to five hundred bushels with a good winter, has yielded only seventy-five."

Julia's life is very confined, tied to her obstinate husband's attempts to be a dirt farmer.

"She has never been ten miles from home, except to come to the city, since her visit to Covington."

I just realized, this letter was written on Julia and Ulysses' wedding anniversary! They would have been married for nine years. They had three children, a fourth baby on the way, over two years of separation, and years of poverty and struggle—and happiness.

St. Louis, Mo.
August 22nd, 1857.

Dear Sister:
Your letter was received on last Tuesday, the only day in the week on which we get mail, and this is the earliest opportunity I have had of posting a letter.
I am glad to hear that mother and Jennie intend making us a visit. I would advise them to come by the river if they prefer it. Write to me beforehand about the time you will start, and from Louisville again, what boat you will be on, direct to St. Louis,—not Sappington, P.O.— and I will meet you at the river or Planter's House, or wherever you direct.

We are all very well. Julia contemplates visiting St. Charles next Saturday to spend a few days. She has never been ten miles from home, except to come to the city, since her visit to Covington.

I have nothing in particular to write about. My hard work is now over for the season with the fair prospect of being remunerated in everything but the wheat. My wheat, which would have produced from four to five hundred bushels with a good winter, has yielded only seventy-five. My oats were good, and the corn, if not injured by frost this fall, will be the best I ever raised. My potato crop bids fair to yield fifteen hundred bushels or more. Sweet potatoes, melons and cabbages are the only other articles I am raising for market. In fact, the oats and corn I shall not sell.

I see I have written a part of this letter as if I intended to direct to one, and part as if to the other of you; but you will understand it, so it makes no difference.

Write to me soon and often. Julia wears black. I had forgotten to answer this part of your letter.

> *Your affectionate Brother,*
> *Ulyss.*

P.S. Tell father that I have this moment seen Mr. Ford, just from Sacketts Harbor, who informs me that while there he enquired of Mr. Bagley about my business with Camp, and learns Camp is now at Governor's Island, N.Y., and intends sailing soon for Oregon. If he is stopped he may be induced to disgorge. Tell father to forward the account immediately.

Julia's last visit away from home, to Covington, Kentucky, was probably three years ago, when she and Ulysses visited his father, to plead with him for a job. This was in 1854. So, she had not been ten miles from home in about three years.

Christmas is often a time to sit back in the secure comforts of one's home, to reflect on the good fortunes of the past year and enjoy its bounty, to look ahead to the future with hope of more good times to come. For Ulysses S. Grant, the Christmas of 1857 provided neither. Looking back at the past was painful, looking ahead, even more frightening.

Poverty-stricken, with a new baby on the way, Ulysses was forced to pawn one of his few possessions remaining, a gold pocket watch, to buy Christmas presents for his family. With his pregnant wife's due-date fast arriving, Ulysses wanted Julia to have a happy Christmas.

The pawn broker never revealed the pawn ticket of his famous customer, until after Ulysses became president. The pawn broker was hesitant to go public with the pawn ticket for fear of offending the Grants, revealing one of Ulysses' lowest moments. In fact, it was one of his finest moments. Nothing could reveal so poignantly his tender feelings for his family.

It is so sad! This pawn ticket of Ulysses is dated December 23, two days before Christmas. The pawnbroker's son, who sold this ticket after Ulysses won the Civil War, fears it might shame Ulysses' family. On the contrary, it shows his soft heart. It is also poignant to see Ulysses only gets one month to try to come up with the money to buy his watch back. I wonder if he did?

PAWN TICKET

St. Louis, Dec 23rd 1857

I THIS DAY CONSIGN TO J.S. FRELIGH, AT MY OWN RISK FROM LOSS OR DAMAGE BY THIEVES OR FIRE, TO SELL ON COMMISSION, PRICE NOT LIMITED, 1 GOLD HUNTING (WATCH) DETACHED LEVER & GOLD CHAIN ON WHICH SAID FRELIGH HAS ADVANCED TWENTY TWO DOLLARS. AND I HEREBY FULLY AUTHORIZE AND EMPOWER SAID FRELIGH TO SELL AT PUBLIC OR PRIVATE SALE THE ABOVE MENTIONED PROPERTY TO PAY SAID ADVANCE—IF THE SAME IS NOT PAID TO SAID FRELIGH, OR THESE CONDITIONS RENEWED BY PAYING CHARGES, ON OR BEFORE JAN/58

U.S. Grant

Their new baby, Jesse Root Grant, was born at Hardscrabble on February 6, 1858. It must have been a rough time for Julia, suffering through childbirth in a "crude shack" she felt wasn't good enough for her. But Ulysses was there to hold her hand. It would have been easy for her to feel this was all his fault. But she loved him so much, she couldn't help but feel happy whenever he was near.

Though his home life with Julia was happy, the pressures of poverty weighed increasingly heavy on Ulysses. With four little ones to feed, he was becoming more and more anxious. Friends saw him on the street, and saw in his eyes the look of a hunted animal.

James Longstreet made a brief stop at the Planters Hotel, the inn where Ulysses was a guest on his wedding day, although he spent the whole day with Julia. Longstreet, who was Ulysses' best man, was still an officer in the army, and dressed in a spiffy new uniform. When he met the disheveled Ulysses on the street, dressed in a faded army jacket and broken old slouch hat, Longstreet's heart went out to him.

Longstreet and other officer pals of Ulysses invited their down and out friend to join them for a game of "brag." It was clear that Ulysses had nothing to brag about, now.

He refused alcohol and only drank water, but they all knew about his resignation from the army, and the bad luck which dogged him. One look at his tired, worried face told the story.

Ulysses had reached his lowest point. Pitied by his friends, despised by everyone in his family except Julia, one can imagine his old pal Longstreet may have let his old friend win a hand, out of kindness.

The next day, Ulysses approached Longstreet, again. Ulysses had a gold piece which he pressed into Longstreet's hand, repayment of a long ago debt, in the army. Longstreet at first refused to take it, but Ulysses pleaded, "Please take it. I cannot bear to live with anything that is not mine."

Seeing the pain in Ulysses' face, Longstreet accepted the gold piece, to save him further humiliation.

Ulysses and his old friend parted. Longstreet probably wondered what would become of Ulysses? They did not meet again, until the surrender at Appomattox.

In this letter to his sister, the struggling Ulysses, though only thirty-six years of age, is so discouraged and worn out, he feels at the end of his life—not knowing, it was only the beginning.

"I am anxious to make one more visit home before I get old."

Toward the end of this letter, Ulysses refers to having a debt with payment due, which he doesn't see how he will pay. He works hard, but is forever in debt and can't seem to get his head above water. Still, he does not complain but just keeps working as hard as he can. The fact that Julia is near keeps him going and trying his hardest. I find his positive attitude inspiring. I wonder how Julia felt? Surely, his hard work touched her heart. But it must have been depressing to see him work so hard and fail so continuously. Their love was the light that warmed them both and kept them alive.

White Haven
March 21st 1858

Dear Sister;

Your letter was recieved one week ago last Tuesday and I would have answered it by the next Mail but it so happened that there was not a sheet of paper about the house, and as Spring has now set in I do not leave the farm except in cases of urgent necessity. Fathers letter, enclosing Mr. Bagley's, relative to the Camp business, was recieved one or two weeks earlyer, and promptly answered. My replay was long, giving a detailed account of my whole transaction with Camp, and a copy of which father can have to peruse when he comes along this way next.

Julia and the children are all well and talk some of making you a visit next Fall, but I hardly think they will go. But if any of you, except father, should visit us this Spring, or early Summer, Julia says that Fred. may go home with you to spend a few months. She says she would be afraid to let him travel with father alone for she has an idea that he is so absent minded that if he was to arrive at Cincinati at night he would be just as apt to walk out of the cars and be gone for an hour befor he would recollect that he had a child with him as not. I have no such fears however. Fred. does not read yet but he will, I think, in a few weeks. We have no school within a mile & a half and that is to far to send him in the winter season. I shall commence sending him soon however. In the mean time I have no doubt but he is learning faster at home. Little Ellen is growing very fast and talks now quite plainly. Jesse R. is growing very rapidly, is very healthy and they say, is the best looking child among the four. I dont think however there is much difference, in that respect, between them.

Emma Dent is talking of visiting her relations in Ohio and Penna. this Summer, and if she does she will stop a time with you. Any talk of any of us visiting you must not stop you from coming to see us. The whole family here are great for planning visits but poor in the execution of their plans. It may take two seasons yet before any of these visits are made, and in the mean time we are anxious to see all of you. For my part I do not know when I shall ever be able to leave home long enough for a visit. I may possibly be able to go on a flying visit next fall. I am anxious to make one more visit home before I get old.

This Spring has opened finely for farming and I hope to do well but I shall wait until the crops are gathered before I make any predictions. I have now three negro men, two hired by the year and one of Mr. Dents, which, with my own help, I think, will enable me to do my farming pretty well, with assistance in harvest. I have however a large farm. I shall have about 20 acres of potatoes, 20 of corn 25 of oats 50 of wheat, 25 of meadow, some clover, Hungarian grass and other smaller products all of which require labor before they are got into market, and the money realized upon them. You are aware, I believe, that I have rented out my place and have taken Mr. Dents. There is about 200 acres of ploughed land on it and I shall have, in a few weeks, about 250 acres of woods pasture fenced up besides. Only one side of it and a part of another has to be fenced to take the whole of it in and the rails are all ready. I must close with the wish that some of you would visit us as early as possible. In your letter you ask when my note in Bank becomes due! The 17th of Apl. is the last day of grace when it must be paid and I dont see now that I shall have the money.

Give Julia's, the children's & my love to all at home and write soon.

Your Brother
Ulysses.

In the previous letter, Ulysses mentions William for the first time. William is the slave given to Ulysses by Colonel Dent, presumably, to turn Ulysses into a slave owner.

Typhoid strikes Ulysses' family. Their son, Frederick almost dies, and Ulysses and Julia both fall ill. Yet, to me, Ulysses still sounds happier than when he was in California. It is because Julia is beside him. And even though they are both sick, his heart is still content. I can feel that he just loves to say, "Julia and I."

"Julia and I are both sick with chills and fever."

Ulysses is funny. He describes rampant illness in his house, then implores his sister:

"Can't some of you come and pay us a visit?"

One can almost hear her say, "Uhhhhh—maybe some other time!"

St. Louis, Mo.
Sept. 7th 1858.

Dear Sister;
Your letter was recieved in due time and I would have answered it immediately but that I had mailed a letter from Julia to Jennie the morning of the receipt of yours. I thought then to wait for two or three weeks and by that time there was so much sickness in my family, and Freddy so dangerously ill, that I thought I would not write until his fate was decided. He come near to being taken from us by the Billious, then Typhoid, fever, but he is now convelescing. Some seven of the negroes have been sick. Mrs. Sharp is here on a visit and she and one of her childre(en) are sick, and Julia and I are both sick with chills and fever. If I had written to you earlier it would have been whilst Fred's case was a doubtful one and I did not want to distress you when it could have done no good to any one.—I

have been thinking of paying you a visit this fall but I now think it extremely doubtful whether I shall be able to. Not being able to even attend to my hands, much less work myself, I am geting behind hand so that I shall have to stay here and attend to my business. Cant some of you come and pay us a visit? Jennie has not answered Julias letter yet. Did she recieve it? I was coming to the city the day it was written to hear a political speech and it was late to get it in the P.O. so I gave it to a young man to put in the next morning. It is for this reason I ask the question. Write to me soon. I hope you have had none of the sickness we have been troubled with.

Your brother
Ulysses.

All around him, everyone thought Ulysses had hit rock bottom. They were wrong. He had much, much further to fall.

In a poignantly underplayed remembrance, Ulysses himself recalled in his memoirs: "In the fall of 1858 I sold out my stock, crops and farming utensils at auction, and gave up farming."

Ulysses' losing streak continued.

Julia's cousin, Louisa Boggs, took pity on Julia and convinced her husband to give Ulysses a job in his real estate office.

Ulysses struggled to attract new customers, but usually just ended up chatting with them about the Mexican War. Then, he became stricken with malaria.

It was so tragic, it seemed almost comedic. What had happened to the "man of fire," Captain Grant? And what had Julia Dent gotten herself into by marrying him? He had gone from the bright, shining "little prince" who captured the hearts of the ladies at White Haven, to the decrepit man in the faded Army coat with the arthritic hands, rumored to be a drunkard, stooped over and shaking so badly with fever that his friends had to help him into a buggy to send him home to his wife.

Ah, but there is the beauty in the scene. They sent him home to his wife. Though the cold wind blew through his thin old coat, and he could barely drag himself home, his wonderful wife was waiting for him. Waiting to take his broken body in her arms. Waiting to fuss over him and make sure his feet weren't wet and sit with him in the evening by their hearth, holding hands.

With Julia he was welcome, always welcome.

In the evenings, after their children were in bed, Ulysses read to Julia from books by Charles Dickens, and poetry by Walt Whitman. They sat by the fire and held hands.

Through-out their lives, many witnesses spoke of the Grants sitting and holding hands, sometimes for hours, not saying a word. Others reported on their kissing, "in full view of staff officers" during the Civil War.

No matter what struggles befell them, kissing and holding hands were at the core of their romance.

Their romance was like a bright candle that stayed lit no matter the darkness that threatened from the outside world.

But surely Ulysses' sad state broke Julia's heart. Where once his youthful arms trembled with passion as he held her, they now shook with fever. His once "beautiful hands," so gentle and loving, were now bent and gnarled with rheumatism. But she found him just as beautiful as before, perhaps even more beautiful. He was trying so hard to support their family, against terrible odds. She saw that though sometimes he was shaking so hard he could hardly walk, he never lost his dignity, or his honesty, or his charity toward others. Every morning, he courageously got up, determined to go out and try again.

To the world, it's no wonder Ulysses S. Grant seemed like "one of life's failures." Here is a list of his seemingly endless, now famous "failures:"

At Fort Vancouver: growing and selling potatoes, barley, onions, oats, corn, selling chickens, cows, pigs, ice, (which all melted before delivery) timber, renting a men's billiard club, loaning money, renting out donkeys, renting out a horse, a coal yard.

Back home in Missouri: wheat farming, real estate salesman, debt collector, custom house man, applied for county engineer— twice!—and lost. (He actually succeeded at selling cord wood, although he eventually gave it up, because of poor health.)

Worst of all, he was reportedly forced to resign from the Army for drinking.

This was the failure that hung heaviest over Ulysses. It was painful for him, running into his old Army buddies on the streets of St. Louis. They had heard all the rumours. When they ran into Captain Grant in his faded army coat, they tried not to look too closely at him. It was painful for them, too, remembering him in his youth, once known as a "man of fire" in the Mexican War. It seemed now, that this man's fire had gone out.

As Marshall Cornwall, author of "Grant as Military Commander" so poignantly wrote, "No one would ever had guessed that out of this shabby chrysalis would emerge the victor of the Civil War."

Ulysses S. Grant was teetering on the edge of the abyss. If Julia had left him at any time, he would have been destroyed. And perhaps, it could be argued, would the future of the Union Army in the Civil War.

The truth is, the more run down her husband's body became, the more clearly she saw inside his heart.

Ulysses struggles with chills and fever.

"I arrived at home on Tuesday, and it being my "chill" day of course felt very badly."

      Ulysses considers an offer to work for his father. Despite his desperate situation, Ulysses still has his self esteem and hopes of someday being in business for himself.

"There is a pleasure in knowing that one's income depends somewhat upon one's own exertions and business capacity."

St. Louis,
Oct. 1st, 1858.

Dear Father:
      I arrived at home on Tuesday evening, and, it being my "chill" day, of course felt very badly. Julia had been much worse during my absence, but had improved again so that I found her about as when I left home. Fred. has improved steadily, and can now hear nearly as well as before his sickness. The rest of the family are tolerably well, with the exception of Mr. Dent whose health seems to be about as when I left. Mr. Dent and myself will make a sale this fall and get clear of all the stock on the place, and then rent out the cleared land and sell out about four hundred acres of the north end of the place. As I explained to you, this will include my place. I shall plan to go to Covington towards Spring, and would prefer your offer to any one of mere salary that could be offered. I do not want any place for permanent stipulated pay, but want the prospect of one day doing business for myself. There is a pleasure in knowing that one's income depends somewhat upon his own exertions and business capacity, that cannot be felt when so much and no more is coming in, regardless of the success of the business engaged in or the manner in which it is done.

Mr. Dent thinks I had better take the boy he has given Julia along with me, and let him learn the farrier's business. He is a very smart, active boy, capable of making anything; but this matter I will leave entirely to you. I can leave him here and get about three dollars per month for him now, and more as he gets older. Give my love to all at home.

Yours truly,
Ulysses.

In this letter to his father, Ulysses sounds like a man who is trying to convince himself he likes selling real estate. He sounds so awkward talking about this stuff, compared to his vivid descriptions of battles in Mexico. Even his descriptions of farming vegetables had more life to them. Why would any one want Ulysses to submit real estate deals for them? It's obvious they could do a better job all by themselves. But, like everything Ulysses does, it's cute because he's trying so hard—in this case, trying hard to be something he's not, for the sake of feeding his family and finding something useful to do in the civilian world. He sounds like a ne'r do well relative, drifting from one failed occupation to another. He always does his best to sound optimistic, while you can feel the reader on the receiving end of each letter cringing and thinking, "What now with this poor, pathetic loser?" And yet, we can relate to Ulysses continuing to try while others look down on him. Funny how Ulysses misspells the word, "succeed."

"I can hardly tell how the new business I am engaged in is going to sucseed."

St. Louis Mo.
March 12th 1859.

Dear Father;
It has now been over a month, I believe, since I wrote to you last although I expected to have written again the next week. I can hardly tell how the new business I am engaged in is going to sucseed but I believe it will be something more than a support. If I find an opportunity next week I will send you some of our cards which if you will distribute among such persons as may have business to attend to in this city, such as buying or selling property, collecting either rents or other liabilities, it may prove the means of giving us additional commissions. Mr. Benton was here for some time and used to call in to see me frequently. Whilst he was here I submitted to him some property for sale belonging to a Mr. Tucker. Since Mr. B's departure

Mr. Tucker has called several times and wants me to submit his propositions again and say that if he is disposed to buy, and pay conciderable cash, he will make his prices such as to secure to him a good investment. I enclose with this a list of the property, and prices, as first asked, one third cash, bal. one & two years. Please tell Mr. Benton if he feels like making any proposition for any part of this property to let me know and I will submit it and give him an answer.

We are living now in the lower part of the city, full two miles from my office. The house is a comfortable little one just suited to my means. We have one spare room and also a spare bed in the childrens room so that we can accomodate any of our friends that are likely to come to see us. I want two of the girls, or all of them for that matter, to come and pay us a long visit soon.

Julia and the children are well. They will not make a visit to Ky. now. I was anxious to have them go before I rented but with four children she could not go without a servant and she was afraid that landing so often as she would have to do in free states she might have some trouble.

Tell one of the girls to write soon.—Has Simp gone South?— Are you going to the city to live?

Yours Truly
U.S. Grant

To J.R. Grant, Esq,
Covington Ky

On October 1, 1858, Ulysses had written to his father of his hopes to work for him. Sometime between that letter and this, that hope had vanished. Ulysses moved to St. Louis where he entered a real estate partnership with Julia's cousin, Harry Boggs. Their business cards read:

H. BOGGS. U.S. GRANT. BOGGS & GRANT,

General Agents, Collect Rents, Negotiate Loans, Buy And Sell Real Estate, Etc., Etc,. No. 35 Pine Street, Between 2nd And 3rd, Saint Louis, Mo.

Unfortunately, Ulysses was so kind-hearted and honest, he made a terrible real estate salesman.

A lawyer who worked in the office with Ulysses explained: "He just doesn't seem to be calculated for business, but a more honest, more generous man never lived. I don't believe that he knows what dishonesty is."

Julia herself felt it was hopeless, recalling, "I cannot imagine how my dear husband ever thought of going into such a business, as he never could collect a penny that was owed to him, if his debtors only expressed regret and said, "Grant, I regret, more than you do, my inability to pay you." He always felt sorry for them and never pressed again, saying, "I am sure they will send to me, knowing now, as they do, how much I need it, all they owe me as soon as they possibly can." We never heard from these "fine" debtors."

When he first came to the city to work, Ulysses left his family back in the country, and stayed with Julia's cousins, Harry and Louisa Boggs, in their spare bedroom.

"We gave him an unfurnished back room and told him to fit it up as he pleased," Mrs. Boggs remembered. "It contained very little during the winter he lived there. He had a bed, and a bowl and a pitcher on a chair, and, as he had no stove, he used to sit at our fire almost every evening."

"He would smile at times, but I never heard him laugh out loud," she recalled. "He was a sad man. I don't believe he had any ambition other than to educate his children and take care of his family."

On Saturdays, Ulysses walked the twelve miles home to see his beloved Julia and their children. The next day, he trudged the twelve miles back to the city, again, hoping to provide for them.

Mrs. Boggs recollected, "He was always a gentleman and everybody loved him, he was so gentle and considerate. But really we did not see what he could do in the world."

Here is a man who just kept trying to do the right thing. Despite his poverty, Ulysses frees William Jones, the slave given to him by Colonel Dent. The sale of William Jones would have given Ulysses about $1,500, big money in those days, especially for someone in Ulysses' sad financial state. He desperately needed the money. But he freed William instead. Imagine the scene. What did Julia say? She herself had no problem with slavery. She must have been completely exasperated with Ulysses. Yet, she loved him anyway. Ulysses was such a "nobody" at that time. He had no idea anyone would ever know or care about his actions on that early spring day, March 29, 1859.

[March 29, 1859]

Know all persons by these presents, that I Ulysses S Grant of the City & County of St Louis in the State of Missouri, for divers good and valuable considerations me hereunto moving, do hereby emancipate and set free from Slavery my negro man William, sometimes called William Jones of Mulatto complexion, aged about thirty-five years, and about five feet seven inches in height and being the same slave purchased by me of Frederick Dent—And I do hereby manumit, emancipate & set free said William from slavery forever

In testimony Wherof I hereto set my hand & seal at St Louis this (29th) day of March A D 1859

U.S. Grant (Seal)

Witnesses
J G McClellan
W. S. Hillyer

The two men shook hands and parted into the unknown. As William Jones looked back and watched Ulysses walk away, he saw a shabby ex-soldier, down on his luck, but with a tender heart—exactly what Julia saw.

Ulysses is so sincere and earnest, but I think his reputation as a drunk and discard of the Army kept people from hiring him.

To Board of County Commissioners

St Louis, Aug. 15th 1859

Hon. County Commissioners,
St. Louis County
Mo.

Gentlemen;
    I beg leave to submit myself as an applicant for the office of County Engineer, should the Office be rendered vacant, and at the same time to submit the names of a few Citizens who have been kind enough to recommend me for the Office. I have made no effort to get a large number of names, nor the names of persons with whom I am not personally acquainted.
    I enclose herewith also a statement from Prof. J.J. Reynolds, who was a class mate of mine at West Point, as to qualifications.
    Should your honorable body see proper to give me the appointment I pledge myself to give the Office my entire attention and shall hope to give general satisfaction.

Very Respectfully
Your Obt. Svt.
U.S. Grant

Ulysses gets some glowing endorsements from people in the Army, all deserved. But even bringing up his Army background at all is a two edged sword. It also reminds prospective employers of why he reputedly left the army. No one brings this up as a reason for his failure to get these jobs, but it all fits to me. His reputation dogged him for the rest of his life after leaving the army, and made him have to try harder than anyone else at every task, a daunting, uphill battle, but it did make Ulysses all the stronger, on the inside as well as the outside. Even referring to him as "Captain Grant" was asking for trouble—a reminder of his disgrace.

Professor Reynolds wrote, August 1. *"Captain U.S. Grant was a member of the class of the Mil Acady, West Point, which graduated in 1843—he always maintained a high standing and graduated with great credit, especially in mathematics, mechanics, & Engineering— From my personal knowledge of his capacity and acquirements as well as of his strict integrity and unremitting industry I consider him in an eminent degree qualified for the office of County Engineer."*

Joseph Jones Reynolds, then professor of mechanics and engineering at Washington University in St. Louis, had been appointed to the United States Military Academy at West Point from Indiana to the class of 1843. Below Professor Reynolds' statement, D.M. Frost, wrote: *"I was for three years in the Corps of Cadets at West Point with Captain Grant and afterwards served with him for some eight or nine years in the army and can fully endorse the foregoing statement of Prof. Reynolds."*

The endorsement on Ulysses' letter read, *"The undersigned take pleasure in recommending Capt U S Grant as a suitable person for the office of County Engineer of St Louis County August 1 1859*

Thos. E. Tutt	*J O'Fallon*
Jno P Helfenstein	*John How*
L.A. Benoist & Co	*T Grimsley*
J.G. McClellan	*Saml B. Churchill*
Chas. A. Pope	*Jas M Hughes*
W.S. Hillyer	*J.W. Mitchell*
C.S. Purkitt	*Lemuel G. Pardee*
Wm. L. Pipkin	*James C Moody*
J Addison Barret	*Felix Coste*

K. MacKenzie　　　*Baman & Co.*
Daniel. M. Frost　　*C.W. Ford*
Robt. M. Renick　　*A.S. Robinson*
Robt. J. Hornsby　　*Geo M Moore*
G.W. Fishback　　　*R. A. Barnes*
J McKnight　　　　*Thomas Marshall*
N.J. Eaton　　　　*John F. Darby*
Taylor Blow　　　　*Ed Walsh*

Ulysses offers to take care of his sick brother, Simpson Grant. Unemployed again, Ulysses adds real estate agent and bill and rent collector to his string of failures. But he refuses to ever give up hope.

"What I shall do will depend entirely on what I can get to do."

"I do not want to fly from one thing to another, nor would I, but I am compelled to make a living from the start for which I am willing to give all my time and all my energy."

St. Louis,
Aug. 20th, 1859.

Dear Father:

On last Wednesday I received your letter, and on the Monday before one from Mr. Burk, from both of which I much regretted to learn of Simpson's continued ill health. I at once wrote to Orvil, whose arrival at Galena I learned from Burk's letter, to urge Simpson to come by steamer to St. Louis and spend some time with me, and if it should prove necessary for anyone to accompany him, I would take him home. Cannot Jennie and Orvil's wife come this way when they start for Galena? We would like very much to see them.

I am not over sanguine of getting the appointment mentioned in my last letter. The Board of Commissioners, who make the appointment, are divided, three free soilers to two opposed,— and although friends who are recommending me are the very first citizens of this place, and members of all parties, I fear they will make strictly party nominations for all the offices under their control. As to the professorship you speak of, that was filled some time ago. And were it not, I would stand no earthly chance. The Washington University, where the vacancy was to be filled, is one of the best endowed institutions in the United States, and all the professorships are sought after by persons whose early advantages were the same as mine, but who have been engaged in teaching all their mature years. Quimby, who was the best mathematician in my class, and who was for several years an assistant at West Point, and for nine years a professor in an institution in New York, was an unsuccessful applicant. The appointment was given to the most distinguished man in his department in the country, and an author. His name is Shorano. Since putting in my application for the appointment of County Engineer, I have learned that the place is not likely to be filled before February next. What I shall do will depend entirely upon what I can get to do. Our present business is entirely overdone in this city, at least a dozen new houses having started about the same time I commenced. I do not want to fly from one thing to another, nor would I, but I am compelled to make a living from the start for which I am willing to give all my time and all my energy.

Julia and the children are well and send love to you. On your way to Galena can you not come by here? Write to me soon.

Ulysses.

One day, Ulysses came back from town and Julia asked him if he had heard any news of the election for County Commissioner, for which he had applied. Ulysses replied, "Yes. I am defeated." Yet, he takes it like a man. To his father, Ulysses simply writes:

"The question at length has been settled and I am sorry to say adversely to me."

He writes to his relatives, but never hears back.

St. Louis, Sept. 23d/59

Dear Father:

I have waited for some time to write you the result of the action of the County Commissioners upon the appointment of a County Engineer. The question at length has been settled, and I am sorry to say, adversely to me. The two Democratic Commissioners voted for me and the freesoilers against me. What I shall now go at I have not determined but I hope something before a great while. Next month I get possession of my own house when my expenses will be reduced so much that a very moderate salary will support me. If I could get the $3000 note cashed which I got difference in the exchange of property, I could put up with the proceeds two houses that would pay me, at least $40 pr. month rent. The note has five years to run with interest notes given separately and payable annually.

We are looking for some of you here next week to go to the fair. I wrote to Simp. to come down and see me but as I have had no answer from him, nor from Orvil to a letter written some time before, I do not know whether he will come or not. I should like very much to have some of you come to see us this fall.

Julia and the children are all very well. Fred. & Buck go to school every day. They never think of asking to stay at home.

You may judge from the result of the action of the County Commissioners that I am strongly identified with the Democratic party! Such is not the case. I never voted an out and out Democratic ticket in my life. I voted for Buch. for President to defeat Freemont but not because he was my first choice. In all other elections I have universally selected the candidates that in my estimation, were the best fitted for all the different offices and it never happens that such men are all arrayed on one side. The strongest friend I had in the Board of Comrs. is a F.S. but opposition between parties is so strong that he would not vote for any one, no matter how friendly, unless one of his own party would go with him. The F.S. party felt themselves bound to provide for one of their own party who was defeated for the office of County Engineer; a Dutchman who came to the West as an Assistant Surveyor upon the public lands and who has held an office ever since. There is, I believe, but one paying office in the County held by an American unless you except the office of Sheriff which is held by a Frenchman who speaks broken English but was born here.

Write to me soon. Julia & the children join me in sending love to all of you.

Yours Truly
Ulysses

This poignant line sums up Ulysses life at this point.

"I am still unemployed..."

To Simpson Grant

St. Louis, Oct. 24th 1859

Dear Brother;
    I have been postponing writing to you hoping to make a return for your horse, but as yet I have recieved nothing for him. About two weeks ago a man spoke to me for him and said that he would try him the next day and if he suited give me $100 for him. I have not seen the man since but one week ago last Saturday he went to the stable and got the horse saddle and bridle since which I have seen neither man nor horse. From this I presume he must like him. The man, I understand, lives in Florisant, about twelve miles from the city.
    My family are all well and living in our own house. It is much more pleasant than where we lived when you were here and contains about as much room, practically. I am still unemployed but expect to have a place in the Custom House from the 1st of next month. My name has been forwarded for the appointment of Superintendent, which, if I do not get, will not probably be filled atal. In that case there is a vacant desk which I may get that pays $1200 per annum. The other will be worth from $1500 to $1800 and will occupy but little time.
    Remember me to all at home. There is a gentleman here who has lands in San Antonio de Bexar Co. Texas, that would like to get you, should you go there this Winter, to look after them. If you go, and will attend to his business, drop me a line and he will furnish me all the papers, and instructions, to forward to you.

Yours &c.
U.S. Grant

P.S. The man that has your horse is Capt. Covington, owner of a row of six thr(ee) story brick houses in this city and the probabilities are that he intends to give me an order on his agt. for the money on th(e) 1st of the month when the rents are paid. At all eve(nts) I imagine the horse is perfectly safe.

U.S.G.

Hmmmm—.I wonder if that man ever came back with Simpson Grant's horse? Or when and if he ever paid for it? It's so funny—typical Ulysses, trusting the guy to just take off with his brother's horse without signing any kind of agreement, and possibly never seeing him again. Yes, Ulysses S. Grant is the man I want conducting my business—NOT! A terrible businessman—with an amazing belief in humanity, though he's been conned and taken advantage of over and over again. It just makes me love him all the more.

He held the job in the Customs office a mere month. Poor Ulysses! I wonder why he lost that job so fast? It must have been a blow when they came and told him they were letting him go. But as always, he went home to Julia, then shuffled back into the world to resume looking for work.

Here, Ulysses humbly re-applies for the job of County Commissioner, the job for which he was recently turned down.

To Hon. J.H. Lightner

Hon. J.H. Lightner:
Pres. Board County Comrs;

Sir:
     Should the office of County Engineer be vacated by the will of your Hon. body I would respectfully renew the application made by me in August last for that appointment. I would also beg leave to refer to the application and recommendations then submitted, and now on file with your Board.

> *I am Sir*
> *Respectfully Your Obt. Svt.*
> *U.S. Grant*

Ulysses did not receive the job.

I wonder if Colonel Dent did not know how to write? Ulysses suggests if he wants a certain letter written, perhaps he should tell Julia what to write. She was a terrible letter writer, but her papa must have been worse.

At the time this letter was written, Ulysses is going to his father, hat in hand, to ask for a job in Jesse Grant's leather goods store. Ulysses arrives in his father's town with a splitting headache, and just misses his father, who is leaving town just as Ulysses arrives. "Down on his luck" does not begin to describe Ulysses' condition. Nearly thirty seven years old, he had no prospects and was reduced to begging his father for a job. But only five years after this letter is written, Ulysses will be the most famous man in the world, victor of the Civil War, and soon, President of the United States—states united by his own determination, courage and military genius. Yet, there is no hint of his glorious future in this hard luck letter—except for the way Ulysses persists from day to day to do the best he can with his modest, often humiliating circumstances. There is also, as there always is in his letters, affection for the wife who would help to carry him there.

"Kiss the children for me and let them kiss you in return for their pa."

Covington Ky.
March 14th 1860.

Dear Julia:
I arrived here at 1/2 past 11 to day with a head ache and feeling bad generally. We were detained on the road last night by the train going to St. Louis Smashing up on the road ahead of us. The result was our train had to go back and the passengers walk around the breakdown and get in another train and come on. This is why I arrived here so late and this caused me to miss seeing father for the next day or two. As I was walking up the Street home I saw him turn down another street not more than half a square ahead of me but I supposed he was just gowing down town for a few minuets and would

be back home for dinner. But I found that he had gone over to the City to take the 12 m packet to go up the river and may not return before Friday evening. I shall have to remain until his return and as the river is in fine boating order I think I shall return that way, particularly if I can get started this week. Clara has gone to Bethel and will not return for a week or two. Mother Jennie (&) Mary asked many questions about you and the children. They were quite disappointed that Fred. & Buck were not along. My head is nearly bursting with pain and I would not have written to you to-day but I wanted to make shure that my letter would be in St. Louis by Saturday now that it is not probable that I shall be there by that time.

Kiss the children for me. I should have written to John Dent before I left giving him instructions about what it was necessary for your father to have done in Washington to enable him to carry his Carondelet suit up. Tell your father that I have not written to John on the subject and if he wishes it done he had better tell you what to write.

Again kiss the children for me and let them kiss you in return for their pa.

Your affectionate
Dado

Dado! This is the first time Ulysses signs his letter this way. Julia's nickname for him was "Dudy." Perhaps their children called him "Dado." Ulysses S. Grant had more nick-names than anyone I've ever known! Nicknames being signs of affection, he was the object of much affection from his wife and children. His lack of worldly success did nothing to alter their love for him. This gives me a warm feeling inside, and it surely gave Ulysses a warm feeling, too.

P.S. I forgot to say that all here were well except Simp. I think he is about as he was last fall. He does not think there has been much improvement. I have not been through the house to see how things look though I have been here three or four hours. The dining room is the only one I have been in.

Cute—Ulysses has only been at his parents' house for three or four hours, when he sits down and writes Julia a letter.

The purpose of Ulysses' trip to Covington was probably to plan for Ulysses' move from St. Louis to Galena. Ulysses went to work at his father's leather store in Galena as a clerk. Ulysses and his family moved to Galena in the early spring of 1860.

Reading this letter to a friend, I was struck by how open Ulysses is about his feelings. For someone so manly, it shows, as always, that he is unafraid to admit his weaknesses and humanity. He admits to feeling anxious. I love the way he refers to his hopes that he will someday "be above the frowns of the world" when it comes to money. He must have felt people frowning down at him for many years. Everyone knows Ulysses did not really like selling leather, but he always tries to be upbeat and do the best with what he's got. And as long as he's got Julia, he is happy.

"Since leaving St. Louis I have become pretty well inniciated into the Leather business and like it well."

"...I have evry reason to hope, in a few years, to be entirely above the frowns of the world..."

Galena, August 7th 1860.

Mr. Davis;
Dear Sir:
When I left St. Louis you will remember you enquired of me if I had the Deed for that Carondelet property recorded. I told you that it had not been recorded and that the Deed had been left with Gibson. I feel anxious to know if you found it and if it has been recorded yet.
Since leaving St. Louis I have become pretty well inniciated into the Leather business and like it well. Our business here is prosperous and I have evry reason to hope, in a few years, to be entirely above the frowns of the world, pecuniarily.—I presume you had an exciting time of it in St. Louis Yesterday! I feel anxious to hear of Blairs defeat but as yet the Telegraph has brought me nothing Satisfactory. One rumor is that Barret is 45 ahead for the short term and Blair far ahead for the long. Another that Blair has gained in both. I cant help feeling more interest in the contest you have just

gone through than I shall in the November election. The fact is I think the Democratic party want a little purifying and nothing will do it so effectually as a defeat. The only thing is I dont like to see a Republican beat the party.—How is Gibson now? Myself and family are all well and highly pleased with this place.

Yours Truly
U.S. Grant

P.S. Not being certain of your first name I shall have to send this through the Collector to whom please present my best respects. Please write to me soon.

The above letter also shows that Ulysses enjoys following politics and he makes a very clever observation about the Democratic party needing a little purifying, and nothing will do it so effectually as a defeat. Very clever!

Ulysses now has a safe, boring job as a leather salesman. His job involves traveling to small towns. As always, he writes to his beloved, and the image of their cozy home together is always a comfort to him.

"Tomorrow will be New Years day. I wish you all a Happy New Year and wish I was at home with you."

Decora, Iowa
Dec 31st/60

Dear Julia:

This is the day I had set for being at home, but various detentions, particularly the one at Prairie du Chien of four days has set us back considerably. The weather has been very cold but I have not suffered any. We have had a fine snow up in these parts so that traveling in a buggy is out of the question. We have our buggy set up on runners and in that condition travel along finely and of course attract attention of evry passer. Have you all kept well. I dreamed night before last that Jesse was sick. I hope in this case dreams may go in contraries.—Tomorrow will be New Years day. I wish you all a happy New Year and wish I was at home with you. To-night, if we can get off, we want to go to West Union, twenty five miles from here. It will be sun down however before we can start and possibly we may not be able to get off to night atall. You may look for me home about the next Teusday after you recieve this.—I enclose a letter from Orvil which have sent to him at once.

Kiss all the children for me. I did not get a letter from you at Prairie du Chien. I shall enquire at the P.O. in West Union. I have not got anything to tell you about the trip until my return so wait patiently for

Ulys.

This will be my last letter.

It was surely difficult for Julia to leave Missouri and the nearness of her family, to follow her husband to a strange new city. But follow him she did. Would everything go wrong, as it always had? Let's see now. Counting the dead chickens and cows, the waterlogged lumber and the frostbitten cornfields, her "little prince" "Dudy" had had exactly twenty failures in a row, twenty-one if you count the melted ice. *Thirty*-one if you count the bad loans that were given out but never paid back. Thirty-two if you count—well you get the idea.

Did Julia still believe in her husband? You bet.

They set up housekeeping in Galena, and Julia got to work right away making a homey nest for her Ulysses to roost at night, after returning from the boredom of his going nowhere job.

In her memoirs, Julia recalled Ulysses had a humble job and a small salary, "But we were happy."

The weekly paycheck did bring a sigh of relief to them both.

Dudy's duties included keeping track of inventory, balancing the books and traveling to small towns, to buy hides. He was quiet and shy.

John E. Smith, a Swiss immigrant who liked to stop by the store, remembered, "Grant was a very poor businessman" who "never liked to wait on customers" and "hardly ever knew the price of anything."

More to his liking was coming home at night to Julia, and their love.

Outside, people eyed his rundown appearance with curiosity.

Inside, Julia tenderly removed his shabby coat.

Outside, the neighbors murmured rumours about his resignation from the army.

Inside, Julia's kisses warmed his heart.

He might have remained a seedy shopkeeper, ignoring the whispers about him while clinging to his wife and family, had not his destiny emerged from the shadows of his past.

CHAPTER TWENTY
Revolution!

In November, 1860, Abraham Lincoln was elected President of the United States. Fearing Lincoln's abolitionist views, slave states defiantly began to secede from the Union. They boldly formed the Confederate States of America, with former Secretary of War Jefferson Davis as their president.

The new Confederate constitution gave individual states more power than the Federal government, and protected the right to own slaves. More than anything, it protected the Southern dream of aristocracy, where any man with slaves might be a king, and his lady fair, a pampered princess.

On April 11, 1861, the Confederate Army opened fire on Fort Sumter, one of only four Federal Forts in Confederate territory still flying the Union flag. The fort stood sadly at the entrance to Charleston Harbor, in South Carolina. As enthusiastic Charleston citizens watched and cheered from the rooftops, the Confederate Army bombarded the Federal garrison with 4,000 rounds of ammunition. The Union flag fell, but the Union soldiers hoisted it back up again. Finally, after a two day fight, the Union flag came down for good.

Fort Sumter surrendered, and its fall electrified both North and South.

The North was outraged. The South had fired upon their flag!

The South was unified. The war for Southern independence had begun!

President Abraham Lincoln called for 75,000 patriotic volunteers to save the Union.

Confederate President Jefferson Davis declared, "All we ask is to be let alone!"

As Ulysses S. Grant himself described it, "It was revolution."

It was a time of great emotion and passionate debate. All over the country, people were choosing sides. Many were friends of Ulysses from the old days at West Point. William T. Sherman, who had quit the Army to become a banker, re-enlisted on the Union side. James Longstreet, best man at Ulysses' wedding, quit the U.S.

army and joined the Confederacy. Simon Bolivar Buckner, who had so kindly helped the then penniless Ulysses with money to return home from California, also resigned and joined the Confederacy. In fact, Ulysses had even more close friends and acquaintances join the Confederacy than the Union.

And right in the middle of the whole controversy was Ulysses' Southern belle wife and family, all waited on from birth by slaves.

Slaves were the cornerstone of Colonel Dent's dream. How could one run a plantation "kingdom" like White Haven, and sit on the porch ruling it, without slaves? It was simply unthinkable. Needless to say, Ulysses S. Grant's father-in-law was pro-Confederate, as was most of Missouri.

Missouri was a border slave state, with close ties to the deep South. St. Louis, the nearest city to the Dent estate, was Southern in culture and in loyalty. The steamboats along the Mississippi River connected St. Louis to all the cities of the Deep South, and they all shared the same lifestyle of slave-assisted luxury.

How did Ulysses' wife Julia feel about the coming rebellion? She was clearly torn.

Julia wanted to be loyal to her husband, who was pro-Union, but her heart still drifted back at White Haven, gathering birds nest with a train of little slave girls who she thought were quite happy attending "Miss Julia."

Julia's memoirs are full of wistful reminiscence of her idyllic childhood, of carriage rides fit for a princess, with her very own coachman and footman, of moonlit nights on the veranda with her family, while the "servants" did the work, of delicious meals cooked up by her very own Mammy.

"Mammy was an artist," Julia recalled. "Such loaves of beautiful snowy cake, such plates full of delicious Maryland biscuit, such exquisite custards and puddings, such omelets, gumbo soup, and fritters—these were Mammy's specialty. She sometimes made them of strawberries and again of pineapple. She even became so esthetic as to make these dainty morsels of flowers from our acacia, rose tree, and from the locust flowers, telling Nell and me that such dainty, delicate young ladies should live on such food."

One slave, or "servant," as she preferred to call them, made the preserves, pickles and jellies. One cooked dinner, and another supper and breakfast. One kept the wood supply for cozy fires. Julia had three slaves all to herself, who obeyed her every whim and treated her like royalty.

Clearly, she would never have abandoned this life of bounty had her heart, body and soul not been wrenched away from it by her passion for the shy Lieutenant Grant.

Her memoirs reveal her sadness the night Lincoln called for volunteers to crush the Rebellion, and so many in Galena answered the call. She feared it would be the end of her father's political party.

"I remember now with astonishment the feeling that took possession of me in the spring of 1861," Julia wrote. "When reading patriotic speeches, my blood seemed to course more rapidly through my veins, and I remember how enthusiastic I was when Governor Jackson called for 20,000 troops to protect my native state..."

Governor Jackson was a Confederate!

In 1861, at the beginning of the Civil War, Julia Grant, wife of Ulysses S. Grant, was a hot-blooded Confederate!

Julia was enthusiastic about protecting Missouri against the Federals, in other words, from her own husband!

Her most telling quote of all, coming long after her husband's death, recalls the "comforts of slavery" like an aging woman crying for her youth.

"I think our people were very happy," Julia recalled with a sigh. "At least they were in mamma's time, though the young ones became somewhat demoralized about the beginning of the Rebellion, when all the comforts of slavery passed away forever."

No, Julia Grant had been raised a Southern belle, and she was still a Southern belle at heart. But there was no escaping this annoying subject.

At night, when her Yankee husband read to her now, it wasn't from humorous novels or poetry books, it was from newspapers about the coming conflict. He asked Julia her opinion, and she hotly replied that the South had a right to secede—but, obviously trying to please her husband, she guessed the United States government had a right to try to stop them, too. Ulysses thought his "Jujy's" opinion amusing.

But it would not be so amusing later on. For at some future date, the fate of the Union would depend on the loyalty of this simple Southern belle. The fate of the Union, if not the world.

While Ulysses' friends ardently chose sides in the War of the Rebellion, Ulysses himself was still a clerk in his father's store. It was a modest life, but his family was finally free from the desperate poverty and bad luck that had dogged him for so many years.

Life was simple, but good. Ulysses' wife and children wore new clothes, instead of rags. They could buy their children toys, and send them to school. Ulysses himself no longer had to go without dinner to save fifty cents, as he had in St. Louis, just a year before.

His family was at last secure. He must have felt in his heart that Julia deserved that. The worst was over.

Or was it?

Ulysses was clearly concerned over events in the paper. He wrote his Confederate father-in-law: "Dear Sir: The times are indeed startling but now is the time, particularly in the border Slave states, for men to prove their love of country." Ulysses insisted that every true patriot should be for maintaining the integrity of the "glorious old *stars* and *stripes*, the Constitution and the Union." Ulysses warned his father-in-law, "In all this I can but see the doom of slavery." But Colonel Dent rejected this idea. Why, the doom of slavery would mean the doom of his own dream, his dream of Southern aristocracy with himself Lord and master. Besides, who was his disgraced ex-soldier, drunkard, loser son-in-law to tell the fine, upstanding Colonel what to do?

Ulysses' parents were abolitionists and intensely pro-Union. Julia's father, passionately pro-Confederate.

Colonel Dent argued in favor of secession with Julia, insisting that secession was protected in the constitution. Julia recalled, "I was dreadfully puzzled about the horrid old constitution..." The wife of U.S. Grant then suggested, "Why don't they just make up a new one?" Even Colonel Dent groaned and shook his head at his daughter's naiveté.

Vivacious, happy-go-lucky Julia wanted to enjoy "one long day of flowers and sunshine," as she had in her youth. Now here was this question of that "horrid old constitution" dogging her. And it wouldn't go away.

Ulysses knew he was pro-Union all the way. As far back as West Point, he was intensely patriotic about his country. In his first letter written from West Point, to his cousin, young Ulysses described Benedict Arnold as "that *base* and *heartless* traitor *to* his country." One can feel the passion in his heart, his passion for his country. Now, Ulysses viewed the rebels as traitors to their country.

But would he do more than just give his opinion about it? Julia admits feeling confused, and certainly wished things could just stay the same. She loved hearing her husband come home from work every night, climbing the steps to their front door. He and their youngest son Jesse would make the same humorous exchange every night: "Mister, do you want to fight?" the three year old toddler would challenge his Pa. "I do not feel like fighting, Jess," Ulysses would reply, "But I can't stand being hectored in this manner by a man of your size." Then Jesse would pummel his Pa with his "dimpled fists," until Ulysses fell on the floor, laughing, "I give up! I give up!"

In the evenings Julia had the comfort of his presence as he read to her, then they would sit and hold hands. They had their passionate love for each other, night after night, and the warm security of each others' bodies as they slept. It was "always sunshine when he was near." And each morning held the prospect of another happy day. The last seven years had been a brutal struggle, but this was their modest reward. Their world was now peaceful and secure. Why did anything have to change?

Julia reminded herself that her husband was out of the Army, for good, and the rebellion might not affect them. Her Papa said the Confederacy was going to win, anyway.

Then, one night, Julia's husband attended a meeting. The pro-Union group asked Ulysses to conduct the meeting, since he was the only soldier present. (Albeit, a former soldier.) Shy Ulysses was embarrassed, and conducted the meeting most awkwardly, by his own admission. Like dancing, public speaking was never one of Ulysses' strong points. To his relief, a dark-eyed man stood up to speak. His name was John Rawlins, and he would be inexorably linked to Ulysses for the rest of his life.

With fanatical emotion, Rawlins admonished every man present to fight with every last breath in their bodies to keep the Union from falling apart. "We appeal to the God of battles!" he cried.

Rawlins oratory lit a fire in Ulysses. And after that night, Ulysses never returned to work at his father's store.

Ulysses decided to re-enlist on the Union side.

Colonel Dent was appalled. He considered Ulysses a traitor, and insisted, "There will always be a place at my table for Julia, but never for him."

Julia's older brother Louis joined the Confederacy. Her other brother Frederick, a close friend of Ulysses, joined the Union, which certainly stuck in the Colonel's craw.

Caught between the two strongest male figures in her life, her pro-Confederate father and pro-Union husband, Julia tried to figure out how *she* actually felt. Her statement to her husband that the South had a right to secede says it all. She had loved the comforts of slavery. "Our people," meaning the Dents' slaves, were "very happy." Slavery seemed completely natural to her.

Her family, friends and neighbors in St. Louis were Confederates. They were fighting to protect their way of life, a way of life that Julia cherished. It is obvious Julia would have remained Confederate, too, had not she been madly in love with a Yankee.

It has been stated that Julia was "indifferent" to the question of secession. In reality, she was trying to walk the line by pleasing both her husband and her father, difficult, since they were on opposite sides. She didn't want to rock the boat.

For the moment, her Yankee husband's Union sentiments were not causing much of a problem. His decision to re-enlist may have alarmed her at first, but the truth slowly dawned on them: the U.S. Army did not want U.S. Grant.

While other old army buddies instantly received high commands, becoming generals as soon as the first shot was fired, the only work Ulysses could find was helping raw, volunteer troops fill out army forms in the state capital of Springfield, Illinois.

His downtrodden presence must have been a curiosity to the brand new generals in their polished uniforms, who knew all too well, the reason Ulysses had resigned from the army. They must have snickered behind his back, to see the infamous drunkard trying to find a way back into the service.

One old Army acquaintance, Brigadier-General John Pope, eyed the shabby Ulysses, and patronizingly offered to help him.

"He spoke of his acquaintance with the public men of the state," Ulysses remembered, "and said he could get them to recommend me for a position and that he would do all he could for me."

Pope's condescending attitude hurt Ulysses.

But Ulysses still had his pride, telling the snooty General Pope, "I decline to receive endorsement for permission to fight for my country."

Ulysses felt hurt, but determined. As usual, he went home to Julia.

From their home in Galena, Ulysses penned the following appeal:

Galena, Illinois
May 24, 1861

Col. L. Thomas,
Adjt. Gen. U.S.A.,
Washington, D.C.

Sir: Having served for fifteen years in the regular army, including four years at West Point, and feeling it the duty of every one who has been educated at the Government expense to offer their services for the support of that Government, I have the honor, very respectfully, to tender my services, until the close of the war, in such capacity as may be offered. I would say, in view of my present age and length of service, I feel myself competent to command a regiment, if the President, in his judgment, should see fit to intrust one to me.

Since the first call of the President I have been serving on the staff of the Governor of this State, rendering such aid as I could in the organization of our State militia, and am still engaged in that capacity. A letter addressed to me at Springfield, Illinois, will reach me.

> *I am very respectfully,*
> *Your obt. svt.,*
> *U.S. Grant*

Poor Ulysses never received a letter, because no letter was ever sent. The Adjutant General's office stuck it in some out of the way place, the way people do when they're unsure what to do with something.

Receiving no answer to his heartfelt letter, Ulysses went to Cincinnati in an attempt to see his old army acquaintance, George Brinton McClellan, who had instantly become a Major-General and was known as the hope of the Union Army.

This was the same McClellan that became enraged when Ulysses was under the influence of alcohol, while fitting up an expedition for McClellan, at Fort Vancouver.

Ulysses called on McClellan on two successive days, but "failed to see him on either occasion."

While all around him, offices were buzzing with activity, planning the war, nobody had time for Ulysses S. Grant, former war hero. Nobody, that is, except his loving wife, Julia.

Julia felt badly for Ulysses. Nobody ever appreciated him. His reputation as a drunk still haunted him, and yet, she knew that since he came home from California, he had not touched a drop. For when he was with Julia, he did not need to drink.

When Ulysses was with Julia, the innate melancholy that haunted him was assuaged. He felt whole. He did not need liquor to escape his loneliness. He also cared so much about what she thought of him, that in her presence, he had the strength to resist his weakness. He did not want to shame her. In California, when his friends insisted he stand trial rather than resign the Army, Ulysses said he would not for all the world let his wife know he had been tried on such a charge (drinking.) He wanted Julia to be proud of him. As a junior officer in New Orleans, on his way to the Mexican War, he wrote her, *"If I feel tempted to do any thing that I think is not right I am shure to think, "Well now if Julia saw me would I do so" and thus it is absent or present I am more or less governed by what I think is your will."*

Yes, Julia was the key to Ulysses' sobriety. But of course, the Army didn't know this, and still bad-mouthed him.

Rumours had begun to circulate about Ulysses' drinking. Politicians looked down on Ulysses and whispered that he was a "military deadbeat" and "just another decayed soldier."

Another witness to Ulysses' despair, remembers seeing him on the street, and noting, "he was fagged out, lonesome and dejected."

A desperate Ulysses confided to an friend, "I've tried to re-enter service in vain. I must live and my family must live. Perhaps I could serve the army by providing good bread for them. You remember my success at baking bread in Mexico." (As quartermaster in Mexico, young Ulysses once took charge of baking bread for his regiment.)

Ulysses just wanted to be useful.

Badly as Julia felt for her unappreciated husband, she must have been relieved at the thought that maybe he wouldn't be leaving her, after all. She affectionately looked over at him, silently smoking his pipe in the twilight. It was spring, 1861. The month they first fell in love. The world thought him a has-been, worthless, one of life's hangers-on. But to Julia, he was everything. If he stayed right here with her forever, holding her hand, she would be content.

And then, a letter arrived.

Ulysses had been accepted into the Union Army.

It was probably the worst assignment one could be handed: an unruly regiment which no one else could control. No one else wanted the job, and so it was given to Ulysses S. Grant, the honored Mexican War hero with the dishonorable reputation.

The 21st Illinois Regiment had been commanded by a Colonel so wild that he often took the guard from his post to go to town and "make a night of it." It didn't take much reasoning to see that this man was untrustworthy to lead them into battle.

Captain Grant had been given the task of mustering in this regiment into the Illinois State service. With a real prospect of battle ahead, they chose him to lead them.

Ulysses' first regiment was a rowdy bunch, "easily led astray," but with the application of a little old fashioned army punishment and discipline, Ulysses whipped them into shape and they liked it! They quickly grew to respect the quiet little man with the calm manner and unflappable self-confidence.

Ulysses was proud of his men, and they trusted him. They could see that here was a professional soldier.

Ulysses' first assignment was to move his regiment from the State capital of Springfield, Illinois, to Quincy, Illinois, near the Illinois River. Though they could have taken "the cars," or railroad, he preferred to have them march, for the experience and self-confidence it would give them.

When they reached the Illinois River, orders were received to change direction, to await a steamer to take them to St. Louis. The steamer became stuck on a sand-bar, and by the time it unstuck, their orders were changed again.

Through it all, Colonel Ulysses remained cool and his men were surely comforted by his quiet confidence.

At last, a prospect of battle appeared, when Ulysses was ordered, with his men, to "move against Colonel Thomas Harris, on the Salt River."

Colonel Harris was a "notorious" Confederate Colonel, rumored to be encamped at the little town of Florida, Missouri.

Ulysses and his men were now encamped at the town of Palmyra, Missouri. They began a march they felt would lead them to their first engagement with the enemy.

Ulysses recalled this unforgettable moment in his life, "Harris had been encamped in a creek bottom for the sake of being near water. The hills on either side of the creek extend to a considerable height, possibly more than a hundred feet. As we approached the brow of the hill from which it was expected we could see Harris' camp, and possibly find his men ready formed to meet us, my heart kept getting higher and higher until it felt to me as though it was in my throat. I would have given anything then to have been back in Illinois, but I had not the moral courage to halt and consider what to do, I kept right on. When we reached a point from which the valley below was in full view I halted. The place where Harris had been encamped a few days before was still there and the marks of a recent encampment were plainly visible, but the troops were gone. My heart resumed its place. It occurred to me at once that Harris had been as much afraid of me as I had been of him. This was a view of the question I had never taken before; but it was one I never forgot afterwards."

Only a few weeks after this life altering experience, Ulysses was promoted to Brigadier General!

Ulysses' promotion sent Julia's Papa into an ever increasing tirade about his worthless Yankee son-in-law. Julia became a source of curiosity to her Southern belle girlfriends. Julia Grant was back at White Haven, being waited on by slaves, while her husband was a general in the Union Army!

Julia was definitely caught in the middle.

Ulysses was soon posted at Cairo, Illinois, near the slave states of Kentucky and Missouri. In previous, telling letters from Ulysses S. Grant to his Southern belle wife, he speaks of her father's traitorous attitude, praises the loyalty to the Union of Julia's Aunt Fanny, then admonishes Julia, "*I hope by this time you feel as loyal to the Union as Aunt Fanny.*"

Ulysses hoped that "by now" Julia was loyal to the Union, indicating that previously, she was not.

Mrs. U.S. Grant was in quite a pickle. (Fitting, since her husband's favorite food was cucumbers!)

Julia had strong feelings of loyalty to the South, and her beloved Papa hated Ulysses more than ever. Yet, Julia couldn't help being proud of her husband. She could tell this job was a boost to his self-respect. He moved with a new energy, sense of confidence and purpose.

After years of being scorned and looked down upon, people were seeing Ulysses in a new light. And her dear husband was trying so hard. She couldn't help but feel for him. His noble, well-meaning efforts always did move her.

Julia didn't understand why "the Union" meant so much to her husband. But she knew his feelings were sincere. And it was his sincere, noble heart that made her love him so much.

It wasn't long before Brigadier General Ulysses S. Grant began to miss his wife. In his early letters, we can see the pattern beginning again: "*I begin to want to see you and the children very much.*" "*I am anxious to hear from you and the children as well as see you.*" "*I should like very much to go into camp some place where you could visit me.*" "*Kiss the children for me and a hundred for yourself.*"

Julia did go to visit Ulysses at his Union headquarters. Whenever she made a visit, they were both like giddy young lovers. As Ulysses' assistant adjutant-general, John Rawlins recalled, "When Mrs. Grant was present, all would be merry as a marriage bell."

The war did not seem so serious yet. Certainly her own role in it did not seem serious. Her husband was a low ranking general, and they had fun when she stayed with him in the Army Camp. It was unusual for a woman to be in the camp, but it was difficult for them to be apart, especially for the amorous, uxorious Ulysses.

Sometimes the Grant children visited their "Pa" along with Julia. Ulysses' staff officers recall hearing Julia and her children singing hymns on Sundays. Julia was a devout Methodist. Ulysses rarely went to church, but he liked it that she did. He usually hated singing, but he liked it when she sang. In his eyes, she could do no wrong. Everything about her was beautiful.

Whenever Julia paid a visit, the usually somber Army Camp was light-hearted and gay. It seemed a little like they were just playing at war, the way Julia and Ulysses played at keeping house in the early days of their marriage.

While Brigadier General Ulysses S. Grant prepared his Army and enjoyed frequent visits from Julia, Major General George McClellan was Commander in Chief of the Union's most prestigious Eastern Army, the Army of the Potomac. Known as the "young Napoleon," the pompous young McClellan realized that the Union was looking to him to win the war, and even wrote to his wife that if he wanted to, he could become a dictator! But he chose not to do it. "Admirable self denial!" he bragged to her.

Directly below McClellan, and directly over Ulysses, was Major General Henry Halleck, desk general par excellence. Known as "Old Brains," Halleck was famously known for his tactical genius, because of a book he had written about military tactics. Halleck was in command of the Department of the Missouri, which made him Ulysses' superior.

Pompous, stuffed shirt, pencil pusher Halleck and plain, quiet, soldier Ulysses did not exactly hit it off. Halleck looked down his nose at Ulysses. Like everyone else, Halleck had heard the rumors of General Grant's drinking, and was wary of him. So far, Ulysses had given the Army nothing new to talk about. He kept busy, and before his loneliness could get the best of him, lovely Julia would pay him a visit.

CHAPTER TWENTY-ONE
The Battle of Belmont

Deep down inside, Ulysses knew the only way to win a war was to fight. When the first opportunity came, he gratefully grabbed it.

In November of 1861, Ulysses received word that 3,000 rebels were afloat on the nearby St. Francis River. Ulysses dispatched Colonel Richard Oglesby, with a command sufficient to compete with the rebels, to confront them.

When Ulysses received word that more rebels had been sent to destroy Oglesby, Ulysses was ordered to "make a demonstration" near the Kentucky border, to distract the rebels and hopefully stop them from pursuing the now vulnerable Oglesby and his men.

Ulysses made the decision, on his own, to do more than make a demonstration. With the aid of gunboats and a force of 3,000 Union troops, he staged a daring raid on Belmont, a rebel camp in Missouri, near the Kentucky border.

Both Missouri and Kentucky were slave States with Confederate sympathies, who had not officially left the Union. As of now, both were "hot beds" of rebel activity.

Disembarking from their naval transports, near Belmont, Ulysses surprised the rebels, and his men were under fire for the first time. They drove the rebels from their tents, but rather than capture them, the men became so excited about their first victory, that they stopped to celebrate and pick up "trophies," items stolen from the rebel camps.

This gave the rebels time to sneak back toward Ulysses' men, and when a boat load of rebels arrived to join the fight, Ulysses' frightened men realized they who had won the first contest were now surrounded!

Ulysses remained cool.

"We cut our way in, and we can cut our way out!" he announced.

Their hope renewed, Ulysses' men fought their way out, and soon drove the rebels back.

Ulysses made sure his troops gathered up their wounded, and headed for the boats.

Ulysses was the last man left between the now pursuing rebels and the boats loaded with Union troops. The last boat was about to leave, and Ulysses was left behind!

In a wild ride through a cornfield, with the rebel army in pursuit, Ulysses later told Julia, that all his thoughts were of her and of their children.

The last Union boat was about to push off and head for home, when someone recognized Ulysses tearing toward the riverbank, on his horse. The Captain ordered the boat to delay its departure, and a plank was extended for their General.

Ulysses' horse slid down the riverbank, and trotted onto the boat just in time, with the rebels firing away.

Ulysses' daring raid had prevented the rebels from sending troops against Colonel Oglesby, saving him and his three thousand men.

Despite its modest gains, the Battle of Belmont was the greatest Union success of the war so far. The only other engagement of note, the first battle of Bull Run, had ended with frightened Union General Irvin McDowell in full retreat—a precedent many other Union generals would soon follow.

The Battle of Belmont established Ulysses as a fighting general.

Suddenly, people began to notice Ulysses. Major- general McClellan, from his pedestal on high, turned and looked in Ulysses' direction for the first time. Shortly after Belmont, Ulysses received his first ever telegram from McClellan: "Inform me fully of the number & condition of your command. Tell me your wants & wishes— communicate fully and often."

It sounds innocent and helpful enough, but the roots of jealousy were just beginning to take hold—a jealousy of Ulysses that started at the top and quickly spread through the ranks.

People either loved Ulysses or they hated him. Those who loved him saw his virtues: kindness, modesty, decision. Those who hated him were higher-ups jealously guarding their own inflated stature. How could they go on doing nothing, while pretending to be doing something, when this unassuming little soldier was *actually* doing something? Ulysses was a threat to every cowardly desk general in the country, and they knew it as soon as they heard about his wild horseback ride through the cornfields at Belmont. (Major General McClellan, the "young Napoleon," never came within two miles of a battlefield during the entire war!)

There were also swindlers trying to take advantage of Ulysses, who, when their illicit activities were halted by him, sought revenge.

Ulysses was an easy mark for revenge. All you had to do was play the "drunk" card.

It must have been during one of Julia's visits home, that allegations of Ulysses' drinking at his headquarters in Cairo, Illinois, began to spread.

Benjamin H. Campbell of Galena, recently returned from St. Louis, wrote to his Congressman, Elihu Washburne, who was a big supporter of Ulysses:

"I am sorry to hear from good authority, that General Grant is drinking hard, had you not better write to Rawlins to know the facts."

Rawlins wrote a lengthy and passionate defense of Ulysses to Washburne, insisting the accusations must have been made in malice. Rawlins promised that if General Grant ever drank to an extent to cause danger to the U.S. Army, Rawlins would resign.

Another letter written soon after was by William Bross of the Chicago Tribune to Secretary of War Simon Cameron:

"Evidence entirely satisfactory to myself & Associate Editors of the Tribune has become so convincing that General U.S. Grant commanding at Cairo is an inebriate, that I deem it my duty to call your attention to the matter."

Secretary of War Cameron forwarded the letter to Abraham Lincoln.

Ulysses was now under attack from all sides.

Captain William J. Kountz, a quartermaster hired by Halleck to oversee the steamboats which supplied Ulysses' army, was placed under arrest by Ulysses, for showing disrespect for his commander. Out for revenge, Kountz then preferred a long list of charges against General U.S. Grant: Kountz accused Ulysses of "drunkenness on duty," and "becoming beastly drunk," "conduct unbecoming an officer," and for being so drunk that "he lost his uniform and sword," and "had to crawl up the stairs on all fours," which Kountz considered "conduct unbecoming a man."

Ulysses, with his Victorian code of honor, never answered the charges. Though, sadly, he was forced to sign a copy of the charges, verifying he had seen them, before passing them on to the higher authorities.

Was loneliness claiming Ulysses again?

If his weakness for Julia could not be satisfied, his weakness for liquor certainly could.

The Army was a hard drinking outfit, and alcohol was easy to find.

The rumors of Ulysses' drinking reached Abraham Lincoln himself.

President Lincoln carefully read the allegations made by William Bross, as well as an attached letter, author unknown, which accused General Grant of "frequently being too drunk to fill his station and of being perfectly inebriate under a flag of truce with rebels."

The author also took a swipe at Julia, ranting, "All these things are facts which the world ought to know. Until we can secure pure men in habits and men without secesh wives with their own little slaves to wait upon them, which is a fact here in this camp with Mrs. Grant, our country is lost."

President Lincoln must have been alarmed, for General Grant commanded one of the most important districts in the country. Lincoln had heard of Ulysses' bravery at Belmont, but most everything else he had heard of the sad-faced little general, was scandalous.

Lincoln wrote to Secretary of War Cameron, "Bross would not knowingly misrepresent. General Grant was appointed chiefly on the recommendation of Hon. E.B. Washburne. Perhaps we should consult him."

Cameron endorsed Lincoln's letter and sent it on to Congressman Washburne.

It is sad to note that while Ulysses defended himself to Washburne against other charges, such as loss of life in his battles and his decision not to run from a fight, he never defended himself against the drinking charges.

As has poignantly been noted by General Grant's supporters, if Ulysses was drinking, he never did harm to anyone but himself. And historians all agree, he drank because he missed Julia.

It is important to remember Ulysses S. Grant was extremely shy. His wife, Julia, was the only one with whom he felt comfortable enough to share his inner most feelings. When long away from her, he was engulfed by loneliness.

Long periods of inactivity were especially dangerous for Ulysses. He was better off when there were battles to be fought. This kept the Union Commander's mind off his Southern sweetheart, and his hands off the bottle.

We will never know what the outcome of the court martial against Ulysses would have been. Before Ulysses could be brought to trial on charges of drunkenness, he won the most smashing victory of the war up to that time, and overnight, became a national hero.

CHAPTER TWENTY-TWO
Unconditional Surrender

In January of 1862, Ulysses asked permission to visit his chief, Henry Halleck, in St. Louis. Ulysses outlined a plan for taking two rebel forts: Fort Henry and Fort Donelson.

In General Grant's own words: "The enemy at this time occupied a line running from the Mississippi River at Columbus to Bowling Green and Mill Springs, Kentucky. Each of these positions was strongly fortified, as were also points on the Tennessee and Cumberland rivers near the Tennessee state line. The works on the Tennessee were called Fort Heiman and Fort Henry, and that on the Cumberland was Fort Donelson. At these points the two rivers approached within eleven miles of each other. The lines of rifle pits at each place extended back from the water at least two miles, so that the garrisons were in reality only seven miles apart. These positions were of immense importance to the enemy, and of course, correspondingly important for us to possess ourselves of. With Fort Henry in our hands we had a navigable stream open to us up to Muscle Shoals, in Alabama. The Memphis and Charleston Railroad strikes the Tennessee at Eastport, Mississippi, and follows close to the banks of the river up to the shoals. This road, of vast importance to the enemy, would cease to be of use to them for through traffic the moment Fort Henry became ours. Fort Donelson was the gate to Nashville—a place of great military and political importance—and to a rich country extending far east in Kentucky. These two points in our possession, the enemy would necessarily be thrown back to the Memphis and Charleston road, or to the boundary of the cotton states, and, as before stated, that road would be lost to them for through communication."

Halleck scoffed that Ulysses' plan was "preposterous," and sent the dejected Ulysses back to Cairo.

"I was very much crestfallen," Ulysses remembered.

Determined, Ulysses gained the support of Flag-officer Andrew Foote, who commanded the small fleet of gunboats about Cairo. Ulysses also gained support from General C.F. Smith, for his plan. The much older General Smith was once Ulysses' professor at West Point, and was highly respected by Halleck.

Persistent Ulysses telegraphed Halleck once more proposing his plan:

With a combined force of troops and gunboats, Ulysses wished to attack Fort Henry, on the Tennessee River, then Fort Donelson, on the Cumberland River, eliminating these two Confederate strongholds in the state of Tennessee.

Now, Halleck reluctantly gave in, and gave Ulysses the go-ahead to do what he did best: take action.

On February 2, 1862, Ulysses left Cairo and headed up the Tennessee River with 17,000 troops, on three separate steamboats. Flag-officer Foote accompanied them, with seven gunboats.

"How pretty the steamers looked as they swung out into the stream laden with troops and bright with flags!" Julia romantically recalled.

Ulysses left his adoring wife waving good-bye on the Cairo shore, and headed down the river, toward his destiny.

The gunboats opened fire on Fort Henry, while the troops were delayed by lack of roads and dense forests. Despite the delay, the Commander of Fort Henry, General Lloyd Tilghman, knew General Grant was coming to get him. Terrified of the aggressive General Grant, the rebel commander panicked and evacuated Fort Henry, leaving one hundred men in the fort to man the guns and cover the escape of his retreating army.

General Tilghman was captured, but most of his men escaped to the much larger Fort Donelson. Of course, Ulysses immediately made plans to pursue them.

The rebels must have been surprised to see such an aggressive Union commander!

Ulysses notified General Halleck of his success at Fort Henry, and announced that he was now prepared to attack Fort Donelson.

Halleck made no reply. He wasn't exactly a "hands on" commander!

Ulysses soon started from Fort Henry, with 15,000 men. Fort Donelson, high on a bluff overlooking the Cumberland River, was much more formidable than Fort Henry. It was surrounded by seemingly impenetrable rifle pits, and manned by around 21,000 men.

Here, the combined forces of both Fort Henry and Fort Donelson prepared to make their last stand.

Fort Donelson stood upon one hundred acres of woods, high above the river. It was fortified with felled tree limbs which had been trimmed and sharply pointed.

The Fort seemed impenetrable—to anyone but General Grant.

The rebels had more troops than General Grant, and the weather was also to their advantage. The temperatures fell below freezing, and as Ulysses' men surrounded the fort, they were forced to sleep in the ice and snow. Many of the men had discarded their coats and blankets on the way to Fort Donelson, to lighten their load. Now, they huddled and shook together, unable to light fires because it might attract the attention of the enemy.

Back at General Grant's headquarters, in Cairo, Julia waited. She was disappointed when Ulysses did not return with a boatload of troops. She did not know her husband was now facing the defining moment of his life.

During the first day's bombardment of Fort Donelson, by the navy, the rebels manning the fort had severely damaged some of the gunboats, wounding Flag-officer Foote and sending his boat careening downriver.

Foote asked General Grant to visit him on board the boat, for a conference.

While he was away, the rebels inside the surrounded fort suddenly broke out, fighting all the way. Without his leadership, Ulysses' soldiers panicked, and fell back.

A messenger on horseback raced away to find Ulysses and tell him the dire situation. Pale with fear, Captain William Hillyer, Ulysses' assistant, informed him that all seemed lost.

Ulysses jumped on his horse and headed for Fort Donelson.

Down icy paths and the darkest fears of his soul he rode, to face the enemy.

Arriving at Fort Donelson, he quickly saw that all Union leadership had collapsed. Terrified officers were immobilized by fear. There was no one giving orders. Shaken soldiers cried that they were out of ammunition.

Taking charge, Ulysses noticed piles of unused ammunition nearby. He coolly told his men to load their guns and cartridge boxes and get into line of battle.

They had only wanted someone to lead them, and Ulysses was that man.

Ulysses took in the situation at once. The rebels had attacked the Union right. He realized that in doing so, they must have weakened their own right, to strengthen their left. He determined to attack the Rebel right, at once.

Ulysses ordered his most trusted general, General C.F. Smith: "All has failed us on our right. You must take Fort Donelson."

Electrified by his commander's confidence, General Smith ordered his men to fix bayonets, and in they went.

"You joined the army to be killed, and now you can be!" the old man cried.

Surprised, those rebels who survived fell back inside the fort.

In command of Fort Donelson were three men. First in command: John B. Floyd, former United States Secretary of War. Taking advantage of his station before the war, he had sent as many war materials as possible down South, for use in the rebellion. He knew he might be hung for treason if he was caught, and so he decided to flee, and handed over authority to the next in command, General Pillow.

General Pillow was simply a coward, who gulped, decided to flee with Floyd, and passed the command to the only brave general in the bunch: General Simon Bolivar Buckner, Ulysses' old friend from West Point, who had taken pity on Ulysses and loaned him money when Ulysses was on his way home from California.

Though Buckner was his friend, Ulysses showed no pity, now. Buckner sent a message to Ulysses:

Headquarters, Fort Donelson,
February 16, 1862

To Brigadier-General U.S. Grant
Com'ding U.S. Forces.
Near Fort Donelson.

Sir: In consideration of all the circumstances governing the present situation of affairs at this station, I propose to the Commanding Officer of the Federal forces the appointment of Commissioners to agree upon terms of capitulation of the forces and fort under my command, and in that view suggest an armistice until 12 o'clock to-day.

> *I am, sir, very respectfully,*
> *Your ob't se'v't,*
> *S.B. Buckner,*
> *Brig. Gen. C.S.A.*

In reply, Ulysses penned the words that would define him for all time, words that would make him immortal:

"No terms but an unconditional and immediate surrender can be accepted. I propose to move immediately upon your works."

Buckner was stunned. How could his old friend be so cold?

He probably swallowed hard, thought it over, and realized there was nothing left to do but surrender. Under threat of an immediate attack by General Grant, Buckner replied:

To Brig. Gen'l U.S. Grant,
U.S. Army.

Sir: The distribution of the forces under my command, incident to an unexpected change of commanders, and the overwhelming force under your command, compel me, notwithstanding the brilliant success of the Confederate arms yesterday, to accept the ungenerous and unchivalrous terms which you propose.

> *I am, sir,*

Your very ob't se'v't,
S.B. Buckner,
Brig. Gen. C.S.A.

Ulysses now had a new nickname, which made his previous load of nicknames like "Uncle Sam" "Texas" and "Dudy" obsolete. His nickname became "Unconditional Surrender" Grant—a name which would become prophetic for his Southern belle wife.

Julia was at Cairo when she heard the news. "Everyone went wild!" she recalled with pride.

But not everyone she knew was proud of Ulysses.

Colonel Dent was at White Haven when the news came that there had been a surrender—the biggest surrender in history.

The Colonel, sipping a julep on his front porch, probably thought McClellan had surrendered to Lee. Imagine his shock when he learned Fort Donelson, with 15,000 prisoners, had surrendered to his Yankee son-in-law!

It was impossible for Southern belle Julia to stay neutral any longer, for her Yankee husband had become the greatest Union hero of the Civil War.

CHAPTER TWENTY-THREE
Caught in the Cross Fire

Mrs. U.S. Grant made the unique decision of announcing she was a loyalist to the Union—while being waited on hand and foot by slaves.

Her Southern girlfriends looked askance at Julia. As Julia remembers, she tried to insist she was for the Union, but they weren't buying it.

Julia recalled her Southern friends knowingly shaking their heads, and chiding her, "It is right for you to say you are Union, Julia, but we know better, my child; it is not human nature for you to be anything but Southern." "We know how you have been brought up and an oath would not be more binding than the sanctity of your roof."

Julia was still walking the line, being supportive of her husband, while living the life he was duty bound to destroy.

While Ulysses was at Fort Donelson, he wrote his wife beseeching her to stay with his own family, in Covington, Kentucky, until he could call for her, again. In Kentucky, she would be closer to where he was. He promised to send for her as soon as "war matters" allowed.

Julia reluctantly obeyed. She knew Ulysses' family did not like her.

On the train to Kentucky, Julia was so lonely for Ulysses, that she began to cry. Her wracking sobs became so loud, a kind lady on the train, though a stranger, came in to console her.

Her husband was a hero, but she wanted his arms to hold her, his lips to kiss and comfort her.

She would not see him again, until he had a new battle to his name: the battle of Shiloh.

CHAPTER TWENTY-FOUR
Shiloh, the "Place of Peace"

Ulysses did not enjoy bloodshed. The smells of his father's tannery made him queasy, and he always insisted on eating meat which had been blackened, because the sight of blood made him sick.

From Mexico, he had written Julia, "*If we have to fight, I'd like to do it all at once, and then make friends.*"

Ulysses hoped to keep advancing while he had the initiative, and end the war quickly, to avoid gratuitous bloodshed. He wrote Julia that the way to avoid "*terrible battles*" was to "*push forward as vigorously as possible.*"

Unfortunately, Ulysses' superiors did not see it that way. Jealous of Grant's acclaim and hoping to further his own career, General Halleck stalled the whole operation in a gamble to get himself promoted to commander of a new department made just for him, the "Department of the West."

He first sought to dilute Ulysses' achievement at Fort Donelson by calling for promotions for two other generals who hadn't even been there. He wrote to George McClellan, now Commander in Chief of the Army: "Make Buell, Grant and Pope major-generals of volunteers and give me command of the west. I ask this in return for forts Henry and Donelson."

Halleck was demanding rewards for the fall of Forts Henry and Donelson, even though he wasn't there! He even stuck Ulysses' name in the middle with the other absent generals, in an attempt to further diffuse Ulysses' fame. This ruse failed, as Lincoln was way ahead of him. Having heard of Ulysses' brilliant success on February 16, Lincoln promoted Ulysses that very night to Major-general. Lincoln knew who was responsible for the success at Fort Donelson. It was not "Buell, Grant and Pope," but Grant alone.

This must have made Halleck's jealous blood boil.

Now, Halleck ordered Ulysses to "stay put" "avoid a general engagement" and other words meant to bog down the operation, while he insisted that without full command of the West, he could not and would not advance. Halleck was blackmailing McClellan in an attempt to grab more power for himself.

Ulysses is blamed for the thousands of ensuing deaths that became necessary to win the Civil War. But it was really the envious Halleck that halted the Union progression long enough to lose the initiative and the chance for an early victory. This allowed the rebels to regroup, sealing the fate of hundreds of thousands of soldiers who died needlessly over the next three years, at places like Shiloh and Cold Harbor.

The lengths to which Halleck and McClellan went to tarnish Ulysses' fame are amazing.

With the fall of Fort Donelson, Ulysses knew "the gate was open" to Nashville, a Confederate city of great military and political importance. Ulysses wanted to move on Nashville as soon as possible, and traveled there to check it out.

While he was away, McClellan asked Halleck to report on the size and condition of his command, as Halleck was demanding "50,000 men from the Army of the Potomac," for a hodge podge of small ventures, none of which had anything to do with smashing the rebel armies.

Halleck telegraphed Ulysses to inform him of the size and condition of his command.

A rebel spy had intercepted the telegrams from Halleck to Ulysses, so that Ulysses had no idea what Halleck was asking of him.

Rather than trust the victor of the most brilliant success of the war, Halleck fumed to McClellan that Ulysses had gone to Nashville without permission. Equally jealous of Ulysses, McClellan quickly gave Halleck permission to have Ulysses arrested! Halleck followed this up by suggesting to McClellan that Ulysses was drinking again, even though Halleck knew it wasn't true.

Meanwhile, Ulysses finally received a threatening message from Halleck, who fumed, "You will place Maj.-Gen. C.F. Smith in command of expedition, and remain yourself at Fort Henry. Why do you not obey my orders to report strength and position of your command?"

Ulysses was surprised. Following his victory at Fort Donelson, Ulysses had been named commander of the District of West Tennessee, "limits not defined." He believed Nashville was not out of bounds for him. He politely defended himself, but asked to be relieved from further duty under Halleck.

Thinking it over, Halleck probably had to admit to himself that Ulysses was the only commander in the field to win a major Union victory, and his own success was tied to the fighting little general, whether he liked it, or not.

Halleck blinked, and announced to Ulysses that he, Halleck had made everything right in Washington. They were going to arrest him, but he, Halleck, like a knight on a white horse, had ridden to Ulysses' rescue.

"Instead of relieving you, I wish you, as soon as your new army is in the field, to assume immediate command, and lead it to new victories." He wrote Ulysses, as if he was somehow General Grant's guardian angel.

"In consequence, I felt very grateful to him," Ulysses later recalled, "and supposed it was his interposition that had set me right with the government." He never knew the truth until after the war, when General Adam Badeau unearthed the facts in his researches for his history of General Grant's campaigns.

Inwardly, Ulysses was hurting.

The men who had fought beside Ulysses knew his value, both as a Commander and as a man. Ulysses' men presented him with a beautiful sword and the following words of encouragement: "At this moment when the jealousy caused by your brilliant success has raised up hidden enemies against you," presenting the ornamental sword "affords us an opportunity to express our renewed confidence in your ability as a commander."

Overcome with emotion, Ulysses was unable to reply, and his assistant, Captain William Hillyer, made an acceptance statement on his behalf.

Meanwhile, Julia was having her own problems.

Following Ulysses' wishes, she and her four children had gone to Covington, Kentucky, to stay with Ulysses' parents, the austere Hannah and the miserly Jesse. It was not long before the pampered Southern belle did not feel wanted by her husband's Yankee family.

Julia wrote Ulysses that his sisters were complaining of the expense of caring for her children.

As Julia put it in her own memoirs, describing the rift between herself and Ulysses' family, "They considered me unpardonably extravagant, and I considered them to be unpardonably the other way."

Though maneuvering for the biggest battle of the war so far, Ulysses wrote his wife advising her to take their children, leave his parents' home, and go to stay with her aunt in Louisville, Kentucky, until he could send for her.

"*It will be impossible for you to join me*," he laments, "*I will soon be in the tented field, <u>without</u> <u>a</u> <u>tent</u>, and after the enemy.*"

He also wrote her that he had been sick, probably because of the unfair way in which he had been treated, but that he was feeling better now that he was restored to command, and feeling useful again.

Ulysses outlined his hopes for moving quickly upon the enemy, but said he did not think "war matters" would be interesting to her. Loving husband Ulysses closed his letter by saying, "*good night dear Julia.*"

If "war matters" did not interest Julia, her dear husband's well-being certainly did.

While Ulysses awaited Buell's Army of the Ohio, so he could take the initiative, the displaced Julia waited in Louisville, hoping Ulysses would call for her, soon.

Julia spent much time daydreaming about Ulysses.

It was March, 1862. All around her, the jasmine was opening and the peach trees awakening, with the first signs of spring.

Spring—the season when Julia and Ulysses first fell in love. She could still see him approaching White Haven on his horse, as pretty as a little doll, his need for her love lighting his pale blue eyes and bringing a blush to his porcelain cheeks. There was a sweetness to Ulysses' eyes that was there even now. She wondered if anyone else ever noticed. He was so far away, but as she gazed at the lovely peach trees with their filmy blossoms, she hoped he might be seeing the peach blossoms, too, somewhere—wherever he might be.

Ulysses was seeing peach blossoms. In fact, the fields around Shiloh church were infused with trees dotted with delicate peach blossoms.

As he gazed out at the peach blossoms, Ulysses couldn't help but be reminded of White Haven and Julia—riding side by side on their horses at sunrise, sharing their dreams beneath the peach blossoms. Sometimes a soft breeze would stir, and the peach blossoms rained down all around them like a fairy land.

In Hebrew, "Shiloh" means "place of peace." Ulysses' friend, William "Cump" Sherman, sometimes called "Uncle Billy," had chosen this lovely place to camp his Army.

It was the first time Sherman and Ulysses had been paired up since their days playing cards at West Point.

It was pleasant to see each other again.

Together, they would face what Sherman called, "The Devil's own day."

CHAPTER TWENTY-FIVE
The Devil's Own Day

When General Grant reassumed command of the Army of the Tennessee, on March 17, 1862, he found the army divided. About half were on the east bank of the Tennessee River at Savannah, while one division was at Crump's landing, an important Union supply center on the west bank, about four miles higher up, and the remainder at Pittsburg landing.

Pittsburg landing was the closest point to Corinth, Mississippi, twenty miles south.

Corinth was the "great strategic point of the West," containing the junction of the two most important railroads in the Mississippi Valley.

Corinth was also swarming with Confederate troops, close to eighty thousand, according to reports.

Albert Sidney Johnston, the Confederate commander at Corinth, was the highest ranking Confederate officer in the West. He was blamed for the defeats at Fort Henry and Fort Donelson, and was especially ashamed of a rebuke by his president, Jefferson Davis. Now, Johnston felt the only way to redeem his honor, was to make a bold move.

Ulysses did not anticipate the Confederates making a move, because they were strongly entrenched at Corinth. They had a better chance of holding off Ulysses' army, if they stayed where they were.

True to his aggressive nature, Ulysses planned to attack Corinth—but he decided to wait.

Ulysses was waiting for reinforcements from Don Carlos Buell, Halleck's old pal and the Commander of the Army of the Ohio. Buell was expected any day at Savannah, where Ulysses was waiting to meet him. As soon as Buell arrived, Ulysses planned to mass all his armies, move all his men toward Corinth, and crush Johnston's' army.

Without reinforcements, Ulysses would be vastly outnumbered. With Buell's expected force of 40,000 veterans added, Ulysses knew there was a much greater chance for success.

Another decision Ulysses made, was not to entrench his troops at Pittsburg Landing. Most of the soldiers were "raw," having never been in an engagement.

Ulysses decided that drill and discipline were more important than hiding behind entrenchments, and so, he left them out in the open.

Waiting, and leaving Yankee troops out in the open, created too big a temptation for Albert Sydney Johnston.

While Ulysses waited for Buell, General Johnston decided this was the chance he had been waiting for.

Johnston sent skirmishers near the Union camp. There were occasional shots fired, as they probed their opponents.

On the night of April 4th, the rain fell in torrents. While riding to the front, where firing had been heard, Ulysses' horse slipped in the mud and fell on top of his master.

Ulysses was injured and in great pain, his ankle swelling so badly his boot had to be cut off.

He had no idea how much worse the situation was going to become.

The morning of April 6, 1862, dawned sunny and bright. While the soldiers yawned and stretched and prepared their breakfasts, there was a feeling more akin to a picnic than an army camp.

At his headquarters in Savannah, Ulysses took an early breakfast, planning to ride out and meet Buell, who was expected that day.

But he had no more than taken a few bites, when cannon fire was heard up the river.

At first, Ulysses was unsure if the attack was being made at Crump's Landing, or Pittsburg. A quick ride up the river proved the attack on Pittsburg Landing was "unmistakable."

At Fort Henry and Fort Donelson, the Confederates fended off their attackers from behind giant fortifications, made of pointed tree limbs.

Ulysses' men were right out in the open, and this made the carnage terrible.

This must have been the longest day of Ulysses' life, as the Confederates hurled themselves, wave after wave of them, against men who did not even have arms in their hands.

With terrified Union soldiers who had never been in battle before, Sherman held his position in front of "Shiloh," the little church which meant "place of peace." The poor men barely knew how to load their rifles. They had scarcely had time to learn, but they had learned a little, in the time providence had given them.

Five Yankee divisions held off the onslaught of warriors in gray:

Sherman, two or three miles from Pittsburg landing, was in front of the log meeting house known as "Shiloh." His troops were all raw, but his own self-confidence calmed their terror.

General McClernand, a former Congressman from Illinois, was on Sherman's left, with troops who had been engaged at forts Henry and Donelson, and so, had more experience themselves, but a far less talented commander.

Next to McClernand was General Benjamin Prentiss, a General who early in the war, had bickered with Ulysses over which one of them was senior in rank, with a raw division. General Stephen Hurlbut, who would loyally serve Ulysses through the whole war, was in rear of Prentiss. The Division of Ulysses' old West Point commander, General C.F. Smith, was on the right. Smith was sick in bed in Savannah, and his division was now being led by W.H.L. Wallace, an honored officer who would be one of the first to die.

Sherman, the tough soldier, McClernand, the former Congressman, Prentiss, the former enemy, Hurlbut, the loyal friend, and Wallace, the doomed officer.

They all looked to Ulysses for the verdict: would they run, or would they fight?

Ulysses decided to fight.

To most, the battleground was a mass of confusion: the deafening crash of musketry, the cries of frightened horses and of men, but to Ulysses', it was an opportunity. If they could hold their ground until reinforcements arrived, they would win.

Sherman held his ground all day, Prentiss and his men fought like mad, but finally surrendered, late in the day. When William

Wallace fell dead, his division fell apart. Despite dead comrades piling up at their feet, the divisions of McClernand and Hurlbut managed to hold on, preventing the Confederates from killing them all.

Ulysses rode from one bloody and diminishing division to the next, all day, encouraging them to hold their ground. All must have nearly collapsed, when "night and night alone closed the contest," as General Grant recalled.

Buell's reinforcements never showed up on that fateful Sunday. To the Army of the Tennessee, and to their sad-faced commander, General Grant, goes all the credit for holding Pittsburg landing that long, bloody, horrible day, against nearly impossible odds.

William T. Sherman was a rugged man. But that night, even he was thinking about retreating before morning.

Sherman sought out his old friend, to discuss plans for a retreat.

He soon found his commander, a lone figure standing beneath a tree in the rain.

Something about General Grant made Sherman abandon any talk of a retreat. Instead, he merely probed him, sighing, "Well, Grant, we've had the Devil's own day."

"Yes," said General Grant. "Yes."

Then, amid lightning flashes and pounding rain came General Grant's answer to the question Sherman dare not ask:

"Lick 'em tomorrow, though."

CHAPTER TWENTY-SIX
The Solitary Man

General Grant alone had faith his troops could win tomorrow.

But he surely spent a heartbreakingly lonely night in the rain. I just love his own poignant words, in his memoirs, recalling of that darkest of nights:

"During the night rain fell in torrents and our troops were exposed to the storm without shelter. I made my headquarters under a tree a few hundred yards back from the river bank. My ankle was so much swollen from the fall of my horse the Friday night preceding, and the bruise was so painful, that I could get no rest. The drenching rain would have precluded the possibility of sleep without this additional cause. Some time after midnight, growing restive under the storm and the continuous pain, I moved back to the log-house under the bank. This had been taken as a hospital, and all night wounded men were being brought in, their wounds dressed, a leg or an arm amputated as the case might require, and everything being done to save life or alleviate suffering. The sight was more unendurable than encountering the enemy's fire, and I returned to my tree in the rain."

During the night, Buell's Army of the Ohio finally arrived, nearly doubling Ulysses' force. General Lew Wallace, with one division from Crump's Landing, also arrived and took their place beside the heroes of April 6th, the bloody, ragged Army of the Tennessee.

As sunlight dawned, the Confederates were amazed when Ulysses S. Grant attacked them. Exhausted from yesterday's battle, the Confederates were quickly driven from the field. Thus ended the bloodiest battle of the Civil War, up to this time.

At first, the battle of Shiloh was claimed as a victory for the Union. But as the horrific casualty count mounted, support for the victor of Fort Henry and Fort Donelson began to erode. Shiloh was pronounced an atrocity by both sides. And both sides blamed Ulysses.

Ulysses had followed his own advice, "When in doubt, fight." The result was more deaths at the battle of Shiloh than in all American wars up to that time, put together.

Ulysses was now hated by Confederates and Yankees alike. They called him a "butcher" and cried out for his removal.

Southern belle Julia's marriage to a Yankee general was no longer something to be shrugged off. At home at White Haven, Julia was surely under pressure from all sides to separate herself from Ulysses, for the sake of her children.

McClellan, Halleck and a host of others flocked to Washington to demand Ulysses' removal. Only Abraham Lincoln felt sympathy. "Poor Grant," said Lincoln, "He hardly has a friend left." In the end, Lincoln stuck by Ulysses. "I can't spare the man," Lincoln grimly stated, "He fights."

Why was Julia's husband so unlike the other Yankee generals? Why didn't he run when the battlefield got too hot? Because he knew the only way to win the war and save the Union, was to destroy the Confederate Armies. There was no other way. To retreat accomplished nothing, and in the end, even more lives would be lost.

It's also important to note, if General Halleck would have let Ulysses advance when he wanted to, right after the victory at Fort Donelson, Shiloh would have remained the unknown name of a tiny church, rather than an infamous name forever associated with blood, butchery—and bravery.

Ulysses alone had the moral courage to take responsibility for what was necessary to win the war.

But did Julia have the courage to stick by Ulysses? Growing up the belle of White Haven, her home was the focal point for the neighborhood of sunshine and Sunday pleasures. Oh, how life had changed. She now felt the bitter scorn of friends and family, not to mention the whole country, weighing on her. Closing her eyes, she could still see the anguished faces of neighbors who had lost loved ones because Ulysses wouldn't walk away from a fight. It was painful to awake each morning knowing everybody hated her husband.

They said he wasn't the man she thought he was. Were they right? Ulysses' mother had never given him affection, never even kissed him. Had it made him cold to the sufferings of others? He always seemed so warm hearted to Julia. How could her kind-hearted, gentle husband, the one who could never collect money owed him, who couldn't bear to see someone mistreat an animal, who couldn't even stand the sight of blood, how could he lead so many men to their deaths?

As spring blossoms faded under the summer heat, Julia suffered under the scorching hatred of friends turned to enemies. Ulysses had his command taken from him, and General Halleck himself left his comfortable desk chair to command the Army of Tennessee. But Halleck was so inept in the field, the men complained loudly. Fate intervened, and Halleck was called to Washington, to be placed in charge of all Union armies. This put Ulysses back in charge of the Army of the Tennessee, and Halleck back behind the comfortable security of his desk.

Julia and Ulysses had been apart a long while.

What joy it was when he called for her again!

The scorn of grieving Southern neighbors faded at the thought of holding her beloved once again.

Julia and her children were soon on their way to Ulysses' new headquarters in Corinth, Mississippi.

Julia wrote of their happy reunion:

"When we visited Corinth for the first time, we found the General's ambulance awaiting us at the depot. The General and two or three of his staff officers accompanied us on horseback to headquarters. The General was so glad to see us and rode close beside the ambulance, stooping near and asking me if I was as glad to see him as he was to see me. He reached out and took my hand and gave it another and another warm pressure. Dear fellow! How kind he always was to me!"

Many romantic rendezvous took place between Julia and Ulysses in the coming months, as he moved from place to place in pursuit of the enemy.

Julia's visit to Corinth was cut short when Ulysses suddenly sent her and the children back to White Haven, just before the bloody battle of Corinth.

But as soon as he was able, Ulysses sent for Julia to join him in Jackson, Tennessee, and in November, 1862, Julia trysted with her husband in LaGrange, Tennessee, his headquarters as he planned a new campaign deeper into the heart of the Confederacy, into Mississippi.

Julia occupied a home whose secessionist occupants had been forced to flee. Julia felt sorry for them, and hoped they were as comfortable as she.

Upon her arrival, she looked up and saw Ulysses observing her. She exclaimed, "Ulys, I don't like stationary washstands, do you?"

"Yes, I do, why don't you?" he queried.

Julia replied, "Well, I don't know."

Ulysses replied, "I'll tell you why. You have to go to the stand. It cannot be brought to you."

This exchange always makes me laugh!

Ulysses was always amused by Julia and her pampered, Southern ways, though future generations would feel she was putting on airs.

His affection for her, and hers for him, kept a warm glow in their hearts, wherever they might be.

It was when Julia was not near, that Ulysses struggled, and he struggled mightily with the bottle, that winter of 1862 to 1863.

His men tried to keep Julia with him as often as possible.

Brigadier General Charles S. Hamilton, a fellow Union officer and friend of Ulysses, wrote of Ulysses' struggles to U.S. Senator James B. Doolittle of Wisconsin:

*"*You have asked me to write you confidentially. I will now say what I have never breathed: *Grant is a drunkard.* His wife has been with him for months only to use her influence in keeping him sober. He tries to let liquor alone but he cannot resist the temptation always. When he come to Memphis, he left his wife at La Grange, and for several days after getting here, was beastly drunk, utterly incapable of doing anything. Quinby & I, took him in charge, watching with him, day & night and keeping liquor away from him, and we telegraphed to his wife and brought her on to take care of him." He then insists, "Now this is in the *strictest confidence.* Grant is a warm friend of mine, & I of him, and although he is not a great man—yet he is a man of nerve and will not let an opportunity slip to strike the enemy a blow, whenever he can do it.*"*

I cried when I first read this quote from Charles Hamilton, who I knew liked General Grant. I only felt compassion, and was glad that Julia took care of him.

While Julia loved and cared for Ulysses, Abraham Lincoln renewed his commitment to the Civil War.

"We cannot escape history," President Lincoln declared, reasserting his belief that the cause of saving the Union and freeing the slaves was the nation's destiny.

When Ulysses took forts Henry and Donelson, it was said that the "back bone of secession had been broken," forcing the Confederates out of Kentucky and much of Tennessee.

At Shiloh, Ulysses kept the Confederates from gaining ground further north, and they were soon forced to evacuate Corinth, the great railway center.

In the East, McClellan had had no luck taking Richmond, considered the ultimate prize.

But in the West, there was perhaps a prize of equal allure: Vicksburg, the Confederate fortress on the Mississippi River.

Their stronghold atop a bluff at Vicksburg enabled the Confederates to control the Mississippi River, which divided the South. If Vicksburg fell, so would the Confederates' use of the Mississippi River. And the Confederacy would be split in two.

The fight for control of the rivers was of equal value to control of the land.

The Confederates knew the value of Vicksburg, and were holding on as hard as they could, with 30,000 men and enormous fortifications.

The taking of Vicksburg seemed impossible. And so, Lincoln turned to the master of the impossible, Ulysses S. Grant.

Of course, Ulysses' reputation was battered. He was decried as a "butcher" and a "drunkard." The only thing that kept him sober, it was whispered, was the love of his Southern wife.

Still, Ulysses was the only Union general to win a victory as brilliant as Fort Donelson. So Lincoln decided to take a chance.

On October 25, 1862, Ulysses officially became Commander of the Department of the Tennessee. (Previously, he had only commanded a district. This was the first time he commanded an entire department.)

On the 12th of November, Ulysses received a dispatch from General Halleck, giving Ulysses command of all the troops sent to his department, and permission to "fight the enemy where you please."

At 1:00 P.M. on January 9, 1863, Ulysses telegraphed Halleck: "I will start for Memphis immediately & will do everything possible for the capture of Vicksburg."

It was in Memphis that Ulysses was apart from his wife, and suffered from extreme loneliness and drinking bouts, until she came to care for him.

From Memphis, on January 13, 1863, Ulysses telegraphed to one of his favorite officers, General McPherson, "It is my present intention to command the expedition down the river in person."

Julia was left behind in Memphis, and Ulysses faced the daunting task of taking Vicksburg, alone.

CHAPTER TWENTY-SEVEN
Vicksburg

The Union now held Memphis, Tennessee. Heading south from Memphis, Vicksburg was the first high land coming to the river's edge.

The problem was that the area between Memphis and Vicksburg was a torturous tapestry of waterways, with names like "Steel's Bayou" "Black Bayou" and "Deer Creek."

It would be impossible for Ulysses' troops to march across such a maze of swamps and marshes, in the face of the enemy. Also, it was unknown how many of these intricate creeks and bayous were suitable for navigation by gunboats and steamboats loaded with troops.

The logical strategy, if one played by the rules, would have been to go back to Memphis, establish a base of supplies there, then swing around toward Vicksburg from the East, marching the troops along the line of the railroad toward Jackson, Mississippi, which was about twenty miles East of Vicksburg.

But to do this would have involved a backward movement, returning to Memphis. The troops were already before Vicksburg, and backpedaling north to Memphis would have been viewed by Union loyalists, as a retreat.

Ulysses knew the prevailing sentiment in the North, now, was discouragement. He feared that a backward movement as far as from Vicksburg to Memphis might be so disappointing that "the draft would be resisted, desertions ensue and the power to punish deserters lost."

In his memoirs, he recalls, "There was nothing left to be done but to *go forward to a decisive victory.*"

Julia was surely worried about Ulysses, as he traveled by steamboat to Young's Point, Mississippi—a man who was expected to do the impossible.

Ulysses remembered, "The real work of the campaign and siege of Vicksburg now began."

That winter of 1862-1863 was unusual for its relentless rain and gloom. Ulysses knew there was not much hope of his troops getting a footing on dry ground in this weather, but he did not want them to lie idle and become discouraged. He knew only too well, the negative affects of idleness, in the army.

One order of business was to find out how far boats could navigate into the winding maze of creeks and bayous. Could one of these waterways be used to get them all the way to Vicksburg?

In his memoirs, Ulysses recounts, "Steel's bayou connects with Black Bayou, Black Bayou with Deer Creek, Deer Creek with Rolling Fork, Rolling Fork with the Big Sunflower River, and the Big Sunflower with the Yazoo River."

If they could get into the Yazoo River, they could get into Vicksburg from the rear. But this bewildering puzzle of creeks and bayous would have to somehow take them there.

All of these waterways were mysterious, so far as navigation was concerned, until the Big Sunflower River, which was large and clear enough for free navigation.

Admiral D.D. Porter of the navy explored these mysterious waterways as far as Deer Creek on the 14th of March, and reported Deer Creek as navigable. On the next day he started with five gunboats and four mortar boats. Ulysses went with him, for some distance. In the evening, Ulysses returned to his headquarters to hurry up reinforcements from Sherman.

I love General Grant's instructions to Sherman:

"You will proceed as early as practicable up Steel's Bayou to Deer Creek and thence with the Gunboats now there by any route they may take to get into the Yazoo river for the purpose of determining the feasibility of getting an Army through that route to the East bank of the river and at a point from which they can act advantageously against Vicksburg."

Does this guy know how to write a memo, or what?

Admiral Porter and his gunboats snaked their way through the mysterious bayous, fraught with overhanging limbs and narrow, torturous passageways.

In Black Bayou, rebel sharpshooters were waiting.

The sharpshooters popped up out of the swamps and ambushed Admiral Porter. Porter rushed word back to Ulysses, "We are within a quarter mile of Deer Creek. Send soldiers! I want to see the soldiers!"

Sherman paddled back through the water in a canoe, and led Yankee reinforcements through Black Bayou. It was so dark, the troops had to march across a narrow strip of land, lighting their way with candles.

Sherman and his men arrived just in time to save the fleet.

But they all returned to the Mississippi River, and "thus ended in failure the fourth attempt to get in rear of Vicksburg," Ulysses recalled in his memoirs.

The other three attempts included trying to dig a canal, cut levees and direct water from a lake.

The task before Ulysses was mind-boggling.

The weather was dismal, the rain incessant and "unprecedented." The land was all under water, and the poor soldiers had to pitch their tents on wet ground.

Small pox, measles and malaria spread through the camps.

Ulysses tried hard to provide hospitals for the sick.

In his memoirs, Ulysses recalled those dark days: "Visitors to the camps came back with dismal stories to relate: because I would not divulge my ultimate plans to visitors, they pronounced me idle, incompetent & unfit to command men in an emergency, & clamored for my removal."

On Feb. 9, Ulysses wrote Julia, "*The weather continues dismal here & roads almost impassable.*"

He feared he would not be able to have her with him.

"*It is not atal probable that I will be up the river again until after the decisive action takes place, and whilst here you cannot come down.*" But he promises her, "*I will send for you whenever it is proper that you should come down.*"

In the midst of every hardship, Ulysses longed for Julia.

The months droned on. Everyone blamed Julia's husband for the lack of progress. Even Ulysses' friend, Sherman, began to lose faith in him.

Ulysses had not been with Julia for over three months, and he was starving for her love.

How could such a strong man be so desperate for the love of one woman? In all honesty, there were camp prostitutes about. He did not have to be lonely. But from every account of Ulysses' character, even reports from his enemies, there was never any other woman in his life but Julia.

She alone had saved him from a life of physical coldness and isolation. She alone could comfort him, hold him, connect with his heart.

As the winter wore on, Ulysses sought comfort the only way his faithful character would allow: with a bottle of whiskey.

To Ulysses' friends, Sherman and Rawlins, it seemed their Commander was finished.

And they sensed deep inside that he was the only one who knew how to win the war.

Ulysses was the glue. If he fell apart, they all would.

Then, someone came up with a brilliant idea. Perhaps more brilliant than even the military strategies of Ulysses himself.

They sent for Julia.

And then, everything was all right again.

The story of Julia and Ulysses S. Grant all comes down to one thing: His need for her love, and her need to love him.

When they were together, both were fulfilled in their need.

Not long after Julia's arrival, the sun came out, and the water began to recede.

Everything began to look up, again.

Ulysses' plan now was to get troops below Vicksburg, to attack it from the rear. To accomplish this task, a fleet of gunboats and transports would have to run the batteries on the heights of Vicksburg, braving cannon fire raining down on them as they traveled down the Mississippi.

Julia arrived just in time to watch the perilous running of the batteries.

Observers remember her standing on the deck of a boat with her husband.

"He was a man of iron," the observer recalled with awe, "All the time he held fast to the hand of his wife."

This image really chokes me up!

He was a man of iron—only if he was with his wife.

Her love made him strong. Without her, he was too weak to go on.

In his memoirs, Ulysses remembered that night:

"The enemy were evidently expecting our fleet, for they were ready to light up the river by means of bonfires on the east side and by firing houses on the point of land opposite the city on the Louisiana side. The sight was magnificent, but terrible."

In his memoirs, Ulysses does not mention that Julia was there, nor does he speak of her presence at all in the army camps.

It was just too personal, even for his personal memoirs.

Ulysses soon succeeded in getting his troops on the East side of the Mississippi, on dry land, on the same side of the river as the enemy.

He recalls feeling "a degree of relief unequalled in the entire war."

Several severe battles ensued, followed by a siege.

Citizens of Vicksburg were forced to live underground, as shells exploded in the streets, raining terror all around. There was no way for them to get food, and many were reduced to eating rats to survive.

Confederate General Pemberton, commanding at Vicksburg, realized he could not hold out indefinitely against the iron will of General Grant.

On the fourth of July, General Pemberton surrendered to Ulysses S. Grant.

The North went wild with celebration. Ulysses was again the hero, again the Union's savior, the "man of iron" who could whip the rebels and bring them to their knees. Sherman and Rawlins knew the source of strength and solace that enabled him to succeed—the dainty Southern woman holding his hand, Julia.

Julia had not come to Vicksburg to save a cause, she had come to save a man, her husband, Ulysses.

He needed her love, and she hastened there to give it to him.

Within eight months, her emotionally needy husband was given Supreme Command of all Union Armies. And Julia's love became imperative—imperative to destroying the South.

CHAPTER TWENTY-EIGHT
Commander-In-Chief

When Julia was in camp, she looked after Ulysses' needs in a way nobody else could match. He was her husband, and she was worried about him. Ulysses was so thin, only one hundred and thirty-five pounds. Julia made sure the Army cooks knew his favorite foods, tempting him to eat more. She knew he gained relief from stress by playing with his children, so the boys often joined them in camp.

And of course, there was her wifely affection.

Ulysses' aide, Horace Porter recalled, "They would seek a quiet corner of his quarters of an evening, and sit with her hand in his, manifesting the most ardent devotion, and if a staff officer came accidentally upon them, they would look as bashful as two young lovers spied upon in the scenes of their courtship."

Someone had to baby-sit to give them time alone—someone they could trust. Perhaps General Sherman did his time as a babysitter! Anything to save the Union!

The other officers must have been jealous of the lucky Ulysses, who was living like a bridegroom. He obviously had an active love life, but it never interfered with his powers of concentration. On the contrary, his Army Camp romance only heightened his military skills.

On one occasion, he commanded his troops pantsless, when a Confederate attack interrupted his midnight rendezvous with Julia!

Confederate ironclads were detected approaching in the direction of the general's headquarters, late at night. An officer knocked loudly on his door, warning him of the situation. A few minutes later, General Grant emerged in only a frock coat and boots, with no pants!

His aide, Horace Porter, recalled that the skirt of the general's frock coat reached about the top of his boots and "made up for the absence of trousers."

The unruffled general lit a cigar and began writing dispatches. He showed no expression of excitement except for "rapid and sharp puffs of his cigar."

Julia quickly dressed and emerged from their bedroom. Julia recalled her Ulys was smoking "like a little steam engine."

The ironclads were soon repulsed, and the two lovers returned to the privacy of their bedroom.

The shy, modest General Grant commanding his troops with his pants off, and commanding quite successfully, only proves the old saying that love conquers all!

Julia and Ulysses were back playing house in the Army Camp again. His headquarters at City Point, Virginia, was rather like a honeymoon cottage. Julia did her best to focus on loving her husband, and forget about what he was actually doing to the South.

She petted him, made sure he ate more than those silly old cucumbers, and saw to it he didn't get his feet wet.

But when Ulysses became Supreme Commander-in-Chief, she sensed the playful days could not last forever. For Julia Grant, a day of reckoning had to come.

On March 10, 1864, Ulysses S. Grant was given Supreme Command of all United States Armies.

His mission: to destroy the army of the South's most successful general, Robert E. Lee.

At first, Southern and Northern generals both scoffed at the choice of General Grant.

"Grant has not yet met Bobby Lee," they declared.

But one of "Bobby Lee's" generals had met General Grant: Longstreet. Southerners remember Longstreet's warning:

"Do you gentlemen know Grant? Well, I do. I was with him at West Point. I was best man at his wedding. Served with him in Mexico and observed his methods of warfare in Tennessee. I know him through and through. We must make up our minds to get into line of battle and stay there, for that man will fight us every day and every hour till the end of this war."

Julia was present while Ulysses presented a plan for cordoning Longstreet's army as if in a noose.

Longstreet was Julia's cousin.

"I was sad, and I said so," she recalled.

When she visited Ulysses, she began to see the bodies—dead bodies of Confederates who were executed by order of her own husband.

The South referred to Ulysses, Julia's beloved husband, as "the beast."

For Julia Dent Grant, daughter of the South, daughter of a slave owner, a moment of epiphany had to come.

She had to realize that by supporting her emotionally fragile husband, giving him the inner strength he needed to bring the South to its knees, she was bringing it to its knees, as well.

She didn't have to stay with him. She didn't have to be a party to the destruction of her own world.

She also knew if she left Ulysses at any moment, he would be destroyed.

The bodies of the dead Confederates haunted Julia. And Ulysses had to know.

Julia was part of a gracious world which had embraced Ulysses, when his own parents were cold and indifferent. With her Southern hospitality, Julia had first opened her door, then her arms to the shy Lieutenant who had never known love.

James Longstreet had been Ulysses' best friend, and best man at his wedding. Simon Bolivar Buckner had helped him get home to Julia when Ulysses was down to his last dime.

Time and again the South had embraced him. When Ulysses and Julia set off on their wedding trip on the steamboat, the guests bid them farewell in the Southern style, tossing gay bouquets in the water as symbols that luck would follow them through out their wedded lives. When he returned from California, broke, broken and disgraced, the doors of White Haven opened wide to receive him. He fell into Julia's arms, and she saved him once again.

In a sense, the South had saved Ulysses S. Grant—saved him from a life of coldness and isolation. And this was the way he repaid them?

Ulysses S. Grant believed in the Union. He believed slavery had to come to an end. And he was the only one with the moral courage to take the responsibility upon himself.

Every other Union general had failed against Robert E. Lee. First, George McClellan, the "little Napoleon" had turned and run. Then, Ambrose Burnside led his men to slaughter, and "Fighting Joe Hooker" was too afraid to fight. Lincoln believed he at last had found his general. "Grant is the first real general I've had," Lincoln announced.

But the whole world had trepidations about his reported drinking problem.

And Rawlins, Sherman, anyone who really knew Ulysses, knew that Julia was the key.

At one time, Ulysses hoped to be a mathematics teacher. He used mathematics and logical thinking to help him defeat Lee. If one knows mathematics, one only has to do the math to get from a to c with the following equation: (In Algebra, one of Ulysses' strongest subjects at West Point, one would use the transitive property:)

If Ulysses S. Grant is the only Union general who can win the Civil War, and he falls apart and drinks without Julia, Julia is the key to the Union winning the Civil War.

Yes, folks, Julia Grant, the little Southern belle who never understood that "horrid old constitution," but loved to cover Ulysses S. Grant with kisses, the pampered lady who adored the "comforts of slavery" but thought Ulysses S. Grant "the very nicest, most handsome man I ever saw," the "delightfully feminine" girl who loved to dance and pick flowers and chatter on about china and silverware, she was the one who really brought Robert E. Lee and the Army of Northern Virginia to its knees.

Why has Julia Grant never received the credit she deserves? Because it was a man's world. And no man could admit it was the love of a woman that saved the Union.

General Grant himself kept her out of his memoirs entirely, during the period of the Civil War, which was most of his book. We hear about Sherman and Halleck and Robert E. Lee, but never once does he mention Julia's constant presence by his side in his Army Camps. Because to do so, would be admitting his weakness, both for alcohol and more importantly, his weakness, his heartbreaking hunger for her tenderness and love.

One can see it in his eyes in his photographs from the Civil War. His face, so stalwart and hardboiled, and yet, if you look closely at his eyes, there is a sadness, a love starved look that makes your heart go out to him. The romance of Julia and Ulysses S. Grant cries out from the far corners of the pages of every Civil War book, especially biographies of General Grant. But no one has ever gone so far as to give the lady her due.

In her own memoirs, Julia talks about her time in the Army camps. But she never takes credit for helping her "dear husband," because to do so would be admitting he needed her, that he *desperately* needed her, and she was so loyal to her "Ulyss," she would never have said anything to tarnish his reputation.

And for General Grant himself, it would have seemed unmanly, too embarrassing to admit his soft heart for his wife. Although he was never embarrassed about showing his affection for her in public all the time. His aide, Horace Porter remembers Ulysses, "kissed her repeatedly" and the word "uxorious" seems to have been invented exclusively for Ulysses S. Grant!

Seeing the bodies of dead Confederates, knowing of the slaughter her husband was planning, now that he had control of the entire Union Army, knowing her own role was paramount, Julia Dent Grant, daughter of the South but wife of the Union Commander, had to make a choice.

Would she go back to White Haven, and wash her hands of the blood of the Confederacy? Or would she stick by Ulysses and help him destroy her own world? The world her father cherished, and hoped to pass on to her? The world which was "one long summer of sunshine and flowers?" The world to which she belonged?

Certainly Rawlins must have been nervous all the time. "If she is with him, all will be well, and I will be relieved," he recalled. But if she left?

At some moment in time, Julia had to make the decision to leave or to stay.

She decided to stay.

She never did understand that "horrid old constitution." But she understood that a "love so pure" comes only once in a lifetime, or in this case, only once in all American History.

At some point, Julia had to forgive her husband for slaughtering the South.

At some point, all women must forgive their husbands for destroying their carefree youth, for bringing an end to the world in which they grew up. But none more than Julia Dent Grant.

It seems General Grant never did forgive himself. On his deathbed, he refused to take communion because he said, "I am not worthy."

But she had to forgive him. At some point, she had to say, "I forgive you."

She knew he didn't really want to hurt anyone. As he sadly said years later, "It had to be done."

No one knows when Julia Grant forgave Ulysses, no one knows the moment she decided to stick by the man she loved, at all costs. Whenever it came, it was a defining moment in their romance. For then, he knew she would stay with him. Then, he could do what he knew he *had* to do.

Many people never forgave Ulysses, and as stated, he never really forgave himself. But the one person who really mattered, his beloved Julia, forgave him.

Julia's decision to stay with Ulysses, to forgive him, was her moment of "Unconditional Surrender."

From that moment on, she was with him continually. And there is no record of him ever drinking a drop of liquor again, during the rest of the Civil War.

Grant's first engagement as Supreme Commander confronting Robert E. Lee, was the Battle of the Wilderness. When he rode into battle for the first time as Commander in Chief, everyone noticed he was much better dressed than usual! It is said that Julia probably insisted he look his best. He wore his sword, which was unusual for him, gold braid on his hat, and fancy gloves. Ulysses' aide, Horace Porter, figures Julia must have given Ulysses the gloves, because he refused to take them off, even when they were getting in the way. During the bloody battle of the Wilderness, Ulysses sat whittling and thinking as the shells exploded all around him, still refusing to take off the gloves, until the whittling knife had literally whittled the fingers of the gloves away.

Julia stayed at City Point, Ulysses' headquarters on the James River in Virginia, until the end of the war. At first, there were only tents at City Point. But Ulysses' old West Point roommate and friend, Rufus Ingalls, came to the rescue.

Rufus had been stationed with Ulysses at Fort Vancouver, and seen how his separation from Julia destroyed him. Knowing his importance to winning the war, and of her importance to him, Rufus oversaw the building of a cabin at City Point, just so Julia could stay with Ulysses.

Julia thought this was charming, and recalled of the cozy little cabin, "The Quartermaster Rufus Ingalls built this for the General so I could be with him he said. They all flattered me by saying that I must stay with him and that at headquarters they missed me."

She thought this was wonderful of them, so thoughtful, but they knew the fate of the Union was at stake.

While at City Point, Julia visited the Army hospital, and was besieged by requests to be passed on to her famous husband. But Ulysses forbid her to return. "I don't want you to hear of these things," he told her, "I need rest and sunshine. I need to hear of you and of the children." He needed dainty "Miss Julia" and her carefree ways to distract him, not to remind him of the horrors of the war.

Other requests could not be ignored. One woman begged Julia to plead for Ulysses to free her husband, who was about to be shot. Julia awakened the sleeping general, to plead on the lady's behalf. The lady's husband was a soldier in the Union army, who she claimed, had deserted and come home and see their seven month old baby for the first time. The condemned soldier's wife cried that it was all her fault, that she had begged him to come. The pajama clad General Grant signed an order preventing the execution, which would have taken place in three hours, all thanks to the pleading of his wife. He never could say "no" to her.

While Ulysses was becoming more and more famous, he was becoming more and more attractive to the ladies. Julia noticed this even more than Ulysses did, and she couldn't help feeling jealous and worried.

Julia remembered there were many gentleman callers at her husband's headquarters, "And many ladies, too, who generally asked for a button from the general's coat, which troubled me some, for it was both inconvenient and troublesome to replace them. These loyal and devoted ladies did not consider how the General would appear minus half-dozen buttons or so. And I fear there was a dash of jealousy in my feelings. He was mine, and I did not wish another to have even one of his buttons. I told him I thought it was very silly for them to be cutting buttons off his coat. After that, he referred them to me when they wanted any."

Ulysses was both teasing Julia and being sensitive to her jealousy, with this amusing approach that whenever the ladies asked for a button, he would refer them to his wife.

For the first time in her life, Julia struggled with the attentions of other women toward her husband. It was then, that she began to worry about her appearance.

Julia suffered from "strabismus," a medical condition which caused her to have one crossed eye.

One day, she fretted to Ulysses that she wished she would have tried eye surgery long ago, to correct it, but that she was too afraid.

"Why, Julia!" the great general replied, bewildered. "What put such a notion into your head?"

"You are becoming such a great man," she stammered, "And I am such a plain little wife. Perhaps if my eyes were like others, I would not be so very plain, Ulys, who knows?"

Ulysses was beside her in an instant, and held her close.

"Did I not see you and fall in love with you with those same eyes?" he soothed her. "They are mine. And you'd better not go making any changes, Mrs. Grant," he warned her, fiercely, "because I might not like you half so much with any other eyes."

"My knight! My Lancelot!" Julia sighed, in her book.

There was surely much hugging and kissing and tender lovemaking, for the rest of the night and I am sure that he kissed her eyes again and again, and that she cried tears of happiness.

Ah, and now we come to another reason Ulysses S. Grant wins the award of "Supreme Love God of American History." He stayed faithful to his wife. Not just faithful, but cherished her every moment, at every age, when he could have had any young beauty he wanted.

Imagine what it was like for Ulysses. He had always been shy and awkward with the ladies. In his youth, his Southern pals had outshone him with ease at all the West Point parties and cotillions. Yet, he had always been wistfully romantic and attracted to girls, hoping they'd admire him in his uniform when he came home from West Point, gazing at them dreamily from afar.

And now, as the famous Union Commander in Chief, he could have any woman he wanted. Teenaged coquettes, porcelain skinned beauties from both North and South giggled and paraded and tried to catch his eye.

He was amused. He felt flattered.

But he only wanted Julia.

Even his enemies in the years to come would write that for Ulysses S. Grant, there was one woman and one woman only: Julia.

She had saved him, and he would never forget it.

CHAPTER TWENTY-NINE
Surrender

When Robert E. Lee surrendered to Ulysses S. Grant at Appomattox Court House, Julia was waiting for him nearby on a boat. The first thing he did when he got to shore was bound up the stairs to tell Julia.

Union General Edward Ord purchased the table on which Lee surrendered to Grant, and, in a telling gesture, offered it to Julia. In an equally telling response, Julia modestly declined the soon to be famous table.

She was proud of her "beloved husband," but still may not have felt altogether comfortable in the role she played. At any rate, she was content to let her sweetheart have the limelight all to himself.

At a parade in Detroit honoring General Grant, he sent Julia a message, through Senator Zachariah Chandler, that the women had offered to greet the great General "all along the line with a kiss!" General Grant teasingly inquired of Julia, through the senator, if this would meet with her approval?

Julia admits that her heart pounded with jealousy, but she coolly sent word back that the *senator* should accept the kisses *for* the general, and thus, her husband would receive the kisses "by proxy!"

Ulysses was surely amused by her clever response, and probably got quite a twinkle in his eye.

How lucky Julia was to feel confident enough in her husband's love and loyalty to be able to joke with him about it. One is reminded of other men's less gallant reactions to suddenly being able to have any woman they wanted. Ulysses S. Grant should go down in history as the greatest husband ever! His nobility of character never wavered.

Ulysses' kindness shone through in the way he treated Lee and the South after the surrender. He allowed all the Confederate soldiers to keep their horses, to help with farming when they got home, and did not allow Union soldiers to fire off their guns and exult in the downfall of their foe, who Ulysses insisted, "are now our brothers, again."

Julia had known of Ulysses' soft heart all along. Now that the war was over, she had hopes they could reunite with their children, and spend more time just being plain Julia and Ulyss.

Julia's hopes to get back to the simplicity and comforts of their family life saved her famous husband once again.

The Lincolns invited the Grants to attend Ford's theater with them, that fateful night. Julia wished to get away and see their children, and begged Ulysses to leave that very night for Burlington, New Jersey, where the children were in school. She may have had a premonition. By leaving the city and not attending the theater, Ulysses' life was spared.

From beginning to end, Julia saved Ulysses S. Grant. And he rewarded her with the most tender devotion.

He also rewarded her by making her the great lady she had always wanted to be. Julia was the most popular First Lady since Dolly Madison.

When Ulysses became our nation's eighteenth president, Julia made sure he dressed up for his inauguration, and he did look handsome! He dressed in a tailor-made black suit and yellow kid gloves, surely Julia's choice.

After taking the oath of office, the first thing Ulysses did was kiss Julia and tease her, "And now my dear, I hope you're happy."

In the White House, the romance of Julia and Ulysses continued. Ulysses told his sister-in-law, Emmy Dent, that with Julia, it had been a case of love at first sight, that he had never had but one romance, but the one sweetheart. He was fond of saying that Julia was perfect in every way.

The Washington crowd was jealous of the Grants and their relationship, and women tried to pry them apart at every turn, probably popping out of closets and crying, "I surrender, General Grant!" But President Ulysses never gave them any satisfaction, and it drove the shallow socialites crazy.

The Grants grew stout from sumptuous State Dinners, and living the easy life, settled comfortably into middle age. But when they gazed at each other, it always felt like they were back at White Haven. She was seventeen and he was twenty-one and they were falling in love all over again.

Julia and Ulysses still held hands in public and always insisted on being seated together on trains and in restaurants. They were never parted for longer than two weeks during his entire Presidency.

As during the Civil War, they lived through marital struggles on a grand scale, when the scandals of "The Whiskey Ring" and con-men Jim Fisk and Jay Gould's attempts to corner the gold market, then force up the prices, exposed traitorous friends trying to take advantage of Ulysses to make money. Ulysses handled both crises quickly, and with honesty, expelling all traitors to the government.

The main goal of Ulysses' presidency was to help the newly freed African Americans. He was the last president to have ever owned a slave, and the first president to invite African Americans to his Inaugural Ball. On March 30, 1870, President Ulysses signed the fifteenth amendment to the constitution, giving African Americans the right to vote.

As it was all his life, many people criticized Ulysses, especially those who did not want to help African Americans in their fight for equality. With his Victorian code of honor, Ulysses seldom defended himself. It still hurt Julia when people spoke ill of her husband, because she saw so clearly the good in him.

While standing by her man, Julia was also having the time of her life in the White House, decorating and throwing parties where everyone was invited. After so many years of war and suffering, it was time to enjoy life, and Julia was just the right First Lady for the times.

Julia was having so much fun, that she wanted her "Dudy" to run for a third time, but he cleverly avoided it. He sent a letter saying he would not run again, without her knowing it. By the time she found out, it was too late. He knew that if his wife begged him, he would have to give in, and he did not want to be president again.

To Ulysses' relief, they managed to leave Washington without losing their souls. The soul-less socialites watched them depart, the women all wishing someone would love them like that.

Ulysses had always yearned for the adventure of travel, so not long after he left the White House, he and Julia embarked on a two and a half year journey around the world.

Observers said they behaved like "newlyweds." And the attentions of the ladies all around him were ignored.

Ulysses continued to tease his wife all the time, to show his affection. Once, she pined for a decoration for her hair that she saw in a jewelry shop, but Ulysses insisted she didn't need it, and that he wanted to leave the shop right away. He surprised her with this same hairpiece as a gift on Christmas, whispering that he had wanted to give it to her, himself.

Returning to the United States, the Grants set up housekeeping in New York City, where Ulysses sought to provide for his family by becoming a business man, something to which he was always attracted—with disastrous results.

Sadly, the ever trusting General Grant was swindled by con-man Ferdinand Ward, who told the general that his son, Ulysses Junior, was a "financial genius," and that Ward wanted to found a financial institution with Ulysses Junior and Senior as partners, if only General Grant would lend his name to the enterprise and convince his friends to invest.

Flattered by the attention to his namesake, who he had always believed was gifted, Ulysses lent his famous name to "Grant and Ward." It seemed to be wildly successful, and all its investors thought they were making money—right up to the moment it was discovered to be a pyramid scheme. Ferdinand Ward was actually pocketing all the money, dolling out "interest" when the principal was actually gone.

When he learned the truth, poor General Grant covered his face. He had been duped again. But even worse than losing all he had, he had lost the money of his friends.

Ulysses was humiliated before the entire world. But Julia held him in her arms and the two went on, together. She agreed to sell White Haven and gave all she had to help bail her husband out. She loved him more than anything in the world.

The stress of this public humiliation probably led to a decline in the general's health, and in the summer of 1884, on the porch of their summer home in Long Branch, New Jersey, Ulysses bit into a peach, and felt a painful stinging in his throat. They soon learned the truth: that the pain was caused by throat cancer, and Ulysses did not have long to live.

Ulysses' first thoughts were of his family, and providing for them when he was gone. At the urging of his friend, Mark Twain, Ulysses began writing his memoirs. He had never had any desire to write about himself, but he realized it was the only way he might provide an income for his beloved Julia and their children, after his death.

While Ulysses struggled valiantly against death, he wrote the final words of his memoirs from the front porch of a cottage in Saratoga Springs, New York. A friend of the Grants, Mr. Drexel, had offered the cottage to them because of its location atop a cool, refreshing mountain top. It was summer, and the blistering heat of New York City would have caused much more suffering to the general.

While the world watched and waited, General Grant struggled to complete his memoirs, while death waited in the wings.

Julia never really believed that he would leave her.

When her beloved died at 8:08 in the morning on July 23, 1885, Julia was holding his hand.

Julia outlived Ulysses by seventeen years. She devoted most of her time to her children and grandchildren.

She became emotional at appearances honoring her famous husband. She never re-married, and wore mourning the rest of her life.

In her memoirs, Julia ends by saying that when Ulysses left her, it was "as when some far-off planet disappears from the heavens;" the "light of his glorious fame" still warmed her.

I believe she really meant it was "the light of his glorious love" that kept her warm.

THE END

Made in the USA
San Bernardino, CA
05 March 2013